justice on fire

justice on fire

The Kansas City Firefighters Case and the Railroading of the Marlborough Five

J. Patrick O'Connor

 University Press of Kansas

Published by the University Press of Kansas (Lawrence, Kansas 66045), which was organized by the Kansas Board of Regents and is operated and funded by Emporia State University, Fort Hays State University, Kansas State University, Pittsburg State University, the University of Kansas, and Wichita State University

Library of Congress Cataloging-in-Publication Data

Names: O'Connor, J. Patrick, author.

Title: Justice on fire : the Kansas City firefighters case and the railroading of the Marlborough five / J. Patrick O'Connor

Description: Lawrence, Kansas : University Press of Kansas, 2018. | Appeal in case decided in *United States v. Edwards*, 159 F.3d 1117 (8th Cir. 1998). | Includes bibliographical references and index.

Identifiers: LCCN 2018016615

  ISBN 9780700626717 (cloth : alk. paper)

  ISBN 9780700626724 (ebook)

Subjects: LCSH: Edwards, Darlene M.—Trials, litigation, etc. | Trials (Arson)—Missouri—Kansas City. | Trials (Homicide)—Missouri—Kansas City. | Judicial error—Missouri—Kansas City. | Fire fighters—Missouri—Kansas City—Death. | Arson investigation—Missouri—Kansas City. | Homicide investigation—Missouri—Kansas City. | Marlborough (Kansas City, Mo.)

Classification: LCC KF224.E368 O26 2018 | DDC 345.778/0252—dc23.

LC record available at https://lccn.loc.gov/2018016615.

British Library Cataloguing in Publication Data is available.

Printed in the United States of America

10 9 8 7 6 5 4 3 2 1

The paper used in this publication is recycled and contains 30 percent postconsumer waste. It is acid free and meets the minimum requirements of the American National Standard for Permanence of Paper for Printed Library Materials z39.48-1992.

For Richard Brown, Darlene Edwards, Bryan Sheppard,
Frank Sheppard, and in memory of Skip Sheppard

Contents

      A photo gallery follows page 158.

Prologue

This is a book about prosecutorial abuse on steroids that led to five wrongful convictions. Richard Brown, Darlene Edwards, Bryan Sheppard, Frank Sheppard, and Skip Sheppard were convicted in 1997 of causing the deaths of six Kansas City firefighters killed in an arson-fueled explosion on November 29, 1988, at a construction site located near the impoverished Marlborough neighborhood where they lived.

Each was sentenced to life in prison without the possibility of parole.

They were convicted not because any of them were guilty but because the government, after eight misguided years of investigation, wanted to bring closure to the families of the fallen firefighters. They were convicted because they were indigent and powerless before the awesome power of the federal government. They were expendable due to the desultory lives they had led.

When I decided in 2000 to become an advocate for the five convicted, I had no illusions about how difficult it would be to overturn their convictions; once an innocent person is convicted and sentenced and has lost the appeals available, the prison doors are almost impossible to reopen. This is especially true—as it is in the firefighters case—when there is no DNA evidence involved.

Each innocence case is different but behind every one of them is a deeply flawed investigation and prosecution. The higher the profile of the case, the more likely defendants are at risk of being falsely convicted.[1]

For Kansas City, this was the highest-profile case in history.

Exonerations make news not only because they are rare but also because they inevitably show an almost total breakdown in the justice system, from the investigation to the prosecution right through the trial to the appeals courts. This breakdown is exactly what caused and keeps in place these wrongful convictions.

The road to exoneration is a protracted one full of delays and pitfalls. Even when evidence of innocence is overwhelming, the government, be it state or federal, in almost all cases stridently opposes claims of innocence.

Meanwhile the innocents languish an average of 8.7 years before some judge finally says they can go home.[2] For those released based on DNA evidence, the average time in prison is 14 years.[3]

One factor that encouraged me to step forward was I thought it was obvious who set the arson that killed the firefighters; if I could help bring that to light the government would admit its mistake, free the Marlborough Five, and prosecute the actual perpetrators. I was greatly mistaken about that. The local US Attorney's Office is as invested today in these wrongful convictions as it was when it prosecuted them.

What I never understood was why the investigation did not focus on the security guards. In the afternoon before the explosion, the general contractor informed the mom-and-pop security company it was cutting back its hours by 150 minutes each night. The initial interview a Kansas City homicide detective conducted with guard Debbie Riggs just hours after the firefighters were killed caught her in numerous lies.

Among other things, she concocted a story about seeing two prowlers as the reason she and her brother, Robert Riggs, had left the site unguarded for five or so minutes. During this brief excursion to QuikTrip, her pickup was torched on one side of the site and a construction company pickup torched on the other side right next to where the explosives were stored in a semitrailer.

Instead of the guards, the federal investigation spent six years investigating organized labor's possible role. When that probe dried up, $50,000 reward posters were placed in every jail and prison in Missouri and Kansas and on overpasses and billboards near Marlborough.

More than 150 leads came pouring in. Not one of these informants, over sixty of them convicts, grouped the five eventually convicted. No two witnesses against any of the defendants testified to the same set of facts. The actual statements of the witnesses name a large number of nondefendants involved in the crime. Most of the informants referred to a wide variety of items stolen from the construction site the night of the explosion despite the fact nothing was ever stolen from the site—that night or any other time.

It did not deter the Alcohol, Tobacco, Firearms, and Explosives (ATF) agent in charge of the investigation that Frank Sheppard and Richard Brown passed police-administered polygraph examinations, or that none of the five ever asked to have an attorney present when questioned numerous times by police or ATF agents, or that none ever invoked the Fifth Amendment right to remain silent, or that each of the defendants turned down the government's offer of a five-year sentence to testify against the others.

At the time of their convictions, I owned and edited an alternative weekly newspaper, the *New Times*. In May, two months after the five were convicted but before they were sentenced in July, we published a two-part, twenty-thousand-word article by J. J. Maloney that forcefully and unequivocally stated the defendants were framed by one super-aggressive ATF agent and railroaded at trial by a combative assistant US attorney and a pro-prosecution judge. Later that year those articles won the Missouri Bar Association's Excellence in Journalism award.[4]

The government's star witness at the grand jury was the stepson of defendant Darlene Edwards. Ronnie Edwards was highly compromised, cooperating with the government to avoid being sent to prison on a parole violation for fraud.

During a six-week trial, the government put on a parade of felon witnesses and thirty-two informants from Marlborough. Many of the Marlborough witnesses had issues with the law themselves and all were aware of the $50,000 reward money.

Twenty-four convicts or ex-convicts, incentivized by reduced sentences or other enhancements, testified. One convict saw his sentence cut from twenty-five years in prison to one year in jail for his testimony. At least seventeen others received deals for their testimony, including drastic sentence reductions.

At every stop along the way the Marlborough Five have been barred from receiving judicial relief. In 1998 a three-judge panel at the Eighth Circuit Court of Appeals denied their direct appeal; in 1999 the US Supreme Court refused to hear their case; and in 2003 a federal district court judge denied their habeas corpus petition.

By this time, the only way back to court to challenge their convictions was to develop evidence of their innocence so compelling that no jury would have convicted had this evidence been known.

A private investigator and I began attempting to interview witnesses to see if any of them would recant. Over the course of a year, we developed eight affidavits, four of them from trial witnesses, that indicated the ATF agent in charge of the investigation had used coercive, strong-arm tactics to pressure potential witnesses. One trial witness swore in her affidavit that the ATF agent threatened to put her in prison for eighteen months on a contempt charge and have her two-year-old son placed in social services unless she testified to hearing Bryan Sheppard and Richard Brown making admissions of guilt on two occasions.[5]

In June 2005, I took the affidavits to Mike McGraw, an investigative reporter at the *Kansas City Star*. After more than a year of investigating the firefighters case, McGraw began writing a series of articles that questioned the validity of the convictions, pointed to the guards as possible perpetrators, and exposed the coercive tactics the lead ATF investigator used to compel witnesses to testify falsely.

"Did Pressure Lead to Lies?" was the headline on McGraw's blockbuster article that ran on the front page, June 29, 2008.[6] He detailed how fifteen people told him one ATF agent pressured them to perjure themselves. Five who testified admitted they lied to the grand jury or later at trial. The other witnesses said they refused to change their stories even under pressure.

The revelations of witness tampering prompted John F. Wood, the local US attorney, to ask the US Justice Department to conduct an independent investigation.

The Justice Department went into full damage-control mode. In the interim, Skip Sheppard died of cancer in 2009 at age forty-nine.

In 2011, three years after Wood asked for an independent investigation, the then US attorney, Beth Phillips, held a news conference and released a 2½-page report that stated the Justice Department review "did not find any credible support for *The Star*'s allegations." She did state that the review had uncovered one or more other perpetrators, but those names were kept secret. She took no questions and left the room.

So now on top of these wrongful convictions there is a cover-up.

No grand jury was impaneled to consider indicting these unnamed perpetrators. What does it say to the families of the fallen firefighters that one or more people responsible for killing their loved ones are still free?

It says the government will do whatever it takes to keep the truth of this tragedy buried.

When the US Supreme Court ruled in 2012 that it was a violation of the Eighth Amendment's prohibition against cruel and unusual punishment to sentence minors—those under eighteen years old—to life without parole, Bryan Sheppard, because he was seventeen at the time the firefighters were killed, was entitled to be resentenced. In March 2017, Federal District Judge Fernando Gaitan sentenced Bryan to twenty years. Because he had already served twenty-two years, he was set free the following week.

Under the Missouri Sunshine Law, my son Joe O'Connor, who is working on a documentary about the firefighters case, obtained about fifty crime scene photos from the KCPD in 2016.[7] A series of photos showed Debbie Riggs's Toyota pickup from both the outside and the inside. One interior photo showed her vinyl purse, some sort of yellow garment, and what looked like a plastic shopping bag in the debris of the passenger seat of the badly charred pickup. Everything except the purse, the garment, and the plastic bag was in ashes. The fire had been so intense that all that was left of the passenger seat was the metal coils; the steering column had melted and collapsed with the key to the ignition still in it.

It did not make sense to Joe that these items could have survived such an intense fire. He thought there was a high likelihood that those items had been placed in the pickup after the firefighters had doused the arson fire and gone to the other side of the construction site. To test his theory, he sent the photos to an arson expert.

In an email Joe wrote the arson expert on March 4, 2016, he did not reveal that the photos he was attaching were from the construction site where six Kansas City firefighters were killed in 1988. Referring to the interior photo of Debbie's pickup, he said, "The white purse, the plastic bag, the yellow cloth and a wad of paper all look out of place. Not only do they look like they were not burned in the same way as everything else, none of those materials appear wet from the fire hoses. . . . Is it possible these items were placed there after the initial fire?"

Three days later, the arson expert emailed his report and stated: "As shown in the photographs, it would have been impossible for those items to have been present at the time of the fire nor should they have been in the condition found if they had been in the original fire. It appears the items you referenced were damaged by a separate fire event."[8]

On August 8, 2016, I sent a certified letter to Tammy Dickinson, the US attorney for the Western District of Missouri, that began, "There is evidence in the possession of the Kansas City Police Department that could establish the innocence of the five people convicted in 1997 in the tragic deaths of six Kansas City firefighters. . . . If you will allow the full development of the evidence, I believe you will have a rare opportunity to correct these wrongful convictions and bring the actual perpetrators of this terrible tragedy to justice."

Dickinson never responded.

One thing is perfectly clear: the local US Attorney's Office and the US Justice Department have no intention of allowing the truth about this case to be revealed.

PART I

FRAMING THE MARLBOROUGH FIVE

CHAPTER 1

The Last Alarm

The night of November 28–29, 1988, was crisp and cool with temperatures hovering around thirty-seven degrees. The wind was out of the south, gusting to twenty-seven miles per hour. There was no precipitation and the moon was full, casting its glow through scattered clouds. Visibility was twenty miles.[1]

The call to the Kansas City Fire Department came at 3:41 a.m. from a security guard at a major construction site at 87th Street and 71 Highway in south Kansas City. As the guard was reporting a pickup truck on fire, a female, another guard, could be heard in the background saying, "The explosives are on fire."

The male guard then told the dispatcher that there was a fire on both sides of 71 Highway, "Uh, there may be some—uh, there's some explosives up on a hill that I also see now is burning." Instead of asking the guard to be more specific and find out what type of explosives may be involved, Phil Wall, the fire department's chief dispatcher, terminated the call and summoned Pumper 41, telling the crew, "There is a pickup truck at—south of Blue River and 71 Highway on the west side. Pumper 41, use caution on your call. There's information there may be explosives. It's in a construction area. The pickup truck may be in that area."

It was turning into a hectic night for dispatcher Wall. A few minutes before the call from the construction site, he was busy sending two other pumper companies to a major fire in an occupied building at 12th and Woodland, a low-income neighborhood near downtown.

Within seven minutes Pumper 41, with a crew of three, arrived at the construction site. Captain James Kilventon informed dispatch there were two fires and asked for the assistance of another pumper company. Dispatch radioed Fire Station 30, advising the crew to check with Pumper 41 on arrival. Because it was plainly obvious from the raging fire engulfing the pickup and from the smell of gasoline, Kilventon advised dispatch that it appeared they were dealing with arson fires and the police should be sent.

Twelve minutes after the guard's call, at 3:53 a.m., Pumper 30 arrived. After seeing that Pumper 41 had the fire in the pickup under control, Pumper 30 proceeded across the median of 71 Highway and up a steep access road to the east side of the construction site where it had been reported explosives were on fire.

Before Pumper 30 settled in by the burning trailer, the dispatcher had one last chance to prevent this unfolding tragedy. Based apparently on information Kilventon received from the guards, the Pumper 41 captain now knew the burning trailer contained explosives. With this information, Kilventon contacted the dispatcher at 3:58:58 a.m. to warn Pumper 30 of the impending danger. "If you can get 30, tell them there's a trailer on fire up there, stay away from it, and we better have 107 [Battalion Chief Germann] out here. There's supposed to be explosives involved in this." (Kilventon's asking for the battalion chief meant he considered this a dangerous situation.)

Instead of communicating that information to Pumper 30, the dispatcher proceeded to radio the battalion chief.

Six and a half minutes after arriving on the east side, Captain Gerald Halloran of Pumper 30 asked the dispatcher if he could "confirm that there is explosives in this trailer or not."

Dispatch told him that Pumper 41 had advised "that and we have additional information on the original call that there were explosives in that area, use caution."

In response, Halloran told dispatch to send Pumper 41 up. Kilventon heard the transmission and informed dispatch, "We're en route now." The two security guards followed Pumper 41 in a station wagon up the access road. While Pumper 41 entered the east side and drove toward the trailers over rough, rocky terrain, the guards kept to the access road, parking some 350 feet away with a clear view of the trailers.

What they saw was a trailer burning so hot it was transparent. Through the thin metal walls of the trailer they could see the socks of explosives stacked in pyramids inside the two sides of the trailer. The back end of the trailer had risen up on its end, sticking almost straight up in the air. Although no flames or smoke could be seen, the trailer was convulsed in an orange glow with countless sparks leaping from it, emitting the sounds of hundreds of tiny explosions, like strings of M-80 firecrackers going off.

By now both pumper trucks were parked near the burning trailer.

At 4:02:13 a.m. Kilventon contacted Marion Germann, the battalion chief, en route to the site, informing him, "Apparently this thing has already blowed up, chief. He's got magnesium or something burning up here."

"Are you back up in there now or where are you at?" Germann asked. "Both companies are back up in here," Kilventon answered.

Chief Germann and his driver arrived at the scene at 4:06:23 a.m., pulling in behind the guard's station wagon, unable to get any closer due to the rough terrain. Germann could see several firefighters using a long pole in an attempt to pull a burning construction company pickup away from the trailer. To Germann the burning trailer looked like "a giant sparkler."

Within a minute of his arrival, as one of the firefighters was just beginning to train a powerful gush of water on the trailer, Germann turned on his radio to order the firefighters to withdraw immediately. Before he could issue the order, an enormous explosion erupted, instantly killing all six firefighters. The female guard would say later that the firefighter closest to the trailer seemed to explode from the inside out.

For over thirty seconds rocks and debris rained down over the construction site. A boulder the size of a stove squashed the trunk of the battalion chief's yellow car and hurled his driver, a 250-pound man, several feet behind the battalion chief's car. The female guard was knocked backward into a ditch. A gloved, smoking hand of one of the firefighters came to rest next to the battalion chief's car. Other human remains would be found as far away as seventy yards from the trailer. The battalion chief's car was totaled; the windshield caved in, the hood popped open, the light bar on top pushed back, and the side chrome sheared off. Only the headlights remained on.

At 4:08:19 Battalion Chief Germann reported the disaster to dispatch, ". . . explosion just as we pulled up in here. Get us all kinds of ambulances and at least a couple or three more companies."

The shock wave from the blast propelled hot metal into a second trailer less than a hundred feet to the west, cutting that trailer in two. Forty minutes later the second trailer exploded with much more firepower than the first. Many other firefighters, who were arriving from all over the city, would have been killed by that blast if Deputy Fire Chief Bill Booth, arriving on the scene ten minutes after the first blast, had not ordered everyone to pull back about a quarter of a mile to 95th Street.

The second explosion delivered five times the destructive power of the bomb that leveled the federal building in Oklahoma City in 1995. It broke windows and cracked walls for miles around and was heard all over the metropolitan area and as far away as Warrensburg, Missouri, forty-five miles to the east. Hundreds of area residents claimed to have been knocked out of bed and many thousands said the blast jarred them awake.

Most of the property damage was confined to a ten-mile radius. More than thirteen hundred individuals and businesses would file $18 million in property damage claims against the general contractor, the two subcontractors, and the security guard company. Mountain Plains Construction Company, the subcontractor responsible for the storage of the explosives, was forced out of business when it could no longer obtain bonding after the explosions. It had been a company with more than $1 million in assets.

In terms of disasters experienced by Kansas City firefighters, this one eclipsed them all.

A helicopter from nearby Research Medical Center was summoned by the fire department to fly over the construction site to check for survivors. Pilot David Walton hovered above the site at 1,000 feet but his visibility was blocked by darkness and the smoke billowing up from the ground. He judged the conditions too dangerous and flew back to the hospital, arriving minutes before the second explosion erupted. Had he remained, he and his crew would most probably have been blown out of the sky.

A few minutes after the second explosion, Deputy Fire Chief Bill Booth sent up another helicopter to look for survivors. In it were Deputy Chief Logan Grote, the head of the department's hazardous materials (hazmat) team, and an employee of the construction company. It was still too dark to see below.

By now police had cordoned off the construction area, closing traffic to both southbound and northbound 71 Highway. A command post was established on an overpass at 95th. There all the brass of the Kansas City Fire Department converged, including Fire Chief Edward Wilson. The police advised waiting until daybreak, which was an hour or more away, before sending anyone to look for survivors.

Deputy Chiefs Booth and Grote told Chief Wilson they needed to find out if any firefighters were alive, saying it would be "a grave mistake" to wait for sunrise. The chief gave permission.

Booth and Grote drove north and walked a quarter of a mile to where the trailers had been, seeing instead three enormous craters. The scene was of a moonscape with wisps of smoke lapping skyward.

The two craters created by the first explosion looked like enormous swimming pools. One crater was eight feet deep and eighty feet wide; the other was six feet deep and twenty feet across. The second explosion created a crater eight feet deep and one hundred feet wide.

All that remained of the pumper trucks was the twisted metal hulk of one of the pumpers. Only the motor remained from the other pumper. From there the deputy chiefs split up, each lighting his way with a large flashlight. Their search for survivors was futile; they found only dead bodies and body parts.

When Booth and Grote returned, they went to the command post and met with their superiors and many firefighters who by now had gathered. "I let them know there were no survivors. We had a moment of silence together. There was no prayer, just reverence and silence, and quite a few tears," Booth told a reporter.

Just after sunrise, crews of firefighters and police officers and other officials went to the blast site to secure the area. In the afternoon, companies of firefighters carried away the bodies and remains.

At the thirty-two fire station houses scattered across the city, bells tolled at 9 p.m. after a chaplain said a prayer over the fire department's radio system and ended by reading out the names of the six fallen firefighters.

On the following Saturday afternoon, four days after the explosions, a memorial service for the firefighters was held at Arrowhead Stadium, home of the Kansas City Chiefs of the National Football League.

Two black-draped pumper trucks were parked outside the stadium. Three pairs of empty boots, each topped with a yellow firefighter's helmet, were beside each pumper truck.

A stage was set up in the east end zone. The families of the fallen firefighters sat directly below in Row One. Seats in the lower section of the stadium around the end zone were filled with over fifteen thousand Kansas Citians who came to pay their respects. Above the scoreboard at the west end of the stadium, the American flag was at half-mast.

It took over ten minutes for wave after wave of firefighters, in rows of four or five, to march in and take their seats on the field. Most wore dress blues. They were followed by hundreds of police officers and paramedics. About four thousand firefighters and law enforcement personnel covered about two-thirds of the football field. Firefighters from as far away as Massachusetts and New Hampshire were in attendance.

Under a clear sky, the memorial began at 2 p.m. with the roar of five police motorcycles in an arrow-shaped formation entering the stadium through a field-level tunnel. Three groups of kilt-clad bagpipers entered next and they were followed by numerous color guards. The color guard from the Kansas City Fire Department was one member short—Luther Hurd, one of the firefighters killed in the blast, was there in spirit only.

Among the speakers were Terry Conroy, president of the local firefighter's union; Mayor Richard Berkley; Mayor Pro-Tem Emanuel Cleaver; Fire Chief Wilson, and Alfred Whitehead, president of the International Association of Fire Fighters. When the fire department's chaplain, Arnett Williams, brought the one-hour-and-twenty-minute memorial to an end, the staccato reports of a rifle salute echoed through the stadium. After a bugler played "Taps," four helicopters flew over the stadium in a diamond formation, and then one peeled away in a traditional tribute to "the missing man."

A year after the memorial, voters approved a five-cent-per-pack increase in the cigarette tax to fund a hazmat unit in the fire department. The new unit was named Hazmat 71 in honor of the firefighters killed on Pumpers 30 and 41. The budget to start and equip the new unit was set at $1.9 million with an annual operating budget of $900,000 to staff the twenty-one-member team under a battalion commander. Two years later the Firefighters Fountain was dedicated in midtown Kansas City, listing the names in granite blocks of the more than eighty-five firefighters killed in service since the establishment of the Kansas City Fire Department in the late nineteenth century. The 30-41 Firefighter Memorial was dedicated six months later near the site of the explosions.

CHAPTER 2

What Went Wrong?

Firefighters, probably more than any other group of public servants, pride themselves on their brotherhood. The three-person crews that form a fire company not only work together and depend on each other for their safety but also live together, eat together, watch TV, play cards, and sleep under the same roof at the station house. Over time many of them become best friends, closer than any friends they've ever had before, even their own siblings.

A lot of firefighters "are looking for a close-knit family," said Jim Gibson, the Kansas City Fire Department's administrative deputy chief. "They may be looking for something they lacked in their personal lives."[1]

Most firefighters would not trade their jobs for any other. In addition to the great camaraderie they feel working in a station house, there is also a heroic aspect to the work. "It takes a certain panache to walk into a building that everyone else is running out of," said Alvin Hacker, an emergency medical technician who often works alongside firefighters. "That's what sets them apart."

"They look at risk-taking and the macho image," Gibson said. "Most jobs are boring to them. They look at the police and the fire department as excitement. They want to see how far they can go to demonstrate that macho. It's a challenge to them, not the same old grind of factory or office work."

Becoming a firefighter often runs in the family. Two of the firefighters killed in the blast, Captain James Kilventon and Michael Oldham, were sons of firefighters. Battalion Chief Germann followed two of his brothers onto the force. Another brother followed him. His older brother, John, was also a battalion chief.

At the time of the explosion, Kansas City employed about 750 firefighters of various rank. In addition to the fire chief, there were 4 deputy chiefs, 25 battalion chiefs, 165 captains, 323 fire apparatus operators, and 326 firefighters. Salaries for firefighters averaged around $30,000. Each of the thirty-two stations is staffed by three shifts of three-person crews.

Firefighter crews work a twenty-four-hour day beginning at 7 a.m. and then are off for two days. Almost all work part-time jobs on their days off to supplement their income—painters, plumbers, roofers, handymen in general.

The crew from Station 41 consisted of Captain James H. Kilventon, apparatus operator Robert D. McKarnin, and firefighter Michael R. Oldham. From Station 30 the crew that went out was comprised of Captain Gerald Halloran, apparatus operator Thomas M. Fry, and firefighter Luther E. Hurd. Each pumper truck was equipped with a fire hose, a water pump, and a tank that holds 300–500 gallons of water.

For Halloran it was his first day back after a ten-day vacation. He had told some intimates he planned to retire at the end of 1988, just a month away. For Hurd it was the first time he ever worked out of Station 30. He was substituting for Lloyd Greenfield, who was off sick. The other regular member of that crew was Ernie Jackson, but he was on vacation. Hurd usually worked out of a station in northeast Kansas City and even though he had a touch of the flu he was the type to help out when called upon. Besides that, he and his family lived only blocks away from Station 30 at 75th and Prospect.

The captains, Kilventon and Halloran, were, through cousins, connected by marriage—sort of shirttail relatives. Although they didn't socialize much away from work, they had excellent rapport.

Halloran, fifty-nine, was the longest-serving captain in the fire department. He had been in charge of a shift at Station 30 since 1970 when the station opened. He and his siblings were the first generation of Hallorans to be born in the United States. His parents emigrated from Ireland. At the station he had set ways of doing things. He always sat in the same place to watch television and he always watched the same shows. He liked nothing better than arguing a point—on any subject. "People would come in here with the express purpose of arguing with Gerald," one firefighter said. "He had an opinion on everything."[2] He was survived by his wife, Leota, and three adult children, Patrick, Steven, and Cynthia Caffrey.

The word that came to mind when firefighters at Station 41—even to this day—talk about Kilventon is "aggressive."[3]

Over his seven years as a captain at Station 41 he had come to miss the action he had experienced as a firefighter at a station close to downtown. Even at age fifty-four, he was lobbying for a transfer back to that area.

He prided himself on being the chief cook at Station 41. His specialty was chili, every now and then a stew, but mostly chili. He was a spirited, handsome Irishman with an infectious smile. Once he was suspended from high school for painting his hair green on St. Patrick's Day. He was survived by his wife, Cecilia, son James Michael, and daughter Alice Marie.

Robert McKarnin, forty-two, an apparatus operator at Station 41, had been a firefighter since 1968, following two years of active duty in the navy. Like his grandfather and father before him, he joined the Carpenters Union. "The guy could fix anything," a fellow firefighter said. He spent many off-duty hours at the Lake of the Ozarks, where he built his own house. He was survived by his wife, Debbie, son Sean, twenty-one, and daughter Cassie, sixteen. To honor his father's memory, Sean became a Kansas City firefighter.

Michael R. Oldham, thirty-two, had been a firefighter since 1976. His father, Charles Oldham, was a retired Kansas City fire captain. Two months before the explosion he and his family moved into a new home. He was known as a man of few words. Bill Markey, a deacon of St. Catherine's Catholic Church, said Michael's reticence could best be described by a John Wayne quote Michael taped to his refrigerator door: "Talk low, talk slow and don't say too much." He was survived by his wife, Karen, son Kyle, six, and daughter Jacqueline, three.

Thomas M. Fry, forty-one, joined the fire department in 1973 after serving in the army in Germany. For recreation he drove off-road vehicles. In the summer he water-skied. He tried his hand at skydiving, taking a couple of lessons and then making a couple of jumps. After the second jump he told his sister, "Well, I've done this," and he stopped.

Luther E. Hurd, thirty-one, was a star football player at Northeast High School in Kansas City. His dream was to play pro football, but when his mother got sick he saw his duty as staying around and taking care of her. That led him to join the fire department in 1977. "The night before he died, we talked about jobs other people had. He said he wouldn't give up firefighting for the world," his widow, Jewell Hurd, wrote in her tribute to her husband. Hurd loved to volunteer. Deputy Chief Charlie Fisher said Hurd "volunteered for any project that came along. He truly exemplified what our fire department is all about." In addition to his wife, he was survived by his daughter Giovanna, 11, a son Sean, 3, and daughter Crystal, age 2½ months.

As revered as these fallen firefighters were, what gnawed most at their colleagues was how was it possible that two such experienced crews, led by seasoned captains, could have been killed in a hazmat explosion.

Fire Chief Wilson, at a news conference held the day after the explosions, said the fire department would conduct a formal inquiry, which would include going over the dispatch tapes and attempting to reconstruct "as well as possible the steps the firefighters took before" the explosion. "We'll look to see if anything could have been done differently, anything that could have changed the outcome."

Although he had not listened to the dispatch tapes, he opened the door to second-guessing the actions of the two pumper captains when he said, "If I was a company officer and found explosives, I would withdraw."

The six dead firefighters had a combined 124 years in the fire department. Both captains were highly respected throughout the fire department for the concern they showed for the safety of their crews.

The basic rule for responding to a fire involving hazardous materials is to secure the area and let the fire burn out without any intervention.[4] This is particularly the case when the hazardous materials are located in an area away from housing or business units. If there are people living or working in the area of the hazardous material, the plan would still be to secure the area and let the fire burn and to proceed to evacuate any people in the area.

One thing that did survive the blast and was found inside the demolished cab of the remaining pumper was a Department of Transportation *Emergency Response Guidebook*, detailing the proper way to deal with hazardous materials. There are fifteen variations of ammonium nitrate listed in the guidebook. Next to each type of material is a guide number that leads to information on the potential hazard and the appropriate emergency response. Each variation of ammonium nitrate also has a hazmat identification number with the sole exception of ammonium nitrate fuel oil mixtures (ANFO), which is listed as a blasting agent rather than as a hazardous material.

In dealing with blasting agents, the guidebook warns that the material may explode and throw fragments one-third of a mile or more if the fire reaches the cargo area. The guidebook directs responding firefighters not to fight the fire in the cargo. Under the subheading "Cargo Fires," directions given are not to move the cargo or vehicle if the cargo has been exposed to heat and not to fight the fire when it reaches the cargo. The instructions are to withdraw from the area and let the fire burn.

Four of the six firefighters, including both captains, had completed the National Fire Protection Association's course on hazmat training, "Recognizing and Identifying Hazardous Materials." Above all else, the course stresses safety and the use of caution. The acronym "D.E.C.I.D.E." is used repeatedly throughout the text to guide the firefighters through the emergency intervention process and to minimize personal risk. The acronym stands for "Detect hazardous material presence; Estimate likely harm (without intervention); Choose response objectives; Identify action options; Do the best option; Evaluate process."

What may have confused the crews that night and led them to try to hose the trailer was their assuming they were dealing not with a "cargo" fire but a "truck and equipment fire." The guidebook has a separate subsection for dealing with hazmat fires in trucks and equipment. The directive is to flood them with water, or if no water is available, to use Halon, a dry chemical, or dirt.

Firefighters finding a trailer that is normally attached to a semitruck on fire, as well as a pickup truck and a compressor on fire next to the trailer, most probably thought the proper remedy was to douse the trailer and equipment with water. Within seconds of applying that remedy, the trailer exploded.

Further complicating matters for the arriving pumper crews was that the trailers were less than 100 feet apart. If either captain was familiar with the distance tables as set out in the Bureau of Alcohol, Tobacco, Firearms, and Explosives (ATF) regulations, he may have assumed the contents of the trailers consisted of construction equipment or material. The ATF regulations required trailers containing explosives to be set a minimum of 224 feet apart if there was no berm or barricade between them—as there was not at this site.

ATF regulations also called for trailers containing explosives to be at least 933 feet from any highway and at least 680 feet from any city street. These trailers were located less than 600 feet from 71 Highway and less than 350 feet from 87th Street.

But likely the most confusing thing about the contents of the trailers was that the trailers bore no placards. En route to the construction site, Department of Transportation placards indicating explosives were clearly visible. At the site, flaps covered the placards to deter tampering by possible intruders. Although this was a routine safety precaution used at many blasting sites, and one the government agency in charge of regulating explosives, the ATF, at least tacitly condoned, for these arriving pumper crews it would result in disaster.

What the crews could plainly see 250 feet or so away from the burning trailer were two well-marked, tall, boxy, yellow explosive lockers sitting on the ground that housed blasting caps and dynamite. It is reasonable to speculate that when the crews saw these locked steel lockers they assumed they contained the "explosives" referred to by the dispatcher.

Another oddity was that all permits issued to the construction contractors were under the Kansas City fire code, but there was nothing in the regulations requiring the City Engineer's Office to notify the Kansas City Fire Marshal's Office of any blasting operations. Nor did the permit application require specific information regarding the type, quantity, or site location of the explosives being used.

Likewise, the ATF, which oversees the manufacturing of explosives and the licensing of any user of explosives, is under no obligation to inform the fire marshal or fire department about any explosive material being used in any given jurisdiction. The ATF did not once use its authority to inspect this particular construction site. If it had the matter of the placarding may have been at issue, although probably not, but the location of the trailers, within less than 100 feet of each other, was a violation that most probably would have been acted upon. This correction would not have saved the firefighters but it most likely would have prevented the second trailer from exploding off of the debris and shock wave from the first trailer's explosion. Thus millions of dollars in property damage resulted from this lack of oversight.

Construction of the Bruce R. Watkins Memorial Drive had been under way at 87th Street and 71 Highway in south Kansas City since just after Labor Day.

Bruce R. Watkins, 1924–1980, was a prominent local politician and elected official. In 1962 he co-founded Freedom, Inc., a coalition of black leaders intent on advancing civil rights issues such as fair housing and integrating electoral politics.[5] In 1963 he and one other African American were the first blacks to be elected to the city council. Watkins would later serve as circuit clerk of the Jackson County Court, again the first black to do so. Although he lost his bid to become the first black mayor of Kansas City in 1978, his work at Freedom, Inc., paved the way for Emmanuel Cleaver II to win that office in 1991.[6] (In 2004 Cleaver was elected to the US Congress from the 5th District of Missouri, a seat he still holds.)

The construction, a project of the State of Missouri Highway Department, was a $200 million venture to link the memorial drive to downtown Kansas City, ten miles away. The project to excavate a rock quarry and use the rocks and dirt to build up the roadway at the south end of the project—at 87th Street—was a $4.2 million undertaking for which Brown Brothers Construction was the general contractor.

The construction site was split into two sides. The west side was flat ground where at night the big equipment—earthmovers, bulldozers, and Bobcats—was parked. During the day the equipment was used to haul away the rocks and dirt from the quarry on the east side. The general contractor also had three office-type trailers parked in the median between southbound 71 Highway and northbound 71. At night the west side was brightly lit with two tall, generator-powered overhead lights.

On the east side, up a steep hill, a limestone rock quarry sat atop a high bluff overlooking the Blue River. Excavation of the limestone had flattened the area to a low plateau with an eight-foot earthen berm. Two semitruck trailers were parked about 350 feet behind the berm.

Both trailers contained a mixture of ammonium nitrate and fuel oil, commonly known as ANFO, in long, nylon socks weighing thirty pounds.[7] Each night, the foreman of the excavating company locked each trailer. At night the east side was pitch dark.

Ammonium nitrate in its pure form is simply fertilizer and is used widely in agriculture. Many people use it on their lawns in the form of white granular beads. Essentially it is a salt. When mixed with a fuel oil it becomes a blasting agent known as ANFO and is used throughout the United States for blasting at construction sites, mines, and rock quarries.

As such it is one of the safest and most economical blasting agents available and it is not easily detonated. One way to get rid of excess ANFO is to light it on fire in an open field and simply let it burn out. Because it is a salt, it will dissolve in water.

On April 19, 1995, Timothy McVeigh used 4,200 pounds of ANFO in a homemade bomb loaded with blasting caps and detonators to blow up the Alfred P. Murrah Federal Building in Oklahoma City, killing 168 people and wounding many hundreds more.[8] Without the blasting caps and detonators, the ANFO in his rental truck was harmless.

The ANFO in most of the socks at the construction site also contained 5 percent aluminum pellets to increase the blast force—giving it a "hotter load"—because the contract for the excavation called for the bedrock to be broken into rock chunks no more than fifteen inches in diameter. This particular mixture of ammonium nitrate, fuel oil, and aluminum pellets was known as "Maynes Mix," named after the company that supplied it, Maynes Explosives. The aluminum pellets introduce a measure of volatility to ANFO.

In the first trailer to explode, there were about 3,500 pounds of ANFO without the aluminum pellets mixed in and 17,000 pounds of Maynes Mix. Each pile of socks was stacked in a pyramid at one end or the other of the trailer, leaving the middle clear. The other trailer had a full load of 30,000 pounds of Maynes Mix, also stacked at opposite ends in pyramids.

This storage pattern was one reason the second trailer was cut in half at the middle by the shock wave and hot debris from the first explosion.

To excavate the limestone, the blasting company drilled thirty-foot holes in the bedrock, stuffed in the long cylindrical socks, and ignited the Maynes Mix with blasting caps and a charge of dynamite. The dirt and rock excavated was then hauled by large earthmovers from the quarry to the west of 71 Highway where it was used to build up a new roadway—sometimes as high as thirty feet—in a lowland near the Blue River. On average, the excavation company, Mountain Plains, used between 10,000 and 16,000 pounds a day of Maynes Mix.

Igniting Maynes Mix in a confined space, such as inside a semitrailer, could cause it to explode if it were allowed to burn for up to forty minutes—the time it took the second trailer to explode. The trapped heat inside the trailer could cause pressure to build up to such an extent that the aluminum pellets would begin firing inside the socks. This agitation and combustion could eventually trigger a shock wave to move through the ANFO and make it explode.

That said, ANFO had never exploded inside a trailer before—despite being stored in thousands of them in the United States—and no one could have predicted it would have the night of November 29, 1988, at a construction site in Kansas City. There is a good possibility that without the aluminum pellets in the socks, the ANFO would have burned itself out or been extinguished by the firefighters.

CHAPTER 3

Investigating the Crime

The deaths of six firefighters in a colossal, arson-fueled explosion shocked Kansas Citians. For the tens of thousands of area residents who were shaken awake, and even more so for those thousands who sustained property damage, this was personal. Not since the Union Station Massacre in 1933—in which four law enforcement officers were gunned down in a hail of machine-gun fire—had one crime created such notoriety and outrage.[1]

Complicating matters for the Kansas City Police Department homicide team assigned to investigate the crime was that the two enormously powerful explosions obliterated all physical evidence from the east side of the crime scene.

Because the arsons involved explosives, the Bureau of Alcohol, Tobacco, Firearms, and Explosives (ATF) also had investigative jurisdiction. When the ATF soon came to suspect labor unrest was at the bottom of the disaster, the US Labor Department, Racketeering Division, was invited to assist in the federal investigation.

The first two people the Kansas City police wanted to interview were the guards at the site. Just before daylight, Detective Victor Zinn picked up Debbie Riggs, thirty-three, the female guard, at her mother's home in Grandview, three miles south of the construction site. Her brother, Robert Riggs, the president of the security company hired to guard both sides of the construction site, was also brought in for questioning that morning. How his company, Ameriguard, came to acquire the security contract is a curious story of its own.

Robert Riggs spent his first five years after high school working as a janitor at a high school in Ruskin Heights, a low-income neighborhood in southeast Kansas City. He took courses at Longview Community College and got an associate's degree in a program called "police science." His first job in security was two months of undercover work at a Sears store.

In October 1976 he was hired as a detention officer at the Dallas, Texas,

County jail. While working at the jail he met and married a female deputy, Jennet McDanald.

His career at the jail hit a road bump in May 1978 when he had a physical altercation with one of the inmates. The inmate, William Hinton, sued Riggs in federal court for assault, claiming Riggs pinned "my arm behind me and ran my head in[to] the bars twice, then kicked me in the stomach and started chocking me. I ended up at Parkland Hospital that afternoon."[2]

The case was heard on September 21, 1979. Judgment was entered in Riggs's favor, but there was a price to pay. The sheriff's office suspended him for three days "for using poor judgment" and transferred him to the Dallas County jail in Woodland.

Not long after that transfer, Robert and Jenny Riggs moved to Kansas City in 1980 where Robert opened a small private-security company he named Ameriguard.

Ken Brown of Brown Brothers Construction originally hired Robert Riggs in October 1988 as a private investigator to surveil a former employee he suspected of sabotaging some equipment at the construction site. The former employee suspected of sabotage never returned to the construction site and there were no further acts of sabotage.

When Ken Brown learned that the guard patrolling the west side of the construction site had been found asleep on the job, Brown opted to replace that guard service with Ameriguard. The job called for posting a guard on duty between 6 p.m. and 6 a.m. each night.

Brown Brothers had hundreds of thousands of dollars' worth of large earth-moving equipment parked at night on the west side adjacent to 71 Highway and easily accessible to anyone with larceny or sabotage on their minds.

The first day for Ameriguard at the construction site was October 20, 1988. Ameriguard deployed six security guards, one of whom was Robert's wife, Jenny; another was his sister, Debbie. The other four were Donna Costanza, Debbie's live-in partner for the last four years, Kevin Lemanske, Robin Hammonds, and Melvin Stanton. Each night two of the guards worked separate six-hour shifts at the construction site: the first guard between 6 p.m. and midnight and the second between midnight and 6 a.m.

To create the impression that Ameriguard was not some kind of mom-and-pop organization, the three Riggses—Robert, Jenny, and Debbie—used aliases on their work sheets and written reports to the construction company. Robert was "Officer Mason." Robert worked thirty-two six-hour shifts between October 20 and the night of the explosions, more shifts than any other guard. Debbie was "Officer Fiser." She worked the second-highest number of shifts, twenty-four. Robert's wife, Jenny, worked twenty-one, and Donna Costanza, who usually worked alongside Debbie, worked twenty-one also. Not even the other guards, other than Costanza, knew that any of the Riggses were related.[3]

The use of aliases also had a benefit for Debbie. It concealed that she, who was on maternity leave from the Ford auto plant, had an income-producing job in violation of her maternity leave arrangement.

In the two months the construction site had been in operation there had been no reported acts of vandalism on the east side where Mountain Plains, the subcontractor that did the excavating, kept dynamite and blasting caps in secure bunkers and about 50,000 pounds of ANFO in two semitrailers.

On consecutive nights in the first week of guarding the west side, Riggs reported seeing and confronting dangerous intruders on the east side.[4] He said the first occasion placed him in a life-threatening standoff with three people in a large SUV, one of whom, the driver, looked to him like Charles Manson. Riggs reported he narrowly escaped major injury or death when the SUV he was pursuing made a U-turn and drove straight at him on the access road, forcing him to the shoulder of the road where he ducked down in his front seat to avoid being shot. In the mayhem, Robert was unable to get the SUV's license plate. He documented the incident by calling the police and writing a report.

The following night, working alone again, he used his spotlight to intimidate a Plymouth Duster with two people in it to exit the east side. Again, he was not able to get a license plate number. When Kevin Lemanske came on duty at midnight, Riggs drove him over to the east side just so he would become familiar with the terrain in case other intruders might appear. As they drove over by the ANFO trailers, Riggs noticed there were wire cutters on the ground. Looking around further, he saw that a trailer door was open—its lock cut off. Robert called Norm Collins of Mountain Plains, who came out to the site in the middle of the night to see the wire cutters and the open trailer door.

By the next evening, Ameriguard was hired by Mountain Plains to post a guard on the east side every night.

While Detective Zinn was interviewing Debbie, Detective William Wilson was questioning her brother in a separate room.

Before the videotape was turned on, Debbie drew an elaborate sketch of both sides of the construction site. When the interview began at

9:30 a.m., Debbie and Zinn stood before an easel holding this drawing as he began his questioning. For someone who just a few hours earlier had undergone such a traumatic experience, Debbie seemed composed. Her shoulder-length hair fell lankly over the sweatshirt she wore. At the time she was five months pregnant.

Zinn began by asking her to tell him "the chain of events that occurred this morning, immediately after the explosion."[5] In a low, emotionless voice, Debbie launched into an uninterrupted response of over fifteen hundred words. Her account began not after the first explosion, but some thirty-five minutes or so before.

Her basic story was she was sitting in her pickup on the west side around 3:30 a.m. when she saw two large men walking in behind the trailers Brown Brothers used as offices in the median of 71 Highway. When the men did not come back into view, she radioed her brother on the east side. When he promptly came over she got into his station wagon and they drove down by the trailers with their headlights off. Not seeing anyone, Robert put the headlights back on and he began flashing a spotlight around the area. Not finding the intruders, they decided to drive about a half mile north to the QuikTrip, where Debbie went inside to ask the night manager if he had seen two men on foot. After the manager said he had not, she came back out and got in the station wagon.

A woman drove into the parking lot and raced into the store. The night manager came out and told the guards that some of the equipment at the construction site was on fire. They drove back to the construction site and saw Debbie's pickup ablaze, its headlights on and its horn blaring. As her brother was calling the fire department, Debbie could see flames rising above the ridge on the east side. She told Zinn,

> I glanced over this way, and beyond the ridge, there's a ridge right there, and you can't see the trailer because of the ridge, but we could see flames, or I saw flames coming up and I said the trailers are on fire too. But it looked more like the truck, but I had said the trailers are on fire too, so he told, he was still on the phone, and told them that there was two fires then.

In a few minutes Pumper 41 arrived, pulling in alongside Debbie's burning pickup. By the time the firefighters put out that fire, Pumper 30 arrived, stayed about a minute, and then headed up the access road to the east side. Not long after, Pumper 41 drove up the access road to the east side. Debbie and Robert followed in his station wagon, parking about 250 feet away from the burning trailer, unable to go farther because of the rough terrain in the rock quarry where the trailers were located.

A yellow fire department car arrived a few minutes later, pulling in directly behind Robert's station wagon. It too could go no farther due to the terrain. The driver approached the passenger side of the station wagon where Debbie was sitting, holding a tiny barking poodle in her lap. She got out and walked around to the back of the station wagon and could see another person sitting in the front seat of the fire department car. The driver was asking her what was in the trailers. "I told him as far I knew it was blasting caps and fertilizer," information the driver relayed to the man in the car, "and that's when the explosion occurred, and it knocked us back in behind" the fire department car.

She could hear her brother yelling if she was all right. She stood up, but by now boulders and metal and debris from the explosion were raining down so she lay back down in the ditch and covered her head with her hands. The driver got up but stumbled toward the back of his car and fell against the trunk. She and her brother tried to help him. The driver was screaming, "Is the chief okay?"

When she saw the other trailer was on fire she became afraid of a second explosion so rather than get back in Robert's station wagon as he suggested, she began walking back down the hill. She got about twenty feet and Robert picked her up in the station wagon. They headed back to the west side. On the way a police officer in the median of 71 Highway stopped them and said for them to go park behind the heavy equipment near her demolished pickup and wait there until the police could take their statements. After waiting twenty-five minutes they decided to leave the area. As they drove away the second blast erupted. "And that's it."

Zinn asked her why she was at the site. "I brought him down a meatloaf sandwich, and he didn't have another officer on duty, so he asked me to stay."

She said she could not identify the two men she saw, never saw their faces, but it looked like they had hoods on and wore dark clothing.

From her vantage point on the west side she could see every car going by on 71 Highway in both directions, but it was "a real dead night."

Zinn asked her if she left anything in her pickup. "My purse, that's about it." Did she leave the keys in the pickup? "Yeah, the keys in the vehicle."

She estimated it took four or five minutes to go to the QuikTrip and drive back. When they got back and saw her pickup on fire, there was no one around.

Was there anything out of the ordinary that night? "No. Nothing."

Zinn asked her if she or her brother were normally armed when guarding the site. She said her brother was.

Several of Debbie's answers and statements did not add up to Zinn. Her leaving her keys in the ignition and her purse in plain view in her pickup after just seeing prowlers seemed counterintuitive in the extreme.[6] The fact both guards left the site in response to seeing prowlers did not make sense. Maybe one guard would go looking for the prowlers but you don't leave the construction site totally unguarded. As he assessed what Debbie was saying, he found himself not buying the prowler story.

Robert was telling Detective Wilson a somewhat different story.[7] He and Debbie were in his station wagon on the west side when Debbie told him she saw prowlers. Debbie was sitting next to him making out a new work schedule for the guards because earlier that afternoon Ken Brown of Brown Brothers Construction informed him he was cutting back the security detail's hours by 150 minutes per night.

Another point of departure popped up when Robert told Wilson it was impossible from the west side to see any of the equipment or the trailers on the east side because "the west side it's down low, [the east side] is way up on a cliff, on a rock." This meant Debbie could not have seen that it was the ANFO trailer shooting off flames—and most certainly not the construction company pickup—because her view was obstructed by a steep ridge and an eight-foot earthen berm.

More elements of Debbie's story fell apart when police interviewed the night manager at QuikTrip. Dave Miller said Debbie purchased milk and breakfast rolls and then used the microwave to heat the rolls and Robert bought coffee. They were sitting in the station wagon having a snack when a woman in a black Camaro sped into the parking lot and rushed into the store to report a fire at the construction site.[8]

Debbie told Zinn they left immediately after the manager told them of the fire, but the woman in the Camaro, Vivian Rhodes, told police she was concerned because the manager did not call 911, and the guards seemed so indifferent she got back in her car and flagged down a patrol wagon.[9] "Ms. Rhodes stated both of the security guards were eating and did not appear to be too excited about the burning vehicle . . . Ms. Rhodes stated that she drove away from the lot and observed that the security guards were still in the parking lot," Detective Ed Glynn wrote in his report.

Thirty-six hours after the explosions, Police Chief Larry Joiner held a news conference to announce a $35,000 reward for information leading to the conviction of the person or persons responsible.[10] He encouraged anyone with information to call the TIPS Hotline. Captain Gary Van Buskirk, who would supervise the homicide investigation, said at present there were no suspects but there were some conflicts between what guards on duty said happened and what other witnesses told police. He said he did not consider the guards suspects. (It was standard practice for Van Buskirk not to identify people under investigation as "suspects" to ward off their hiring lawyers and clamming up.[11])

Detective Zinn's interview with Debbie left him with some serious doubts about the story she told of seeing two prowlers. To check out the veracity of her claim, he and his partner, Detective John Fraise, arranged to meet Debbie at the shut-down construction site three nights after the explosions. He wanted Debbie to show where she was parked and where she saw the prowlers.

Debbie said she was parked facing due east on a level area on the west side in among the large earth-moving equipment. From there she saw two large people walking about a quarter or a third of a mile away near Blue River Road toward the office trailers parked in the median of 71 Highway.

Leaving Fraise in the police car with Debbie, Zinn positioned himself at Blue River Road and radioed Fraise he was ready. Zinn then began walking toward the office trailers. When Fraise said he could not see him, Zinn, who was wearing a tan trench coat, began waving his arms like a windmill. Fraise still could not see him.

When Zinn returned to the police car and sat down in the front seat he noticed the glare from the two large overhead lights made it difficult for him to see out. When he flipped on the interior dome light, as Debbie said she had while filling out new scheduling assignments, all he could see was his own reflection in the window. This convinced Zinn that Debbie could not have seen the prowlers from where she sat.

The next night, around 7 p.m., Zinn and Fraise were back at the construction site to re-interview Debbie and to interview Robert separately. During each interview Zinn drove around the construction site, getting them to track their movements from point to point the night of the explosions.[12]

This time Debbie admitted she made some incorrect statements to Zinn in her initial interview: she was in her brother's station wagon when she saw the prowlers; she left her brother's gun in her pickup; she was not near her burnt pickup when the second blast occurred, but walking toward the command center while her brother returned to her pickup to retrieve his gun. She did not correct her fabrication about not being scheduled to work that night, something Zinn found out by looking at Ameriguard's scheduling logs.

Robert, in his interview, also mentioned giving his handgun to his sister and going back to get it before the second blast. He told Zinn he went back because it was a "collector's item of limited edition," that only two thousand of these snub-nosed .38s had been minted. (It was not.[13])

After Zinn asked Robert to hand over the gun, Robert said the gun was being cleaned at a gun shop, but he would bring it in when he got it back in a day or two. (Zinn never got the gun.[14])

In his written report, Zinn described the interview with Robert as "a very strained affair. Robert would seldom answer questions first hand [sic]. Most of his responses to questions or accounts were quotes of varying sources, i.e., 'My sister said'; 'I heard that'; 'I read'; 'The paper said'; and/or 'The news reported.'"

He also wrote Robert "seems more preoccupied with his reputation and business than with the conversation at hand. Robert was visibly unhappy with the information his sister Deborah had given detectives. His displeasure was almost to the point of saying his sister was lying."

Robert, in particular, did not like his sister saying he nodded off in the station wagon and she had to awaken him to tell him about the prowlers. In his initial interview with Detective Wilson he addressed this point: "I heard her say 'Robert,' and I, you know I wasn't there to take a nap or anything such as that. I, she was working on some paperwork and I had eaten a sandwich and my eyes were shut and I'm telling you that because that's what Debbie has told me over the telephone just a little while ago."

The simulation Zinn and Fraise conducted to test the veracity of Debbie's prowler story and the subsequent interviews the detectives conducted of the two guards led Captain Van Buskirk to tell reporters on Friday, December 2, 1988, that police were taking a closer look at the activities of the guards that night. He said Robert Riggs would be given a polygraph later that day but a medical condition (pregnancy) prevented the police from polygraphing Debbie.

Van Buskirk told reporters he had doubts about some of the accounts given by the security guards, but they were not suspects. "They're saying four to five minutes at the most (they were away from the construction site). Don't you have a problem with that? There's a lot of distance involved. In my opinion it would have taken longer," referring to the amount of time the arsonists would have needed to set fires on both sides of the construction site.

That same day, Richard Miller, an attorney for Mountain Plains, told a reporter Ameriguard was still in charge of security at the construction site. "We haven't really talked about whether they provided adequate security," Miller said, adding he was unaware the guards spent extra time at QuikTrip purchasing and consuming snacks.

The next day, Van Buskirk reported Robert Riggs passed the lie detector test. (At the time Robert took the test, he had been administering polygraph examinations for his security company for the last eight years.[15]) With that the investigation into the Riggses lost its momentum and went into a deep freeze once each of them retained attorneys.

In the days immediately after the explosions, the Kansas City Police Department set up checkpoints in the wee hours going north and south on 71 Highway for several nights. The police wanted to see if any of these drivers had gone by the construction site on November 28–29 between the hours of 11 p.m. and 4 a.m. to find out what they had seen.

A number of witnesses were identified. One thing that came out from the reports was the Riggses were not alone at the site. From what the passersby reported there was a high probability another guard, Donna Costanza, was at the site in her VW and there was a fourth person as well.

Sometime around 3 a.m., passerby Christy Miller saw four people sitting in Robert's station wagon parked near Debbie's unoccupied red pickup.

That one of those four people sitting in Robert's station wagon was Costanza was buttressed by what three other passersby saw. Around 12:30 a.m. passerby James Collins saw a VW with a handheld spotlight turned on traveling around the construction site. He said he saw three people in the VW. Just after 2 a.m., passerby Richard Lackland saw a yellow hatchback parked on the west side. He said he had seen that vehicle there during other early mornings. He saw a male in the driver's seat and a female leaning into an open door. (Costanza's VW Fox was a 1988, two-door hatchback.) At 2:30 a.m. passerby Koper (first name unknown) saw a light brown, two-door VW parked at the site.

At 3 a.m. and at 3:07 a.m. separate passersby reported seeing a female sitting in the front passenger seat of a station wagon with the dome light on. At 3:15 a.m. another passerby saw a female security guard in a station wagon.

And then there is passerby Terry Butts. He told police at 3:42 a.m., just a minute after Robert called in the fire, that he saw security guards parked next to each other. By the time the firefighters arrived, the second security guard vehicle was gone.

Somehow these revelations did not bring the Riggses back into focus.

Nor did a police report taken on February 22, 1989, that raised grave suspicions about Robert and Debbie Riggs.[16] Melvin Stanton, one of the guards Ameriguard used at the construction site, told Detective Fraise that Debbie Riggs called him around 9:30 p.m. on the night of the explosions and told him to report to work because another guard was not coming in. When Stanton arrived fifteen or thirty minutes later, Debbie was alone on the west side so he took up a position on the east side. At 11 p.m., Stanton said, Robert called him and told him to go home.

Asked by Fraise who he thought was responsible for the explosion, Stanton said "Robert Riggs." He also stated that "Debbie Riggs told him that Robert Riggs was about to lose the account at the construction site because the Browns (Brown Brothers Construction) were not satisfied with Ameriguard's performance."

Stanton further stated that several days before the explosions, Robert told him, "If anything happens out here, you keep your mouth shut."

Three other points Stanton made had significance: Debbie normally had a large boxer dog with her, but this night only her miniature lap dog; Debbie always carried a one-gallon red gas can with a yellow spout in the bed of her pickup because her gas gauge was broken; she told Stanton she was about to lose her truck because she had spent so much money on her pregnancy (artificial insemination).[17]

Stanton would never be reinterviewed.

More opportunities to refocus the investigation on the Riggses came through the TIPS hotline. The $35,000 reward money generated scores of leads.

Buried in among those calls to TIPS were messages from two separate friends of Debbie's that directly implicated her in causing the explosions.[18] Even though one of these tipsters made a second call a month later to follow up, she was never contacted. Neither was the other one. The one who called in twice said Debbie told her two nights before the explosions she was going to torch her pickup to collect insurance; the other said a few days after the explosions, Debbie admitted pulling an insurance scam on her pickup.

A third caller left information with the TIPS operator that implicated both Robert and Debbie. Gloria Nolen, a recent graduate in radiology, thought what she saw the night of the explosions was something the police should know.[19] As the investigation into the firefighters' deaths dragged on, she sought out a friend of hers who was a detective in the KCPD homicide department, Rita Stawicki, and told her what she saw that night. Stawicki advised her to call homicide and make a formal report.

On August 2, 1990, Nolen called homicide and spoke with Detective John Fraise. By now the investigation had morphed into a task force comprised of the ATF, the US Labor Department, and a couple of homicide detectives from KCPD, neither of whom were Zinn or Fraise. For their parts, the ATF and the Labor Department were concentrating almost exclusively on investigating organized labor's possible role in the blasts.

Nolen, twenty-four, told Fraise, who just happened to be the one who answered the phone, that around 3:30 a.m. on the night of the explosions she was driving southbound on 71 Highway by the construction site when she saw a pickup on the west side of the roadway fully engulfed in flames. In the police report, Fraise quoted her as stating she "also observed two white cars (unknown occupants) circling the area from the burning pickup to Blue River Road . . . 'as if they were looking for someone.' She stated these cars bore no markings and the only thing that stood out was the position of their spotlights which were shining around the area in the median that separated 71 Highway." She told Fraise the spotlights were "higher up on the cars" and not positioned "like the police cars have theirs."

Fraise ended his report by writing the witness told him she called 911 the moment she arrived home to report her observations and was informed she would be contacted by the police, but never was. Not long after making that call she said she heard the first explosion.

Fraise sent his report to his supervisor, Sergeant Troy Cole, who signed it and passed it on to the task force. Although what the eyewitness reported seeing that night completely undermined the stories Debbie and Robert Riggs told about being at QuikTrip when they first learned of the fire at the construction site, no one in the task force took the opportunity to interview the eyewitness, either by phone or in person, and her revelations just slipped through the cracks.

Investigators would be given two more chances to link the guards to the blasts. On June 1, 1993, ATF Special Agent Dave True, who led the federal investigation, wrote a report based on what Johnnie Ray Neil told him.[20] Neil is the brother of Jessica Vernon, who worked at Stack's Drive-In with Donna Costanza. Neil said two months after the explosions, he was present in 1989 at Stack's Drive-In when he overheard Donna Costanza telling his sister that she assisted a female security guard,

Debbie Riggs, in setting fire to her pickup at the construction site on the night the firefighters died to collect insurance. Neil said he also heard Costanza say, "We set the trailer on fire after placing the [construction company] pickup right next to it so that the pickup would catch fire, but the fire got out of hand."

Over eight months later, on February 16, 1994, Agent True and Special Agent Eugene Schram of the Department of Labor took a signed statement from Jessica Vernon that in part stated:

> Approximately five years ago, shortly after the explosions which
> killed the six Kansas City firefighters . . . I believe some television
> news program mentioned the explosion, which caused Sandy
> DiGiovanni to say she had information about the cause of the
> explosion. DiGiovanni said a friend of hers, Donna Costanza,
> claimed to have worked as a security guard on the construction site
> where the explosion occurred. Donna Costanza said that on the night
> of the explosion, she assisted a fellow female security guard [to] burn
> her private pickup truck. This was done to collect insurance on the
> truck.[21]

Vernon also said she heard DiGiovanni—the owner/operator of Stack's Drive-In—say she heard Costanza claim the reason they burned the pickup was because it had mechanical problems.

Even though over five years had passed since the explosions, and the task force was no nearer to solving the case than it was the night it happened, neither agent followed up personally. It would take almost a year for anyone to contact Debbie Riggs. Costanza was never contacted.

On February 10, 1995, Detective Don Emerson went to see Debbie Riggs at the Ford assembly plant in Claycomo where she resumed working in 1989 after giving birth to a daughter. Before proceeding with the interview, Emerson had her read the Miranda warning, which she signed.

When Emerson asked her if she had intentionally burned her vehicle, Debbie said no. He then told her he had received information Donna Costanza burned her vehicle for her because it had a lot of mechanical problems. Debbie denied that, advancing the theory disgruntled union members were responsible. She said two had to be hiding behind her vehicle and the others on the east side near the trailers.

In his report, Emerson wrote, "She stated Donna Costanza does not have the guts to set a vehicle on fire . . . Donna has a cocaine problem," and she had not heard from Donna in over two months. "She further stated she would take a polygraph to clear her of any involvement in this offense."[22]

Three days later Emerson received a phone call from John Cullom, an attorney representing Debbie Riggs, who told Emerson if the police wished to contact Debbie he must be notified first. "He further stated she will not make any additional statement and will not submit to a polygraph examination," Emerson wrote in his report.[23]

From this point on, the investigation never got back to the guards. (When Special Agent True met with Robert Riggs, on April 17, 1990, the interview centered on how long the guards were gone from the construction site. Riggs said he did a test run and the answer was seven minutes. Did Riggs have any suspicions? Well, there were gay parties on the weekends up in the woods behind the quarry and he heard there were some doing devil worship in an abandoned house near the site.[24])

CHAPTER 4

Investigating the Marlborough Neighborhood

By the late 1980s, the Marlborough neighborhood had fallen a long way from the days when it was a lower-middle-class enclave of mostly small, ranch-style homes. It was now, more than anything else, a monumental failure in urban planning; for those who lived there it had become a place to escape; for most others it was a neighborhood to avoid.

Higher aspirations prevailed when Marlborough began as a suburban real estate development around 1900, attracting new home buyers who wanted a more bucolic setting. The neighborhood was named after John Churchill, the duke of Marlborough in eighteenth-century England.

In the two decades before the City of Kansas City annexed Marlborough in 1947, it had the appearance of a self-contained village. Its main commercial road, 71 Highway, ran through the heart of it. Various businesses and a few small factories operated on both sides of the highway, a two-lane state road that connected downtown Kansas City to the rural farming communities farther south and east.

The annexation would prove to be the neighborhood's downfall. With it soon came a city landfill next to the Blue River that brought a growing mound of garbage to the 250-foot-high bluffs overhanging the river. Being a part of Kansas City did not bring the infrastructure improvements the neighborhood expected. Very few residential blocks had sidewalks and sewers. Rainwater and water runoff collected in two-foot-deep ditches that ran along the streets throughout the community. The city did nothing to improve these defects and they remain today.

The blow that sent Marlborough spiraling downward, and from which it is unlikely to ever recover, was a proposal by city planners in the 1960s to convert 71 Highway into US 71—into what would eventually become the Bruce R. Watkins Memorial Drive. Because the proposed ten-mile route would physically cut off numerous largely black neighborhoods on the east side from the rest of the city with a six-lane concrete barrier—

and displace 10 percent of the city's black population—lawsuits alleging "economic racism" delayed the project for over twenty years.

No one knew it was going to take that long, but everyone knew the disruption was coming sooner or later. Shops and businesses along 71 Highway closed and real estate values began to plummet as those who could afford to move elsewhere got out. Those who could not afford to leave saw the equity in their homes evaporate. They were stuck.

Real estate speculators moved in and bought up many of the homes at bargain prices and turned them into rental properties, many of them run by slum landlords. The once neatly kept streets of Marlborough took on the look of Appalachia. Drug houses sprang up; motels that rented by the hour became fixtures on 71 Highway. Jack Stack Barbecue, one of the city's most frequented restaurants, shuttered. Fairland Park, an eight-acre amusement center that opened in 1923 and drew people from all over the metropolitan area, particularly to ride the "Wildcat" roller-coaster and the eight-story Ferris wheel, shut down in 1977. Over the next thirty years the population of Marlborough would drop from ten thousand to under nine hundred. It had become a ghost of a neighborhood.

For Marlborough residents in late 1988 and early 1989, the explosions at the nearby construction site became topic one. Gossip in Marlborough was rampant. At the time there was a widely publicized $35,000 reward for information leading to the arrest of the perpetrators. With no other leads to go on, the police investigation of Marlborough became intense, with detectives chasing down tips that implicated a wide array of suspects from the neighborhood.

It was widely assumed in Marlborough that Frank Sheppard and his brother Skip, two large, forbidding Native Americans, had to be involved. Both were drunks, druggies, and notorious brawlers. A number of bars in Marlborough had banned both. Frank had served prison time for armed robbery. So it was to be expected fingers would be pointed at Frank and also at Skip, who was constantly at his side.

The police heard of these rumors. One early rumor was started by Darlene Edwards, Frank Sheppard's longtime girlfriend, with her claiming she saw a black pickup resembling the one driven by teenager Richard Brown go racing down the street outside her house shortly after the first explosion. The pickup, she said, was soon followed by a maroon-on-white vehicle that looked like one owned by Chuck Jennings, one of Richard Brown's closest friends.

Nine days after the explosions, around 8:30 p.m., police stopped Frank and Darlene on their way to a laundromat, informing them they were being arrested "for homicide" in connection with the firefighters case.[1] At the police station, two detectives grilled Darlene for over four hours while Frank was kept in an adjoining room. From time to time, he could hear one of the detectives screaming at Darlene and Darlene screaming back. Before they released her they had her draw a map of where she lived in relation to Richard Brown and draw the direction she saw his truck driving by.

Darlene was then taken back to her vehicle in a squad car. When the detectives got around to Frank, well after midnight, they found him asleep on the floor, curled up under a table. After ten minutes of questioning, they released him. With no money on him, not even enough to make a phone call, Frank had to wait around for his bail bondsman's office to open so he could get bus fare back to Darlene's house.

The next day, December 9, 1988, police came to see Richard Brown. When the questions turned to his possible involvement in the firefighters case, it quickly became apparent Darlene was the one linking him to the crime.[2] To clear his name, he volunteered to take a polygraph. The test was administered that day at police headquarters by Officer Harold D. Oldham. In his report, Oldham wrote, "No deception shown by Richard W. Brown."[3]

Over the years, as the police continued to pull him over and question him about the firefighters case, the mistrust he felt for Darlene would fester.

The investigation took on a desperate quality as the years passed. While the families of the dead firefighters ached for those responsible to be brought to justice, there was no getting away from the impression that both sides of the investigation had reached dead ends.

There were growing reasons for this pessimism. Back in 1989, the State of Missouri charged a teenager, Bryan Sheppard, with six counts of second-degree murder in connection with the deaths of the firefighters only to have to turn him loose three months later when his attorney established that the two jailhouse informants lied about his confessing. (Bryan Sheppard, Frank and Skip's nephew, was in jail for a probation violation stemming from his conviction for stealing a bicycle, a misdemeanor and the only criminal offense on his record.)

The high-powered ATF/Labor Department investigators spent six fruitless years trying to connect organized labor to the crime. The major problem with this line of inquiry was there had been no real labor strife at the construction site, a fact attested to by Ken Brown of Brown Brothers Construction, the general contractor at the site, and by Norm Collins, the president of Mountain Plains, the blasting subcontractor. Both companies used unionized labor. The only real sticking point was that concrete was being supplied by a nonunion company.

The lead investigator for the ATF was Special Agent Dave True, a twenty-six-year veteran of the agency. An attractive man with silver hair and a pencil-thin mustache, he carried a certain swagger. He would not have been out of place in a Dashiell Hammett detective story. Now in his early fifties, he was set to retire and move on to a high-paying job in security at Yellow Freight, a major trucking company headquartered in Kansas City, but he did not want to retire with the biggest case of his life unsolved.[4]

With nothing to lose, the local ATF office and the Kansas City Police Department decided in 1993 to join forces and conduct one investigation. To accommodate the ATF, the police department agreed to replace its Crime against Persons (homicide) detectives with detectives from its Bombs and Arson unit. This seemingly innocuous switch would put ATF's True in firm control and give full throttle to the "cowboy" tactics for which the ATF nationally had come to be known in the wake of the disastrous sieges it initiated in the early 1990s at Ruby Ridge and at the Branch Davidians compound outside Waco, Texas.

As such, this realignment brought with it an entirely different culture in terms of how the rest of the investigation would unfold. As an ATF special agent, True had investigative powers that were unavailable to any city's police force. When facing recalcitrant witnesses, he, unlike city police, had a hammer with three prongs. With civilian witnesses, he could threaten them with an obstruction of justice charge if he believed they were withholding information; with felon witnesses, he had a stick and carrot depending on what the situation called for. He could threaten to bring additional charges such as upping a pending state charge into a federal crime with a longer sentence without parole or he could entice cooperation with the promise of leniency for pending charges. True would use these powers repeatedly in cobbling together his case against the Marlborough Five.

In late 1993, at the request of Captain Joe Galetti of the Kansas City Fire Department, True approached the producers of the TV series *Unsolved Mysteries* to do a segment on the firefighters case. He also announced a $50,000 reward—paid for mostly by the International Association of Fire Fighters—for information leading to the arrest and conviction of the people responsible for the firefighters' deaths. The announcement of the reward money was published widely in the news media.

As the *Unsolved Mysteries* episode was in production, the ATF received a call in November 1994 from Amy Pederson, an eighteen-year-old with social ties to Marlborough. She told ATF Agent Pete Lobdell that Richard Brown made admissions to her four years ago that he and his uncle, along with Frank and Bryan Sheppard, took dynamite to the construction site, placed it under the [ANFO] trailer or nearby equipment, and blew it up just to see what would happen. They did it "just for kicks."

Agent True would later say this call was "the starting point for investigating the Marlborough area" even though the statement Pederson gave Lobdell contradicted the known facts of the explosion. True knew the explosion was caused by a gasoline-fueled arson, not by dynamite, and he knew that other assertions she made were false.

She claimed Richard talked about his uncle always having a large quantity of explosives at his house. "She stated that the uncle (first name unknown, last name Brown) is an arson/bomb freak and has been involved in burning or blowing up buildings and sheds before," Lobdell wrote in his report. (Richard has no uncles with the surname Brown.) She stated Bryan Sheppard had recently married Valerie Rocha and they were living in an unincorporated area of Jackson County. (Bryan has never married.)

She told Lobdell she "decided to contact law enforcement and provide the information now before the TV show airs and law enforcement is deluged with information," i.e., before others began calling and trying to cash in on the reward money.

Based on this one tip, as implausible as it was, True pivoted from labor and put all of his energy and powerful resources into investigating people from Marlborough.

Two days before the *Unsolved Mysteries* segment aired, the *Kansas City Star* ran a front-page article that quoted Richard Cook, the ATF agent in charge of the Kansas City office, as saying, "We've identified some individuals we believe are at least connected to the fire."

Unsolved Mysteries reexamined cold cases, missing person cases, conspiracy theories, and unexplained phenomena such as alien abductions, ghosts, and UFO sightings. Although the show strove for the legitimacy of the documentary, its frequent focus on the paranormal greatly undermined that ambition. It was in no way the *Dateline* or *48 Hours* of its day. It ran on NBC from 1988 until 1997. After short stints on CBS, Lifetime, and Spike TV, it went out of production in 2010. In its heyday, Robert Stack, who played Eliot Ness on the popular TV show *The Untouchables* from 1959 through 1963, was the show's host. His melodramatic narration was delivered in a somber tone. For heightened dramatic effect, there was chilling theme music.

When the program ran on February 10, 1995, it featured interviews with various members of the fallen firefighters' families and a vivid re-enactment of an exploding trailer, a special effect the Kansas City Fire Department assisted in creating. During the program, Stack said because the arson led to the explosion and deaths of the firefighters, the crime was "nothing less than cold-blooded murder." At the end of the segment, Stack looked into the camera and asked the audience to help solve this crime by calling the local TIPS hotline or 1-800-ATF-GUNS with any information they might have, emphasizing the $50,000 reward.

Around this same time, in a highly unorthodox move, True had $50,000 reward posters placed in all Missouri and Kansas jails and prisons. Large posters were also plastered on highway overpasses and billboards, particularly those close to Marlborough.

Within a few days of the airing of the program, the two hotlines took calls from over 150 people, more than 60 of them convicts or ex-convicts. Another high percentage of the calls came from Marlborough residents.

The fact Bryan Sheppard had been indicted by the state for this crime in 1989 made him an easy target. The fact Richard Brown was his best friend did the same for him. Some of these callers harbored long-held grudges against Bryan Sheppard's uncles, Frank and Skip Sheppard, and implicated them in the explosions. Frank, who was twenty years older than Bryan, had by now two felony convictions and had been in and out of prison for years. He was back in state prison for violating his parole.

As a result of all of these calls to the hotline, these four and Darlene Edwards all of a sudden became Agent True's primary focus.

On March 14, 1995, the *Kansas City Star* ran a front-page story written by reporter Tom Jackman saying the government's investigation was focusing on the Sheppards and Darlene Edwards. Jackman quoted an ATF spokesperson saying, "It's a case that needs to be solved. The people of Kansas City want it to be solved."

The article cited possible physical evidence, "including a two-way radio that may have been stolen shortly before the explosion. . . . Some witnesses said the suspects were stealing construction equipment, while others said they intended to steal dynamite. Some said the fire was a diversion. Others said it was done for spite."[5]

Jackman's article—which made him a propaganda surrogate for the ATF—would become a script for many of the witnesses who came forward from Marlborough and from the prisons and jails. Over and over these informants would claim the Sheppards were up at the construction site stealing equipment, or dynamite, or walkie-talkies, and the fire was a diversion for these thefts or the fire was done out of pure meanness.

Anyone reading through the investigative reports would see none of the convicts told the same story. The same was true of all the numerous Marlborough witnesses.

Dozens and dozens of possible perpetrators were named in these reports, many of them in groups of three or four, but no two of these reports listed the same cast of characters. Among the names frequently cited were Ronnie Edwards, Darlene Edwards's stepson; Jackie Clark, Darlene's brother; Larry Baker, Frank and Skip's brother-in-law; Chuck Jennings, a friend of Richard and Bryan; Mike DiMaggio, the boyfriend of Richard's half sister; Johnny Driver, one of the informants who lied about Bryan confessing to him in 1989; Lonnie Joe Pugh, a friend of Richard and Bryan who lived next door to Larry Baker; the Bohrn brothers—Pooh and Buddy; and Shawn Roma and Ed Massey, woodcutters at the construction site.

Despite the wild inconsistencies in these reports and the dubious claims they contained, Agent True opted to focus the investigation exclusively on Frank and Skip Sheppard, Darlene Edwards, Bryan Sheppard, and Richard Brown. The fact none of the informants ever grouped these five as acting together did not dissuade him.

CHAPTER 5

The Marlborough Five

If Special Agent Dave True had conducted an in-depth investigation of the Marlborough Five, he would have learned that three of his targets—Darlene, Frank, and Skip—were so impaired from severe physical injuries they were incapable of participating in the lightning-fast assault over the rugged terrain of the construction site.

Skip had not worked since a barroom fight in 1984 left him permanently disabled; Frank was recuperating from being hit by a car on June 9, 1988, a collision that broke his left ankle and fractured his left elbow, requiring the surgical insertion of metal rods; and Darlene was recovering from a motorcycle accident on September 10, 1987, that broke her back and left her in a body cast for three months, with Harrington rods implanted in her back. (Those were surgically removed in February 1989, three months after the explosion that killed the firefighters.)

If True had asked anyone in Marlborough who knew about the dynamics operating among the Marlborough Five, he would have learned they were divided into two distinct camps of allegiance: Bryan and Richard, who in 1988 were seventeen and eighteen years old, respectively, in one group and the much older three in another.

It was common knowledge Bryan and Richard went out of their way to avoid Frank and Skip. As a Sheppard, Bryan had grown up under the black cloud his Uncle Frank emanated. It was second nature for Bryan to disavow Frank. For their part, Frank and Skip found Bryan and Richard to be cocky kids. They never socialized or "partied" with Bryan and Richard—or any other teenagers. On the rare occasions when Bryan and/or Richard came in contact with Frank or Skip it was inadvertent—Darlene was the only common ground among them and she was only that because from time to time she rented her upstairs bedroom to girlfriends of Bryan and Richard.

How the Marlborough Five spent what would turn out to be the most fateful day of their lives is a typical example of the separate worlds they inhabited.[1]

Monday, November 28, 1988, was the end of the long Thanksgiving weekend, a day to return to work or school. But there were no jobs that day for Skip, Frank, and Darlene, and no school for Bryan and Richard to attend. Both had dropped out in the tenth grade.

Larry Baker, who was married to Frank and Skip's sister, Diddi, saw it as a good day for a cookout. Frank limped up to Larry's around noon and was soon joined by Skip and his girlfriend, Liza Harrigan. Diddi dropped by Darlene's house and invited her and her eleven-year-old daughter, Becky, to join the party. They arrived about 2 p.m.

The beer flowed. People from the neighborhood were in and out all day, including Naomi and Earl Sheppard, the parents of Frank, Skip, and Diddi. They only stayed for a drink or two.

During the afternoon, while Frank and Skip were doing cocaine and drinking beer after beer, Darlene sat in the kitchen with Diddi drinking beer and smoking a joint. Around 5 p.m. Frank threw something at Darlene, and she knew it was time to go. She and Becky ate dinner at home. Becky went to bed around 10 p.m. and Darlene fell asleep watching *The Tonight Show.*

Frank, Skip, Liza, Diddi, and Larry ate dinner about 6:30 p.m. and then watched television. Around 11 p.m. Skip and Liza went to sleep on a sofa bed in Larry's front room. Frank, Diddi, and Larry continued to watch TV until about midnight. "I finally was going to walk home about midnight or so, but Larry told me it was cold outside and I still couldn't walk very good so I should get in the car and he'd drive me," Frank wrote in a letter in 2012. "We sat in front of Darlene's house, 2016 E. 83rd Street, and drank the beer we brought. I was kinda drunk, so when I got out of Larry's car I fell into the ditch in front of her house and got somewhat dirty. . . . I was laughing at myself for falling and Larry was helping me up and into the house. He yelled for Darlene to come help."

When the two of them got Frank inside, it was about 1:30 a.m. By this time he had consumed about a case of beer. He made it to the front bedroom and passed out on the bed. "I finally woke up in bed and asked Darlene to fix me some baking soda water for my stomach and also something to eat," Frank wrote. She made some scrambled eggs and then went back to bed. "It must have been about 3:30 a.m. then. So I stayed in the living room and was falling asleep on the couch. I just smoked my last cigarette and I was drifting off and then Booooooom!" he wrote.

It was amazing. It picked up the couch I was on and it was a very heavy couch—a hide-a-bed. Anyway, the couch slammed back to the floor after being about 2½ feet in the air. I was still in the air. It knocked me kind of sideways. I landed on the coffee table where my empty breakfast plate was. I broke the coffee table, broke my plate, and spilled the ashtray. When I got to my feet, I looked out the picture window of the living room and saw cars moving and trees swaying like in an earthquake. . . . There was a vacuum in the air and it was making my ears pop.

He heard Becky screaming, "Mommy, mommy, mommy," as she exited her bedroom. Darlene ran to her in the hallway and hugged her. Frank, thinking it was a gas explosion, yelled to Darlene to turn the thermostat off. Frank checked all the burners on the stove, put his pants back on, and went outside to check the gas meter. He saw the explosion had blown open the side door to Darlene's house so he nailed it shut. While he was outside, he saw some of his neighbors checking for damage to their houses. He saw Bill Grande, a letter carrier, outside his house across the street and he saw his next-door neighbors, Bear and Carole Williams, trying to nail plastic sheeting over the shattered windows in the front of their house.

Becky went back to her bedroom; Frank and Darlene to their bedroom. Then the second explosion, much louder and more forceful than the first, erupted at 4:48 a.m. It knocked out all of the electricity in Marlborough. There was no thought of sleeping after that.

Richard and Bryan spent a good part of November 28 together. For the last year or so, they had become inseparable. Bryan has a hard time remembering the day in any detail. "I'm sorry that I can't remember that day or night. I really am," he wrote in a letter in 2012.

I would give anything to be able to remember what I did all day and all night on November 28, 1988. . . . All I can say about that day is that I sure as hell wouldn't have been up early. . . . My days in 1988 were more or less the same. I'd wake up around 10, 11, or 12, get dressed and hit the streets. Start hustling, drive from house to house, friend to friend, always looking for things to scrap, looking for things to buy cheap and sell for a profit. Just driving around all day.

Bryan and Richard's main goal was to come up with money to party.

I do know that if you are hanging out with Richard he likes to be the one driving. We may have picked up a few items to take to the scrap yard—just junking old metal like we always done. Started drinking, smoking some pot, driving from house to house, park to park, up and down the streets of Marlborough, blasting the radio and looking to hook up with the neighborhood girls. Just like every day. We did that until we were too tired and too drunk to go on.

Bryan's best recollection is Richard dropped him off at his parents' house around midnight and he was "drunk as hell and he passed out on the couch in the front room." He remembers his girlfriend Debbie Howard coming upstairs and laying down beside him.

Throughout 1988 Richard lived with his grandparents in Marlborough. He moved in after his maternal grandfather had an incapacitating stroke. He helped by changing his grandfather's diapers, giving him his meds, and cooking some of his meals.

Richard remembers spending most of the day on November 28, 1988, with Bryan, scrapping for metal. As he recalls, he dropped Bryan off about 6 p.m., went to his grandparents' house, took a shower and then went to pick up Alena Fantauzzo about 7:30 p.m. at AB's, a topless bar where she worked. They bought some beer and drove over to Brenda Carpenter's house at 80th and Brooklyn where Alena's cousin, Stephanie Webb, was babysitting. They played cards for a couple of hours until Brenda Carpenter got home and then Richard drove Alena and Stephanie to QuikTrip to get some food.

"Then I took Alena back to her motel. I think the motel was called Best for Less," he wrote in a letter in 2012. He took Stephanie home and went to his grandparents' house to sleep.

"The next thing I know my grandma and grandpa are waking me up and saying go check the furnace to see if it blew up. I went downstairs, out the basement door to the front yard." Across the street he sees neighbors outside and they see him.

Frank Sheppard had the intelligence to be a top student but his impulses ruled him, dropping out of high school in tenth grade to get a job as a concrete worker. By then he had started smoking pot and using harder drugs—speed, sedatives, and prescription narcotics. At age nineteen, in 1969, he enlisted in the army. Three days before he was assigned to Fort Leonard Wood in central Missouri for basic training, he got married.

Joining the army made his family proud of him, especially his father, who had served in World War II. During his twelve weeks of basic training Frank scored high on rifle training and physical fitness, earning a promotion to corporal and then to acting sergeant, being responsible for training new enlistees. For the first time in his life Frank was showing promise and purpose. From there he was sent to Fort Ord in Carmel, California, for twelve weeks of advanced infantry training, once again becoming a squad leader.

Instead of sending him to Vietnam as a corporal, which is what he wanted, the army sent him to Fort Benning, Georgia, for noncommissioned officer school, wanting to make a sergeant out of him, something he did not want. When he came home on leave in December 1969 he was disillusioned. Shortly after he arrived, his son was born.

He reported to Fort Benning four days late and told the captain there he did not want to be an NCO because he did not want the responsibility. The captain said he intended to make a good sergeant out of him. Frank refused to attend the classes and was put on kitchen duty as a punishment. When his new orders arrived, he was ordered back to NCO school and given leave. He returned to Kansas City and went AWOL. His wife was soon pregnant with their second child.

MPs rounded him up and sent him to the army base at Fort Leavenworth, Kansas—35 miles northwest of Kansas City—to serve out the rest of his enlistment, but he kept going AWOL. To make that more difficult, the army sent him to Fort Riley, Kansas, 120 miles southwest of Kansas City. He continued to go AWOL until he was put in the stockade and from there mustered out of the army with an undesirable discharge in late 1971.

The long slide down for Frank, the Sheppard with the most inherent intelligence, the best looks, and the most charm, was now in an irreversible gear. He became, by his own admission, "a functioning drunk," doing concrete jobs by day and drinking beer and using drugs to oblivion most nights.

After his wife divorced him in 1972 and left with their two small children, Frank began living with another woman. In a letter he wrote in 2015, he described this period of his life: "But I blew that too. I was still drinking, working and partying and it all caught up with me. So I guess that you can get the drift of what my life consisted of. And what is strange is so did I and I could have changed it all, but I thought I'll change it tomorrow. Tomorrow never came."

By 1973, at age twenty-three, he had come to view his life as such an utter failure he attempted suicide by shooting himself in the stomach with a 12-gauge shotgun at a friend's apartment. The friend called 911. Following emergency surgery, Frank lingered near death for several days in intensive care but managed to pull through. Two weeks later he was released. "God didn't want him and the devil didn't either," said Virgie Sheppard, his sister-in-law, recalling this episode in 2015.

Frank's life would never turn around. Early in 1975 he pulled a strong-armed robbery at a QuikTrip in Grandview, Missouri, about three miles from Marlborough, beating up the clerk and taking about $450 from the cash drawer under the counter. The clerk took down the license plate on Frank's car and called the police. "I just did it to see if I could. I didn't need the money. I was working at the time. I was caught later that same night while I was still riding around in my dad's car, planning to rob another QuikTrip."

He pled guilty and was set to get a five-year probation sentence. His grandparents posted bond, "but I screwed up that probation by committing another burglary and getting caught while I was out on bond." He burglarized a Revco drugstore in Grandview and was arrested coming out of the store about 2 a.m. "I did not steal anything because I could not find what I was after—it was some drugs but they were locked up in the pharmacy department. I only had minutes to pull this off and I wasted too much time looking around and I got busted."

Instead of probation, he was sentenced to ten years in the Missouri State Penitentiary. He was paroled six years later in 1981 and returned to his job as a concrete finisher. On the side, he and Skip made extra money by collecting scrap metal and selling it to junkyards.

Frank was able to stay out of prison until 1994 when he was sentenced to five years for a house burglary. "I got a stereo and some other appliances and tools. I was going to sell them. I took some of them to the 4-Acre Motel in my Marlborough neighborhood and the cops sometimes patrol the motels. At least they drive by just looking. Just my luck. I had stereo speakers hanging out of the trunk of my car and got busted," he recounted in a letter.

For the house burglary he was sentenced to five years at Algoa, a medium-security prison about five miles from the state capital, Jefferson City. Fourteen months later he made parole and was sent to an honor center, a halfway house, in Kansas City. If he could remain sober from drugs and alcohol, keep a job, and pay part of his earnings to the honor center, he could do the rest of his parole on his own. Instead he backslid.

He was next sent to a drug and alcohol treatment facility at Tipton,

Missouri, about 110 miles east of Kansas City, for a twelve-week program. When he finished that program he was allowed to go back home on house arrest. "I violated that by not staying home and drinking. I had a leg monitor on with the actual machine attached to the telephone at home. I wasn't supposed to be 50 feet away from the monitor or else it would notify my parole officer. I was hard-headed, but I knew also if I got rolled back I would make it out again. So I got rolled back." He was sent to another halfway house in Kansas City, but broke the rules by going home. This time the state sent him to the diagnostic prison in Fulton and that is where he was when he and the other four of the Marlborough Five were indicted in the firefighters case.

Skip Sheppard did not have any of Frank's gifts. He struggled in school and dropped out in the ninth grade. He was the silent type, totally reserved. He knew nothing about glad-handing or making small talk. He never tried to impress people to get them to like him. To many he seemed remote and emotionless. He was big and strong and had such a stone face that he scared people.

It was hard to get to know Skip, but to the few close friends he had, he was loyal. He idolized Frank. Skip showed signs of settling down when he got engaged to Kella Ward in 1981.[2]

In January 1982 Skip was in a terrible car accident in Belton. Kella was driving when a pickup being driven without its headlights on broadsided the driver's side of the car. Kella was mashed in under the dash of the car and Skip was thrown outside, knocked unconscious under the tailpipe.

Kella was a pitiful mess but still alive. Her back and neck were broken, so were her cheekbones and pelvis. Her spleen was ruptured. During the thirteen days she survived, her kidneys failed and her lower left leg was amputated.

Skip spent thirty-three days in a coma at Truman Medical Center. He sustained burns on the upper thigh of his left leg from the tailpipe. The damage to his left shoulder required a metal rod being inserted down that arm. He was awarded $650 a month in disability income for the rest of his life. Although his physical recovery was excellent—he was able on the side to resume his job as a tree trimmer—Kella's death greatly depressed him. To cope, he came to rely much more on alcohol and drugs, particularly cocaine.

In 1984, two years after the car accident, Skip was out drinking after work at a bar with some of his tree-trimming co-workers when he got into an argument with a man who hit him over the head with a pool cue, knocking him unconscious. Following emergency brain surgery, Skip again went into a coma, this one lasting two weeks. There would be no recovery from this injury; he was now totally disabled, his short-term memory was impaired, and for the rest of his life he suffered from recurring headaches. Now, instead of turning over his monthly disability checks to his mother, he began cashing them and going to dope houses to buy cocaine.

Until he was convicted in federal court in 1995 for interstate transport of firearms, Skip had no felony record. He was sentenced to twenty-eight months and was doing that time when he and the others were indicted in 1996 for causing the deaths of the firefighters.

Darlene Edwards had traces of Native American ancestry on her father's side, but she came from a different background than her co-defendants. Her parents, Jack and Doris Clark, were churchgoing Southern Baptists who moved to Marlborough with their four children at the end of 1968 when Darlene, the oldest of the Clark children, was fourteen. Jack Clark was a self-employed cement finisher and Doris was a data processor for Amaco Oil in midtown Kansas City.[3]

Doris Clark, a teetotaler, was in many ways the opposite of her oldest child. As Darlene entered tenth grade at Center High School she was developing a wild, independent side. She no longer accompanied her parents and younger siblings to church. She spent her high school summers working at Mug's Up, flirting with the boys who dropped by for the five-cent frosty root beers. She began smoking pot.

By the time she entered her senior year she was pregnant. When she began to show, the school administration told the seventeen-year-old she had to drop out. She appealed and won, becoming the first girl in the Center School District to be allowed to attend classes while pregnant. Thomas Lee Clark was born on December 13, 1971. Two months later she married her son's biological father, John Parrish, and once again had to fight the school system to remain in school as a married student. Her marriage to Parrish lasted two years.

After graduating from high school, she and her son moved into an apartment in Marlborough and she got a job at Fairyland Park, the city's largest amusement park, and a second job at Ed's Drive-In. After divorcing Parrish, she moved back home with her parents and began dating Steve Edwards. In 1974 she enlisted in the army reserves. In the reserves she was a clerk for a supply officer in Kansas City, and when she and Steve Edwards moved to Dallas in 1976 she became a captain's clerk, holding the rank of E4. The army invited her to go to NCO school to become a drill sergeant, but that she did not want. While in Texas, she became pregnant. She and Steve moved back to Kansas City. She decided not to reenlist in the reserves and was generally discharged in 1977 under honorable circumstances.

Later that year, in September, she gave birth to Rebecca Renee Clark and two weeks later married Steve, Rebecca's father. Darlene was now an Edwards. She submitted paperwork to change both of her children's names to Edwards. By marrying Steve, she also, fatefully, became a stepmother to six-year-old Ronnie Edwards, Steve's son from a previous marriage. Ronnie was raised by his mother, Kathy Utter. Darlene and Steve separated in 1980 and soon thereafter Darlene began dating Frank Sheppard. Her life would never be the same.

Darlene was now on her own, with two small children. Becky was just three and Tommy nine. She rented a house in Marlborough and supported herself and her children by working as a maid in a Marlborough motel. She also helped a man publish and distribute a travel magazine. During the Christmas holidays she worked as a waitress. Later on, in the mid-1980s, she mowed lawns in the neighborhood for fifteen to twenty regular customers. Money was always tight.

By the time Frank started living part-time with Darlene in 1982, he had already served a lengthy prison term and was a confirmed alcoholic and regular cocaine user. When he was not living at Darlene's, he lived with his parents a few blocks away. Frank was a new sort of man to Darlene, who was 5 feet 2 and pudgy. He was handsome and could be charming and fun to be with; his major avocation was partying. The most common description of Frank at that time was that he was a Dr. Jekyll and Mr. Hyde, a good guy when he was sober but a lout when he drank and snorted cocaine. He worked only sporadically as a concrete finisher, paving driveways. His primary source of income was scrapping metal with his brother Skip and selling it to junkyards. He and Skip also mowed lawns.

"Things were good for a long time," Darlene wrote about Frank a few years ago:

> He never raised his voice, cursed me or hit me. That change was gradual. Becky and Tommy both saw me get knocked around. They both got angry, not only at Frank for doing it, but at me for allowing

it to happen, forgiving him and letting it happen it again. I am so ashamed that I let him come back after the first time and that I let my children witness that abuse.

Six years after Frank moved in, Tommy had seen his mother with enough black eyes that he hated Frank and he wanted out. One time when Tommy tried to intervene, Frank roughed him up. After that episode, Darlene allowed Tommy to move to Des Moines to live with her parents, who had transferred there as part of Doris Clark's job at Amaco Oil. Darlene's parents saw Frank as the greatest curse to ever strike their family. Becky, too, detested Frank, particularly now that he had driven her half brother out of the house. This enmity would only build over the years.

"I'm not saying that everything that happened to me in my 30s was Frank's fault, just that I was shown a different lifestyle, a different culture—way different," Darlene wrote.

Part of that different lifestyle was Darlene's graduation from smoking pot to free-basing cocaine, something she relied on more and more to numb the back pain she had from being in a motorcycle accident in 1987. The driver's insurance company paid her a settlement of $50,000 in June 1988. After paying part of her medical expenses and her attorney's fee she netted $29,000.

That money did not last out the year. She paid $8,000 in cash for a used Datsun 280ZX sports car; she rented a house in Marlborough next door to Bear and Carol Williams, paying the first six months in advance. She bought furnishings for the house and new school clothes for Tommy and Becky. She also paid a vet bill for one of her sister's horses and helped her father buy a fishing boat. Some of the money went to buying cocaine.

With the money all but gone, Frank came up with the idea of torching her Datsun to collect the insurance. The car was hidden in Larry Baker's garage in early November where it was stripped of its T-tops and stereo system. Following the explosions at the construction site, Baker insisted on getting rid of the car. Frank drove it to a secluded spot in Marlborough called Whore's Hollow and set it on fire.

When it came to filing a police report to trigger the insurance claim as Frank urged her, Darlene refused. Cops had been all over Marlborough after the explosions. She and Frank had been taken downtown where she was questioned for four hours before being released. She did not want any further contact with KCPD.

Once the prepaid rent on the house ran out, Darlene could not make the next month's payment and was evicted. She stored her furnishings and belongings in an empty trailer a friend let her use, and she moved in with a woman friend. Frank returned to his parents' house and Becky, now eleven, began living with her father, Steve, who shared a house with his brother nearby. Darlene went to see Becky almost every day.

Darlene got a job at Venture, a discount department store, which lasted six months, but she got fired because Frank kept showing up drunk and acting belligerent. For a year she worked at a gas station convenience store outside of Marlborough on US 50. After that, up until the time she was busted for selling drugs to her stepson, her main source of income was from mowing lawns in the summer.

There was much more of Oliver Twist than Tom Sawyer in Bryan Sheppard. Born in 1971, he lived a usually chaotic life regularly punctuated by devastating traumas. Although his parents, Jack and Virgie Sheppard, were loving, if not doting, parents they had their own demons. Both Jack and Virgie were raised by alcoholic parents and they in turn became alcoholics themselves. With this, a great deal of unpredictability permeated domestic life at 8521 Flora and later at 8444 Wayne.[4]

Growing up with her maternal grandparents in Marlborough, Virgie saw her grandfather, Paul Henry Kelly, sent off to prison for ten years for robbing a drugstore to get opiates for her grandmother, Hazel Kelly, an addict with needle marks all over her arms.

Virgie, an only child, was forced to drop out of high school in the tenth grade and take over household duties when her grandmother died and her mother resigned herself to being a self-appointed invalid too overwhelmed by life to cope.

Virgie and Jack, who was a year older, had known each other since childhood. At age seventeen, she became pregnant. A daughter, Glynnis, was born in 1966. Thirteen months later, Jack and Virgie married. If it was not a marriage made in heaven, it was one that would somehow manage to endure for almost fifty years through countless heated, alcohol-fueled arguments. The one thing that could always bind them together was their love for their children.

Jack, unlike his brothers, worked steady jobs as an automobile mechanic at Midas Muffler and later at the Ray Smith Ford dealership; Virgie, beginning in 1968, worked full-time in the stockroom at Lab Conco, a medical supply company. They owned their own homes in Marlborough.

Jack, the oldest child in his family, was well acquainted with stern dis-

cipline from both his parents. His mother Naomi, a full-blooded Cherokee from a reservation in Oklahoma, brooked no dissent. His father Earl,
the strong silent type who worked two jobs—one in construction and
the other as a bartender—had taken the strap to him and his brother
Frank so often, particularly Frank, that Jack took corporal punishment as
a child-rearing given. Virgie didn't see it that way and would physically
intervene to stop Jack from hitting their children; for this she sometimes
came away with black eyes. Bryan's other sister, Katie, would sometimes call 911 to report Jack's physical abuse in progress, usually as part
of a drunken rage. One time Virgie's father tried to intervene and Jack
knocked him out the front door. To avoid his father's discipline, Bryan,
at age thirteen, moved in with his friend David Baird, into the basement
of Karen Baird's house.

Marlborough's degeneration was nearly complete. The neighborhood
was dotted with drug houses, with most adult residents living on welfare;
poverty, alcohol, and drug abuse had become a way of life. The Baird
home was no exception; under the guise of providing licensed massage
services, Karen Baird was operating a prostitution ring and selling a variety of illegal drugs.

By his own admission, Bryan was well into becoming a juvenile de-
linquent. "Put it this way: I was just an everyday, trouble-making kid at
13, 14, 15, 16," Bryan wrote in a letter. "I wasn't there hurting people, just
stealing bicycles, having fun sneaking out at night to run the streets and
ride my little Honda 50 and smoke pot."

For the three years he lived in the Baird's basement, he and David
Baird turned it into an entertainment destination—called "The Cave"—
for Marlborough teens. They staged parties complete with sixteen-gallon
kegs of beer. Admission was $3 per person and $5 per couple. They did
this on some weekday nights and had live bands on some weekend nights.
As many as 75 to 100 teens could turn up. Back then, the cops had more
pressing crimes to police than busting teenagers for drinking in a private
residence.

In 1985, Bryan began a disastrous relationship with Carie Neighbors.
She had just moved to Marlborough and was in his tenth-grade class at
Center High School. At a party at "The Cave," while Bryan was passed
out from drinking, two of Carie's cousins began kicking him on the
floor, trying to get him to drive them back to Raytown, about five miles
away. The next day, Denise Howard drove Bryan and David Baird to
Raytown to settle the score with the cousins. When they arrived, Carie
ran around the back of her grandfather's house, carrying a .22-caliber

rifle, and hid by a tree. She told Bryan that if he didn't leave she would shoot him.

"Go ahead and shoot then, bitch," Bryan shouted out. The bullet entered the right side of his chest just below the nipple, missing his heart by inches. He spent a week in the hospital where blood transfusions were required. Carie was confined to a juvenile detention center for a month and released.

Center High School expelled him shortly after he returned to school. "They expelled me because I was a troubled kid and I wouldn't go to class or stay in class—that was even if I went to school at all. Getting shot was just the last straw," Bryan wrote. For the next year and a half, Bryan attended a special-behavior development school with about twenty other at-risk kids in Belton, but dropped out of there at age sixteen.

One day after school, on May 4, 1986, Bryan came home to find his maternal grandfather, Virgil Bryan, sitting in the living room recliner drinking whiskey. Virgil, fifty-nine, moved in with Bryan's family shortly after his wife—and Virgie's mother—died in 1977. Six months earlier, he lost his job as a night watchman and had gone into a funk. Bryan asked him for some cigarettes and his grandfather told him to get a pack from his room. Bryan got the cigarettes and went into his parents' bedroom. A few minutes later when he heard a gunshot, Bryan ran into the living room and found his grandfather slumped in his chair and saw a .25-caliber handgun on the floor.

When the ambulance and police arrived, his grandfather, who shot himself in the right temple, was still alive but grievously wounded. Because Bryan was home alone at the time of the shooting, the police did a gunshot residue test on his hands but found no traces. When his grandfather died seventy-two hours later, his death was deemed a suicide.

Later that year, Bryan—now dating Debbie Howard, Denise Howard's younger sister—was driving Denise's car with Debbie when the car ran off the road at 61st and Paseo and smashed into a tree. Debbie sustained multiple lacerations to her face and eight of Bryan's front teeth were knocked out. Even with dental insurance, the expense of the new teeth came to $4,000. Virgie paid.

Over the July 4th holiday in 1988 at a park near Marlborough, Bryan and a bunch of other teens from Marlborough engaged in a fireworks war. Two groups were doing battle about thirty to forty feet apart, shooting bottle rockets and Roman candles and heaving missiles at each other. One of the combatants came running at Bryan as he hid behind his car lighting a Roman candle. When Bryan reared up he took a direct hit in his left eye. Surgeons saved his eye but since then he is only able to see light and motion. "I don't remember if I had two or three surgeries, but the pain was out of this world. I took pain medication just to knock myself out," Bryan wrote.

When Bryan writes about himself he frequently uses the expression "Young and dumb" to explain why so many things went awry in his life as a teenager. What might better describe him then is totally undisciplined and irresponsible. Another adjective that comes to mind is spoiled. As dedicated as Jack and Virgie were in their own way to Bryan's welfare, they were basically enablers rather than parents, abandoning him to his own impulses by the time he was thirteen. With nobody to answer to but his own immature whims, Bryan's young life was set on a downward path from which he had no clue how to escape.

A young girl he dated for a few months in late 1987 and early 1988 had his baby in September 1988 and cut off all contact with him. Five months before that baby was born, Debbie Howard became pregnant. She was four months pregnant when Bryan suffered the eye wound. Once Bryan recovered from the second eye surgery, he moved out of his parents' house to go live up the street with Richard Brown, Lonnie Joe Pugh, and another friend in what Bryan described as "one big party house."

For the last four months of her pregnancy, Debbie moved in with Jack and Virgie and slept downstairs in a refurbished bedroom next to Katie, Bryan's nineteen-year-old sister. Bryan only came home to eat, shower, and change clothes. Occasionally, he would stumble in the door drunk after midnight and flop down on the sofa in the living room. Jack wouldn't allow Bryan and Debbie to sleep together even though she was well along in her pregnancy.

The incident that initiated Bryan into the maw of the criminal justice system seemed innocuous when it happened. He was with David Baird at the upscale Ward Parkway Mall when Baird broke a display window at a Sears store and stole a $600 bicycle and rode off on it by himself. Maggie Weaver, a young Marlborough woman who had gone to school with Bryan, was working in a kiosk about fifty yards away. She called police and reported that she saw Baird and Bryan steal the bicycle. As first-time, youthful offenders, Bryan and Baird were sentenced to two years' probation plus restitution for the bicycle. The lawyer Bryan's parents hired, the court costs, and the restitution for the bicycle came to $1,200. Virgie paid.

A few months later, Bryan violated his probation by testing positive for marijuana. When he told his probation officer that he wasn't about to quit smoking pot, he was taken back to juvenile court and sentenced to twenty-eight days in the Jackson County jail. While there homicide detectives questioned him several times about the firefighters case. He told them he knew nothing about who was involved, but word of these interviews got around the jail.

One inmate, Chris Sciarra, who was in jail on a credit-card fraud charge, told Detective John Fraise on August 9, 1989, that he overheard Bryan making admissions to another inmate, Johnny Driver, while they were in the common room one Saturday morning watching a particular cartoon program. Sciarra said he overheard Bryan telling Driver that he and some friends would go to the construction site to steal batteries. Bryan said they broke into a shack and then set it on fire to distract the guards. Bryan said his uncle didn't make it because he was too drunk. Bryan said his alibi was his grandmother who would say he was at home sleeping that night. It seemed to Sciarra that Bryan saw the deaths of the firefighters as a "big joke."

Detective John Fraise subsequently interviewed Driver, who was being held on a high bond for several felonies. He confirmed what Sciarra said. For his cooperation, Driver was released on a signature bond.

Based mostly on the information provided by Driver and Sciarra, the Jackson County Prosecutor's Office charged Bryan the following month in Jackson County Circuit Court with six counts of second-degree murder in connection with the deaths of the firefighters. They also transferred him to the Clay County jail to await trial.

Bryan's parents mortgaged their house and came up with $20,000 to hire defense attorney John O'Connor, a former Jackson County assistant prosecutor. O'Connor succeeded in getting the charges against Bryan dropped when he proved through jail records that Bryan was in the visitor's room, in a different part of the jail, when the TV program that Sciarra and Driver referenced was airing. On December 28, 1989, he walked free, escaping for the time being the pernicious force of jailhouse snitches.

But even though the charges against him in the firefighters case were dropped, the stigma would not go away. Shortly after his release, Bryan got a job at the Appliance Recondition Center store. When it came time for his annual raise, none was forthcoming, nor was he allowed to take any paid vacation. "They knew it would be hard for me to get work elsewhere," Bryan wrote to me. "So I was stuck. After a year and a half I told them to give me a raise and my paid vacation or I was quitting. I was told no, so I quit."

It was difficult to find another job. When he did start a new one it wasn't long before the employer realized he had been indicted in the firefighters case and let him go. One such job was at the House of Lloyd, a major international direct selling company with a large warehouse in Grandview, Missouri. Bryan started at the bottom packing boxes. He was promoted to maintenance and was getting ready to start forklift training when two supervisors called him in for a meeting. They said he lied on his application about being convicted of a felony and fired him. The fact that he had not been convicted but released did not matter. "That sucked. I liked that place," Bryan wrote.

His next job was at a shop that replaced car transmissions. "I worked there one week; hell the boss even seemed to like me," Bryan wrote. The boss handed him his paycheck and told him he didn't want "his kind" working for him. "The boss said he had a firefighter friend that died on the job when he was crushed by a fire truck."

After losing so many jobs because of the indictment, "It was off to the drug game. I couldn't get any respect working honest jobs so I got my respect from buying and selling stolen goods and buying and selling drugs or buying old cars and then selling them for profit," Bryan wrote. The drug selling caught up with him in 1995 when he got busted selling meth to an undercover cop and sentenced to three, seven-year sentences in state prison.

Richard Brown has always been peripatetic and most likely always will be. It runs in the family. Words burst out of him in torrents. Although he is also enigmatic, it can still be said that he is well-meaning and sincere, and there is an endearing quality to his unadulterated frankness.[5]

Born in Kansas City on April 4, 1970, his parents divorced three years later. His mother, Nadine, worked various jobs, including bartending and as a nursing home attendant, trying her best to provide for Richard and his older brother, Carl. But without any support from her former husband, the family periodically was forced to go on welfare.

"It was hard for me as a kid to hear my mom cry at night because she had to feed us corn or baloney sandwiches because she was broke," Richard wrote in a letter. "'I'm hungry, Mom,' I'd say, and she'd say 'It's Wednesday—two days to payday.'"

Nadine, whose great grandmother was a full-blooded Osage Indian, had two more children by two other men. Shannon was born in 1974 and Trance, a son, in 1977. The family moved around. They lived at 69th and Jackson in Kansas City until that house burned down. They moved to 39th and Virginia. At Knotts Elementary School, there were two other white children besides Richard and his older brother. Fights with black kids were regular occurrences. Later Nadine moved her family to 9th and Benton. "We moved so much I never had time to stay in one school for a year, but I got good grades when I was in school," Richard wrote.

Richard's first exposure to arrest involved—just as Bryan's had—a stolen bicycle. When he was thirteen, he stole a bicycle for his younger half brother, Trance. "Man, I never saw him so happy in my life," he wrote. "Then the cops showed up and took me and the bike. Then mom showed up at the police station. She got me in a room and beat the shit out of me for telling the cops I stole the bike. She told me don't ever tell them shit and don't ever steal again." In juvenile court he was given three years' probation.

Nadine packed him off to live with his father, Coral Edward Brown Sr., something she sometimes did when she felt he needed more discipline. These stays never lasted long. Ed Brown, a long-haul diesel truck driver who was on the road for extended periods of time, was stern and short-tempered. "My dad was a strict man. After all these years I realize he just wanted me to get a good education that he didn't get," Richard wrote.

By the time Richard was ready for high school, Nadine purchased a home at 23rd and Overton in Independence. Richard enrolled at Van Horn, a school torn by racial strife and years of neglect. "Rough school," Richard wrote. "I made it through 10th grade and then I ran away from my dad's because he kicked the shit out of me because he was drunk. So I went back to my mom's to live." But soon after that Richard and his brother Carl moved to Marlborough to help take care of Nadine's father, Louis Smith, who had suffered a severe stroke.

There he would meet Bryan, who was living in the basement of Karen Baird's house—the locale of "The Cave"—where Bryan and David Baird threw parties on most weekends. Before long Richard and Bryan were inseparable; if you saw one you saw the other.

When he turned sixteen, Richard got a job at Kentucky Fried Chicken and worked there for a year and then he worked on a lawn and garden crew. "In 1987–88, me, Bryan and Lonnie Joe Pugh began scrapping for metal," he wrote. "We would go to neighborhoods and see junk in front of a house or behind it and knock on the door and see if we could have it. Then we would go to Langley's junkyard and sell the scrap metal. They paid by check. We'd go right around to the corner store and cash the check, take out gas money, then split the rest."

They would use the money to buy beer and then begin hitting the various parks around Marlborough to check out the girls. "In the two years leading up to the explosions, I did all that kids do: chase girls at parks and parties, and mow grass, clean out gutters and scrap for metal."

On his seventeenth birthday he was ticketed in Grandview, Missouri, for doing sixty-five in a fifty-five-mile-per-hour zone. This minor event would have dire consequences. His license was confiscated pending a court date for the infraction. He was given a piece of paper that allowed him to drive until then. One night not long after that he was stopped in Kansas City for driving without his van's headlights on. (The ex-boyfriend of the girl he was dating had loosened the lug nuts on one of the van's front tires. When Richard turned the corner onto 85th Street, the tire wobbled, causing the wire for the headlights to come off the battery.)

When Richard could not produce the temporary driving permit, the officer arrested him. "The next morning in court, after sitting all night in jail, they said if I pled guilty to driving without a license they would drop the driving without headlights charge," he wrote. "I said, 'Can I go home?' They said yes, so I said okay. I didn't realize they just took my license away."

Richard never got his driver's license back, something that did not stop him from driving any time he wanted. Up until he was indicted for the firefighters case, Richard was ticketed as many as twenty times for driving on a suspended license.

At age twenty-five, in 1995, Richard married Melissa Jones in a ceremony in Oklahoma witnessed by his parents. As soon as they were married, Richard and Melissa witnessed the remarriage of Nadine and Ed Brown—a reconciliation that was twenty-five years in the making, but did not last.

By the time the indictments came down against the Marlborough Five in 1996, only Richard was not in prison on other charges. Because he had only misdemeanors on his record, his bail was set at $50,000. His mother mortgaged her house on Overton Road and posted his bond. Before Richard was sent to prison in 1997, he and Melissa had two boys, Levi and Sheldon. Earlier, in 1990, his daughter Kaylee Brown was born.

CHAPTER 6

Indicting the Marlborough Five

As Agent True went about building his case against the Marlborough Five, he seemed to be pursuing a three-pronged strategy: put the Marlborough Five behind bars on unrelated charges as quickly as possible; identify as many people as possible who said they heard these five implicating themselves in the arsons; turn one or more of them against the others.

The first two phases of his strategy were interrelated. There is no richer source for government witnesses than jailhouse snitches.

Frank Sheppard was already in state prison for violating his parole. (He had been convicted of a home burglary in February 1994 but released on parole fourteen months later.)

Bryan Sheppard was arrested a day after the February 1995 airing of the *Unsolved Mysteries* episode on the explosions for making three sales of methamphetamines to an undercover cop. One sale was for $25, the second for $50, and the third for $125. It was normal practice for the court to place first-time drug offenders in a drug-treatment program and suspend the sentence. This is what happened to a woman busted around the same time in Marlborough by the same undercover cop. Although her two sales came to $750, she was discharged by the court to a 180-day drug-treatment program. That would not be the case for Bryan. When he appeared in court for the arraignment, Agent True was there, asking the judge to set a high bond because he claimed Bryan had been threatening witnesses in the firefighters case. This claim had no substance but it worked and was publicized in the media.

Bryan ended up spending ten months in the Jackson County jail before going to court and pleading guilty. During the sentencing, a Jackson County assistant prosecutor asked the judge to sentence Bryan to the maximum sentence of fifteen years on each count because he had just recently been re-indicted in the firefighters case. This request was too much for the judge. He sentenced Bryan to three seven-year sentences of state time on each of the drug charges, to run concurrently.[1]

Richard Brown was not as easy a target. He did not sell drugs or steal. He alone of the Marlborough Five had no criminal record. His vulnerability was his persistence in driving with a suspended license.

Throughout a good portion of 1994 and into early February 1995, the KCPD and the ATF had been harassing Richard. In mid-1994, a Kansas City police officer stopped a car Richard was riding in as a passenger, took the keys out of the ignition, threw them at Richard's feet, and arrested him for driving with a suspended license.[2]

At the police station, detectives questioned him about the firefighters case. During these interviews Richard told the same story about his whereabouts in the hours leading up to the explosion that killed the firefighters: he spent the night playing cards at Brenda Carpenter's house with his girlfriend, Alena Fantauzzo, and her friend Stephanie Webb. Sometime after midnight, he drove Alena and Stephanie to the QuikTrip on 85th Street to get some food and then drove them both home before returning to his grandparents' house to sleep.

About twenty minutes into this interview, the detectives brought Alena into the room. She had told the detectives that when they stopped at QuikTrip they had seen Frank, Skip, and Darlene walking toward the convenience store with a gas can. At one point she asked Richard if he didn't recall seeing Frank, Skip, and Darlene. "Hell no," he said, "Are you out of your fucking mind?" As Alena persisted in her claim, Richard's anger at her grew so intense the detectives escorted her from of the room.

The detectives clearly believed Alena, pressing Richard now to confirm her account. When he adamantly refused, the detectives threatened to put him in jail for six months for driving on a suspended license. When he still refused to provide any information, Richard was arrested, sent to municipal court and sentenced to six months at Leeds Farm, a city detention center.

Not long after Richard was released from Leeds Farm in late January 1995, police came to his grandparents' house and took him to the police station, holding him for the maximum seventy-two hours allowed without bringing formal charges, questioning him ad nauseam about seeing Frank, Skip, and Darlene walking toward the QuikTrip. He denied seeing them. As he was leaving the police station, police arrested and detained him for another seventy-two hours. As he was leaving the jail for the third time, he ran through the front door but only made it two blocks before police tackled him and brought him back. This time, with Agent Eugene Schram of the Labor Department present, they told him he would not be let go unless he implicated Darlene, Frank, and Skip in the explosions.

"The next thing you'll want me to say is that I saw Diddi and Larry Baker and Johnny Driver and 10 other people that night," Richard said. "I ain't no fucking stoolpigeon. Fuck you, I'm not saying another fucking thing." (Driver was one of the jailhouse snitches who implicated Bryan Sheppard in 1989.)

Before departing, Richard signed a statement that contained only his account of how he spent the hours leading up to the explosions. The agents, however, added to his statement their summary of what Alena had said about seeing Frank, Skip, and Darlene, and Richard's mentioning Larry and Diddi Baker, as well as Driver.

Nonetheless, even though Richard had refused to allow the agents to videotape this interview and had refused to sign the summary prepared by the agents, his offhanded and sarcastic remarks were now down on paper and would soon be used to turn one of the Marlborough Five against him.

Darlene Edwards was Agent True's target. Thirteen days after getting the signed and unsigned statements from Richard, True orchestrated the arrest of Darlene on drug charges, using her stepson, Ronnie Edwards, in an elaborate ruse to entrap her.[3]

Ronnie's rap sheet from that time shows he was convicted of credit-card fraud in April 1992 and placed on probation. In January 1994 a probation revocation hearing was set on a forgery charge and in November 1994 a bench warrant was issued. Enter Agent True with his offer of assistance in return for Ronnie's cooperation in the firefighters investigation. Ronnie agreed and his parole was not revoked.

Ronnie consented to wear a wire and approach Darlene in February 1995 about buying crack cocaine for him. He told her he needed some fast money because his ex-wife was going to put his young son up for adoption and he could use the money from the resale of the crack to hire an attorney to fight the adoption. After Darlene told him she would help him get an attorney and he could pay her back in installments, Ronnie said he had to have the money now.

After Darlene agreed to help him, he returned later that night with $300 in cash the ATF supplied. Darlene spotted a drug dealer at 72nd and Prospect and told him she wanted to see him. Ronnie drove eight blocks south on Prospect with the dealer following, turning in at a 7-Eleven parking lot in Marlborough, directly across the street from a public elementary school. Ronnie gave Darlene the $300. She went back to the dealer's car and bought $100 worth of crack, just over two grams, keeping $200 for herself.

Ronnie gave Darlene some of the crack for her to smoke later and then dropped her back at her house. When Ronnie turned the crack over to the ATF that night it weighed less than two grams, the minimal amount needed for the drug bust to stand. The ATF sent him back to Darlene's to retrieve the crack. She gave it back.

While in the car with Darlene, Ronnie, wearing a wire, asked her what she knew about the firefighters case. She said she knew nothing.

Two weeks later, on February 17, 1995, ATF agents came to Darlene's house and told her they wanted to question her about the firefighters case. She said she knew nothing, but would go because she had nothing to fear.

At the ATF office, True pressed her on what she knew about the firefighters case. When she denied knowing anything, True brought Ronnie Edwards into the room to confront her about making admissions to him. Now face-to-face with his stepmother, Ronnie waffled. This was an attempt at pure intimidation; True knew from listening to the wire tape that she had made no admissions or claimed any knowledge. After Ronnie left the room, ATF agents in another room began secretly videotaping the rest of the interview.[4]

On the videotape, Darlene appears relaxed, friendly, and cooperative, as someone with nothing to hide. When True told her there were people who said she was involved in the explosions, she asked for a polygraph. True asked her about her drug use, which she readily admitted to, and about her drug sales. She also admitted to that.

Now True played his hole card. He opened a door and a Drug Enforcement Agency agent entered. The agent told her she was under arrest for buying crack cocaine within 150 feet of a school and she was looking at years in prison under the mandatory sentencing guidelines. He told her Ronnie Edwards was wired when she bought the drugs and the case against her was ironclad.

The videotape now shows a completely flummoxed Darlene as this reality settles in; it was as though a trap door had opened and she was falling downward, unable to grab onto anything, a sensation True was ready to capitalize on. He leaned forward and said she had a "window of opportunity," all this drug business could go away if she cooperated on the firefighters case.

"It doesn't matter if you put me away forever," she yowled, "it won't change the truth," swearing she knew nothing about who was responsible for killing the firefighters. She again asked True to give her a polygraph.

True: And we're still giving you that opportunity to talk to us. . . .

Darlene: Yeah.

True: . . . to sign this.

Darlene: But I don't know.

True: Darlene, you do know.

Darlene: No, I don't know. I don't know.

True: This is your chance.

Darlene was left alone in a room to ponder her dilemma. On the table next to her were two typed statements federal investigators had recently taken from Bryan Sheppard and Richard Brown. The way Darlene read the statements, both implicated her, Frank, and Skip in the crime. The fact that Bryan's was unsigned caused her to discount its contents, but Richard's made her livid. She had no way of knowing that Richard had only signed a statement saying he was home in bed when the firefighters were killed. The monumental effort on the part of the KCPD and the ATF to wear down and manipulate Richard Brown would soon pay off.

Darlene spent the next two days in an isolation cell at the Clay County Detention Center in Liberty, sixteen miles north of Kansas City—no phone calls, no visitors, no showers—with nothing but time on her hands to think about what was happening to her. She was sickened by the betrayal of her stepson and had now come to believe that Frank's nephew and Richard Brown, whom she considered to be family (her sister was married to one of Richard's uncles and she considered his uncle Louis Smith her best friend), had betrayed her too. She rationalized the reason they were lying about her was because they had something to do with the explosion and were trying to scapegoat her. She began to believe her way out, her way to take advantage of the "window of opportunity," would be to turn the tables and lie about them.

At 8:30 p.m. on Sunday, Darlene had the jail call the ATF and say she was ready to talk. Within an hour Dave True and ATF Agent Harold Lett made the drive to the jail; joining them in the interview room was Detective Bill Forbes of KCPD. Darlene was read her rights and signed away her right to remain silent and have an attorney present.

Before turning on a tape recorder, True told her he knew Bryan and Richard were involved in causing the explosions and she could go home if she could put them close to the site.

Darlene said on the night of the explosions, she was awakened at her home by Richard Brown and Bryan Sheppard, who told her their car had run out of gas and asked her to drive them to QuikTrip.[5] After filling up a gas can and heading back home, they said something about starting a fire at the construction site. She told them they were crazy and told them to get out of her car, dropping them off on 71 Highway at one of the entrances to the construction site.

Instead of opening the "window of opportunity" and letting her go home free of any drug charges, True now wanted her to admit to her own role in causing the explosions. She insisted she played no part.

Within a few days, Darlene was in federal court pleading guilty to one count of distributing narcotics near a school zone and sentenced to sixty-four months in federal prison.

Skip Sheppard fell into True's hands of his own accord. In February Skip was arraigned in federal court on a charge of transporting guns across a state line. (He and some others broke into a house in Kansas, stole some shotguns and rifles, and drove back to Marlborough. One of his accomplices snitched him out.) True appeared at Skip's arraignment to argue for no bail, alleging Skip had been threatening witnesses in the firefighters case. When US Magistrate John Maughmer asked True to identify these witnesses, True did not reference any. The judge released Skip on bond. A few months later, Skip was sentenced to twenty-eight months in federal prison, the first felony on his record.

The first part of True's strategy had now worked almost to perfection—all but Richard Brown were tucked away in prison on unrelated charges. Dozens of prisoners would now come into contact with them and maybe some of them would later allege to hear admissions of guilt. The third part of his plan resulted in Darlene now being at total odds with Bryan and Richard.

Special ATF agents like Dave True have immense power, but it only goes so far. The cases they develop for indictment have to pass muster at the US Attorney's Office. Because the working theory of the investigation was that organized labor was behind the explosions, prosecution of the case was assigned early on to Assistant US Attorney Paul Becker, the head of the office's Organized Crime Strike Force. Becker would be the one to decide if the case True built against the Marlborough Five merited being brought before a federal grand jury.

Becker, who is proud of being from Brooklyn, is a small man with a flinty manner. His intelligence is without question, as is his legal acumen. As the head of the Organized Crime Strike Force, he had set up his own fiefdom within the US Attorney's Office. He reported to the US Justice Department in Washington rather than to the local US attorney. He certainly was not beholden to anyone at the local ATF office.[6]

The Organized Crime Strike Force was created in the late 1960s to prosecute mob members for racketeering and those who derived substantial income from organized crime activities. Labor union leaders were frequent targets of various strike forces.

Originally there were fourteen Organized Crime Strike Forces. Kansas City, because of its well-entrenched Mafia, was one of them. Long before Nick Civella began dominating mob activities in the early 1950s, Kansas City endured a reign of political corruption by Boss Tom Pendergast. From 1925 until he was sent to a federal penitentiary for tax evasion in 1939, Pendergast was the head of Jackson County's Democratic Party. From that post he directed the area's largest concrete construction projects to the cement company he owned. For years he handpicked governors, mayors, and city council members. When Harry Truman was elected to the US Senate in 1934, he was dubbed the "Senator from Pendergast."[7]

By the mid-1990s, most of the strike forces had closed shop, but the one Becker ran was still humming along. He kept it going in the early 1990s by gaining headlines for the way he went about investigating organized crime. Even though the mob controlled narcotics, gambling, prostitution, extortion, and loan sharking throughout Jackson County, Becker's strike force had been unable to bring even one high-ranking Mafioso under indictment.

To break this impasse, Becker began bringing a succession of young Italian American men, some of them the sons of reputed Mafia figures, before a federal grand jury and questioning them about mob-related activities of family members and friends. When they refused to testify, even though the government granted them immunity from prosecution, Becker had twenty of them, one after the other, jailed on contempt of court charges for up to eighteen months.

While law-and-order adherents saw Becker as a fearless prosecutor— the Eliot Ness of the prairie—to civil libertarians and the leaders of the Italian American community in Kansas City he was a pariah. The jailings set off a backlash that came to be known as the "Basta" movement (*basta* is Italian for "enough"), which was launched on September 22, 1991, when a small plane waving a banner that read "Basta! Basta!" flew over Arrowhead Stadium during a Kansas City Chiefs football game. A billboard overlooking the parking lot of the federal courthouse soon carried the slogan. T-shirts and bumper stickers did the same. Demonstrations were held at the steps of the federal courthouse to call for federal grand jury reform and to protest the jailing of the young Italian American men. Ten thousand Kansas Citians signed a petition opposing their incarceration.[8]

Eventually, after up to eighteen months in prison, nine of the twenty were released. To win the release of the remaining eleven, including his own son, prominent mob figure Peter Simone, a reputed underboss, pled guilty in 1992 to gambling charges and was sentenced to four years in federal prison.

And then the firefighters case came along. In something of a perfect storm, Becker not only supported True's investigation but would use the immense power of his office to make deals with a number of felon witnesses to secure their testimony at the grand jury and trial.

Federal grand juries, which consist of between sixteen and twenty-three members, are convened to consider indicting "targets" of federal criminal investigations. The prosecutor, without a judge present, runs the proceedings, which are held in secret. No attorneys for the targets or the witnesses called to testify are allowed to be present. By federal rule at least twelve of the grand jury members must concur that there is probable cause—a much lower standard than guilt beyond a reasonable doubt—that the person or persons being considered for indictment committed a felony.[9]

Indictments from federal grand juries are so routine that it occasioned Federal District Court Judge William Campbell to state, "Today, the grand jury is the total captive of the prosecutor who, if he is candid, will concede that he can indict anybody, at any time, for almost anything, before any grand jury."[10] A former chief judge of the New York Court of Appeals put it more colorfully, saying grand juries were so pliable that a prosecutor could get a grand jury to "indict a ham sandwich."[11]

The federal grand jury for the firefighters case met for eighteen months before handing down indictments—known as "true bills"—against each of the Marlborough Five on June 12, 1996.

There were a number of oddities about the way Agent True put this case together—using the TV show *Unsolved Mysteries* to encourage witnesses to come forward and making an open plea for convicts to testify by posting reward posters in all the prisons and jails in the two-state area are two prime examples. But another unusual aspect of this case was that True kept the investigation going after the indictments were handed down. In most federal prosecutions, the grand jury is not convened until the investigation is considered finished. The primary reason for this is that federal law requires a case to go to trial within seventy days after indictment. In this case, police and ATF agents were interviewing new witnesses up until at least December 1, 1996, just two weeks before the scheduled start of the firefighters trial; a number of these witnesses would turn out to be jailhouse informants.[12]

There are two reasonable deductions that may be drawn from True continuing the investigation so long after the indictments, and they are not mutually exclusive: he wanted this case over as soon as possible so he could resign from the ATF (something he did at the end of the firefighters trial), or he kept developing new witnesses because he felt the witnesses he had might not be enough to convince a jury.

The star witness at the grand jury was Darlene's stepson, Ronnie Edwards, despite the wildly different accounts he gave the police, the ATF, and finally the grand jury about his knowledge of the crime. (By then Ronnie had already been used by the ATF to entrap Darlene in a drug sale.)

He was a highly compromised witness, as he would prove in his statements and testimony about the firefighters case. He had lied so repeatedly over the years about what he claimed to know about the case that— ethically speaking—the government should not have used him as a witness. During his first appearance before the grand jury on March 15, 1995, he stated his testimony "was part of my probation," referring to the deal Agent True worked out to save him from being sent to prison on a parole violation involving credit-card fraud.

Ronnie had been on the police's radar since December 12, 1988—two weeks after the firefighters were killed—when a KCPD detective went to interview him at Center High School, following up on a report that he told people that Bryan Sheppard, Ben Craft, and Derek Smith were responsible for killing the firefighters. When questioned, Ronnie denied any knowledge of the incident.[13]

Ronnie's connection to the case resurfaced on February 16, 1989, when he told KCPD detectives that his housemate, Alan Bethard, was with him at his mother's house at a party when he heard Richard Brown admit he and Chuck Jennings set the fire that caused the explosion. Police subsequently interviewed other people who were alleged to be at the party, but none of them heard any admissions.[14]

Six years later, on January 25, 1995—with Ronnie working off his probation—he would tell a different story when he was brought to the KCPD's Bomb and Arson Unit.[15] He said he was at a bar in Marlborough with Alan Bethard just two hours before the explosion that killed the firefighters when Darlene, Richard Brown, and Bryan Sheppard entered. He said Frank Sheppard and Johnny Driver were waiting outside in Bryan's car.

Ronnie said either Richard or Bryan asked him if he wanted to buy some walkie-talkies. Ronnie said he knew the walkie-talkies were Motorola Intercoms from the 71 Highway construction site because "they had stolen some there before and I bought them and I told them to go back and get some more. They had sold me six for $200 each. I left the bar at 2:30 a.m." He then added, "Richard, Bryan, Darlene, and Frank Sheppard left to go" to the construction site in Bryan's car.

Ronnie said he and Bethard went home, but five minutes later he and Bethard drove to QuikTrip to get gas. This would mean he left his home at approximately 2:40 a.m. and was at most five minutes away from the QuikTrip. Nonetheless, he told the police,

> We left [home] about 3:30 a.m. and got there about 4 a.m. While we were on the way, the first explosion took place. After the first explosion but before the second explosion, I was pumping gas and I saw Bryan Sheppard's black Toronado. Darlene Edwards was driving northbound on 71 Highway, about 70 miles an hour. I saw Frank Sheppard, who was the passenger in the front. Bryan Sheppard was in the back with Richard Brown.

He said Darlene later told him "there was another guy in the back" whom she identified as Johnny Driver. (Bryan never owned a Toronado. At the time he owned a Thunderbird with no front hood.)

A number of factual errors occur in Ronnie's timeline. The explosion that killed the firefighters occurred at 4:08 a.m.; the second explosion, some 40 minutes later. Anyone reading Ronnie's statement about leaving the bar at 2:40 a.m. would realize what he said about his subsequent movements and their relationship to the explosions could not have happened. His saying he heard the first one as he and Bethard drove to QuikTrip and the second as he was pumping gas is not possible.

With no defense attorneys present during grand jury deliberations, the role of questioning witnesses' assertions falls to the government's lawyer, in this case Assistant US Attorney Paul Becker. At his second and final appearance before the grand jury on September 27, 1995, Ronnie was about to make a dramatic U-turn from the sworn statement he had given to police nine months earlier.

This time he testified that the walkie-talkies placed in evidence that day belonged to his friend Alan Bethard, not Bryan Sheppard and Richard Brown.[16] Becker followed up Ronnie's revelation about obtaining the walkie-talkies from Bethard by asking him if he knew where Bethard acquired them. Ronnie couldn't say.

In effect, the government's main witness was backtracking before the grand jury on a key link to Bryan and Richard and Frank and Darlene. Despite what Ronnie had told police earlier, Becker knew Bethard had stolen the hand-held radios from a lawn service company at 85th and Troost six months before the explosion at the 71 Highway construction site. He knew because ATF agents had verified this from a police report filed by the victim.

With the walkie-talkies sitting prominently on the evidence table, Becker was not about to forgo their incriminating value despite their exculpatory provenance. Here is how Becker proceeded to question Ronnie Edwards:

Q. Now, in an earlier report that I have of an interview with you, you talked about Bethard having six of these [walkie-talkies] and that you bought them for $200 each.
A. Yes.
Q. Is that correct?
A. It's somewhere around there. The money might not be precise but the quantity of CBs yes.

This line of questioning misled the grand jurors. By the way Becker formed the question, the grand jurors could not realize Ronnie had originally sworn to police he bought the walkie-talkies from Richard Brown and Bryan Sheppard and the walkie-talkies were from the Bruce R. Watkins construction site.

Under further questioning, Ronnie revealed Bethard sold the walkie-talkies to someone named Curtis [Vedders] for $20 each, which made a farce of the notion that he, a sixteen-year-old high-school dropout at the time, purchased six walkie-talkies from Bethard for a total of $1,200.

Becker still had the problem of trying to establish the relevance of the walkie-talkies to any of his five suspects.

Ronnie was now willing to testify that about ninety minutes before the explosion killed the firefighters, his stepmother, Darlene Edwards, and

Richard Brown entered a neighborhood bar where Bethard and he were drinking. Darlene and Richard approached them and one of them asked Bethard if he wanted to buy some more walkie-talkies. Bethard said he did and he and Bethard agreed to meet them at the QuikTrip in an hour.

Becker, of course, knew Ronnie told police six months earlier he and Bethard were in the same bar when Richard and Bryan came in and approached Bethard about buying walkie-talkies, and Frank and Johnny Driver were outside in Bryan's car.

Despite knowing this, Becker asked him if anyone else was with Richard and Darlene when they entered. No one was, he said, but through the front window of Billy B's bar he could see Frank and Bryan outside in the car.

Becker asked Ronnie if Richard and Darlene offered to sell them some more radios. "Yes," Ronnie said.

Asked Alan if he wants some more radios. Me and Alan sat down at the table with them. We said sure. We'll meet you down at QuikTrip within an hour. They left. We went to my house. By the time we hit the QuikTrip, we heard the explosion. And the windows broke out at QuikTrip and about probably a few seconds later, I seen Darlene drive by in that Thunderbird probably 90 miles an hour just going up 71 Highway.

All Becker wanted Ronnie to do next was to identify who was with Darlene and Richard in the Thunderbird as it sped by the QuikTrip:

Q. Could you tell if there was anybody else in the car?
A. Frank was in the front seat and Darlene was driving and three people were in the back seat but I positively seen Frank and Darlene in the front.
Q. Do you remember ever saying that Johnny Driver was in the car with them that night?
A. I really don't know Johnny Driver too much. I heard something about Chuck Jennings being in the car and I heard something about Johnny Driver being in the car and a fifth person but I'm not for sure.
Q. But I'm—I'm interested in what you saw mostly.
A. Yeah.
Q. So, you saw Frank and Darlene in the front?
A. Front seat for sure, yes.

Q. And then when you looked out the window at Billy B's, you could see Bryan—

A. Uh-huh.

Q. —and Frank, right? Bryan and Frank outside—

A. Yes.

Q. Richard and Darlene inside?

A. Yeah, they were inside.

Q. And then the unknown—

A. Yeah, the unknown person, I didn't see him.

Ronnie was not done. He would enhance his testimony by coming up with another completely new and damaging scenario against the five suspects. He told the grand jury he was at a barbeque at Darlene's house a day or two before the explosions. He was there with Darlene, Frank, Skip, Richard, Bryan, his half brother Tommy Edwards, and Becky Edwards, his eleven-year-old half sister and daughter of Darlene. He testified, "they were all talking about planning the explosion—not the explosion but going up there and stealing from the explosion site."

Ronnie's allegations were so transparently bogus Agent True would try to bolster them by getting Alan Bethard to corroborate them. When True approached Bethard in late 1996 to confirm Ronnie's allegations, Bethard refused to corroborate any of them, even after True offered him the entire $50,000 reward money and safe refuge in the government's witness protection program for his testimony. Bethard stood fast, essentially telling True everything Ronnie had said involving him was a fabrication.[17]

When the carrot did not work, True applied the stick, informing Bethard if he did not corroborate Ronnie, True would see to it that a pending state charge of tampering with a motor vehicle would be converted into a federal charge, which carried a longer sentence and no parole. Bethard still would not budge. (Bethard had stolen a truck in Independence, Missouri, and crossed the Kansas state line during a police chase.)

In retaliation, the government filed a federal charge of auto theft against Bethard.

Throughout the firefighters trial Fridays were days off. Two weeks before the firefighters case would go to the jury, Becker scheduled Friday, February 14, 1997, as the day to prosecute Bethard.

At Bethard's trial in US District Court, Becker admitted he was prosecuting Bethard because of his refusal to cooperate in the firefighters investigation.[18] Bethard had filed a motion with the court saying he told Agent True he would be perjuring himself if he corroborated Ronnie's statements. Bethard's attorney told US District Judge Scott O. Wright, "In another context, what has been attempted here [by the government] would be called extortion."

Judge Wright then told Bethard, "I'm sure the [Federal] Sentencing Commission would never, never in their wildest dreams anticipate that the government would pull something like this, like they've pulled on you." Wright then gave Bethard a so-called downward departure and expressed open disgust with the way the government handled Bethard's case, terming it a "vindictive prosecution." Although the sentencing guidelines called for Bethard to serve twelve to eighteen months in prison without parole, Judge Wright rejected the guidelines and sentenced Bethard to five years' probation, with six months in a halfway house, and restitution for the stolen vehicle.

Without intending to get an answer, the judge asked Becker, "Did it ever occur to you that your witness [Ronnie Edwards] might be the one that's lying?"

So what role did Ronnie Edwards play at the firefighters trial? He was not called as a witness.

The final witness before the grand jury was Agent True, the only government agent to testify. Becker called him to summarize the testimony of the dozens of witnesses who had appeared before the grand jury and asked him as well about several witnesses who did not appear before the grand jury. Immediately following Agent True's testimony, the grand jury indicted the Marlborough Five.

Four months after the federal grand jury handed down indictments against the Marlborough Five, Agent True laid out his case against the defendants in a seventy-eight-page pretrial report for Becker.[19] The document, entitled "Recommendation for Prosecution," was intended to provide Becker with a roadmap of how and why the five defendants committed the crime. The great bulk of it is taken up with True summarizing his version of what the numerous jailhouse informants and Marlborough witnesses said about the admissions of guilt made by individual members of the Marlborough Five.

In his report, True makes no attempt to weave these highly differentiated, and often contradictory, witness accounts into a narrative. It would have been impossible to do that because considered en masse they tell no story, comprising instead a hodgepodge of claims that have various members of the Marlborough Five, and many others as well, going to the construction site for a variety of reasons, stealing a wide array of items, and setting the arson fires for a host of reasons.

The report begins with a "Background and Motive Section." True repeatedly uses such words as "reportedly" and "possibly" and "may have" and "similar to" to make his case seem more convincing. There is no instance in all of these nebulous references where True questions the veracity of any of the government's witnesses even when they directly contradict known evidentiary facts or contradict what other witnesses claimed happened.

For example, True references Frank Sheppard telling Marlborough resident Lorena Deardorff three days after the explosions that he, his brother, and one other person were at the construction site the night the firefighters were killed. Frank said they were "drinking, partying and wanted to play around." One of them set the fire "to see if anybody would show up to see what would happen." Then they broke into a trailer and "found dynamite, and that one of them took a stick of it." They were still there when the firefighters arrived. To scare one of the firefighters, "they lit a stick of dynamite and threw it down there; it landed close to their trailer and then everything went 'boom.' Then they ran home and continued to party."

Three paragraphs into the report, True begins to palter, stating that "certain members of this group were well known in the area as common thieves, specializing at times in thefts from area construction sites. This particular site had been one of their intended targets for a period of time . . . and the area was familiar to the members who had previously frequented the site in the past for both legal and illegal purposes."

None of the Marlborough Five had ever been involved in thefts at any construction site and there was no proof any of them had ever been at this construction site.

In the report's next section, "Chronology of Events," True continues to misrepresent the facts, asserting the contractors routinely left tools and walkie-talkies overnight "that were visible to the general public" driving by. (As would come out at trial when various contractors testified, the workers owned their own tools and took them home with them each night as well as the walkie-talkies.)

In this section he depicts the Marlborough Five as "a small loose-knit group of individuals . . . [who] would periodically interact and communicate with each other, while socializing together and carrying out various criminal activities." True completely misunderstood the inner dynamics of the Marlborough Five. Bryan and Richard didn't socialize with Frank or Skip and they never engaged in any previous criminal activity with them.

Other than the Marlborough Five, True wasn't sure who else to include as perpetrators:

> This group, some of who were related, included but was not limited to Frank and Earl "Skip" Sheppard, and their nephew Bryan Sheppard, Darlene Edwards, who was Frank's girlfriend, Ronnie Edwards, who was Darlene Edwards's stepson, Richard Brown, who was a close criminal associate of Bryan Sheppard, and Alan Bethard, who was a close criminal associate of Richard Brown and Bryan Sheppard and was living with Ronnie Edwards at the time. This group would communicate with each other, as well as with many of their mutual friends, brag about their successful thefts, and display their stolen goods to each other and talk about future theft sites.

Bryan and Richard were friends, not criminal associates. True didn't have one example of the two of them engaging in previous criminal activity and the same was the case in terms of Alan Bethard.

Despite the fact nothing was ever stolen from the construction site, including the night of the explosions, True's report is replete with witnesses' references to items stolen that night. True has Frank and Richard selling concrete saws and concrete saw blades to [name redacted] sometime in the first week of December 1988, items Richard told this person "came from the construction site where the firefighters died." In as far-fetched a scenario as imaginable, True has Richard and Bryan, a few days after the explosion, trying to sell two walkie-talkies "believed to belong to the Kansas City Fire Department." He also has Darlene in possession of walkie-talkies less than a year after the explosion.

True knew Bethard had stolen some walkie-talkies from a lawn service site a few months before the explosions, but in his report he states Bethard stole them "reportedly along with Richard Brown and Bryan Sheppard." No one, not even Ronnie Edwards, had ever made that claim.

Although Bryan's girlfriend, Debbie Howard, told True that Bryan came home around midnight on the night of the explosions and she slept upstairs with him until she left him at 3 a.m. to go back downstairs, True leaves out that Debbie left him at 3 a.m.

This omission allowed True once again to reprise the lies Ronnie Edwards spun for the grand jury about meeting with all five defendants at

Billy B's bar at 2:30 a.m. and planning to steal walkie-talkies from the construction site later that night. "The topic of trying to steal walkie-talkie type radios was once again discussed between Alan Bethard, Richard Brown and Bryan Sheppard, along with other items of value located at the construction site . . . Alan Bethard had agreed to meet the others at the construction site to assist them in the eventual theft of the items from the site."

On page twelve of the report, True advances his theory of the case:

On November 29, 1988 between 3:20 a.m. and 4 a.m., exact time unknown, Richard Brown, Bryan Sheppard, with the assistance of Darlene Edwards, Frank Sheppard and Earl D. "Skip" Sheppard and *several other individuals* [emphasis added] reportedly were at the construction site near 87th Street and South 71 Highway in Kansas City, Missouri. They reportedly set fire to a Toyota pickup truck owned by security guard Deborah Riggs and to a construction site trailer containing a large quantity of blasting agents located at the construction site.

The above individuals allegedly used gasoline purchased from a local convenience store to assist in the acceleration of the fires. One fire was set as a diversion to avoid detection by the security guards and another fire was set to destroy evidence of fingerprints and other evidence of theft, which the above individuals conducted while at the construction site. While at the construction site, the above individuals utilized Richard Brown's older model black Ford pickup, as well as Frank and Skip Sheppard's father's yellowish-gold-and-white pickup truck, along with other vehicles at their disposal. The above individuals also used Bryan Sheppard's dark-colored Ford Thunderbird to assist in the theft.

In the years following this date, each of the above named defendants would brag, confide and lament to numerous individuals about their own involvement, as well as the other individuals' involvement in this crime.

This chronology is proven up by more witnesses than can be listed all inclusive in this section. The proof of the event will be proven circumstantially through these witnesses and admissions by the defendants.

This brief summary contains a number of assertions for which True has no supporting evidence. There was no corroboration from any convenience store employee that any of these defendants purchased gas the night of the explosion. The QuikTrip night manager told police he did not sell a can of gas to anyone that night. In addition, there were no witness reports about seeing any of the vehicles True references entering or leaving the construction site.

True has no basis for claiming these defendants set fire to a security guard's pickup as a diversionary tactic. According to the guards, they were away from the site when both fires were set.

When True wrote that the Marlborough Five "and several other individuals" were involved in the arsons, he was inadvertently stating he had not solved the case.

In crafting this report, True's major problem was that the case he mounted against these five was entirely circumstantial, based on information provided by jailhouse informants and Marlborough witnesses. These statements were so conflicted and contradictory—and they often named perpetrators not indicted—True didn't know how the crime went down. He did not have any idea who of the Marlborough Five allegedly did what.

Despite his Herculean efforts to find one witness who actually saw any of these defendants at the construction site the night of the explosions, True had come up dry, and so had all other investigators before him. All he had for proof were alleged admissions by the defendants themselves.

His witnesses' stories were so diverse he had these five and inconveniently several other individuals arriving at the scene in as many as four vehicles. One witness has Bryan Sheppard departing the scene on a bicycle; another has Frank and Skip running away on foot.

True does not raise the issue of how to account for all of the devious actions the defendants were alleged to have perpetrated in the five minutes the security guards were gone from the site. If the guards had been gone fifteen minutes or even thirty minutes, this rag-tag group could not have stolen all the equipment, set all the fires, and driven away in three or four vehicles undetected as True claimed.

Many other aspects of this case make True's theory unsupportable. True's central notion that these street-smart petty criminals would continue year after year to admit their guilt to others, after being harassed by the police in the weeks immediately following the explosion, and particularly after Bryan Sheppard had been indicted for the crime in 1989, simply collapses when given any thought.

Frank Sheppard read True's report in 2008. He said in a letter he wrote:

The way this report reads is 1988, 1989, 1990, 1991, 1992, 1993, 1994, 1995, and all the way up our indictment date June 12, 1996, we stooges TALKED, TALKED, TALKED about this terrible crime that we had done and seemed to have gotten away with. We talked about it to ANYBODY & EVERYBODY that would listen to us. Can't get any better than that can you? I guess the only thing left would be THE STOOGES HALL OF FAME!!!

Toward the end of his report, True takes up the unenviable task of informing Becker that star grand jury witness Ronnie Edwards had concealed his own role in the crime:

On [redacted date], 1995, Ronnie Edwards told [name redacted] that he was at the construction site along with Darlene Edwards and the Sheppards in the early morning of November 29, 1988 when the firefighters died in the explosion. Edwards said the reason they were there was to steal. There were two vehicles used that night and Darlene Edwards was driving one of them. Edwards said he was there to try to help steal some radios and he was present when the fire was set. Edwards admitted to [name redacted] that he had not told his total involvement to investigating officers and agents.

Obviously, what True was now stating made Ronnie Edwards, by his own admission, an accessory to the deaths of the firefighters. This would explain why Ronnie was not called as a prosecution witness at the firefighters trial, but it begs the question why he wasn't indicted for the crime.

Other than the government wanting to close this case, it is difficult to understand how a prosecution could have been mounted on the report True wrote, considering all the misrepresentations and contradictions it contained. The only thing that made it possible for this prosecution to go forward was the fifty-six witnesses who were willing to say the defendants made admissions of guilt.

CHAPTER 7

The Trial Opens

One of the most fundamental of all the rights the US Constitution provides is the Sixth Amendment's right to a fair trial. The cornerstone of that right is the presumption of innocence afforded anyone accused of a crime. The innocent-until-proven-guilty claim of the US justice system is a bedrock ideal, but the reality is and has been for decades that if a federal grand jury indicts someone, the defendant is going down 98 times out of a 100.[1]

Most go down by plea-bargaining away their right to a trial. The vast majority of federal defendants—some 95 percent—plead guilty in order to evade longer sentences.[2] "A pernicious phenomenon called the 'trial penalty' dissuades many defendants" from going to trial, according to an article in *Vice News*.[3] "The federal conviction rate is an astonishing 97 percent, and studies have shown that defendants who refuse plea bargains are put behind bars for roughly nine times as long as those who take deals." For those with the temerity to go to trial, they are bucking extraordinary odds. Less than 9 percent of those trials end in acquittal.[4]

Despite the odds facing them at trial, each of the Marlborough Five had the guileless confidence that because he or she was innocent, the jury would set them free, a belief that would remain with each of them throughout the trial and during jury deliberations.

Because each of the Marlborough Five was indigent, the court appointed private criminal defense attorneys for each. The defense attorneys would be paid by the court $125 an hour for in-court time and $75 per hour for out-of-court time.[5] (On average, the five principal attorneys were paid about $65,000 each for representing their clients.[6])

Frank Sheppard was represented by Pat Peters, a former Jackson County assistant prosecutor who earned the nickname "Doctor Death" for the numerous death-penalty convictions he had run up. He left that position in 1992 after running for Jackson County prosecutor and losing to Claire McCaskill, who would go on to become a US senator from Missouri.

John P. O'Connor, another former Jackson County assistant prosecutor, was appointed to represent Bryan Sheppard. O'Connor had successfully represented Bryan in 1989 when the state charged him with six counts of second-degree murder in the deaths of the firefighters. O'Connor, though the youngest in his early forties, would prove himself to be the most dogged and effective advocate at trial.

Susan Hunt, a former technician for the KCPD's Regional Crime Lab turned defense attorney, represented Skip Sheppard. Hunt was assisted by attorney Elena Franco.

Will Bunch, a past president of the Kansas City Metropolitan Bar Defender Commission, represented Darlene Edwards. Bunch had spent eight years as a lecturer at the University of Missouri–Kansas City School of Law. He was the author of a chapter on criminal evidence for the *Continuing Legal Education* handbook used by the Missouri Bar Association.

The attorney for Richard Brown was John Osgood, who had recently gone into private practice after spending nineteen years as a federal prosecutor. This appointment would represent his first high-profile experience on the other side of the courtroom. Being forced to work so closely with five other defense attorneys made him something of a fish out of water. At the first planning session of defense counsel, Osgood told his colleagues he intended to defend his client by pointing the finger at the other defendants. This rupture in the defense would persist and lead to dire consequences for all five defendants.

If there had been any intention of providing these defendants with any semblance of a fair trial, the government would have tried them separately or at least severed the trial of Richard Brown and Bryan from that of Frank, Skip, and Darlene. Due to the accusations Darlene made against Richard and Bryan there was a built-in schism within the defense that would not be surmounted at trial—a schism so deep that members of Darlene's family would testify against Richard, and Richard's half sister would testify against Darlene and Frank. Darlene's family, her parents and sisters, sat on the other side of the courtroom—with the families of the firefighters—rather than with the families of the other defendants.

It also made sense to try Richard and Bryan together because almost all of the witnesses against them linked the two of them without connecting them to Frank, Skip, or Darlene. The same was the case for the majority of witnesses against Frank, Skip, and Darlene. Only one government witness, Darlene's daughter Becky Edwards, had ever put the five defendants together—along with two others, including Ronnie Edwards—in a plot to rob the construction site.

But in a federal trial in a federal courthouse, the government gets what it wants and what it wanted was these five tried together as co-conspirators who acted in union to pull off a theft that resulted in the deaths of six firefighters. All motions for severance—separate trials—both pretrial and during the trial, were dismissed, and there was nothing the defense attorneys could do about it.[7] For the government, it was not only more efficient and enormously more cost-effective to try all five together, but it provided a key strategic advantage to be able to parade over fifty witnesses in front of the jury who would say they heard one or more of these defendants making admissions of guilt. Because the case against each defendant was thin on its own—particularly the government's case against Darlene and Skip Sheppard—it would not be unreasonable to say that there may well have been no convictions in separate trials.

When it came to prosecuting the firefighters case, Becker would display a hard-nosed style of prosecution.[8]

His first salvo was to invoke a seldom-used and outdated evidentiary rule that designated the firefighters case "closed file," meaning the government would withhold witness statements and their addresses and phone numbers until shortly before trial, leaving the defense little time to investigate these witnesses. The normal purpose of invoking a "closed file" case was to protect witnesses against reprisals in organized crime cases. Of all the assistant US attorneys in the Western District of Missouri, Becker is the only one who routinely designated cases he prosecuted as "closed file" ones.

Under discovery rules, the government is compelled to turn over to the defense the statements of government witnesses who might be called to testify at trial. Using the "closed file" case designation allowed Becker to release several hundred pages of these witness statements in redacted form, blacking out the names of the witnesses and any other information that might identify them. This made it impossible for defense investigators to interview these witnesses, something they would have done in preparation for trial.

The witness statements did show the defense what an incredible jumble of accusations the government had pieced together. The statements were in great conflict with each other on which defendants were allegedly involved in the crime, what their motives were, and what they had stolen the night of the explosion. No two of these witness statements made the same claims and none of them put the Marlborough Five together. Many of these statements listed perpetrators not under indictment, but acting with one or more of the Marlborough Five in the commission of the crime.

Becker additionally thwarted the defense by withholding discovery material. As a result of a 1963 US Supreme Court decision in *Brady v. Maryland*, prosecutors are compelled to turn over to the defense any material that tends to support the innocence of the defendant or which will impeach a government witness.[9] In *Brady*, the Supreme Court held, "the suppression by the prosecution of evidence favorable to the accused upon request violates due process where the evidence is material either to guilt or to punishment, irrespective of the good faith or bad faith of the prosecution."

When Bryan Sheppard was charged by the state in the firefighters' deaths in 1989, the Jackson County Prosecutor's Office turned over about twenty-five hundred pages of discovery, a great deal of it *Brady* material.

Although Becker early on agreed to turn over all *Brady* material, he initially released only a small amount. In response, the defense filed a detailed *Brady* motion with US Magistrate Sarah Hays, listing a great deal of *Brady* material that was in the state's 1989 file but absent from Becker's filing. The magistrate, who oversees pretrial rulings, ordered Becker to turn over all *Brady* material by November 26, 1996, listing in detail the type of material that Becker must provide the defense. When that day arrived, Becker, clearly not intimidated, turned over only forty-seven additional pages. The defense was expecting to receive fifteen hundred pages or more.

The defense reacted by filing a motion seeking sanctions against the government for Becker denying a direct court order. One of the sanctions the defense asked for was for the magistrate to force the government to turn over the full transcript of the grand jury proceedings that led to the indictments and give the defense access to the Department of Labor files, both of which the government kept secret. Magistrate Hays sidestepped the issue of sanctions by ruling that a decision on that matter would be taken up by the trial judge during or at the conclusion of the trial.

With the trial scheduled to begin on January 13, 1997, Becker waited until Christmas Eve to turn over thirty-three hundred pages of discovery, including witness statements with the names of the witnesses and rap sheets for the numerous felons involved as witnesses—but not their addresses. A good deal of this discovery turned out to be *Brady* material—information that pointed to the innocence of one or more of the defendants—and should have been turned over to the defense on November 26, 1996.

This late dumping of so much discovery led four of the defense attorneys to ask for an additional thirty days to prepare for trial, but the court granted only a ten-day postponement.

While the trial date was approaching, the defense team got another stark look at Becker's disregard for *Brady* material. In early January, John P. Ryan Jr., an attorney for government witness Mary Hawks, sent a copy of a letter he had sent to Becker to the defense attorneys. The letter stated Hawks no longer would agree to testify at the firefighters trial because she had lied at the grand jury. At the grand jury, she testified Skip Sheppard made incriminating admissions about his role in the explosion. Now she said Skip never said anything to her about the crime.

Becker still wanted her to testify. Because she was related by marriage to the Sheppards, her testimony would carry the patina of "inside knowledge." Becker wrote back to Ryan straight away and said he wanted to talk to Hawks about her decision on testifying, adding "nothing she says in this interview would be used against her, directly or indirectly in any criminal prosecution including a prosecution for perjury or contempt."

The defense now waited to see if Becker would reveal what was in Ryan's letter. No call, no fax came from the prosecutor.

When Becker turned over his list of trial witnesses on January 8, Hawks was still on it. The next day, during a conference call among all the defense attorneys, the prosecutors, and Federal District Judge D. Brook Bartlett, who was slated to preside at trial, one of the defense attorneys asked Becker if there would be any more *Brady* material disclosed to the defense. Becker said no.

What Ryan told Becker about Hawks saying she lied at the grand jury was as pure a *Brady* matter as they come.

Becker, in addition to Hawks, had 167 names on his witness list, but had not provided addresses as ordered by Magistrate Hays and had not indicated which of these he actually intended to call. When Bartlett asked him how many witnesses he intended to call, Becker said between 115 and 117. (At trial, the government called 24 felons, 32 witnesses from Marlborough, and 21 others for a total of 77 witnesses.)

When Bartlett asked Becker to give the defense the names of the witnesses he was going to call. Becker's response was: "The answer is I think they can figure it out themselves."

The judge, always one to search for a compromise, asked Becker why he did not want to give the defense the first week's witnesses right now and the second week's witness list by Friday, two days away:

> It's not unusual for your office to furnish an order of proof at about this time before trial where you lay out the people that are going to be called. Some summary of what they're going to say or what you

believe they're going to say, and the order which you are going to call them, all of which is very helpful to, not only to me in figuring out how to plan the trial schedule, but also it's helpful to the defendants.

"Well, Judge, I agree," Becker responded. "It's sort of something in a normal case that we would do, I would do or anybody else would do. This isn't a normal case."

Bartlett asked him what was "abnormal about it?"

"Six people are dead because of what these defendants are charged with, six firemen," Becker said.

The judge said he understood the case was about six firefighters being killed,

but what's that got to do with whether you do this? I mean, that's the issue the jury is going to have to decide is who, if any, of these folks are responsible. But why not give it to them? I mean, we've got to try the case. I mean the fact that six people are dead is a terrible tragedy, but, still the case has got to be tried.

Becker was not about to budge. "I agree, Judge, but I don't see why I should have to give them a roadmap of my case prior to the trial. I see no reason to make their life easier."

Eventually, after more than a half hour of back and forth, Becker agreed to turn over a list of the witnesses he intended to call and provide their contact information by noon the next day.

Over eight years after the six firefighters were killed, the trial of the Marlborough Five was about to begin at the federal courthouse in downtown Kansas City.[10]

With Judge D. Brook Bartlett presiding, the impaneling of jurors began on January 13 with 105 potential jurors in the pool. Two days later, a jury of seven men and five women was sworn in, with two men and two women as alternates.

Just before the first day of the trial got under way on January 21, the attorneys for the defense and prosecution were summoned to the judge's chambers. There they learned Judge Bartlett had been diagnosed recently with bone cancer and was to begin treatment immediately; a federal district judge on senior status, Joseph E. Stevens Jr., would be taking over the trial. Stevens had been on the federal bench for the last fifteen years.

(Once federal judges reach the age of sixty-five they may retire at full pay or continue, on a more limited basis, to preside at trials. Stevens, like more than five hundred federal judges throughout the United States, had opted to keep his day job.[11])

Once Judge Bartlett recused himself and Judge Stevens stepped in, there was scant discussion in chambers about postponing the trial. The jury was out in the courtroom, the early government witnesses were present, and the courtroom was packed.

Probably no development in this far-flung odyssey of a case could have been more detrimental to the fates of the defendants than Stevens replacing Bartlett. For one thing, Stevens taking over the trial just minutes before it was to begin meant he had missed out on all the pretrial developments and knew no more than what he may have read in the newspaper or seen on television about the substance of the case. And now that the trial was about to begin, he was out of time to catch up. Any hope the defense had of getting sanctions imposed on Becker for his pretrial maneuverings became a dead letter. (The defense team never mentioned the issue of sanctions again.)

Although Stevens had earned a reputation as an accomplished trial lawyer and had served as president of the Missouri Bar Association before President Ronald Reagan appointed him to the federal bench in 1981, it was his courtroom manner that most concerned the defense team. Stevens could be intolerant and unyielding and he was quick to irritation. He was known as a judge who liked to move a trial along "smartly."

Even on senior status, he was a man in a hurry, as though he was already late to be somewhere else. Where Bartlett was painstakingly fair to the point of agonizing over the meaning of a word and would give considerable deliberation to any objection raised by either team of attorneys, Stevens would rule on an objection almost before an attorney could utter it. Sometimes, but only when a defense attorney was speaking, he would even make an objection of his own and cut the attorney off, shattering the normal courtroom protocol.

As an example, while John Osgood was cross-examining government witness Jerry Rooks, Stevens interrupted him to say that what he was asking Rooks was "argumentative." He then said, "Sustain the objection" even though no objection had been made.

After trial the first day, Stevens ordered attorney John O'Connor to turn over the interviews he had conducted with eleven of the government's jailhouse witnesses. Pat Peters, the former Jackson County assistant prosecutor who represented Frank Sheppard, told the judge it was the first time in the history of the United States a federal judge was ordering a defense attorney to produce witness interviews prior to the witnesses testifying. Stevens's response, after a testy debate, was to uphold his order.

On the sixth day of the trial, Susan Hunt, the attorney representing Skip Sheppard, was cross-examining a government witness. As soon as Hunt mentioned the name of a defense investigator, former KCPD police officer Mark Reeder, Stevens cut her off. At the bench, with attorneys for both sides present, Stevens said he did not trust defense investigators. After some heated debate with several of the defense attorneys, Stevens sustained his own objection and instructed Hunt not to pursue the line of questioning developed by the investigator.

In an almost unprecedented step—some court observers would say "suicidal"—all six defense attorneys filed a joint motion the next day asking the judge to recuse himself "for the reason that the remarks by the Court regarding defendants' investigators demonstrated bias and prejudice of such magnitude as to deny defendants due process."

Stevens denied the motion. If the defense thought asking this crusty judge to step down would in some way soften him up, something akin to a basketball coach screaming at a referee and taking a technical foul in hopes of getting a favorable call later in the game, this strategy was misguided.

The judge's bias against the defense permeated the trial. Time and again when one defense attorney or the other attempted to cross-examine government witnesses, the judge would sustain prosecution objections, ruling the question went beyond the scope of the prosecution's direct examination. In federal court, cross-examination in criminal trials is limited to the ground covered during the direct examination of the witness, although there is a great deal of leeway or discretion the judge may deploy in ruling on the admissibility challenge. In the case of three of the government witnesses—ATF Agent True and the two security guards, Robert and Debbie Riggs—Stevens limited the cross-examination on the basis the defense would have its opportunity to question them more widely when the defense put on its case.

Another area of judicial bias concerned the judge's handling of "offers of proof" made by the defense.[12] Offers of proof arose numerous times during trial when one of the prosecutors objected to a line of questioning one of the defense attorneys was pursuing. When the judge ruled with the prosecutor that the line of questioning was either irrelevant or was delving into inadmissible evidence, the defense attorney was allowed to counter with an offer of proof in an attempt to overcome the objection. If the offer of proof convinces the judge the line of questioning is proper and might lead to proper evidence being admitted, the attorney will be given a chance to show how the expected answers will be both relevant and admissible. Judge Stevens ruled against every offer of proof the defense made.

The major problem Assistant US Attorney Paul Becker faced in making his case against the Marlborough Five was that no one claimed to see any of them at the construction site the night of the explosions. Plus there was no physical evidence linking any of the defendants to the crime. All of the evidence accumulated was based on alleged admissions the five defendants made over the years.

Another significant hurdle Becker had to somehow get over, or at least get around, was that jailhouse informant testimony, for good reason, was suspect, and the testimony from Marlborough residents could easily be considered tainted by the government's offer of a $50,000 reward. In addition, a number of the Marlborough witnesses had issues with law enforcement themselves.

To deal with both of these problems there was only one solution: get as many felons and neighborhood people to testify as available. It appeared that the entire working strategy of the prosecution was to throw as much mud up on the wall as possible, not just in the hope that some of it would stick, but that the sheer tonnage would sway jurors into believing that these many witnesses, despite their unreliability and the wildly different accounts, could not all be lying.

Jailhouse snitch testimony, as every judge, prosecutor and defense attorney knows, is extremely unreliable not only because it is coming from convicted felons but because there is almost always a quid pro quo attached. For testifying on behalf of the prosecution, the inmate is promised or at least expects something major in return such as a reduction in sentence or a get-out-of-jail card.

In a profound way, Federal Sentencing Guidelines, with their draconian mandatory-minimum prison terms that do not allow for parole, have created a snitch culture where "cooperation" with the government is the only way federal inmates can obtain a reduction in sentence or an outright release.[13]

Up until the passage of the Sentencing Reform Act in 1984, federal judges decided sentences on a case-by-case basis.[14] Depending on mitigating or aggravating factors—or the whim of the judge—the sentences imposed could vary drastically for the same crime, say an armed robbery.

The Comprehensive Crime Control Act of 1984[15] was intended to take the arbitrariness out of sentencing by replacing the US Parole Commission with the US Sentencing Commission and in the process not only standardize sentencing but abolish parole for federal prisoners.[16]

The US Sentencing Commission, composed of seven members appointed by the president, was an independent agency within the judicial branch that was tasked with drafting rigid sentencing guidelines that federal judges would be mandated to apply based on two factors: the crime's offense level, which ranged from a low of one to a high of forty-three (first-degree murder), along with the defendant's criminal history, ranging between one to six (habitual criminal). Using these two factors, the judge would mete out punishment by consulting a "sentencing table," a matrix of offense levels and criminal history with a 258-box grid of punishment ranges.[17]

The first mandatory-minimum sentence promulgated by Congress imposed a minimum sentence of fifteen years for a felon in possession of a firearm if the criminal had three prior convictions for a violent felony or a serious drug offense. Two years later, Congress passed the Anti-Drug Abuse Act of 1986—aimed specifically at crack cocaine—imposing mandatory-minimum terms of imprisonment for violations of the federal controlled substances laws.[18] People caught selling fifty grams of crack—the great majority of them blacks—now faced a minimum of ten years in prison. (Fifty grams of crack weigh the same as a five-cent piece. For defendants in powder cocaine cases—the vast majority of them whites—it took five thousand grams to merit a ten-year sentence—a disparity of 100 to 1.)[19]

In later years, more and more crime categories were given mandatory-minimum sentences, from child pornography to identity theft.

What ingrained snitching into the fabric of the justice system was Congress directing the US Sentencing Commission, soon after the passage of the 1986 Anti-Drug Abuse Act, to establish major incentives for "cooperating witnesses." As a result, the Sentencing Commission promulgated a new section of the sentencing guidelines—known as 5K—that allowed judges to make a "downward departure" from a guideline sentence if the defendant provided "substantial assistance" to the prosecutor.[20] The original intent of 5K was to enable prosecutors to ring up far more drug convictions by turning drug dealers into government witnesses to bring down other, presumably higher-placed, drug dealers. The 5K section would soon find uses in prosecuting organized crime suspects and then it would seep into all manner of prosecutions. Prosecutors simply could not resist the leverage 5K offers had on closing cases that seemed unsolvable without such witnesses.

As Ethan Brown observed in his book *Snitch: Informants, Cooperators and the Corruption of Justice*, "While section 5Kl.1 was an invaluable tool to federal prosecutors—'flipping' was suddenly a foregone conclusion for most defendants—it also created huge incentives for defendants to fabricate evidence, particularly when faced with harsh prison terms."[21]

In the years since 1984, snitching has become embedded in the justice system and has become one of the primary factors responsible for so many wrongful convictions. According to Northwestern University's Center on Wrongful Convictions, 45.9 percent of documented wrongful capital convictions have been traced to false informant testimony.[22] This makes "snitches" the leading cause of wrongful convictions in capital cases in the United States.[23]

Since 1989, there have been over 2,100 exonerations in the United States according to the National Registry of Exonerations, a joint program of the University of Michigan Law School and the Center on Wrongful Convictions at the Northwestern University School of Law.[24] Most of those set free had been convicted of murder, rape, or other sexual assaults. The Death Penalty Information Center reported in 2017 there had been 160 exonerations of prisoners on death row in the United States since 1973.[25]

It's not known how many innocent people are in prison, but a conservative estimate would be between 2.3 and 5 percent, or 53,000 to 115,000 prisoners, according to the Innocence Project at the Benjamin N. Cardozo School of Law in New York City.[26] For all but a few hundred of these who have their cases taken up by innocence projects or by lawyers mostly working pro bono, they will leave prison only after serving their sentences or, in the case of those sentenced to life or execution, they will die in prison.

Barry Scheck and Peter Neufeld, the founders of the pro bono Innocence Project, reported in their 2000 book *Actual Innocence* that fifteen of the seventy-four men ultimately freed through DNA exonerations between 1989 and 1999 were the victims of perjured testimony by jailhouse snitches.[27]

Actual Innocence quotes a career criminal by the name of Leslie Vernon White, who never served close to his full sentence because of the deals he worked with the Los Angeles D.A.'s Office for testifying against fellow inmates, as saying, "Among inmate informers, the jokes were: 'Don't go to the pen—send a friend.' Or: 'If you can't do the time, just drop a dime.'

And: 'Trouble? You better call 1-800-HETOLDME.'" White said informants like him "will swarm to a hot case—the hotter the case, the higher the reward for snitching."[28]

An often overlooked or underplayed aspect of convicting innocent people is that this allows the actual perpetrators to remain free and commit more crimes. The Innocence Project states that in the process of exonerating 351 innocent people through DNA evidence, 150 actual perpetrators were identified. "Those actual perpetrators went on to be convicted of 147 additional violent crimes, including 77 sexual assaults, 35 murders, and 35 other violent crimes while the innocent sat behind bars."[29]

More than anything else, the use of snitch testimony makes the firefighters trial stand out as a judicial aberration. Of the fifty-six informant witnesses the government called to testify, twenty-four of them had been convicted of a total of seventy-six felonies for crimes that included assault, drug sales, prison escapes, embezzlement, counterfeiting, fraud, forgery, sexual assault, witness intimidation, explosives violations, and manslaughter. A large number of Marlborough witnesses had criminal backgrounds and all were aware of the $50,000 reward potential for their testimony. The trial set the record, by a wide margin, for using more informant testimony than any trial in US history.[30]

It is not known what deals the government made with all twenty-four felons who testified at trial, but details concerning the deals made for eighteen of the informants can be documented through court transcripts of the trial and individual case records. The deals the government made with them will be presented alongside their testimony.

In addition to the felons and the witnesses from Marlborough, twenty-one witnesses were drawn from various departments of law enforcement, the fire department, and from the construction companies. Guards Debbie and Robert Riggs were the second and third witnesses the government called; ATF Special Agent Dave True would be the last. In an attempt to bring some cohesion to the prosecution's case, the first set of informants testified against Frank, the next set against Skip, then Darlene, Bryan, and finally Richard.

No matter how conscientious the jurors could be—and several of them took copious notes throughout the trial—the task of evaluating the evidence against the Marlborough Five was an overwhelming one. In addition to all the witnesses, the government entered over 450 exhibits into evidence, the defense more than 40. With two prosecutors (Becker was assisted by Dan Miller of the Jackson County Prosecutor's Office) and five defendants represented by six attorneys, just trying to make sense of what was being presented was a daunting task, a task complicated greatly by the scores of objections that frequently led to prolonged sidebar conferences at the bench out of the hearing of the jury or were argued in the privacy of the judge's chambers.

Approximately one-third of the trial's time was taken up by these conferences. Although the jurors could not hear what was being argued at the bench, they were free to observe the often animated exchanges between the defense attorneys and the prosecutors and between the defense attorneys and the judge. When, invariably, the judge ruled in favor of the prosecution at the end of these conferences, an inevitability about the righteousness of the government's case took on its own subtle momentum.

Complicating matters more for the jurors was a pretrial decision the defense attorneys made that prevented the jury from hearing the complete testimony of many government witnesses because the defense had invoked the "Bruton Rule."[31] In multidefendant trials, the Bruton Rule is designed to protect co-defendants from being implicated by the statements made by one of the other defendants. If, for example, a witness said Richard Brown told him that he, Bryan Sheppard, Chuck Jennings, and Lonnie Joe Pugh caused the explosion, the witness would only be allowed to testify that Richard told him that he and three others were involved.

By taking this strategy, the defense not only deprived the jury of hearing numerous government witnesses name alleged perpetrators who were not on trial, but the jurors did not get to hear these witnesses say other co-defendants were not implicated. In the example above, for instance, no reference was made to Frank, Skip, or Darlene. Witness after witness who testified against Frank did not mention anyone other than Skip and his sister Diddi being with him. Not one witness testified Richard ever made admissions that linked him to Frank, Skip, or Darlene. Many linked him to Bryan, some to Chuck Jennings, some to Lonnie Joe Pugh, and some to his girlfriend at the time.

Another unfortunate consequence of using the Bruton Rule was it made it possible for the jurors—despite any admonition from the judge to the contrary—to deduce the "unnamed others" being mentioned by the witnesses were none other than the co-defendants sitting in the dock.

The Bruton Rule crippled the jurors' ability to hear for themselves that not a single one of the informant witnesses put these five defendants together in commission of the crime.

At the end of the trial, in closing arguments, each of the defense attorneys could have made a strong case for reasonable doubt by simply going through, one by one, the dozens of witnesses who made no reference to his or her particular client and referencing all the other people named as perpetrators.

There is no polite way to say this: the defense attorneys made a colossal error by invoking the Bruton Rule and muzzling these informants.

CHAPTER 8

The Case against the Marlborough Five

At the time of the explosion that killed the firefighters, Frank Sheppard was the only one of the Marlborough Five with a felony record. He had lived the sort of desultory life that made it possible for those who knew him—and later for law enforcement—to see him as someone capable of not only being involved in the deaths of the firefighters but of being the mastermind. In a sense, the others indicted with him were collateral damage, the victims of their connections to him, particularly after he turned himself into an object of hatred to the firefighters' families.

Following his appearance before a state grand jury in 1989 that would indict his nephew Bryan Sheppard in the deaths of the firefighters, Frank told reporters gathered outside the grand jury room that in his opinion "the stupid fucking firemen actually killed themselves." This widely aired quote "put me and all of us in a very bad light as far as being an innocent citizen," Frank wrote years later.

> But it was the truth—as insensitive as it turned out to be. And this statement of mine has haunted and followed us for years. And as bad as it is—the firemen and families of these dead guys—hate it to no end that their guys actually knew what was on fire that fateful morning and still yet they chose to fight this non-emergency fire and it was a fatal mistake they made. And that is why they hated me and us.[1]

At trial, the government called fourteen informant witnesses to testify against Frank Sheppard.[2] Six of them were felons and the others were from Marlborough. Later in the trial, two others would implicate him when testifying against his brother Skip. Shannon Reimers, Richard Brown's half sister, would provide damaging testimony against him when testifying about him and Darlene. And Darlene's daughter, Becky Edwards, would provide the most devastating testimony the jury would hear about the Marlborough Five.

• John Barchers, thirty-four, a Marlborough neighbor, said Frank told him they set the fire as a diversion without realizing there were explosives in the dump truck. Frank said the firefighters were stupid for rushing in before finding out what was up there. Frank, Skip, and their sister Diddi went to the construction site to remove metal out of deserted houses and to steal construction equipment. They remained at the site until the firefighters showed up and then all three of them went to the QuikTrip, where Frank talked to a construction site guard who was eating donuts and drinking coffee. (There were no explosives in a dump truck; there were no vacant houses within a quarter of a mile of the trailers; the guards did not return to the QuikTrip after the firefighters arrived.)

• Peggy Barchers, thirty-four, John Barchers's wife, heard Frank say the firefighters were stupid and that he, Skip, and Diddi set the fire where the ANFO trailers were located as a diversion to draw attention away from where the metal and copper were being stolen from vacant houses at the site.

Special Agent True and Agent Schram of the Labor Department met with the Barchers on February 19, 1995. Later that year, both Barchers pled guilty to a state charge of marijuana possession and got a sentence of three years' probation. In 1996, after they testified at the grand jury, Peggy pled guilty to larceny and got two years' probation despite violating her parole.

• Lisa Landon, thirty-four, John Barchers's sister, overheard either Frank or Skip say they knew what was in those trailers and "just wanted to see what would happen" if they caught fire.

• Virgil D. Whitt, forty, testified Frank told him at a tavern in 1990 no one was supposed to get hurt and the guards were not supposed to be there. Whitt told Kansas City police about this in 1990 when he was in jail for receiving stolen property. Whitt had previous felony convictions for burglary, interstate transport of forged securities, and cocaine sales. (Whitt's testimony contradicted the heart of the government's theory that the Marlborough Five set fires on both sides of the construction site while the guards were away from the site.)

• Charles E. Elliott Jr., forty, a jailhouse informant with eight felony convictions, shared a cell with Frank at an honor center in Kansas City in 1995. Frank, who he said introduced himself as "George," told him someone drove him to get the gas they used to start the fire. To establish an alibi, they used a detonator so they could be somewhere else when the fire started. (There was incontrovertible evidence from arson investigators that gasoline was the source of the fires on both sides of the site.)

Elliott was getting out of prison the day after he testified. ATF agents came to see him in May 1995 at a prison in central Missouri and took an unsigned statement from him. During 1996, after his grand jury testimony, he wrote six letters to Becker seeking reward money and a cut in his sentence. During cross-examination, he admitted he would do almost anything to get out of jail, including lying. (Some time after the firefighters trial, Elliott committed another federal crime, occasioning Becker to file a motion on October 9, 1998, with the US District Court for the Western District of Missouri, requesting the court to depart from the sentencing guidelines and to sentence Elliott below the statutory mandatory minimum. In the motion, Becker cited Elliott's "substantial assistance" in the firefighters case.[3])

• Jerry Rooks, a Marlborough resident who was thirteen at the time of the explosions, said the only time he met Frank was six months after the explosions. Frank told him they went to construction site to get into trucks, but couldn't so they poured gas on them. Frank said he could hear sirens on the way home and was home before the first explosion. Not much later, Rooks ran into Richard at a park where Richard told him he was at the site but left before the explosions. On the witness stand when asked to identify Richard, he said he did not see him in the courtroom. Could he identify Bryan Sheppard? No.

Rooks was in Platte County jail in 1995 serving a three-year sentence for violating his parole—he had been convicted of burglary and sentenced to three years' probation—when he called KCPD homicide to implicate Frank and Richard. When detectives showed him a photo array, he was unable to identify either. After talking with detectives, he only had to serve four months in prison and one month in jail.

• Tracy Cauthon, twenty-six, was at Darlene's house in March 1989 and heard Darlene tell Frank they needed to get their stories straight for their state grand jury testimony the next day. Cauthon informed police about this when he was arrested the next month for forgery. By the time he testified, he had three felony convictions, two for forgery and one for burglary, but was not on parole or probation.

• Gary Fugate, a drug user and confidential informant for the ATF and the Jackson County Drug Task Force, said Frank told him in 1989 he was at the construction site with one other person to steal equipment. Frank said he gained access to one of the buildings and stole some "devices which I do not recall specifically what the devices were." Frank used a crowbar on one of the trailers but couldn't get in. "He became angry and set it on fire." When Frank saw headlights, he left the scene. Frank was standing on the crest of a hill when the trailer ignited. The explosion knocked Frank off the hill and he suffered back injuries from rolling down the hill.

• Ronald Williams, three felony convictions, testified Frank told him in 1991 he went to the construction site to steal dynamite, but was "spotted" by security guards so a fire was set as a diversion. Frank never said who set the fire. Frank then hid out in some woods and watched as the firefighters arrived and was still there when the first explosion went off. No one was supposed to get hurt. At the grand jury he testified Frank told him he went to the construction site with his brother-in-law, Larry Baker. Frank told him that Bryan was not at the site because he was home in bed.

• Stephen Kilgore. In 1971 at age fifteen, he accidentally shot and killed Frank and Skip's younger brother, fourteen-year-old Phillip Sheppard. For the next twenty-three years, he avoided Frank and Skip. In 1993 Kilgore went to see Naomi Sheppard, Frank and Skip's mother, about buying a headstone for Phillip's grave. After visiting with Naomi, Kilgore testified he gave Frank and Skip a ride to mow a lawn in Marlborough. During the ride, Frank told him there was a guard with a Polish last name who had been allowing them to steal from the site for some time. The night of the explosions, they walked to the site with two purposes in mind: to torch the guard's truck as part of an insurance scam and "to loot the place."

After setting the guard's pickup on fire, they went into a shack and were rummaging around when Skip accidentally kicked over the small lantern he had brought with him. As the shack began to burn, Frank and Skip exited in a hurry. (There was no shack.)

After Frank and Skip finished mowing the lawn, Kilgore drove them back to their mother's house where Frank showed him some of the items they had stolen from the construction site: six Motorola radios, three or four 100-foot extension cords, concrete saws, a sledgehammer, drills "and all kinds of equipment," and acetylene torches, adding, "He had a set of torches there." Frank told him he also stole jackhammers from the site. Kilgore said Frank told him they ran from the construction site all the way to the 4 Acres Motel, which he estimated to be a distance of a half mile. (A number of witnesses claim acetylene torches were stolen the night of the explosions. Only one mechanic had an acetylene torch and he kept it in his truck and took it home each night.)

• Glen Shepard, forty-nine, no relation to the Sheppard family of Marlborough, was a career criminal. In December 1992, he said he saw Frank standing on a street corner in Marlborough and Frank asked him to give him a lift to Bryan's apartment. When they got there, Bryan, who had been drinking for several days, asked Frank and Glen to go get him more to drink or some drugs. Before they left, Bryan told Frank, "I'm not like you and the other guys. I can't live with myself because of the death of them firemen, and it's eating me up." Glen said Frank told Bryan to shut up. A few days later Frank told him that on the night of the explosions they got drunk, sobered up, and went to the construction site to steal tools, but ended up "burning the place." Frank said killing the firefighters wasn't supposed to happen. Frank didn't tell him why they set the fire, only that he was there.

In December 1995 Glen was convicted in Cass County of four felonies and two misdemeanors. On January 10, Agent True came to see him at the jail. Based on what he told True about Frank making admissions to him, he was called before the grand jury. Facing a long prison sentence, he did not like his chances of surviving if he ratted out Frank Sheppard. He refused to testify. Becker told him he could be forced to testify or be held in contempt of court. While still at the federal courthouse, True told Glen about bringing up a gun charge in Blue Springs. Glen called his lawyer and his lawyer worked out a deal for Glen's testimony. True and other agents reinterviewed Glen in April and this time Glen stated Bryan made admissions also.

When Glen went before a Cass County judge a couple months later, in June 1996, he had seventeen felony convictions. As a prior and persistent offender under Missouri law he would have to serve 80 percent of any sentence. At sentencing, True testified Glen was cooperating in the firefighters case—that Glen had been of "substantial assistance." The judge sentenced Glen to thirteen years on the first count (possession of drug contraband with intent to distribute) and to twelve years on count two (possession of a controlled substance with intent to sell), with the sentences to run consecutively, i.e., twenty-five years. Then the judge suspended execution of the sentences, placing Glen on probation. On count three (possession of a controlled substance), the judge sentenced him to seven years; on count four (possession of burglary tools) to five years. The judge ordered those sentences to run concurrent with the twenty-five-year sentence. On the misdemeanor counts, including possession of drug paraphernalia, the judge sentenced him to two one-year sentences in county jail to run concurrently.

On cross-examination, Glen admitted that without his cooperation in the firefighters case, he would be serving a twenty-five-year sentence in state prison instead of a one-year sentence in a county jail.

• Lorena Deardorff, a twenty-nine-year-old who worked at a mini-mart gas station in Marlborough, testified that a few days after the explosions Frank told her he and some friends were at the construction site partying, getting drunk, and playing around when one of the guys went down to a trailer and came back with a stick of dynamite. Then "one of them decided to set a vehicle on fire just to see what would happen. So they set it on fire; they were sitting up there on the hill and the firemen came. . . . One of them decided, well, let's see what would happen if I threw this stick of dynamite down there." Frank said the dynamite caused an explosion "and then a few minutes later there was another explosion, so they got scared and they ran and went home and started partying some more and just getting drunk more." (There was no dynamite in any trailer, nor did anyone throw a stick of dynamite near the firefighters, nor would throwing a stick of dynamite cause it to explode.)

• The last two direct witnesses against Frank were his and Darlene's next-door neighbors, Bear and Carol Williams. Bear said he did not go outside until after the second explosion and that was the first time he saw Frank and Darlene. Carol testified Bear went outside after the first explosion to nail up two blown-out windows by their front door. The second explosion blew off the plastic from the windows and they had to go outside and renail the plastic to the windows. She said it was after the second explosion when Frank Sheppard hollered over, "Hey, man what's going on?" or something "to that aspect."

Becker asked her if she talked to her husband about that. "Yeah, I said, 'Yeah, what are they going to do, use us for an alibi?' and that was it." (This was a far-fetched comment for her to make because at the time no one in Marlborough knew what caused the two explosions.)

In addition to the four witnesses who had implicated Skip Sheppard when testifying against Frank, the government called nine witnesses to testify against him, including three jailhouse informants. The first three witnesses were from Marlborough. Each recounted him making admissions at Lee Ballinger's house in Marlborough in August 1989.

• Douglas Bayliff, twenty-six, testified he overheard Skip say he almost got some dynamite the night of the explosions; the fire at the trailer was set as a diversion to distract a guard, and Skip drove to the site. (Bayliff contacted KCPD in September 1989 after his house had been burglarized. He told police he thought Skip was responsible and also mentioned hearing Skip making admissions at Ballinger's house the month before.)

It came out on cross-examination that when Detective Fraise conducted a videotape interview with him that afternoon, Bayliff said the fire was started in security guards' shack—not at the trailer—as a "distraction." (The so-called diversionary fire was the burning of Debbie Riggs's pickup on the west side of the site.)

• Tracy Ownby, twenty-six, Bayliff's girlfriend at the time, overheard Skip speaking in a low voice to Bayliff, asking him if he remembered the explosions, and saying he was there. She heard Skip say they were running when the first explosion erupted. She did not hear Skip make any comments about setting a fire, or guards, or dynamite. (Bayliff had made no claim about Skip saying anything directly to him.)

• Megan Williams, twenty-three, said the only thing she heard Skip say was he was at the construction site.

• Carl Nettles, thirty-four, a three-time convicted felon who was incarcerated with Skip at the St. Clair County jail in Osceola, Missouri, in mid-1995, testified Skip told him they went to the construction site to steal jackhammers, generators, and lots of tools. They set a trailer on fire, with gas purchased from QuikTrip, to cover up the "stuff they had taken." His alibi was he was at his mother's house. They had stolen from the site previously.

After being sentenced to 6½ years in federal court on November 13, 1996, for possessing methamphetamine with intent to distribute, Nettles had his attorney contact the ATF to get "some leniency in my sentence." True had him brought up to Kansas City for an interview where he said Skip made admissions. Nettles's reward came on February 25, 1997, when Federal District Judge Howard F. Sachs recommended he serve his sentence in a camp-type facility.

• John White, forty-seven, a three-time felon, also met Skip in the jail in Osceola. A month before the explosions, Skip cased the construction site and vandalized a bulldozer by putting rocks and dirt in its transmission. He also stole an acetylene torch. On the night of the explosions, he and Frank drove to the site to steal tools. They parked by some railroad tracks and waited for the guards to leave. In the meantime, others joined them. To get the guards to leave the side where the ANFO trailers were parked, two of the people who joined Skip and Frank went to the west side and set a pickup on fire.

With the guards gone, they tried unsuccessfully to break into a trailer by using a small crowbar. In frustration, they set the trailer on fire. They went back by the railroad tracks and were still there when the firefighters arrived and the first explosion occurred. After the explosion, they went to the home of one of Skip's brothers. Skip didn't feel any blame because the firefighters "had been stupid and killed themselves, basically."

In 1991 White was convicted in federal court of mail fraud and sentenced to twenty-seven months. He had also served a ten-month sentence for promoting prostitution. In 1995 he was convicted in federal court of threatening a witness and was sentenced on August 12, 1996, to forty-six months. White had his attorney call the ATF. True came to see him on December 6, 1996. After he testified at the firefighters trial, he was sent to a federal prison in Michigan and released thirteen months later, knocking thirty-three months off his sentence. (Many years later, in October 2015, John White swore in an affidavit that everything he testified to at trial was a lie. "I come now to recant the testimony I previously gave at the [firefighters] trial. During my time in jail I met Skip Sheppard. . . . There was a lot of motivation to testify against Skip. It is no secret that there is one way to extract yourself from jail and that is to cooperate with the government. I wanted out of jail so I decided to offer my services to the government." He said he spent less than five minutes with Skip and the only thing Skip ever said to him was, "Do you have any coffee?"

• Patty Smith, twenty-eight, began dating Skip in August 1990 but ended the relationship after Skip assaulted her. Skip told her he stole a crate of dynamite from the site and buried it under his mother's house. Each time the police came to look for the dynamite they couldn't find it and Skip laughed about that. He also said they used the stolen dynamite to cause the explosion. She also testified that Frank told her that the explosion caused dirt and rocks to rain down on them "and it hurt as the rocks hit them."

• Michael Whitelaw, thirty-four, another felon who did time with Skip, said Skip told him they were out driving around the night of the explosion and stopped at the construction site where the trailers were and he was there when the fire started.

On July 13, 1995, Whitelaw was sentenced to twenty-five years in federal court for distributing cocaine and carrying a gun. Federal District Court Judge Fernando Gaitan denied his habeas corpus appeal in June 1996. His attorney contacted ATF. Three months later his attorney informed him that the government will take a new look at his habeas corpus appeal. (After the firefighters trial ended, Gaitan denied it a second time.)

Two of the other witnesses against Skip had him in two places at once after the first explosion.

• Carolee Ann Smith, thirty-nine, who lived next door to Naomi Sheppard, Frank and Skip's mother, testified that five to ten minutes after the first explosion she heard a loud truck pull up in Naomi's driveway. She saw four people get out all wearing dark clothes, two of whom were Frank and Skip, with Skip exiting the driver's side. The other two she didn't recognize and could not make out their gender. All four walked around to the back. She said they usually entered through the front. The truck, which she said belonged to Skip's father, was still there after the second explosion.

• Lonnie Joe Pugh, who lived next door to Larry and Diddi Baker, saw Larry outside after the first explosion and saw a dark Ford pickup pull up in front of Larry's house. Skip got out with a beer in his hand and went inside his sister and brother-in-law's house. Two other people were in the pickup whom he did not recognize.

In late 1989, Detective Fraise of the KCPD came to see Pugh, telling him his name had come up in the investigation. He denied involvement and told Fraise the only one he saw after the first explosion was Larry Baker, adding that his memory of that night was hazy due to heavy drug use and drinking. When Fraise asked him what time Skip got to Larry's that night, Pugh said, "I didn't see Skip at all."

On cross-examination, Pugh said in 1995, Agent True contacted him, telling him a confidential witness who was religious and a well-respected woman in Marlborough was saying Pugh saw Skip after the explosion. From the description, Pugh thought True must be referring to the wife of Pugh's boss. Pugh told True he never talked about the explosion with this woman. True told him that posed a problem: the word of a respected woman against his. This comment caused Pugh to say that maybe he did see Skip. True then asked him to come down to the ATF office. Pugh wanted to bring an attorney with him. When they got to the ATF office, True would not allow the attorney in the interview room. "She was locked downstairs is what it was," Pugh told the jury.

The government's case against Darlene Edwards was extremely thin. Four of the six witnesses against her were classic jailhouse snitches, three of whom made it clear on cross-examination their testimony was predicated on the government providing assistance with their own cases. One of two Marlborough witnesses was a drug user with scant credibility, the other was Richard Brown's half sister.

• Shannon Reimers, twenty-three, the voluble, rapid-talking half sister, personified the fissure between Darlene and Richard. Shannon testified that on the night of the explosions she returned to Darlene's house after the second explosion. She and her boyfriend, Mike DiMaggio, and their baby were living upstairs at Darlene's at the time. When they walked in the living room she saw Frank, Darlene, Becky, and someone else sitting in the dark. No one spoke to her. Becky was in a nightgown but the other three were fully clothed.

• Joe Denyer, twenty-four, was a down-and-out drug addict who slept in unoccupied houses in Marlborough. When asked his occupation, he said he sorted through garbage for a living. He had three convictions for burglaries and one for aggravated escape. He testified he was at Darlene's house not long after the explosions when she told him she was at Quik-Trip when the first explosion erupted and "freaked out" when the ceiling tiles fell.

• Lisa Frederick, thirty. Before bonding out on a bad check charge, she spent fifteen to twenty minutes with Darlene in a holding cell at the Clay County jail in 1995 after her drug bust. When she asked Darlene what she was being held for, Darlene said, "For killing six firemen."

• Rosemary Quiroz, thirty-nine, met Darlene in August 1995 when she was incarcerated at the Leavenworth Detention Center operated and owned by the Corrections Corporation of America under contract with the US Marshals Service. Quiroz was awaiting trial on charges of distributing cocaine and unlawfully purchasing food stamps in the trade of cocaine. When she testified at trial she had been convicted in federal court of those charges and was serving a five-year sentence at a prison in Texas.

She was scheduled to testify the day before, but refused to take the stand because so far she had not received any assistance from the government on cutting her sentence. Becker had to go to see her.

Quiroz testified Darlene told her the explosion that killed the firefighters was "an accident." She said Darlene discussed the case "with practically everybody [at CCA]. She told everybody she was involved in it." Quiroz said Darlene told Carolyn Woods and Bridgette Dornhoffer "and many others." (Dornhoffer would be the only other inmate from CCA to testify.)

Becker asked her if she made any notes about what Darlene told her. "When I was first indicted I was afraid I was going to have to do time in the federal prison so I thought this would help me get out but it didn't. And I wrote this down in case I needed more information to get a plea agreement."

> Becker: Let's talk about that. Has anyone, myself or anyone from the United States Department of Justice or ATF, made any promises to you about getting you out of jail in exchange for your testimony?
> Quiroz: Not that I know of.

This answer prompted John O'Connor to ask for a bench conference. O'Connor told the judge and the other attorneys that last night he talked with Quiroz's attorney, Dan Ross, who was also representing Bridgette Dornhoffer. Ross told him that when Agent True interviewed her in September 1996 he told her he would try to get her a sentence reduction for her cooperation in the firefighters case. He said Ross also quoted Becker as saying, "The government will recommend a drug program within six months." Ross said Quiroz was told that if she got in the drug program it would cut a year off her sentence. O'Connor said the reason she did not agree to testify the day before was because she had not received any sentence reduction.

When O'Connor cross-examined her, she admitted she told ATF agents she wanted a sentence reduction for testifying against Darlene; also that she and Bridgette Dornhoffer had been on the phone this week trying to get a deal for their testimony.

Quiroz said she made notes of what Darlene told her. Quiroz had written, "Blew up a highway"; "robbed a highway for machinery"; "set fire to draw distraction"; "Darlene said the walkie-talkies set off the transmitters," meaning the firefighters' walkie-talkies set off the explosion.

• Bridgette Dornhoffer, thirty-eight, had been convicted of three separate felonies for passing bad checks in Clay County in 1988 and had been sentenced to four years on each count, to run concurrent. The next year she was convicted of another forgery, this one in Platte County, and was sentenced to three years to run concurrent with her Clay County sentence.

Dornhoffer testified Darlene told her she drove to a gas station, went back home, and then drove to the construction site to steal tools; she bought the gas "to cover up the fact that they had robbed the site, and it was going to keep them busy awhile." Darlene told her "there were various practice runs or drills run prior to the night of the explosion." Also various planning sessions: one at a park, one at her house, and one at another location "to avoid suspicious neighbors." Darlene's primary job was to get the gas and she went to several gas stations to get it. Darlene was at the site when the fire started and was in the vicinity when the trailer erupted.

Darlene told her a crowd gathered at the site so quickly after the explosion they were afraid of drawing attention to themselves if they tried to leave in a hurry. They were still waiting to exit when the police arrived and tried to move people away. The police had to move a car so Darlene and the others could get out on the highway and make their escape. (No crowd gathered at the site because police had cordoned it off.)

Dornhoffer said Darlene told her they poured gas at various areas at the site and added charcoal fluid to set various fires. They set a shed on fire. There were several areas heavily gassed, including around a trailer with office equipment. Darlene mentioned stealing walkie-talkies and a fax machine out of a trailer. (These were references to nonexistent thefts on the west side of the site where the office trailers were located in the median.)

Darlene stole lots of expensive tools the night of the explosions, as well as building materials and cement. In particular, Dornhoffer referenced an acetylene torch.

In December 1993, while incarcerated at the Chillicothe Correctional Center, Dornhoffer testified against another inmate in a federal case. This cooperation paid off when she was convicted of two separate forgeries in 1994. Instead of having to serve two concurrent sentences of eight years with five years of probation, the judge gave her parole at the request of US Assistant Attorney Dan Stewart.

Five months later Dornhoffer violated her parole by tampering with the ankle bracelet but remained out of jail.

Less than two weeks later she violated her parole again by stealing three checks from her employer, Panel Systems. The checks were in the amount of $12,500, $641, and $710. This embezzlement was deemed a bank fraud—a federal crime. On May 1, 1995, she was sentenced in federal court to eighteen months, with five years of supervised parole, and restitution of over $26,000, twice the amount embezzled.

For this parole violation she now had to serve the eight-year sentence she was convicted of in 1994 in Clay County.

While awaiting sentencing in federal court, Dornhoffer was housed at CCA in Leavenworth in the same pod as Darlene and Rosemary Quiroz. After she began serving her state time, Dornhoffer, through her attorney, made it known Darlene made admissions to her at CCA. Agent True came to see her twice in July 1995 and took a taped statement.

What Dornhoffer wanted for her testimony was to start serving the remainder of her federal sentence so she would not have to serve it in full after her state sentence had been completed. This arrangement would have the effect of cutting her total sentence by allowing the federal sentence to run concurrent with her state sentence, i.e., shave eighteen months off the state sentence. Becker informed her attorney that he would look into having her transferred from the state penitentiary to a federal one.

(Becker delivered. Dornhoffer was moved from state prison to the federal prison for women in Fort Worth, Texas.)

—Linda Mynhier, forty-nine, met Darlene at a federal prison camp in Pekin, Illinois. Darlene told her they planned the heist at her kitchen table and the fire was set as a diversion "so the security guards would go toward the fire." Darlene said there was dynamite in a trailer and the fire ignited the dynamite. She remembered Darlene telling her five fire-fighters were killed. Mynhier said Darlene and the people with her stole dynamite from the construction site and Darlene stored it in an oven at a house. Darlene drove a van the night of the explosions. One of the people with her was her stepson. (Darlene's only stepson was Ronnie Edwards.)

In 1992, Mynhier was convicted in federal court of possessing counterfeit Federal Reserve notes and got four years' probation. Probation was revoked in 1993 for embezzling from her employer. She had a gambling problem. She was sentenced to ten months. In 1994, she was convicted of conspiracy to commit wire and bank fraud in connection with the embezzlement of $350,000 from her employer and sentenced to eighteen months at Pekin, where she was from May 1, 1995, to May 7, 1996. On November 7, 1995, she began calling FBI Agent James Purcell in northwest Indiana and talking to him every day she was in prison. On September 25, 1996, she met in Hammond, Indiana, with Agent True. Instead of serving her eighteen months—there is no parole in the federal system—she was released after only serving a year.

When Mynhier stepped down, it was a few minutes after 3 p.m. The jury was excused for its afternoon break—usually about fifteen to twenty minutes. The next order of business was for the jury to hear the twenty-minute audiotape recorded on February 19, 1995, at the Clay County jail where Darlene, attempting to take advantage of the "window of opportunity" Agent True promised her, told True that she drove Bryan and Richard to get gas and then—against her better judgment—dropped them off at the construction site and went back home where Frank was asleep.

The government, because of the Bruton rule, deleted the names of Bryan and Richard from the tape so that the jury would only hear that Darlene had driven "them." The defense attorneys pressed the judge to allow the jury to also view the one-hour videotape made at the ATF office two days earlier wherein Darlene denied knowing anything about who was responsible for the deaths of the firefighters and volunteered to take a polygraph. They argued it was not until after Darlene was left alone and allowed to read the statements the ATF had of Bryan Sheppard and Richard Brown that she later called the ATF and made the damaging charges about Bryan and Richard's involvement in the blast.

The argument consumed the rest of the afternoon. The jury was excused at 4 p.m., an hour early. The next day Judge Stevens, as he did on every important defense request, refused to allow the viewing of the one-hour videotape.

To provide context for the twenty-minute audiotape, the government put ATF Agent Harold Lett on the stand to recount Darlene calling him from the Clay County jail at 8:30 p.m. on Sunday, February 19, 1995, saying she wanted to talk to him about where the drugs came from that she purchased for Ronnie Edwards. Lett told her he did not care; he only wanted to come see her if she would talk about the firefighters. She said she would. Lett then called Agent True and the two agents met at the jail about 9:30 p.m. Detective Bill Forbes of the KCPD joined them in the interview room.

Darlene was read her rights, the standard Miranda warning, and she signed a waiver, forgoing her rights to remain silent and to have an attorney present, agreeing that anything she said could be used against her in court.

With that established, the tape was played. Darlene states on the tape that two people came by her house between 1:30 and 2:30 a.m. to ask for a ride to get gas.

> Darlene: After I had come home from being over at Frank's brother-in-law and sister's, okay, Frank and I had come home. He was drunk and wanting to argue as usual, right? We went to bed. I pacified him, he passed out. Someone [the government redacted the names of Richard Brown and Bryan Sheppard] come up and said they'd run out of gas. Wanted to know, could I take them down to get some gas, right?
> ATF Agent Lett: Uh huh.
> Darlene: Okay, and I took them down to QuikTrip. I had, I usually kept a joint rolled beside the bed because at that time, that's all I did was, you know, I'd just indulge in smoking pot once in a while. Just the worst of my vices. So, I took them down. They took a joint. I parked behind the building, behind the QuikTrip, because I was smoking a joint.
> Lett: Yeah.
> Darlene: And if. . . .
> Lett: That's the QuikTrip at?

Darlene: The QuikTrip at 85th and 71 Highway. Yeah, they went around. They got some gas. They got in the car. They said the car was up the road. I said what are you doing up there? They said, well, we're just doing 4-wheeling up in the hills, right? So, we get up there. Like we're going to go over here and over there, and I said, what are you doing? Well, we're going to steal something. We're going, we're gonna take care of something. I said, well look, I'm not staying here and playing if you are playing with gasoline. I'm not getting my funky ass blown up because I love the fuck out of me, and I left them there, period! And then after I had gotten home and gotten in bed . . . is probably what must have woke Frank up, you know, when I'd gotten undressed and got back in bed.

For the jury, listening to Darlene on that tape was likely the most captivating part of the prosecution, a break from the tedium of direct and tortured cross-examination. Instead of some felon or ne'er-do-well from Marlborough claiming to have heard admissions of guilt, here was one of the five defendants speaking directly to federal agents about her role in the deaths of the firefighters.

Without knowing anything about the contents of the one-hour videotape the judge excluded, the jury only heard Darlene saying two other people, albeit unnamed, caused the deaths of the firefighters.

Will Bunch, as Darlene's attorney, asked Lett if he was present two days previous when Darlene was videotaped at the ATF office and said she knew nothing about the explosions and denied any involvement in the crime. He said he was aware of that and he was aware, when asked, that a statement implicating Darlene, Frank, and Skip by "another person" was shown to her at the ATF office after she denied any involvement. This was the best Bunch could do to make the jury aware of the existence of a preexisting, much longer tape Darlene had given the ATF.

Darlene's tape-recorded statement, even though it exonerated her, Frank, and Skip, would turn out to be the most important exhibit the government introduced at trial.

The prosecution of Bryan Sheppard got off to an inauspicious start when the first witness, drug dealer Shawn Furrell, pointed to Richard Brown when John O'Connor asked him to identify Bryan. It was also brought out that Bryan was in jail in 1989 when Furrell claimed Bryan made admissions to him about going to the site to steal blasting caps and setting the trailer on fire to burn evidence.

The next two witnesses, although together when they heard Bryan and Richard making admissions, recounted sharply contrasting stories of what was said and where they were when they heard these admissions.

• Carie Neighbors, twenty-six, the ex-girlfriend who shot Bryan in the chest with a .22 rifle when he was fourteen, testified she was with Shannon Newcomb at Swope Park in the spring of 1989 when she heard Bryan and Richard saying they went to the construction site to steal batteries and they set the fire to cover their tracks after they saw two guards. They ran to Richard's grandmother's house and faked being asleep. Two weeks later she and Shannon Newcomb ran into Bryan and Richard on a street in Marlborough between 1 and 3 a.m. Once again they told them what they had said at Swope Park.

• Shannon Newcomb, twenty-six, testified that she and Carie Neighbors were at a party at Tim Laddish's house in the spring of 1989. They were standing outside on the front porch with a small group of people that included Bryan and Richard while a larger group of people was milling about. She heard Richard talking about the explosions, saying he was at the explosion site, saw the guards, and for a diversion set a pickup on fire and ran away toward the woods. As Richard spoke, Bryan was standing next to him "agreeing, interjecting a comment every once in a while, like talking with Richard about this." She said Richard was acting like it was no big deal, he was "nonchalant, kind of just joking about how they, how they ran." She also was with Carie Neighbors at a Swope Park shelter house when Bryan and Richard were present but did not hear any admissions from either of them about the explosions.

• Brian Atterbury, twenty-nine, felon and jailhouse informant, said Bryan told him they were at the construction site to steal explosives out of a trailer and were about to open the trailer with a crowbar when a guard came up. To divert the guard, they started a fire. There was an "older gentleman" who would pay $500 to take dynamite from the trailer. Bryan rode home on a bicycle, entering his house through a bedroom window and went to bed.

On March 1, 1995, Atterbury was indicted on first-degree burglary and witness tampering. (He threatened to kill the woman whose house he robbed if she testified against him; he also offered her a $500 bribe.) He called ATF, claiming Bryan made admissions. (Atterbury had been in the Clay County jail on a domestic violence charge.) The ATF promised him help for his testimony. On August 11, 1995, he was allowed to plead guilty to witness tampering in the second degree and was given a ninety-day sentence. During his direct testimony he said the government hadn't given him anything for testifying, a misrepresentation the government did not correct.

• Kevin Smith, twenty-five, a three-time felon, heard Bryan bragging at Minor Park in the spring of 1990 about getting off the state charges for killing the firefighters and admitting he set a fire as a diversion to steal explosives.

Smith was convicted in 1994 of felony burglary and felony stealing. He was sentenced to two three-year sentences to run concurrently but as a first-time offender he was given parole. He soon violated his parole by committing felony robbery and was sentenced to five years to run concurrent with his previous two concurrent three-year sentences. Agent True came to see him at the Ozark Correction Center in March 1995. He told the agent Bryan made admissions to him in 1990. Smith testified at the grand jury. When he testified at the firefighters trial he did so as a free man. Instead of serving his five-year sentence, he was released from prison in September 1996, only twenty-one months into his sentence.

• Christine Mall, twenty-five, a bartender at Amigo's Cantina in south Kansas City, met Bryan when she and her boyfriend, John McGovern, went to Bryan's house on July 7, 1992. She overheard Bryan telling McGovern he had some dynamite and was going to blow up a truck so someone could collect insurance. She called the TIPS hotline but no one called her back. In 1995 she called again. During the summer of 1996, Agent True visited her. She told True about Bryan using dynamite to blow up a truck owned by a friend named Darlene. (Darlene never owned a truck. John McGovern was not called as a government witness to corroborate Mall's testimony, but would be called by the defense to rebut her claims.)

• Wesley Romans, thirty, was in the Clay County jail on a parole violation—he had been convicted of sexual assault—in December 1989 when he overheard Bryan talking about the explosion, saying he drove up there with others and was sitting in a car when it happened. Bryan went to the site to steal dynamite and explosives and set a fire to cover their tracks.

Under questioning by O'Connor, he said he came forward with this information after seeing *Unsolved Mysteries* and learning of the $50,000 reward.

• Travis Small, thirty-five, four felony convictions, testified that Bryan made admissions to him in March 1989, saying, "I fucked up. Some people got killed."

Small was serving a five-year sentence in Arizona for transporting cocaine when ATF Agent Paul Marquardt came to see him on February 9, 1995, about implicating any of the Sheppards in the firefighters case. In an affidavit, Small swore he didn't know any Sheppards and had only heard of Skip. He wrote that no Sheppard ever told him anything "because I never met them."

To ramp up the pressure on him to testify, a federal indictment was returned against him in the Western District of Missouri on August 5, 1995. Count one charged him with possession with intent to distribute methamphetamine, count two possession of marijuana, count three aiding and abetting distribution of marijuana. His pregnant wife, Krista, was also named in count one of the indictment. On count one they were facing five to forty years and a fine of $2 million each; on count two he faced five years and a fine of $250,000; he faced the same punishment on count three.

Small hired an attorney who offered a proffer for him and his wife.[4] They would admit his crime and cooperate against others in the drug indictment and against other people in general. In return he wanted the charges against his wife dropped and substantial assistance with the charges against him. Six days later, on November 19, 1996, True came to see him. True took a signed statement from him, not an affidavit, i.e., he was not swearing to his statement.

For this testimony, Small was able to reach a plea agreement. The government agreed to drop the charges against his wife and to file a motion for a downward departure, recommending a sentence of between 8.3 and 11.4 years. Gone was the possibility of a sentence of up to 40 years and a fine of $2 million. The week before he testified at the firefighters trial, he pled guilty in federal court to the lesser charges of possession of marijuana and methamphetamine with intent to distribute. On July 15, 1997, Federal District Judge Dean Whipple granted the government's motion for a downward departure for Small and granted probation to his wife.

The government had two witnesses who would claim they saw Richard and Bryan after midnight on the night of the explosions.

• Margaret Weaver, twenty-five, the same person who eight years ago called police to report she saw David Baird and Bryan stealing a bicycle from a Sears store, testified that on the night of the explosions she came out of a 7-Eleven in Marlborough around midnight or later and saw Richard and Bryan and some other man standing next to Bryan's car. In 1989 she told Detective Fraise the other man was Mike DiMaggio and that they were all high on drugs, loud and obnoxious.

• Stephen Morales, a thirty-six-year-old felon out on parole who worked at the time of the explosions as a newspaper delivery driver for a *Kansas City Star* carrier. He testified that between 1:15 and 1:45 a.m. on the night of the explosions he saw Bryan, Richard, Frank, and someone he did not recognize outside a friend's house in Marlborough.

Morales also testified that in March 1989 he met Bryan at the Clay County jail where Bryan was awaiting prosecution on his indictment in the deaths of the firefighters. (Morales had been convicted of a class A misdemeanor for sexual assault.) Bryan told him they were on a "raiding party" going after tools, construction equipment, and batteries. They had a lookout on the west side of the site who set a guard's pickup on fire to draw security away from the east side where the trailers were. On the east side they set a trailer on fire to give them cover to get off the hill.

Asked by prosecutor Miller if the government helped him in any way for his testimony, he said no.

During questioning by the defense, it came out he had been convicted on December 4, 1995, in Jackson County of possessing a controlled substance and sentenced to a five-year suspended sentence and three years of probation. When O'Connor tried to bring out that the ATF had helped him obtain a signature bond—no bail money required—after he was busted on another felony charge in Cass County in late 1996 and given a bond of $5,000, Miller objected and the judge called the attorneys to the bench.

O'Connor informed the court that Morales was caught at a United Missouri Bank trying to cash a $3,700 check that wasn't his. He was charged with forgery, which violated his parole, and his bond was set at $5,000. He posted the required 10 percent ($500) and was bonded out and given a court date on the pending forgery charge. He also was facing another forgery charge in Cass County. The judge there set his bond at $5,000. He could not pay it and was in jail there from late November to December 13, 1996, when the same judge released him on a signature bond at the request of Agent True.

Based on that information, which O'Connor ran down by talking to Morales's public defender and the Cass County judge, O'Connor wanted to prove Morales was induced to testify against three of the defendants and that he gained from it. Another clear sign of the quid pro quo involved in Morales's testimony was that his parole violation hearing in Jackson County had been postponed twice and was not to take place until several days after he testified at the firefighters trial.

Judge Stevens ruled that questioning Morales about any benefit he received from the government for his testimony was not admissible because Morales testified he had not asked for any help. O'Connor, he said, could question Agent True about all of this when he took the stand later in the trial. (Later in the trial, when the defense tried to put True back on the stand, the judge forbid it.)

• Karen Baird, fifty-four. (From the time he was thirteen until he was sixteen, Bryan lived off and on in the basement of Karen's house.) For years she had run a massage parlor out of her house, complete with prostitutes and offering a wide variety of illegal drugs. She was now on permanent Social Security disability and weighed over three hundred pounds; she was carted into the courtroom in a wheelchair; at home she was confined to bed. She told the jury that Bryan and Richard came to her house about four hours after the explosions. They smelled of smoke and gas and Bryan wanted her to massage his neck. When she asked him why he was so tense, he said, "If you'd been through what I've been through, you'd be tight too."

She testified that after Bryan was charged with the firefighters' deaths in 1989, he called her numerous times from the Clay County jail. In one of the calls he told her he was at the construction site and after the first explosion he ran across the road with one other person and hid in a ditch. She said that her friend Kathy Marburger was patched into three or five of the calls.

When the State of Missouri indicted Bryan for the deaths of the firefighters in 1989, Detective John Fraise rousted Baird in an attempt to bolster the state's case against Bryan. When Fraise asked her what she knew about the explosions she had nothing to tell him. Fraise took her downtown to the homicide department and reminded her of a pending drug charge against her for sale and possession of narcotics. (On October 1, 1990, she pled guilty to a felony in Jackson County for possession of a controlled substance and received a four-year sentence and three years of probation.)

The next morning, Fraise and Detective Zinn had her sign a five-page statement. She said no one ever admitted involvement in the blasts and that Bryan never mentioned going to the construction site. She told Zinn that in a recent phone call from Bryan—he was in Clay County jail—she asked him if he was involved in the explosion and he answered, "'Fuck no.' He said if he knew who did it, he'd tell . . . even if it was his uncles."

But she did tell the detectives about Bryan and Richard coming to her house a few hours after the explosions, with Bryan wanting a massage and smelling of smoke and gasoline.

John O'Connor, Bryan's attorney, went to see Baird in November 1989, bringing with him a certified court reporter to make a written record of the interview. Baird told O'Connor she wasn't sure that Richard and Bryan came to her house the morning of November 29, 1988. "It seems like he came home with Richard Brown, but to bet my life on it or somebody else's I couldn't do it." She said she was "70 percent sure Bryan had come to her house and 100 percent that he might not be." She also told O'Connor that Bryan never asked her to lie or even admitted any involvement in the crime. After O'Connor left, Baird called KCPD about being intimidated by O'Connor and said Bryan threatened her. (Although she had been sentenced to four years on a felony drug conviction in October 1990, Baird served no time.)

O'Connor moved his cross-examination to a March 8, 1995, interview where True asked her if during one of Bryan's phone calls when he was crying and being sad, did Bryan say he was present at the explosion? "No, I don't recall him saying that," she answered. "I'm not saying he didn't, but I don't recall if he did."

Four months later, she now testified, she called True and told him that Bryan said he was at the construction site and ran across the road and hid in a ditch after the first explosion.

• Kathy Marburger. Blind from birth, she also ran a "massage parlor" from her home in Marlborough. She testified that she called Karen Baird around 8 a.m. the morning of the explosions, and when Baird told her that Bryan and Richard were there she asked her what they looked like. Baird told her they smelled of smoke and gasoline. Marburger said she could hear Bryan in the background saying, "If you had been through what we had just been through and where we had just come from, you would be nervous too." She also said she was patched into three or four phone calls Bryan made to Baird from the Clay County jail, and during one of these calls Bryan was crying when he said, "I was there, I helped start the fire, but I did not mean to kill the firemen."

Osgood brought out that at the grand jury Marburger testified that when she called that morning Baird told her Bryan had just left. And she made no mention of Richard being there.

The government called fifteen witnesses to testify against Richard Brown, four of them felons and the rest from Marlborough. A number of witnesses against Bryan Sheppard, such as Carie Neighbors, Shannon Newcomb, Margaret Weaver, Karen Baird, Kathy Marburger, and Steve

Morales, had already implicated Richard when they testified against Bryan. The same phenomenon in reverse would occur when eight of the witnesses against Richard implicated Bryan.

• Stephen Caudill, a thirty-one-year-old felon, fell into this category. He testified Richard told him in April 1989 he was at the construction site when the firefighters were killed. Three to five weeks later, Richard told him he was the last to leave the site. Richard was at the site with Bryan, Lonnie Joe Pugh, and Chuck Jennings. When Caudill mentioned Bryan's name, O'Connor asked for a mistrial. The judge denied the request and told the jurors to disregard the reference to Bryan. (So much for the effectiveness of the Bruton Rule.)

One of the few humorous moments in the trial occurred while Dan Miller, the prosecutor assisting Becker, was questioning Caudill about Richard's pickup. "And about this black Ford pickup that you mentioned, what color was it?"

In 1984, Caudill had been sentenced to three years for assault and had served that time. In 1994 he was convicted of two counts of burglary and one for stealing. For these three felonies he was sentenced to ten years. Nonetheless, when he testified before the firefighters grand jury in 1996 he had been released on house arrest following completion of a drug rehab program.

• Pam Barth, whose two sons were friends of Richard and Bryan, testified that a month after the explosions she overheard Richard "blabbing at the mouth" to Bryan out in her living room, saying that after the explosion they stole tools from the construction site. "They set a fire on top of the hill and it got bigger than they thought and they ran out of gas before they had done this crime," she said. "They were going to break into the shed, I guess to get the equipment out, whatever." Richard said they set the fire "because they wanted to burglarize the shed that had the tools in it." She said she heard Richard say, "They went to get gas to start a fire up on the hill and the guards, or whatever, they were down there distracted them."

At the bench, Pat Peters said Barth "was high as a kite on meth— speeding on meth as opposed to cocaine." Becker said she always talked like she was doing now.

Osgood asked her if she was interested in the reward. She said she wasn't although she had asked Detective Robert Guffey about it when she called him with the information about Richard and Bryan in 1996.

• Thomas Butner, twenty-six, another Marlborough resident, testified that in the year following the explosions—when Richard was drunk—he made admissions eight or nine times. Richard told him they went to the site to steal but when they couldn't get the trailer open "got mad and they just started a little fire with gas." Butner said before the explosions, Richard refused to trade him his Ford pickup for Butner's Malibu and some cash, but two or three days after the explosions he traded his Ford for the Malibu straight up. Butner said Richard frequently mentioned being at the construction site with his girlfriend Kelly [Corriston] but he could not remember her last name and one other person.

• Cynthia Butner, twenty-five, the sister of Tom Butner, testified that two months after the explosions she was at a party at her aunt's house where she overheard Richard say he was at the construction site to steal dynamite and he used gasoline to set a fire. Kelly Corriston and two other people were with him. When they couldn't get in "the thing" that held the dynamite, they poured gasoline on it and set it on fire.

• Fern Ayers was the mother of one of Richard's friends. At various times, Richard lived in her house and he called her "mom." A year after the blasts, when they were discussing the deaths of the firefighters, Richard told her it was an accident. About a year later when they were talking about the explosions, Richard asked her if she "wanted to see some of the stuff" and Bryan told him not to do it. Richard said Fern was trustworthy and as he began to open the trunk to Bryan's car, Bryan slammed it down so fast she did not see what was in the trunk.

Shifting gears, Becker asked her what Frank Sheppard told her about the explosions. "He just said the firemen were stupid," she answered.

None of the witnesses other than Becky Edwards would be testifying about the Marlborough Five acting as a group, but Becker was trying to use this witness to link at least the male defendants. He asked her if she ever saw Skip, Frank, Bryan, and Richard together. "It was mostly Bryan and Richard together but Frank, Skip, yes, they have had occasion to be together yes."

If it was difficult for Richard to listen to a woman he considered a surrogate mother testify against him, the next witness would be even harder to take.

• Frank Gile, twenty-four, felon. In 1992, Richard allowed Gile to live with him at his home in Marlborough after Gile was released from prison. Gile testified Richard told him in 1992 that he had been at the construction site to steal and that they set a pickup on fire next to a trailer. Bryan told him he was at the site but gave no specifics.

Convicted of felony auto theft in 1988, Gile got probation and a $1,500 fine. Convicted of felony stealing in 1991, he got a three-year sentence, suspended to 120 days of drug treatment at Farmington Treatment Center. After completing that he got three years' probation; released on parole February 19, 1992; for drug use, charged with violating his parole but failed to appear for a parole violation hearing on October 26, 1994; arrested January 27, 1995, bond set at $10,000, which he couldn't raise; probation revoked on February 10, 1995; three-year sentence imposed. Four days later he called ATF. Agent Lobdell got him to sign an affidavit wherein he averred, "I am providing this information at this time for the sole purpose of potentially reducing my prison time." True told him he would put a letter in his parole file for his cooperation and would attend his parole hearing. On cross-examination he said that during the time he was talking to Bryan he was using "pot, meth, cocaine and LSD."

• Wally Mills, twenty-three, met Richard through Frank Gile. For four months in 1994, while Mills was on the run after escaping from prison, he stayed at Richard's mother's house in Independence. Sometime in 1992 or 1993, Richard told him that he and others were partying at the construction site but Richard's pickup had run out of gas. They found a gas can at the site and went to QuikTrip to fill it up. Back at the site, they poured gas in Richard's pickup and then dumped the rest of it on a trailer and proceeded to start a fire. Then they left.

ATF Agent Lobdell came to see Mills in February 1995. Although Mills had been sentenced to five years on his felony conviction for escape in 1995, when he testified at the firefighters trial—less than two years later—he had been released from jail after serving only a year, had done four months of house arrest, and was now out on probation.

• Amy Pederson, twenty-one, was the one who called the ATF in 1994 as publicity about the upcoming *Unsolved Mysteries* program and the reward money was building in the local media. She testified that when she was sixteen Richard told her that he "and a group of people had gone down to the construction site to set off some dynamite and that they set the explosion off and left. They set the dynamite near or underneath the truck, I don't remember which one." She said they did it "just for fun."

• Brian Studna, twenty-eight, felon, testified Richard told him in 1990 that he'd "started a truck on fire at the construction site, and as a diversion after that he started the rest of it on fire." Richard was at the site to steal items to trade for drugs.

Studna pled guilty in 1992 to forgery in Jackson County and got probation. He violated his parole in September 1992, but he got a second chance. In 1995 he was arrested for drug use. While out on bond, he threatened to jump off an overpass at 103rd and I-435 on April 15, 1995; a rescue team pulled him off. The next month he met with Detective James Shea and implicated sixteen area people in drug use. He told Shea he wanted to be a police informant. Twice he got paid $100 for information. In May 1995 he told Shea that Richard Brown made admissions to him in 1992. Two months later, while still out on bond, he met with True. On November 13, 1996—after the indictments in the firefighters case came down—he pled guilty to another felony—witness tampering—and got a three-year suspended sentence, despite his prior felony conviction for forgery and his arrest for drugs.

•Kelly Corriston, twenty-five, was dating Richard around the time the firefighters were killed. Richard told her he was worried someone saw him filling up a gas can at 7-Eleven; also she heard Richard was angry at his grandmother for telling police he wasn't home until after the first explosion.

When Detective Zinn interviewed Corriston in October 1989, she said she could not remember anything Richard told her. Four days later she said the same thing to Zinn's partner, Detective Fraise. Under this questioning, Corriston began crying and asked Osgood not to yell at her.

Corriston resurfaced as a potential government witness after her sister, Tracy Smith, went to the ATF and gave a videotaped statement, saying Corriston had information about Richard's involvement. Agent True met with Corriston on June 23, 1995, and played the videotape. Corriston told him she didn't want to remember that period of her life; it was a bad time for her, doing drugs.

On February 20, 1996, True called her in again. This time her father came with her. By then she had seen *Unsolved Mysteries* and was aware of the $50,000 reward. She now implicated Richard.

The parade of people close to Richard continued.

• Kimberly Finch, thirty-six, was his aunt through marriage. She testified that in the fall of 1991 she was at a party at Richard's house. A keg of beer was outside. Bryan, Frank, and Skip were there and Darlene was in and out. Finch was in a back bedroom when she heard Bryan yelling at Richard, telling him to shut up. Richard said something about wiping all the fingerprints off a shed or a trailer. Then Richard said Bryan was the one who said he was going to burn the lock "so they could get in there and see what was in there." Frank told Richard to shut up or "I'm going to punch you dead in your mouth."

O'Connor asked her about her interview with Detective Guffey on June 19, 1995, where she said she didn't have firsthand information. She denied telling Guffey that.

• Kimberly Archer, twenty-nine, was dating and living with Richard's brother Carl Brown near Bannister Mall. She testified that about 6:30 a.m.—less than two hours after the second explosion—she was awakened by a knock on the door. She didn't leave the bedroom, but she heard Richard say there was an explosion and a fire "and you should have seen it." When they left about a half hour later, Carl drove her to get an abortion and then she went to stay at her father's.

At the time she testified she was incarcerated in the Jackson County jail on a probation violation for forgery. She was currently participating in a twenty-one-day drug rehab program. She testified that she went to the ATF in January 1996.

• Monica Maggard, forty, testified that on the night of the explosions she was driving her boyfriend, Pat Stewart, on a burglary run to the Silo store at nearby Bannister Mall when the first explosion erupted, causing them to abort their plan. The next day at Swope Park, Stewart was talking to a bunch of his Marlborough friends, including Richard Brown, about having to forgo the robbery when Richard Brown put his arm around Stewart's shoulder and said he and some others were responsible for the explosions.

Almost eight years later Maggard contacted Agent True in hopes of helping Stewart get his sentence reduced. Stewart had been convicted of felony theft and breaking into a home and was serving a sentence at the state penitentiary in Lansing, Kansas.

On cross-examination, it came out that Maggard told True it was Bryan Sheppard who put his arm around Stewart and bragged about causing the explosions. When Osgood asked her if she was working as a drug informant to help Stewart, she said she was not. At the bench, Becker said she was.

The tangled web between Darlene and Richard was on display when one of Darlene's sisters testified.

• Nancy Jill Romi, thirty-five, who was now separated from Tom Romi, Richard's uncle, testified that a few minutes after the first explosion she saw a black Ford pickup with rust spots on the hood and with a front headlight out driving at a high rate of speed past her house, and said out loud, "There goes Richard!" She could not actually see who was driving but Richard lived just two blocks north of her. (Richard's truck was buffed to a gloss and had no rust spots.)

Osgood asked her if she had been arrested recently in Boots & Saddle with drug paraphernalia. Judge Stevens chastised him. Back in February 1989 she told Detective Zinn about seeing the black Ford dashing by but said Richard often lent his pickup to his friends, mentioning one in particular, Chuck Jennings. In February 1995, as the investigation was honing in on the Marlborough Five, Agent True interviewed her on tape.

During a break, Becker made a motion to revoke Richard's bond "for a pattern of intimidating government witnesses." Becker said that earlier in the trial Richard had made an obscene gesture to his former girlfriend Kelly Corriston as she came into the courtroom. The day before, Becker said Richard approached Becky Edwards in the street outside the courthouse and attempted to talk to her. And just now, out in the hallway, he called Nancy Romi "a lying bitch," Becker said.

With the jury absent, Richard was called to the stand and sworn in. Under questioning from Osgood, he said as he was walking out of the courtroom for the current break, he said to one of his cousins, "I can't believe her; she's a lying bitch." Richard said Nancy's parents overheard him, and when her father, Jack Clark, told Richard to watch himself, Richard said he told him, "Fuck you." Richard said he did not see Nancy; she was still in the courtroom when he addressed her father. He said he subsequently apologized to her parents and to her. He then apologized to the judge.

Osgood asked him if he was under a lot of stress lately. Richard said his grandfather died a week and a half ago and that his one-year-old son was in the hospital with IVs in him being treated for pneumonia and may have meningitis. The doctors were about to do a spinal tap to determine that.

Becker asked him if he gave the finger to Kelly Corriston. No, he knew better than to do that. Did he approach Becky? No, he knew that was forbidden. Did he glare at Nancy Romi and Monica Maggard the night before? He only saw them from the end of a long hallway.

Judge Stevens revoked his bond. Osgood pleaded with him to reconsider, saying how helpful it was to the defense to have access to him every night after trial and that he wanted to be with his son in the hospital. There would be no reconsideration. Revoking his bond, the judge said, "would mean everybody had the same [client] relationship and the same situation with their client working now."

The moment in the trial finally arrived for Darlene's daughter Becky Edwards to take the stand. Her mother had been in prison for over two years and she had just been scraping by, living off and on with her father and with a woman she babysat for. For the last year she had been living with a family in Adrian, Missouri, a small town about fifty miles south of Kansas City off of US 71.

She was eleven at the time of the explosions and nineteen now. Becky is petite and soft-spoken; at times she is barely audible. She looks fragile. Without a doubt, she was intimidated to be in this courtroom and terribly conflicted about having to testify as a government witness. Agent True had worked repeatedly with her to shape her testimony.[5]

Under questioning from Becker, she was about to give the most devastating testimony against the Marlborough Five the jury would hear. She said a week or so before the explosions, Darlene, Frank, Skip, Richard, Bryan, and her stepbrother Ronnie Edwards were in Darlene's kitchen getting high. She heard Frank and Richard saying there was copper and stuff at the construction site that they could steal and sell and there were some sheds.

She said they talked about "a Bobcat bucket just laying up there they could take and sell." She heard no discussion about gasoline.

The second explosion awakened her. As she came out of her bedroom her mother was walking down the hallway and Frank was coming in through the front door. Frank had on jeans and a T-shirt; he had a rip in his pant leg and grass stains on his pants and shoes. Frank said he thought the furnace had blown up and turned off the thermostat.

After that she went into her mother's bedroom where Darlene and Frank were talking through a window to their next-door neighbors.

Will Bunch, the attorney for Darlene, made numerous trips to Adrian in an attempt to interview Becky. When he finally did succeed, she made it plain to him that this would be a onetime meeting and that no other defense attorneys should attempt to reach her. She also revealed a deep hatred for Frank Sheppard, telling the soft-spoken attorney that Frank made passes at her when he was drunk, that he abused Darlene continually, and he beat up her half brother, forcing him to move to Iowa to live with Darlene's parents.

Bunch advised the other defense attorneys to leave all the cross-examination to him. He was afraid if she were pushed in any way she would unload on Frank about his abuses and that the jury would feel revulsion not only for Frank, but Darlene too because she had allowed her daughter to live in an abusive, drug- and alcohol-infested environment.

The cross-examination went by in a whiff of smoke. Becky said her mother was in her nightgown when she saw her after the second blast.

Would it be fair to characterize what went on around the kitchen table as "parties" rather than "meetings"? She agreed it would.

Bunch asked her what happened after Agent True showed up with news media cameras in tow at the QuikTrip where she worked on the day the indictments against her mother and the others were announced. She said she quit her job out of embarrassment.

Was it difficult for her to know what the truth really is anymore, after all these intervening years and countless conversations with family members and Agent True? Yes, it was.

The Defense

During cross-examination, the defense attorneys did a good job of discrediting the felon witnesses and chipping away at the credibility of most of the Marlborough witnesses; more chipping away was on its way when the defense called its rebuttal witnesses. To anyone paying attention it was clear that no coherent account of what any of the Marlborough Five had allegedly done had emerged. The testimony the government put on was so disjointed that it told no real story. Did Frank start the fire with a stick of dynamite, or did he do it by remote control, or did Skip start it when he accidentally kicked over a lantern? Did they start the fire to cover their tracks or just out of plain meanness?

Jurors like anyone else want to hear a believable story, not a jumble of unrelated and half-baked accusations. So far, with the exception of Becky Edwards's testimony, they had not heard that. And not even Becky's testimony gave them any clue as to who did what. Plus there was the totally confusing audiotape of Darlene saying she drove two people to get gas and dropped them off, reluctantly, at the construction site. Darlene's version totally exonerated Frank and made her role in the crime a dubious one.

By the end of the prosecution's case there was a palpable feeling among the defense attorneys and the defendants that the government had failed to prove its case.

In addition to calling some rebuttal and alibi witnesses plus a man who admitted to the police that he and a friend were responsible for the blasts, the defense strategy centered around putting Debbie Riggs, Robert Riggs, and Dave True back on the stand and calling Agent Eugene Schram of the US Labor Department to question him about his six-year investigation into the possibility that organized labor was behind the explosions.

The first witness for the defense was Harold Fernau, the general manager of Sealright Corporation, the Kansas City, Kansas, company that Bridgette Dornhoffer testified she worked for. During her testimony, she claimed that Fernau wrote a letter to Judge Howard of the Clay

County Circuit Court urging him to grant her probation on her latest fraud charges because she was such a valuable employee. During cross-examination, Dornhoffer said she knew the letter was genuine because she discussed the letter with Fernau on the telephone.

Attorney Bunch showed Fernau the letter and asked him if he had written it. He said he had not and that the signature was a forgery. Further, Dornhoffer had never been an employee of Sealright, just a temp sent over by Olsten staffing services for a ten-week period. He had never talked to Dornhoffer on the phone.

Pat Peters asked Fernau if anyone from the prosecutor's office had called him about the letter. He said yes, about two weeks ago, and he informed the caller (assistant prosecutor Dan Miller) that he had not written the letter and Dornhoffer had never asked him to write one.

Under the *Brady* rules, once Miller found out that the letter was a forgery, the prosecution was obligated to inform the defense that Dornhoffer had perjured herself about the letter, but neither Miller nor Becker did. It would appear they hoped the defense would not contact Fernau and discover the perjury. No matter, not divulging this perjury to the court and the defense violated Becker and Miller's obligations as officers of the court.

Probably the oddest witness the jury encountered was the next one, Frederick Martindale. The police brought him in for questioning on February 29, 1991, where he denied any involvement in the deaths of the firefighters. A week later, Detectives Fraise and Rosalind Morrison interviewed him again. Word got back to the police that Martindale, twenty, was bragging to several people that he caused the explosions. This time Martindale was subjected to a polygraph, which he failed. When he was told by the police there were some witnesses against him, including a friend of his father's, and that his black Nova was seen at the construction site that night, he lowered his head and said, "I was there."

He said his father was with him (by the time he said this his father had died), and they were there to steal explosives. When they couldn't find the explosives, he set a trailer on fire by stuffing cardboard and straw under the tires of the trailer and igniting it.

Before the detectives booked Martindale on six counts of homicide and held him overnight, they told him he was facing a life sentence and prison was bad for gay men. He repeated he was guilty. The next morning, Martindale gave the police a full statement. In the twenty-one-minute video Martindale stated, "I went to the site. There was a trailer or mobile home, you know, I am not sure which one it was. I got there and I started picking up things and I set a whole bunch on fire and set it basically right underneath and I was setting cardboard on fire. There was straw that caught on fire, a whole bunch of junk lying around." He said he did not mean to kill anyone.

There were several details about the site that gave credence to Martindale's confession. In addition to the cardboard, he mentioned seeing earth-moving equipment, Caterpillars and a Bobcat, at the construction site. He mentioned having to cross a creek to get up to the site. But most telling, he recalled there was a pickup truck parked near the trailer and he actually started the fire under the pickup.

Now when he was asked who was with him, he said it was hard to be a "narc," meaning a snitch, but eventually named his friends Billy Hardin and Shawn Bryant.

After completing the video, he wrote a note to Detectives Fraise and Morrison thanking them "for getting this off my shoulders."

After the police interviewed Hardin and Bryant and they denied any involvement, they turned Martindale loose the next day, pending further investigation.

Attorney O'Connor interviewed Martindale on January 8, 1997, a couple of weeks before the firefighters trial began. Martindale told O'Connor the police did not tell him about the cardboard, the Caterpillars, the Bobcat, or the pickup truck near the ANFO trailer.

O'Connor knew that Agent True met with Martindale two months ago and True did not ask Martindale if he started the fire. When O'Connor tried to bring this out, Becker objected, saying O'Connor could have asked True about this when he was cross-examining him. (This question would have been outside the scope of cross-examination because Becker had not asked True anything about Martindale while he was testifying for the government.) The judge came up with a remedy, "You can still call True and ask him if you want to." (Again the judge cut off questioning on the grounds that the defense could delve into the matter when it recalled Agent True to the stand, something he would later bar the defense from doing.)

When Pat Peters took over the questioning, he asked Martindale, who said he was 6'3" or 6'4", how big Hardin is. "Hardin is 260–300, about 6'3"," he said. Their sizes closely resembled the sizes of the two prowlers Debbie Riggs claimed to see the night of the explosions. This coincidence was something Peters would attempt to draw attention to when the defense called Debbie Riggs as a defense witness.

Why did he confess, Becker asked Martindale on cross-examination? Because he was scared, he said, and wanted to go home. If he told them what they wanted to hear they might go easier on him. "So I told them and they let me go."

O'Connor, in rebuttal to Martindale's claim that he was scared of the police, wanted the jury to see the videotape of his confession. For one thing, the video showed that police considered Martindale a serious suspect. Second, Martindale appeared relaxed and sincere, not fearful. Becker objected to showing the video. The judge barred the video.

Bruce Trammel, another rebuttal witness, operated a newspaper route near the construction site. When Steve Morales testified he claimed he was in a van with Trammel when he saw Richard, Bryan, and Frank outside a friend's house in Marlborough around 1:30 a.m. on the night of the explosions. Trammel said he drove one route in his van and Morales drove another in his van—they were never in the same van together. He also said he had never been in a van with Morales when Morales went to visit someone's house.

The next two witnesses were the two primary KCPD detectives assigned at the outset to investigate the deaths of the firefighters: Detectives John Fraise and Victor Zinn.

Fraise testified that Karen Baird, when he interviewed her for the only time in October 1989, never told him Bryan made admissions to her. Next O'Connor asked him about Kathy Marburger, the blind woman who claimed on the witness stand that she heard Bryan making admissions about his guilt during a three-way conversation with Karen Baird and Bryan. Fraise said that when Marburger called him on September 21, 1989, she never said anything about a three-way conversation involving Baird and Bryan. Nor did she tell him that she overheard Bryan in the background, a few hours after the explosions, telling Baird, "You should have seen what we seen," or anything like that.

If Fraise had heard Marburger claim to have heard Bryan saying something like that, would he have written it in his report, O'Connor asked him. "Absolutely," Fraise answered.

Just as Fraise had testified, Detective Zinn said Karen Baird never alleged Bryan made admissions of guilt. Zinn said Marburger frequently called homicide trying to reach Fraise but talked to him four or five times when Fraise was out. During these calls, she never mentioned anything about participating in any three-way calls with Baird and Bryan during which Bryan made admissions.

Under questioning by Pat Peters, Zinn recounted returning to the construction site after dark on December 1, 1988, to test Debbie Riggs's claim about seeing two prowlers in among the office trailers in the median of 71

Highway. He said he parked the police car close to the spot where Debbie's pickup had burned, leaving Debbie and Fraise there while he walked toward Blue River Road. When Zinn positioned himself where Debbie said she saw the prowlers, Fraise was unable to see him. Zinn concluded she could not have seen the prowlers from where she was sitting in her brother's station wagon the night of the explosions.

When Peters tried to elicit testimony from Zinn about a number of inconsistent statements Debbie made when Zinn interviewed her a few hours after the explosions, Becker objected that it was a backdoor way of impeaching Debbie, arguing that Peters should have attempted to impeach her when she testified earlier in the trial. The judge agreed.

Next up was another detective, Robert Guffey. O'Connor called him as a defense witness to undercut the trial testimony of Kimberly Finch. Guffey interviewed her twice in mid-1995 and had written up reports. In neither interview, he testified, did Finch say anything about Richard telling her he wiped his fingerprints off of something at the site. Nor did she say anything about Richard Brown arguing with Bryan or Bryan telling Richard to keep his mouth shut.

John McGovern, twenty-seven, was a rebuttal witness to impeach the trial testimony of his former girlfriend Christine Mills. She had testified that Bryan made admissions at a party at his house in the early 1990s; also McGovern told her to keep her mouth shut about hearing those admissions. McGovern said he never heard Bryan make any admissions and Mills never mentioned to him that Bryan had.

Becker asked him what happened that night when he showed up with Mills at Bryan's house. He said Richard asked him why he "brought that bitch with him." McGovern told Becker they left the party shortly after that.

This might have been the only time in the trial Becker did something to reinforce a defense point. The answer he elicited from McGovern made it unlikely that she was around long enough to hear much of anything.

One of the guards at the site the night of the explosions was Kevin Lemanske. Elena Franco, one of the two attorneys representing Skip Sheppard, called him as a witness. Franco could have questioned Lemanske about a number of unusual things that occurred among the guards the night of the explosions while Lemanske was working the pre-midnight shift with Donna Costanza. Something happened that caused Debbie Riggs to replace Costanza halfway through her shift. It was never explained why when Robert Riggs showed up about 10 p.m. that he sent Lemanske home early or why another guard, Melvin Stanton, was called into work around 10 p.m. only to be sent home again an hour later by Robert Riggs. All of this Franco could have probed, but not one question came from her about any of that.

The defense was aware of a statement Melvin Stanton gave on February 22, 1989, to Detective Fraise. By the time the firefighters trial took place over eight years later, Stanton was in a mental care facility and unavailable to testify. Considering what Stanton told the detective, this was even more reason to do a thorough examination of Lemanske. Among other things, Stanton said Debbie Riggs always had a gas can in the bed of her pickup because the gas gauge did not work.

When Fraise asked Stanton who he thought was responsible for the explosions, he said Robert Riggs. Debbie had told him Robert was about to lose his only contract because Brown Brothers was not satisfied with Ameriguard's performance. Stanton said the explosions resulted in Ameriguard's hours being doubled. Stanton quit a week after the firefighters were killed. Robert Riggs let Lemanske go three days after the explosions.

Instead of questioning Lemanske about any of Stanton's revelations or what he saw that night, Franco seemed only interested in having Lemanske rebut one of the claims made by government witness Stephen Kilgore. He testified Frank told him there was a security guard with a Polish last name—Lemanske fit the bill—who had been allowing them to steal from the site for some time. The night of the explosions, Kilgore said they walked to the site with two purposes in mind: to torch the guard's truck as part of an insurance scam and "to loot the place."

After establishing he had no criminal record and was now a truck driver, Franco asked him if he knew any of the defendants. No. Nor had he ever allowed any of them to steal from the site. She did not ask him about conspiring with any of them to burn his vehicle as part of an insurance scam.

Oddly, none of the other defense attorneys had any questions for this font of insider information into the workings of Ameriguard at the site. With Lemanske doing no harm to the prosecution's case, there was no cross-examination and he was excused. As he left the stand, so did the defense's final chance to shift the focus to the Riggses.

In the judge's chambers the next morning, the issue of Pat Peters calling Debbie Riggs as a defense witness was hotly debated. By now, Debbie was being represented by one of the most high-profile defense attorneys in Kansas City, J. R. Hobbs of Wyrsch Hobbs & Mirakian. The day before, Peters went over what he intended to ask Debbie with Hobbs; Becker also spoke with Hobbs.

Debbie Riggs had been on Peters's list of defense witnesses since before the trial began. He had a number of questions that had not been raised during her direct testimony. One concerned her having a gas can in the back of her pickup. This is the exchange that followed:

Judge: I haven't heard anything substantive, Mr. Peters, or constructive to your case. You just want to bring her in and chip away at her some more.

Peters: Then I would ask that I be allowed to make an offer of proof. I think that it is relevant to the defendants' case that the guard on duty who left the site has in reports provided by the government told people that her gas gauge wasn't working, she had a gas can in it, and she couldn't—

Judge: Did you know that when you had her on the stand for cross?

Peters: Yes, but—

Judge: Well, then, why didn't you ask her?

Peters: Because it wasn't brought out on direct [examination], and the Court [Judge Stevens] has consistently told us—

Judge: I'm not going to buy that, Mr. Peters.

Peters: Judge, then I'll need to make an offer of proof.

Judge: You may do so.

Peters: In the transcripts of the number of times that we've been told that cross-examination—

Judge: You've had plenty of opportunity exhaustively to cross-examine that lady, and you passed it up. We're not going to prolong this trial by recalling witnesses and going over and over and over what could have been gone over in the first instance.

Peters: I will need to make an offer of proof, Your Honor.

Judge: You may do so.

Peters: Judge, the record I want to make is there's nothing deliberate in this. I complied with the Court's order in turning over the names of my witnesses. I believe that I will show the Court that the Court has consistently said that the defense questioning of witnesses is limited to the scope of direct examination so—

Judge: That's the rule in federal court.

Peters: And, Judge, the government did not bring out that she had said that her car was in trouble, that it had a gas can in it, the working order of the car that night, and it wasn't—there's no implication that I can see that what I was doing was trying to string out a witness or delay the trial or perpetrate any sort of fraud on the Court.

She was endorsed by me as a witness. I covered everything that was covered in direct examination in my cross-examination of her, but the issues, the two limited issues that I wanted to call my witness for, were not covered on direct examination.

And I think the Court is aware the Riggses, the credibility of the Riggses is at issue in this case, and the issues that I want to raise I think are very important to the defense case. And in the length of time, in terms of judicial economy, and I understand the Court's concern about that, Deborah Riggs would have been on and off by now. I have just a few questions.

Judge: Let's stop this now. What is your [Becker's] position on this business of whether this was something that was not covered on her original direct-examination which, therefore, would not have been appropriate for cross?

Becker: I disagree with that. I covered with Ms. Riggs the whole events of that night and all about her truck. If there were—I imagine Mr. Peters is going to ask about the condition of the truck that night. Certainly the fact, on cross, did you have a gas can in the back of that truck, would not have been outside the scope on direct, that night.

Judge: It seems to me the truck figured very prominently in the direct examination.

Becker: The whole matter of the truck and what happened to the truck and where was the truck.

Judge: Okay.

O'Connor: I'd like to make one more argument.

Judge: Let's get on with this, Mr. O'Connor.

O'Connor: One thing, the Court [Judge Stevens] hasn't been in this case the whole time. We got in this case 3,400 pages on December the 24th. I mean, we have done, I think, remarkable to do everything we've been able to do. Now that we have maybe missed in 3,400 pages [of discovery] and being basically forced to trial with a minimal continuance [ten days instead of the thirty requested] on this case, should we get some leeway on a matter like this that is critical to our case?

Judge: A, I don't think it's that critical and, B, I don't see that it's a matter of too many pages to examine. It's a question of whether he [Peters] conducted a thorough cross-examination, knowing what he knew then. There isn't any newly discovered evidence here, he just didn't ask the questions.

O'Connor: What I'm saying is he [Peters] chose as a part of his trial strategy, Your Honor, he was calling the witness himself as a witness. So if he chose as his trial strategy not to ask the witness a question when she was on the stand, I don't understand why he would be precluded when he's now putting on his case to now put her on as part of his case.

Becker: Because Rule 611 allows the Court to control the order of witnesses and the manner of direct and cross-examination. And the rule that I've been aware of here in federal court is that if there's cross-examination to be made, it should be made, rather than withholding some cross-examination until calling the witness yourself late in the trial merely to highlight some point you want to make.

Judge: After the other side [the prosecution] has rested. Okay. Let's go.

After the jury was released for lunch, attorney Peters was allowed in open court, as part of his offer of proof, to ask Debbie Riggs two questions. The first was if she had been working on her pickup the night of the explosions with the pickup's hood up. She said she had not because the pickup was in good working order. The second question was if her paychecks from Ameriguard went directly to her mother to pay off debts Debbie had run up with her. This she confirmed.

Over the lunch hour, Peters interviewed a witness who had driven by the construction site at 10 p.m. on the night of the explosions, taking his daughter to an emergency room at Research Medical Center. As he drove by he saw four people standing around a red Toyota pickup with its hood up. A station wagon was parked next to the pickup. The witness, Greg Pugh, was—and still is—a mechanic for the City of Kansas City. He remembered saying to his wife how lucky the people working on the pickup were to be underneath the bright glare of the portable overhead lights. On his way home from the hospital around midnight he saw the pickup still being worked on and the hood up.

The next day or the day after the firefighters were killed, when it was broadcast that the police wanted anyone with information about the night of the explosions to call the TIPS hotline, Pugh called the hotline with the information about the red pickup with its hood up, but his call was never returned.

Years later, during the firefighters trial, when Pugh read in the newspaper that Debbie Riggs testified that her pickup was not being worked on the night of the explosions, Pugh called defense attorney John O'Connor and told him what he saw that night. Pugh said he knew the guard was lying and was hiding something. O'Connor passed the information to Osgood and Peters.

Peters now wanted to call Pugh, who was waiting outside the courtroom. He said he only wanted to ask him four or five questions.

Judge Stevens was adverse to any sort of curveball surprises. He said he did not like the fact that this witness was showing up eight years after the fact. He found that inherently untrustworthy. Peters said it was important to the defense for the jury to learn that Debbie Riggs had lied about not having her pickup's hood up that night.

> Judge: Why? What are you going to prove was the reason that she had the hood open?
>
> Peters: I don't think it matters why she had her hood open. I think the reason she had the hood open is because her truck stopped working and that's why she torched it. You're asking, and that's what I think.
>
> Judge: You mean she drove it there and it stopped working while she was there and then she decides she's going to burn it?
>
> Peters: Right.

A few minutes later, this exchange wrapped up the issue:

> Becker: I think it's [having Pugh testify] a collateral [not relevant] matter.
>
> Peters: It's new information, it's new evidence that wasn't available when Deborah Riggs first testified. It goes directly to her credibility on the issue of whether or not her truck was operating properly at the time. I made my offer of proof. She said that it was operating and that her hood was never up that night. I've advised the Court that we have an independent eyewitness who is a mechanic who describes the scene, is certain—and it's backed up by medical records if we wanted to go that far as to when he drove past the scene going north to the hospital with his daughter, and when he came back after midnight and the truck was still there with the hood up.
>
> Judge: Well, the government objects to that, and I think on the basis of the record we have now and the Riggses' testimony that it's—well, regardless of the Riggses' testimony, I think it's collateral and not, I'll not admit it.
>
> Peters: Thank you, Judge.

There would be no recalling either of the Riggses.

The trial transcript is replete with intense arguments at the bench or in the judge's chambers or in the courtroom with the jury not present where the judge, in every single instance, sides with the prosecution against the defense. The ones denying Debbie Riggs being recalled as a defense witness or not allowing Greg Pugh to testify are only different in subject matter.

The cumulative effect of the judge's rulings, over the course of this trial, was to cripple the defense, undermining any real chance of advocating properly for the five defendants. The jury, not even aware of these rulings, only got to hear a fraction of the case the defense wanted to present.

All of the Marlborough Five had good, if not strong, alibis, but the jury would hear testimony concerning only Skip and Richard. One might wonder why John O'Connor did not call Bryan's parents, his sister Katie, and his girlfriend at the time, Debbie Howard, as alibi witnesses. Perhaps O'Connor felt his parents and sister were too close to Bryan to have credibility with the jury, but Debbie Howard had married and moved on with her life. Asked twenty years later why he did not call any alibi witnesses for Bryan, O'Connor said he simply could not remember his reasoning at the time.[1] Pat Peters was no doubt afraid that calling Larry Baker, who drove Frank home the night of the explosion, might backfire if he appeared inebriated on the stand. Baker could have been an alibi witness for Darlene and Skip as well but he was such an unpredictable character, who had done prison time himself for DWIs, that there was no telling what Becker might elicit from him during cross-examination.

The only alibi witness for Skip was Elizabeth "Liza" Harrigan. She had dated Skip off and on for three or four years. Although they discussed marriage, the relationship was rocky. One time in a bar Skip hit her in the mouth and knocked out one of her front teeth after she danced with another man. Following that incident, she got a protective order against Skip. She said she did that "probably just to make him mad." She violated the order by going to see Skip.

On the night the firefighters were killed, she was with Skip at Diddi and Larry Baker's house. She said she didn't use drugs that day. After everyone left but Frank, she and Skip went to bed around midnight or 1 a.m. The Baker children woke her up after one of the explosions—she hadn't heard either blast—and Skip was in bed with her. She did not know if Skip got up during the night and left but said, "He never roamed around too much in the night." She said Skip was panicked like everyone else after the explosions.

Becker asked her how she met Skip. She was living with a woman who did drugs and was a friend of Skip's. When the woman got busted, Skip took Harrigan to his parents' home in Marlborough and tried to get her off dirty drugs like crack and crystal meth and onto cocaine.

Asked if Skip stole things, she said he and his buddies stole bikes, hubcaps, and lawn tools.

After Bryan was arrested and charged with the deaths of the firefighters in 1989, Harrigan asked Skip if Bryan was involved in the explosions or knew anything about them. She quoted Skip as telling her, "You don't really need to know anything."

Susan Hunt, the lead attorney for Skip, took the testimony of Frank and Skip's mother, Naomi Sheppard, a full-blooded Cherokee with deep furrows lining her face, a face that in repose had a haunted look. Serene, composed, she was at age sixty-nine the picture of the stoic survivor. She had been through it all from her days on an impoverished Indian reservation in Oklahoma, through her years boarding at an Indian school, through all the grief of losing her son Phillip to watching Frank carted off to prison and seeing her son Skip turn to cocaine after his near-fatal car accident that took the life of his fiancée. At the end of 1988, her husband died. (She herself had lung cancer and would be dead seven months later.) Now she was in a courtroom with prosecutors intent on sending two of her sons and one of her grandchildren to prison for life. Despite it all, here was a woman who had somehow managed to keep it all together.

Naomi would be the only parent of a defendant called by the defense. In terms of rebuttal witnesses, the jury would not encounter a more credible one. There was no hem or haw in her terse, direct answers; she evoked credibility.

She recounted how her fourteen-year-old son Phillip died in 1970 after he was shot in the head by Stephen Kilgore. They were playing hooky at Kilgore's house. After the funeral, she did not see Kilgore for twenty-three years, until 1993, when he showed up at her house saying he wanted to buy a headstone for Phillip's grave in Longview Cemetery. She didn't care one way or the other whether he bought the headstone.

Did Frank and Skip ever go for a ride with Kilgore? "They never." (Kilgore claimed that Frank made admissions to him while he was giving him and Skip a ride to mow a lawn.) Did she ever see Kilgore after he visited her a second time in 1993? "Never." Did Kilgore ever buy the headstone? "Never."

Naomi said the only time Lisa Landon was ever in her house was when she came to tell her that her mother, Naomi's best friend, was in the hospital with only a few hours to live. Naomi rode with Lisa to the hospital and spent the night with her friend. Landon testified that a couple of weeks after the explosions she overheard either Frank or Skip say that they knew what was in the trailers and just wanted to see what would happen if they caught fire.

As for Landon's brother, John Barchers, Naomi said Frank and Skip were always friendly with him but only when they were kids. Barchers and his wife testified that Frank, Skip, and Diddi had awakened them around midnight a few weeks after the explosions. While they were sitting around the kitchen table smoking marijuana, Skip said if Diddi had done her job the blast would not have happened. Frank said the firefighters were stupid for rushing in before finding out what was in the trailers.

Because it had been alleged by various government witnesses that items stolen from the construction site were hidden in an add-on at the back of Naomi's house that contained a washer and a dryer, Hunt asked her to describe the layout of her house. Naomi said there was no add-on and no small room at the back of the house that held the washer and dryer. The dryer is in the kitchen and the washer is in the garage. Those two appliances have never been housed in the same room.

Patty Smith, one of the witnesses against Skip, claimed Naomi warned her in 1993 to stay away from Skip, saying she didn't know who she was dating, that Skip killed six firefighters. Naomi said Skip never dated Smith; they were just friends. "I never talked to her that much," nor did she tell her Skip did this crime.

Carolee Ann Smith, Naomi's next-door neighbor, testified after the first explosion she saw Frank, Skip, and two others get out of a pickup in Naomi's driveway and enter the Sheppard house through the back door. Naomi said neither Frank nor Skip came home that night. After the first explosion, she and her husband Earl went outside on the front porch and Earl's pickup was parked in the driveway.

Becker was not about to let Naomi stand down without trying to dent her credibility. Didn't Liza Harrigan and Skip live at her house in 1988? Skip did but not Liza. Liza lived there for a short while, but that was well before the explosions. Did the two of them do drugs at her house? No. Did Skip have a job in November 1988? He did tree trimming, but not every day. Frank didn't have a job then.

When Becker posed a question about Harrigan coming over to her house, attorney Hunt objected on the basis that Naomi was not asked anything on direct examination about Harrigan. The judge overruled Hunt's objection without providing a reason. Becker asked Naomi if she remembered Harrigan telling her Bryan Sheppard came over to the Bakers' house the night of the explosions and asked Skip to go out with him. Naomi said she remembered that, but when Becker asked her if she also remembered telling Harrigan not to mention to the police anything about Bryan coming over, she said, "I never told her that."

So far Becker had not made much of a crack in Naomi's armor. His next line of questioning was so far out of order that the judge should have stopped him before attorney Hunt made a belated objection. The prosecutor asked Naomi if she told her friend Sylvia Barchers and another one of her sons, Al Barchers, that her family was at the construction site the night of the explosions in her husband's pickup. "No," she answered.

Sylvia Barchers was dead. Al Barchers had not been called to testify by the government. For Becker to represent what Naomi allegedly told Sylvia and Al Barchers was tantamount to making himself a witness for the prosecution. Plus it was double hearsay. The judge did not intervene and Hunt did not object until Becker asked Naomi if she told Al Barchers and his mother that Frank and Skip were at the construction site intending to steal copper and aluminum. "No, sir," she said.

> Hunt: Objection. Your Honor, Al Barchers was not discussed on direct and has not been a witness in this case, and he [Becker] keeps cross-examining her on what she told Al Barchers. It's beyond the scope.
> Judge: I don't think credibility questions are beyond the scope.
> Hunt: There has been no testimony to date about Al Barchers.
> Becker: Because he's a potential rebuttal witness, but there—
> Judge: There has been mention of the Barchers family and the Barchers relationship. I'm not sure that specifically Al Barchers—
> Becker: We've had three Barchers testify, and this is one more.
> Judge: I'll deny that, I'll overrule that.

Becker resumed his questioning, asking Naomi if she told the Barchers that Skip created a diversion when he saw the security guards. "Never."

It would make any court observer wonder how the same judge, within the expanse of two hours, could rule in such opposite fashions when it came to challenging the credibility of trial witnesses. Stevens allowed Becker to question Naomi Sheppard about what Al Barchers, a nonwitness in this case, purportedly claimed Naomi said to him and his mother because it went to her credibility. But when it came to allowing an actual eyewitness [mechanic Greg Pugh] to challenge the credibility of Debbie

Riggs, the ruling was that such testimony was "collateral," i.e., not relevant.

John Osgood put on three alibi witnesses for Richard Brown.

Brenda Carpenter, thirty-six, said that on the night of the explosions she played cards at her sister Janet's house in Marlborough with Richard, Alena Fantauzzo, Stephanie Webb, her boyfriend, Ron McCullough, and her sister Janet, who would be testifying next. Starting around 8 or 9 p.m., they played rummy, spades, and Uno. She said her sister Janet was the only one drinking. Richard left around midnight with Stephanie and Alena, driving away in his black pickup. She never saw Bryan that night and Richard made no phone calls.

During cross-examination, she said Janet passed out from drinking about 10 p.m. and slept on a bed in the dining room while McCullough slept on a couch. She said McCullough slept through both blasts. After the second blast, she went up to 7-Eleven and on her way she drove around the neighborhood to see what had happened. As she was driving around she saw Richard's pickup parked in his grandfather's driveway. She estimated that Richard left her house either an hour before or an hour after midnight.

Her sister, Janet Carpenter, thirty-two, could not say when Richard, Alena, and Stephanie left because she fell asleep about 10 p.m. She remembers waking up after the first blast and going to check on her children.

The final alibi witness was Linda Peak, thirty, who lived across the street from the Romi family, Richard's grandparents. She did not know either Romi personally and only knew Richard by sight. She testified that after the second explosion, she went outside and saw Richard and an elderly woman across the street about two hundred feet away looking around. It seemed like everyone in the neighborhood was out looking around. Richard was wearing blue jeans, but no shirt or shoes. She saw a pickup and a car in the Romis' driveway.

Assistant Prosecutor Miller tried to get her to increase her estimate of how far Richard was away from her, but she would not budge off the two hundred feet. Then Miller began reading from a tape-recorded transcript defense investigator Mark Reeder made of his interview with Linda Peak, asking her a string of questions based on what Reeder recorded. In this interview she said she went outside and saw Richard and his grandmother after the first explosion. Why Miller would want to draw attention to that was mystifying because it put Richard at his grandparents' house at least forty minutes earlier than if he was seen there after the second explosion.

What was even more peculiar was that Mark Reeder was the investigator the judge said he had no faith in when attorney Hunt was attempting to reference a tape-recorded interview Reeder conducted with government witness Stephen Kilgore. Now that one of the government's prosecutors was quoting from a Reeder report, the judge allowed it into the record.

The next morning before the jury was called in, Hunt brought up the matter of Miller's cross-examination of Linda Peak.

> Hunt: Just for the purposes of the record, I am going to ask for a mistrial. When the government produced Steve Kilgore early on in this case and I was attempting to cross-examine him with a tape-recorded conversation he had with Mark Reeder, remember I was precluded by the Court because the Court did not trust Mr. Reeder, the government was allowed to use Mr. Reeder's tape-recorded conversation with Linda Peak. He was allowed to use it; I wasn't.
>
> Judge: Okay.
>
> Hunt: I would ask for a mistrial just for the record.
>
> Judge: Wouldn't you be surprised if I granted it?
>
> Hunt: I would be thrilled. Yes, I would be surprised.
>
> Judge: All right, that will be denied.

When Osgood called Thomas Romi, thirty-three, to the stand, the defense did not know he would be the defense's last witness. The defense strategy was to close by calling Debbie and Robert Riggs and then Eugene Schram of the US Labor Department and end with ATF Agent True. The judge had already ruled the defense could not recall Debbie or Robert Riggs, but the defense had every reason to believe it could call the two agents. In fact, Judge Stevens told Pat Peters when he was questioning Martindale about what Agent True asked him that he could wait to get that answer directly from True when he recalled him as a witness. The judge used the same rationale for limiting O'Connor's questioning of witness Steve Morales, saying O'Connor could ask True about it later when the defense recalled him.

Tom Romi was Richard Brown's uncle. His presence as a rebuttal witness was something like a play within a play, a dramatization of the rupture within the defense team where the interests of Richard and Bryan conflicted so acutely from those of Darlene, Frank, and Skip.

Romi was married to Nancy Romi, one of Darlene's younger sisters. Nancy had testified that while looking out her front window three to five minutes after the first explosion she saw a black Ford pickup racing by her house and yelled out, "There goes Richard!"

After the first explosion, he said, he and Nancy went out the front door and he did not see a black pickup go by nor did he hear her say anything about Richard.

With the jury excused, the defense attorneys made separate offers of proof about calling ATF Agent True and Labor Department Agent Eugene Schram to testify. After prolonged and impassioned debates, the judge denied both offers and that was that—the defense came to an abrupt halt.

Now the matter of whether any of the defendants would testify would play out. The defense attorneys spent an hour the day before in a private strategy session with the defendants considering the pros and cons of this testimony. Each of the defendants fervently wanted to testify, but there were plainly hazards involved. With Richard Brown named last on the indictment, he was entitled to testify last. The other defense attorneys were afraid that if the first four defendants ceded their right to testify that Richard could sandbag Darlene, Frank, and Skip. Having this worry showed how little trust the other defense attorneys had, not with Richard, but in his lawyer, John Osgood. It did not appear that any of them ever recovered from the first time when the six defense attorneys met pretrial and Osgood said his defense of Richard would be to point the finger at Frank, Skip, and Darlene.

The other hazard in having the defendants testify and deny any involvement in the crime and repudiate the alleged "confessions" so many witnesses had sworn to is that it would allow the prosecution to call rebuttal witness after rebuttal witness, affording the government the opportunity to virtually try its case twice. So the decision was made that none of the defendants would testify.

In retrospect, not allowing the defendants to testify was the worst decision this defense team made. Becker and Miller's cross-examination of them would have been ruthless and withering, but most jurors, even though advised not to draw any inference from a defendant's not testifying, have a built-in distrust of defendants who do not assert their innocence.

Closing Arguments and Verdict

Because the prosecution has the burden of proof, the government makes the first closing argument, the defense goes next, and the government gets a final turn. The goal of the first closing argument is to lay out the case against the defendants; the goal of the second closing argument is to rebut the closing arguments of the various defense attorneys.

Assistant Prosecutor Miller led off by saying the case was about admissions. "These defendants could not keep their mouths shut. . . . You don't admit to a crime like this unless you did it."

The only defense that could logically be made was that all of the prosecution witnesses were lying or "grossly mistaken," he said, claiming that the prosecution had produced fifty-seven witnesses "who saw the defendants before the explosion and saw some of them after the explosion."

It is considered poor form for an opposing attorney to make an objection during closing argument—although Becker would not abide by this courtesy during three of the closing arguments made by the defense—and none were lodged despite the fact that what Miller just stated was patently untrue. There were two witnesses who claimed to see Bryan and Richard pre-explosion, and one who saw Frank and two who saw Skip after the first explosion. There were no witnesses who claimed to have seen Darlene that night. The only witnesses who claimed to see Bryan and Richard after the explosions saw them after 7 a.m.

How to explain why so many of the Marlborough witnesses waited until after seeing *Unsolved Mysteries* and learning of the $50,000 reward to come forward? "Some witnesses waited to come forward, sure, because 'I didn't know I was a witness. I didn't know what I knew was evidence that could be used.'"

Another bothersome issue for the prosecution was how to account for all the divergent testimony the jury heard from the government's informant witnesses concerning motive, what was stolen, how the fire was started, where the defendants were, and where they went afterward. To any disinterested observer what it showed was that the government's witnesses were lying their heads off.

To try to spin this problem, Miller said, "and there might be one or two things where one witness doesn't exactly concur with another but, if anything, that shows there is no orchestration here by the government. . . . Amy Pederson was up there saying something almost totally different than what Frank Gile told you . . . but the bottom line is I was there." (Pederson testified Richard told her they took dynamite to the site to set it off just for fun. Gile said Richard told him they went to the site to steal dynamite.)

Miller said Darlene's taped interview with the ATF at the Clay County jail was "tantamount to a confession," even though the opposite was the case. What she said exonerated Frank and showed her to be unwilling to go the construction site with the two she drove there. "Darlene was trying to distance herself, but she goes right up and carries through with the plan that Becky overheard—drives them there with a can of gas."

Becky did not testify to hearing anything about the group taking a can of gas to the construction site, but telling the jurors that Becky said the defendants plotted to rob the construction site at Darlene's kitchen table was a powerful reminder.

Skip's alibi about being asleep at his brother-in-law's house "was phony." Frank consistently told people that "the stupid firefighters killed themselves." Richard could not keep his mouth shut; Bryan had remorse.

Miller had droned on for almost an hour when he concluded by saying, "It is time now to do the right thing, to find these people guilty for what they did . . . 50 people hearing 65 admissions aren't all mistaken and they aren't all lying. I am confident you will do the right thing. It is proof beyond a reasonable doubt. It is proof beyond all doubt."

After a lunch break, Pat Peters, representing Frank Sheppard, began his closing argument by thanking the jurors for the attention they paid over the course of the trial.

As I told you at the beginning of the case, an indictment is simply an accusation. Each defendant is presumed to be innocent. And the burden is on the government. By your oath and by the instructions you can only find a defendant guilty if you are convinced beyond a reasonable doubt. And that is what this case is about, reasonable doubt. This instruction guides you further. There is no burden upon any defendant to present evidence to you to show that he is innocent.

And yet in this case what you have had is consistent—consistent testimony that Frank Sheppard always was, always will be, at home at the time of the explosion, at home before the explosion.

And after listening to the government's opening statement and the hour of Mr. Miller's closing statement, that is not refuted. That has not been taken from you beyond a reasonable doubt.

And now, eight years later, for the first time a jury listening to the evidence will stand up and say Mr. Sheppard is not guilty.

Peters, like the other defense attorneys, believed the deaths of the firefighters were caused by the guards. He believed the government had gotten the case backwards.

Before Debbie Riggs took the stand, he said, she advised the court of a previous insurance fraud involving one of her vehicles. During her testimony, she admitted lying to the police three times: about not being scheduled to work that night, about her brother being on the east side where the ANFO trailers were when she saw the three prowlers, and about not having a gun in her pickup.

Peters points out that the night of the explosions was the first time the guards ever left the site unguarded.

The gang that couldn't shoot straight sees the guards abandon the site and runs down from the east side to Debbie's pickup and sets it on fire as a diversion. The gang leaves her purse in her pickup. Then they run back up the hills to the underground bunkers, open one of them, and take out a crate of dynamite. Then to the trailer where they remove concrete saws, blades, drill bits, acetylene torches.

They stole all this property that was never stolen and broke into a trailer that was never broken into.

They did all this in the four or five minutes Robert Riggs testified the guards were away from the site.

When Debbie Riggs is heard on the dispatch tape saying the explosives are on fire, she could not see the trailers. "Why did she say that? You can use your own deductive reasoning to begin to see that something isn't right with this picture."

Susan Hunt advocated for Skip. She had a chart with all the witnesses against Skip on it and went through them. She pointed out how Carolee Ann Smith and Lonnie Joe Pugh put Skip at two places at once, and how after the indictment three jailhouse snitches came forward trying to get their sentences cut for testifying.

She concluded her argument by saying, "He is not on trial for abusing women. He is not on trial for stealing anything. He is on trial for this case. And I think when you look at this evidence, consider it all, apply the instructions to it, would you hesitate to act on this evidence? Would you hesitate in your own life to make a decision? And I believe you would. We ask you to return a verdict of not guilty. Thank you."

Will Bunch was appalled by the way the government had shoehorned this case to indict Darlene and her co-defendants. After warmly thanking the jurors for their attention and service and promising them he would not go on for more than twenty minutes, he began his peroration:

> I think it is important to recognize that the usual case is one in which there is an investigation leading to a conclusion. That is the way criminal cases are, as a matter of fact, all cases, an investigation leading to a conclusion; in other words, a result.
>
> It is not the usual case where a conclusion is reached and an investigation is conducted to support the conclusion.
>
> I submit to you that is the nature of this case. If that is the case, if you have already reached the result and a conclusion about who did something and then you can conduct an investigation to support that, there can be no other conclusion, that has already been reached.
> . . .
> How did it come about? It came about because the ATF and the Department of Organized Labor Racketeering Section worked on this case for six years, many years, always investigating organized labor. I make no suggestion nor reach any presumption or draw any inference organized labor had anything to do with this. But that is a fact. For many years that is the people accused by the government of having committed this atrocious crime.

With the government investigation at a dead end, Agent True turned away from labor and began focusing the investigation on Marlborough, Bunch said. He reminded the jurors they heard Agent True say the turning point in the investigation was a call he received from a woman in late 1994 informing him that Richard Brown admitted being involved in the explosions.

The fact that Bryan Sheppard had been indicted for this crime in 1989—even though subsequently released—also jibed with True's new interest in Marlborough. Because his name was "Sheppard and he lived in the Marlborough area. And the Marlborough area by the testimony of everybody was ripe with rumor with who done it. It has a unique location to the site. It has a unique constituency of people, presumably capable of being thieves, lowlifes, and so forth. So it is kind of a natural place to look if you want to reach some sort of conclusion."

When *Unsolved Mysteries* aired in February 1995, announcing a $50,000 reward, and reward posters were posted in all the jails and prisons in Missouri and Kansas and in overpasses throughout Marlborough, "most of the witnesses at this trial began coming forward."

Shortly after the *Unsolved Mysteries* broadcast, Agent True orchestrated the arrest of Darlene for selling drugs to her stepson, whom Agent True recruited to entrap her.

"So what happened in January of 1995, the people in the Marlborough area are suspects or the conclusion has been reached so we better set somebody up to see if we can get them to tell us about this," Bunch said.

Here was an avuncular, sixty-two-year-old defense lawyer telling the jury that the ATF had sprung a trap on an unwitting Darlene to break open this unsolvable case.

On February 17, 1995, in a videotaped interview at the ATF offices, Darlene denied any involvement or knowledge of the firefighters case. "After that denial, she was arrested and charged on drugs," Bunch continued. "True told her she now had a 'window of opportunity' to get out of the drug charge if she would tell him about her involvement in the crime."

After spending two nights in a county jail, Darlene gave an audiotaped statement about two people coming to her house well after midnight, saying they needed gas, Bunch went on. She drove them to QuikTrip. One of them asked her to drive to the construction site. She put them out of her car near the site and drove home.

"The government wants us to believe she drove two people to get gas and then drove them to the construction site, but the government doesn't want you to believe that she left," Bunch said. "Why? Well, it is obvious, isn't it, if what she told is the truth, she didn't have anything to do with setting the fire."

If you believe the testimony of the Riggses, Bunch said, there is a fatal flaw in Miss Edwards's statement:

> Why is that? Well, both of the Riggses said they were parked on the west side of 71 Highway and could see both roads leading onto the site. Thus if this was true, she [Darlene] would have stopped in plain view where they were sitting. Their [the guards] only purpose was to let nobody onto the site. So they parked in a particular location so they could see if somebody was trying to. They could have seen her

stop, these two people get out with a gas can and go on up on foot here, turn around. And they said no one drove onto the construction site that night, period—no one. Didn't happen.

After many years in the courtroom, Bunch said he'd learned this about reasonable doubt: "If you don't know, that is reasonable doubt; if you don't know who to believe, that is reasonable doubt."

Darlene told a story to try to take advantage of her "window of opportunity" because she was desperate, Bunch said. "Isn't the government's case to a large degree based upon desperate witnesses trying to find a window of opportunity, out of jail, whatever you can get of the reward, what have you? Isn't it fair to say that is the nature of many of these witnesses: they are desperate people?"

One thing that showed the desperation of these witnesses—"that shows it as clear as the morning sun when it comes up is all the items these witnesses claimed the defendants stole from the site: a transit, a concrete saw, batteries, acetylene torch, dynamite, tools and on and on and on, valuable things."

Yet, as construction executives testified at trial, nothing was ever stolen from the site, he said. "If these defendants were such thieves, why not take at least the checkbook from [Debbie Riggs's] truck?"

Now to the problem of Becky's testimony. "Becky talked about them discussing stealing copper from the site, but there was no copper. Becky never said Darlene said anything about stealing. On the night of the explosion she said her mother was in her nightgown and after the explosion Becky slept with her mother 'because I was scared.'"

Bunch said that "perhaps the most disturbing thing" about Becky was that she had been interviewed so many times over the years about something that happened when she was eleven years old that by her own admission, "'I no longer know what the truth really is.' And by saying that in no way is disparaging young Becky Edwards. This is just what happened."

After going through the testimony of the other witnesses against Darlene and pointing out how divergent it was from the facts of the case, he concluded, "We are here, ladies and gentlemen of the jury, because of the genuine, genuine tragedy, the death of six firefighters, fine men. We are not here to compound that tragedy by convicting five persons who are not responsible."

John Osgood, representing Richard Brown, was disjointed from the start, rushing frantically and incoherently from one point to the next. The one thing he did say that the jurors could follow was he was not going to be "as eloquent as Mr. Bunch." For thirty minutes he stumbled through a whirlwind of cross-references. He mentions Shannon Reimers, Richard's half sister, twice when he was referencing the testimony of Shannon Newcomb. He was impassioned but that was the only real impression he left. Taking a stab at candor he said he was not here "to tell you he [Richard] is a good guy," although he pointed out that Richard was the lone defendant with no felony convictions. It must have been mystifying for jurors to hear Osgood put down Richard.

Somehow Osgood, despite hours of private sessions with Richard, had it in his mind Richard talked carelessly about the firefighters case over the years and said things that made the witnesses against him think he was making admissions. He tried to excuse that by saying Richard "has a personality that likes to talk and he likes to talk all the time about anything and everything."

Throughout the trial John O'Connor had taken on the role of speaking for the defense as a whole. In the numerous sidebar conferences, it was his voice that dominated the record and represented the overall defense interests. It made sense for him to give the final closing argument. Although in his early forties, he has a boyish demeanor and radiates sincerity. He is the type of person people take to automatically. On the other hand, he pursues his work with dedication and has an encyclopedic recall of facts.

His well-organized closing argument would put his diligence on display.

"Mr. Becker, Mr. Miller and members of the jury, I want to thank the court and Bryan Sheppard for allowing me to be here to represent him. And he may be a 'yahoo' to Dan Miller but he is a human being entitled to the protection of the law that he is cloaked with here today," O'Connor began, taking a broad swipe at Miller for his demeaning reference to the defendants during his closing argument.

He also wanted the jurors to cloak Bryan with the presumption of innocence. "Looking at the evidence through the eyes of the presumption of innocence, I believe that evidence will take on newer meaning as jurors in this case. Because the government presumed him guilty, you presume him innocent."

O'Connor wanted to know why Frederick Martindale was not the one on trial. He confessed to the crime twice and named an accomplice. The police had witnesses who said they saw him at the construction site. Where are those witnesses? Martindale told the police about using cardboard to start the fire under the trailer, about a Caterpillar, about a Bobcat, about a platform, and about having to cross a creek to get to the site. The police did not mention any of these five facts to him. "Five things—five things that Bryan Sheppard never told anyone—five things undisputed at that scene."

Then O'Connor went through the witnesses against Bryan.

• Glen Shepard tells the ATF Bryan never made any admissions to him. Two months later, after the ATF threatened him with a gun charge, he's at the grand jury saying Bryan confessed. Instead of having to serve a sentence of twenty-five years as a persistent offender, he gets five years' probation "because he changed his story."

> What happened to the story he told them the first time? We are the government, the big search for the truth. When Glen Shepard was on the stand, did they ask, Mr. Shepard, you remember telling Agent True about Bryan Sheppard not making admissions, can you explain that to us? No. We had to ask it on cross-examination. They didn't want to ask him. They knew the answer. Bryan Sheppard never made any admission to Glen Shepard. But now, if he can get probation . . . a 17-time convicted felon, yeah, you are the kind of witness we would like to take people's freedom, come on, Bryan Sheppard, let's take yours with that kind of evidence.

• Steve Morales was the one who claimed before he ran his paper route the night of the explosions, he saw Bryan, Richard, and Frank around 1:30 a.m. outside the house of a friend of theirs in Marlborough. He claimed he was in the same van as his boss, Bruce Trammel, but Trammel testified for the defense he was never in the same van with Morales that night.

> He [Morales] had been on probation for a couple of months when he told this story [to the ATF]. As we have heard now he has some new forgery probation violation and it wouldn't hurt a guy like that to fudge his testimony a little bit. And he was willing to do so. What else did he say? He said he was interested in the reward money in the sworn affidavit, that was one of the things he mentioned.

In 1989, Morales was in jail with Bryan when Bryan made admissions to him, but Morales waits five years to tell anyone about that until he is in violation of his parole.

• Travis Small told the ATF in February 1995 he didn't know any Sheppards, he'd only heard of Skip. On August 5, 1996, the federal government indicted him and his wife on three new federal drug charges. "The indictment he is facing is for dealing in hundreds of kilos of methamphetamine and drugs," O'Connor said. "Now he remembers Bryan confessing to him."

The ATF didn't offer "one scintilla" of proof that Bryan ever knew Small. "This is the thing to verify. Does this man [Bryan] know Travis Small? Nothing. Oh, we can just take his word for it. He is a perjurer. He committed perjury. . . . That is the kind of evidence they brought with Travis Small. No corroboration whatsoever and another guy that was in jail."

• Kathy Marburger. When O'Connor interviewed her in 1989 she never told him anything about being on the phone and calling Karen Baird and overhearing Bryan and Richard being there. Detectives Fraise and Zinn interviewed Marburger and she never told either of them about overhearing any conversation. Agent True talked to Marburger in 1995, but True never called Detective Fraise even after Marburger told True she had told everything to Fraise years earlier. "Can you imagine he [True] now has a woman who is telling him we have a viable confession in the case and the guy never makes the call? Why? He knows the answer to the call."

• Karen Baird. At the time the Kansas City police came to see her she was worried about being arrested on drug charges. She pled guilty to a felony. "The government knows that Zinn and Fraise got no call from Marburger or Baird about any confessions."

• Wesley Romans was in jail with Bryan. He said Bryan went to the construction site but stayed in the car. Bryan never told Romans he was involved in the explosions.

• Brian Atterbury didn't come forward when he was in jail with Bryan in 1989, only after he caught a new charge [in 1995 for first-degree burglary and witness tampering]. Atterbury said Darren Elder was with him in jail when Bryan made admissions. "Where is Darren Elder to verify the story in their search for verification on Bryan Sheppard?"

• Kevin Smith is a convicted robber, thief, and burglar. He was in jail when the ATF talked to him. He knew of the $50,000 reward. He told you he was strung out on drugs in 1985–1989. He said Bryan told him they couldn't prove he's done the firefighters crime—not enough evidence. O'Connor said the government wanted people like Smith to come into the courtroom seven years later "and have this crystal-clear memory about what people said at the time. Life just doesn't work that way. It doesn't happen that way."

• Pam Barth, O'Connor said, heard 50 million rumors but heard no admissions from Bryan.

• Kimberly Finch had no firsthand information.

• Kimberly Archer lived with Richard's brother, Carl Brown. She said Bryan and Richard came to their apartment at 6:30 or 7 in the morning of the explosions. She detected no smell of smoke or gasoline. They were telling Richard's brother they drove by the construction site but she didn't know if they drove by before or after the explosions.

• Frank Gile was in jail in February 1995 for a probation violation, getting ready to serve a three-year sentence, when he called ATF and said he wanted to make a deal to get his sentence reduced by saying he heard Bryan and Richard make admissions about the firefighters case. He could remember no specifics about what Bryan told him. He said it had been too long, plus at the time he was using pot, meth, cocaine, and LSD.

• Carie Neighbors was with Shannon Newcomb at a party. Neighbors said admissions happened in the living room. Newcomb, however, testified she never went inside. Neighbors said Richard and Bryan told her they went to steal batteries, Newcomb said it was dynamite.

> Neither story is the same. Everyone is there present at the same supposed conversation but it was seven years ago. These people never came forward. And that is why it is so important for you to look at the evidence against Bryan Sheppard, 90 percent of these people never came forward because when they heard it they either didn't believe it or they felt it was drugs talking and or it didn't mean anything to them.

• Christine Mall told Agent True in 1995 that she was at a party at Bryan's house in 1989 and heard him make admissions. She changed her trial testimony to say the party was in 1992. Her boyfriend at the time, John McGovern, testified that he was with her at Bryan's house in 1992 but Bryan made no admissions.

For the rest of his closing argument, O'Connor sounded as though Clarence Darrow was inspiring him. He was disturbed—indignant actually—by how the government mounted its case on the perjured testimony of felons. He brought up how the government put on Shawn Furrell to say Bryan made admissions to him in the fall of 1989 at Bryan's house. "There is just one problem with all that. Bryan Sheppard was in jail. That makes two questions. Did they know he was in jail and they put on that evidence or how could they not know he was in jail and put on that evidence?" Another problem with Furrell was that when asked to identify Bryan in the courtroom he pointed to Richard Brown three times.

O'Connor said the same was the case with the government putting on witnesses such as Bridgette Dornhoffer and Travis Small. The government knew they were lying and put them on anyway. In a reference to Dornhoffer, he said:

> The government let that forger and that perjurer testify. Did they stop—stop everything, this lady has lied to this jury? They don't have to—they are the government. They don't have to, they can make the deals with Small, they can make the deals with [Glen] Shepard. They can do whatever the heck they want. And they have proved it in this case. They will put on perjurers. They will put on testimony after testimony of witnesses that don't appear credible, all in an effort to vindicate what happened in '89 because they had to turn him [Bryan Sheppard] loose and they don't want to face that prospect again— whatever it takes they'll do to take him down. And if that doesn't convince you, there isn't anything I can say that would.

There was a criminal trial a couple of years ago, he said, where the jury had been out two days when one of the jurors asked if there was anyone in the room who would want to be convicted, or anyone they cared about convicted, on the evidence the prosecution presented. Not one juror said he or she would. They immediately voted to acquit.

He was afraid if he did not talk about Becky Edwards's testimony that Becker would point that out during his final argument. "They will say maybe I failed to mention Becky Edwards. Becky Edwards said Bryan Sheppard was at that house party everyone attended a week before. Everyone was drinking, eight or 10 people. Bryan Sheppard never said anything. And that night they were talking about going and stealing copper. We know there is no copper."

In closing, he said the six firefighters who were killed suffered a terrible wrong, but it would be wrong to convict someone who wasn't responsible because everyone knows that two wrongs don't make a right.

> You can never make this right by convicting the wrong person; you just can't do it as much as you want to, as much as I would love to see closure on people in this case. You have that human emotion that is digging at you now. You have seen these pictures. It is a tough, tough, tough, tough decision but the law will help you. Turn to the law.

Turn to the [jury] instructions, follow the instructions and I think you will find the help you need.

As Assistant US Attorney Paul Becker listened to the closing arguments of the defense attorneys, he heard Pat Peters make the case that the guards were responsible by saying Debbie Riggs lied repeatedly to police about what went on at the site that night and that the guards were not away long enough for any outside intruders to wreak all the havoc that went down. She was heard on the dispatch tape to the fire department saying the explosives were on fire when it was impossible for her to see the ANFO trailers from where she was. Her claim that she warned the firefighters and Battalion Chief Germann about what was in the trailers was refuted by Germann when he testified earlier in the trial.

Becker heard Susan Hunt undermine the credibility of all the witnesses against Skip Sheppard, particularly Stephen Kilgore's claim that Skip hid stolen items from the site in an add-on room at his parents' house when there was no add-on room.

Will Bunch's closing argument attacked the government's investigation as being concocted not to find the actual perpetrators but to pin this crime on the five preselected to take the fall so the government could close the case. To make this possible, Agent True set up Darlene for a drug bust so he could compromise her with his "window of opportunity."

O'Connor's onslaught—saying the government knowingly put on perjurers—was the most devastating.

It might be an overstatement to say that Becker had waited all his life to give the rebuttal argument in the firefighters case, but then again it might not be. Without a doubt this was the biggest case of his sixteen-year career as a federal prosecutor and he was deeply invested in its outcome. He worked hand in hand with Agent True to get the grand jury indictments based in large part on the perjured testimony of Darlene's stepson Ronnie Edwards. He vindictively prosecuted Alan Bethard for not corroborating the lies Ronnie Edwards told about the defendants. And he worked to cut deals with a number of the felon witnesses True recruited to testify at the firefighters trial.

Becker caught a major break when the fair-minded Judge Bartlett, for health reasons, was replaced at the last minute by the prosecution-oriented Judge Stevens. It is unimaginable how different both the prosecution and defense presentations would have been if Judge Bartlett had presided.

Things had been going his way throughout the trial with Stevens upholding almost all of his objections. When Stevens prohibited the defense from recalling the Riggses and Dave True and not allowing the defense to put Eugene Schram of the US Labor Department on the stand, the defense was emasculated. Becker even succeeded in getting the judge to not allow the defense to put on mechanic Greg Pugh as a rebuttal witness to Debbie Riggs.

But now it was time to deal with the annoying assertions the defense lawyers made during their closing arguments. He was allotted an hour and he would use it all.

"You sit here and we all have all sat here today through the summations and you wonder have we watched the same trial?" he began. "Is it the same evidence that came from the witness stand I heard—that we all heard . . . I submit to you that you must look at the evidence as a whole of all the witnesses that came in and all of their testimony."

This was a rather jumbled way to say what he meant. It lacked crispness. Although his intent was to be disparaging to the defense, the jurors could have just as easily felt the rebuke.

During the closing arguments each of the defense attorneys went through the testimony of the witnesses against their clients and had discredited parts of their testimony, sometimes by comparing what they said in earlier police reports or at the grand jury to what they said as trial witnesses.

Becker did not like that one bit. "It is fundamentally unfair to put a sentence from one witness's statement when we have 80 witnesses who each have their own bound volume of transcript that must be viewed as a whole." When he enlarged the number of witnesses who testified against the defendants from the fifty-six who did to eighty, no defense lawyer objected.

Now to the rebuttal.

The attorney for Frank Sheppard, he said, "would have you believe that the five-month pregnant Debbie Riggs torched her own truck, planted bombs in the trailers, and then went up to watch it so she could be blown 40 feet away. There is no evidence whatsoever that [the] Riggses had anything to do with this." (Peters had made no claim about Debbie planting bombs in the trailer.)

He conceded that the guards didn't do such a great job of guarding this site, but there is no evidence that they caused these fires. "And it is not a fair inference to get up here and try and argue that."

Peters argued that Frank was home at Darlene's house that night.

Well, the question is, yeah, he was at home. When was he at home? If you look at the time the fires were reported, that is 3:40 in the morning. So is there anybody that says Frank Sheppard is at home at 3:40 in the morning? The only piece of evidence—and it wasn't a half-dozen witnesses—the only piece of evidence that the government introduced, or anybody introduced, is the Darlene Edwards tape, where Darlene, I submit is trying to cover up for Frank, says Frank was at home when she took the other guys up there to get gas and start these fires.

What about all those inconsistencies that Susan Hunt pointed out about the testimony of the various witnesses? Becker said the defendants themselves caused that problem. "We have to live with what the defendants said and they can't give a perfect confession every time and they didn't give a consistent confession every time, but what it came down to, of all they said, we went up there to steal, we set this fire and we got out of there."

Considering that Hunt had gone through a number of the government witnesses by name, Becker's retort did nothing to rehabilitate any of them.

Becker could not see why Will Bunch was saying the government set up Darlene for a drug bust so that the government could ensnare her and the other defendants. He said there was nothing in evidence to support the claim that the government "had preconceived notions who we were going to get and then we went out and got them."

Nor did the prosecutor agree that the guards would have seen Darlene drop off two men carrying a gas can. "On the audiotape she had not said anything about being seen or said precisely where she dropped the men off."

Osgood's closing argument was dispensed with in one paragraph. "Mr. Osgood at least admits that Richard Brown said all these things but then on the other hand he says, well, the witnesses are lying because they want a reward. Well, either they are lying and Richard Brown didn't say these things or Richard Brown did say these things. You can't have it both ways."

It would not be as easy to deflect what John O'Connor said in his closing argument. Becker tried to downplay Frederick Martindale's confession by saying Martindale spoke of setting fire to a mobile home. (What Martindale actually said was, "I went to the site. There was a trailer or mobile home, you know, I am not sure which one it was.")

Becker made a more salient point about Martindale's lack of importance by asking why the defense did not put on any of those witnesses who implicated Martindale to the police. After all, he said, "their names are not state secrets."

O'Connor's comments about the government intentionally putting on perjurers to testify was not something Becker could just blow off. How could he spin that Shawn Furrell testified that Bryan made admissions to him in Marlborough when Bryan was in jail in 1989 and that when asked to identify Bryan in the courtroom he pointed to Richard Brown? "That kid [Furrell] totally went in the tank on the witness stand. But, as Mr. O'Connor said, fine, throw him out. He picked out the wrong guy three times and he told the wrong year. Forget about Shawn Furrell. But that is not some major evidence, evidence of a plot by the government. It gives us some credibility."

It was not clear how putting a known perjurer on the witness stand gave the government "credibility," and Becker did not try to explain how it did. Becker did not even attempt to explain why the government put on Bridgette Dornhoffer after the government found out she forged a letter at a recent sentencing hearing. Becker did not try to counter O'Connor's damnation of the government using the testimony of Travis Small and Glen Shepard.

Setting those witnesses aside, Becker countered, "It is easier as we get older in life, we come to realize it is easier to tear down than it is to build up. We have attempted in five weeks of testimony to build up this case. And now for the last two hours, three hours, we have heard the defense attorneys try and tear it down. It is easy to tear down."

If the jurors were wondering why so many of these witnesses waited to come forward until *Unsolved Mysteries* was broadcast in early 1995, it was simply because they did not want to subject themselves to grueling cross-examination. "Put yourself in their shoes. Would any sane person want to come in here and take that witness stand and have five experienced, professional attorneys dig up your past, rake you through everything you have ever done wrong in your life, yell at you, have you relive times in your life that you probably aren't particularly proud of?"

What made these witnesses get over their reluctance to testify was because "there are six firemen dead here and the witnesses truly felt that responsibility. . . . And when the call went out, do you know anything more, these people felt an obligation to finally—finally get involved."

For the next twenty minutes Becker went through parts of the evidence against each defendant. During these summations of witness testimony,

Becker frequently could not restrain himself from asserting a bald-faced opinion or from distorting the facts. His opinion was that Lisa Landon was more credible than Naomi Sheppard. "Do you seriously believe Naomi Sheppard when she says Lisa Landon was never in my house?"

His explanation for why Chuck Elliott referred to Frank as "George" was because prisoners go by their first names. Elliott said Frank introduced himself as "George." Becker said a "big deal" was made about that on cross-examination but that Naomi repeatedly referred to her son as George when she testified. (This was not the case. When Susan Hunt asked her at the outset to name her children she gave the first names of all of them, but during the rest of her testimony only referred to Frank by that name.)

Ronald Williams testified that Frank asked him in 1991 to help him steal a Bobcat off a trailer parked up the street. Becker turns this into Frank trying to recruit him to steal a Bobcat from a construction site. Becker does not mention that Williams testified Frank went to the construction site the night of the explosions with only one other person, his brother-in-law Larry Baker. Nor does he remind the jurors that Williams was in the Clay County jail with Bryan in 1989 and Bryan made no admissions to him.

All Becker says about Stephen Kilgore, Glen Shepard, and Lorena Deardorff is that they said the same thing Williams did: Frank went to the site to steal and set a fire. Now, maybe Frank did not tell each of them the same story. "Frank doesn't confess the same way every time. But clearly he wants people to know, he can't keep it in, he did this, he is responsible. You just don't go telling more than a dozen people—and that is a conservative list—I committed this crime unless you did it."

In fact, according to these three witnesses, Frank told amazingly different stories. Kilgore said some Polish guard was allowing them to steal frequently from the site and one of the goals that night was to torch that guard's truck for the insurance money. Glen Shepard said Frank told him they got drunk, sobered up, and went to the site to steal tools, but ended up "burning the place." Deardorff said Frank told her he was at the site with some friends just "partying," then one guy went down to a trailer and came back with a stick of dynamite. Then another one of them decided to set a vehicle on fire just to see what would happen. They were sitting on a hill when the firefighters came and one of them said "let's see what happens if I throw this stick of dynamite down there."

Bear Williams, Darlene and Frank's next-door neighbor, was not about to be intimidated by Frank into saying he saw and talked to Frank after the first explosion, Becker said. (Bear testified he did not go out of his house until after the second explosion, but his wife, Carol, who testified right after him, said he went out after the first.)

Moving now to Skip, Becker concedes he is "not a big talker," but he does confess to the Barchers and to Kilgore. (Kilgore testified that only Frank confessed to him.)

Naomi Sheppard's testimony was something that really discomfited Becker and he could not leave it alone. "Do you think Kilgore, as Naomi Sheppard would have you believe, took a ride with the women out to the grave site or do you think he went out to drink beer and carouse around with Frank and Skip, like he testified?" (Kilgore said he drove Frank and Skip to mow a lawn in Marlborough.)

"And Kilgore, you know, he looks a little goofy and he acts a little goofy," Becker said, "but his diagram of the Sheppard household was pretty good. And it turns out that when [Skip's girlfriend] Harrigan testified maybe Kilgore wasn't so crazy after all, when he said there was stolen property in the garage, because Skip's girlfriend said Skip stole things and traded it for drugs and kept the stolen property in the garage. So maybe old crazy Kilgore wasn't so crazy after all." (Harrigan said Skip stole bikes, hubcaps, and lawn tools and she only assumed—she never saw any stolen items in the garage—that he stored them there.)

The government had taken testimony from Tracy Ownby regarding Doug Bayliff telling her not to mention anything she heard Skip say at Lee Ballinger's house "because these guys are dangerous." Christine Mall testified her boyfriend John McGovern told her basically the same thing when they left Bryan's house after hearing Bryan say he was going to blow up a truck owned by Darlene so Darlene could get the insurance money. (McGovern testified for the defense that Bryan made no comments of the sort and that he and Mall were only in Bryan's house for a couple of minutes. Darlene never owned a truck.)

Becker said these two witnesses were "important" because they didn't know each other and yet heard the same type of warning. He said such testimony "had the ring of truth."

The fact that Patty Smith waited until 1995, after she learned of the $50,000 reward, to talk to Agent True could be explained, Becker said, because she feared Skip, who had assaulted her more than once in 1990. Becker did not address her claim that Skip and Frank stole a box of dynamite from the construction site a couple of days before the explosions.

It would take a magician to rehabilitate Michael Whitelaw and John White, the two jailhouse snitches who testified against Skip. Becker said they have credibility because they don't know each other and got admissions from Skip at two different detention centers. In referring to White, Becker said, "Skip Sheppard gives him significant details about this case. Skip and another guy go to the site. They are joined by two other guys. Those two guys go down to set the fire. They go up to get the trailers. Skip Sheppard told John White what happened in this case." (White did give significant details about a host of items Skip and those with him stole from the site that night, but Becker knows nothing was stolen from the site at any time and does not mention those thefts. Becker also does not reference the deals the government—and he in particular—made with each of these jailhouse informants.[1])

Now to the case against Darlene. The audiotape the jury heard, where she said she simply drove two people to the QuikTrip to get gas and then dropped them off and went home, "can't be seen in isolation" because there is other evidence against her, Becker said. "We have the testimony of her daughter that they were all sitting around getting high, talking about ways to steal."

Would Becker have the nerve to mention Bridgette Dornhoffer, the jailhouse snitch whom O'Connor exposed as a "forger and a perjurer" on cross-examination? How about Rosemary Quiroz, who had the same attorney as Dornhoffer and had refused to testify when she was first scheduled to appear because she had not received a sentence reduction? Quiroz would not be mentioned.

"Let's talk about Dornhoffer for a minute," Becker said. "Dornhoffer made up her own letter of recommendation. The defense attorneys dug that up and sprung it on her and, boy, they got her. What did Dornhoffer testify to that wasn't on that tape? What did Dornhoffer testify to that Linda Mynhier didn't testify to?"

The only thing Dornhoffer said that reflected the contents of Darlene's audiotape was she drove to get gas. From then on nothing Dornhoffer testifies to matches anything on the audiotape. Dornhoffer concocted an elaborate admission from Darlene. She talked about various planning sessions Darlene and the others held at numerous locations "to avoid suspicious neighbors," that Darlene was at the site when the fire started, still there when the first explosion erupted, and still there when the police arrived and a crowd began to form and they didn't want to be seen in a hurry to leave. The cops, Dornhoffer said, had to move a car out of the way so Darlene and the others with her could drive away. Darlene told her they stole lots of expensive tools the night of the blasts, including an acetylene torch.

By now Becker must have thought the jurors were so confused they would not remember how divergent Mynhier's testimony was from Dorn-hoffer's. Mynhier had been in federal prison with Darlene in Illinois and she testified Darlene told her she was in prison for killing five firefighters. Mynhier said Darlene told her on the night before the explosions they stole dynamite from the site and she stored it in someone's oven. On the night of explosions, Darlene said she drove to the site in a van and one of the people with her was her stepson, another was someone with the initials J.D.

Becker led off his rebuttal of John O'Connor's closing statement by saying O'Connor "would have you believe that these people are all liars and the government got together to fix it all up so they could come in here and lie about Bryan Sheppard because the state court people were unsuccessful in getting him in '89. I submit there is no evidence to support that statement." By way of proof he said Glen Shepard, "who is a felon from here to tomorrow, but he is a friend of Frank Sheppard, went over and heard Bryan make admissions about this."

It was almost inexplicable how Becker could have chosen Glen Shepard as the exemplar of the case against Bryan. Of all the witnesses against the five defendants, he, as the jurors knew, had the most to gain by testifying. On cross-examination, Glen admitted without his cooperation in the firefighters case he would be in prison serving a twenty-five-year sentence instead of in jail serving a one-year sentence. It was also brought out on cross-examination that Agent True had coerced Glen into testifying by threatening to bring a federal gun charge against him.

As to the witnesses Carie Neighbors and Shannon Newcomb, Becker said O'Connor made "a big deal" about the discrepancies in their testimony:

> Carie Neighbors and Shannon Newcomb don't exactly in lockstep remember the same things. . . . But if they came in here and told you exactly what was said on the street and they each matched each, would any of you believe it but, do you think we would have heard about it from the defense attorneys, these women eight years later come in and tell us exactly the same thing. "Don't you think they got together and hatched this all up, cooked it up?" Use your common sense. We didn't plot to bring these people. We didn't plot to make their stories perfectly fit because they don't.

The important thing is Neighbors and Newcomb heard admissions, Becker said. So did Brian Atterbury, Wesley Romans, and Steve Morales while incarcerated at the Clay County jail with Bryan in 1989.

Kevin Smith heard admissions from Bryan at a park in the spring of 1990, a few months after he was released from jail on the firefighters charges. What is Smith's motive to lie, Becker wanted to know. "He got nothing. He didn't get out of jail one day sooner. He has got no pending charges. What is the reason for this guy to come in here and make all this up? Does he seriously think he is going to cash in on $50 grand? Come on." (In 1994 Smith was convicted of felony burglary and felony stealing. He was sentenced to two three-year sentences to run concurrently but as a first-time offender he was given parole. He soon violated his parole by committing felony robbery and was sentenced to five years to run concurrent with his previous two three-year sentences. Agent True came to see him at the Ozark Correction Center in March 1995 where he said Bryan Sheppard made admissions to him back in 1990 at Minor Park. Smith testified at the grand jury. When he testified at the firefighters trial he did so as a free man. Instead of serving his five-year sentence, he was released from prison in September 1996, only twenty-one months into his sixty-month sentence.)

Next, Becker said, he wanted to talk about Karen Baird and Kathy Marburger, although he never said anything about Marburger. He said O'Connor seemed to forget Bryan and Richard were at Baird's house a few hours after the explosions.

The easiest target for Becker was Richard Brown. It was a given, an admission by his own attorney, he was "a talker" with a tendency to embellish and brag. Richard, Becker said, made admissions to a series of people: his girlfriends, his friends, his neighbors, people he met at parties. One of his girlfriends, Kelly Corriston, said he was worried because someone might have seen him at the 7-Eleven getting gas and Richard told her he yelled at his grandmother to change her story about when he got home the night of the blasts.

Two other Marlborough women, Pam Barth and Fern Ayers, heard Richard make admissions.

On the day after the explosions, Richard made admissions to Monica Maggard and Pat Stewart at Swope Park, Becker said. (Maggard dropped Stewart off at the park and only heard Stewart say Richard talked about his role in the explosions.) "You saw what he looked like back then in those mug shots," Becker said. (Richard wore his hair below his shoulders.)

Although the evidence presented at the trial made it clear to the jurors there were no eyewitnesses or physical evidence linking any of these defendants to the crime and the government's case was based solely on the alleged admissions the defendants made, Becker had four "witnesses to the event" to discuss.

The first was Carolee Ann Smith, the next-door neighbor to Naomi Sheppard, who claimed she saw Skip and Frank and two others get out of a pickup shortly after the first explosion and walk around to the back of the house. "Ask yourself, would you come forward if you lived next door to the Sheppards? What possible motive does this woman have to lie? She is a nurse for 18 years, 16 years. She has lived there for 18 years."

The second was Margaret Weaver. She saw Richard and Bryan at the 7-Eleven the night of the explosions around midnight.

The third was Becky Edwards. "Becky saw all five defendants there, saying on cross-examination they were getting high, plotting ways to get money to buy drugs. On cross-examination there were gas cans, a lot of them at the house."

Last was Lonnie Joe Pugh. Becker said he was another example of people who would rather not get involved who finally came forward to say they saw Skip Sheppard that night get out of a pickup and go in (after the first explosion). The prosecutor thought Pugh's seeing Skip enter Larry Baker's house was proof Liza Harrigan simply did not realize because she slept so soundly that Skip left her in bed during the middle of the night.

Throughout his closing argument Becker had been offering raw opinion and shading facts to his best advantage. His final words to the jurors, instead of being the crescendo expected of a prosecutor in such a high-profile case, were more of the same:

> The witnesses come from all walks of life. They don't know each other. They come in at different times. They talk to different agents. Finally, they came forward when it would have been easier to do nothing.
>
> We have built up this evidence over the past six weeks that has now been torn down by the defendants. We have built up this evidence that proves beyond a reasonable doubt that these defendants are guilty of the crime charged in the indictment. I ask you, on behalf of the men of Pumper 41, Pumper 30, their families and the United States of America, to return a verdict of guilty in this case.
>
> Thank you.

The witnesses did not come from all walks of life. Only one had a college education (John White). None were professionals. The majority of the Marlborough witnesses did know each other. They didn't come forward when it would have been easier to do nothing. Almost all of the felon witnesses were looking for sentence reductions—and got them—just as most of Marlborough witnesses were looking for the reward money. Agent True had to threaten two of the government's felon witnesses, Travis Small and Glen Shepard, with upgraded charges to get them to testify.

It really did not make sense for Becker to say the prosecution has proven beyond a reasonable doubt these defendants are guilty after just saying the defense attorneys had torn down the evidence against them. As he liked to say, "You can't have it both ways."

As Becker left the podium, the defendants and their attorneys felt a sense of optimism. Becker clearly had not delivered a knockout blow. He addressed, but did not scuttle, the primary points the defense team made in their closing arguments. It was still incontrovertible Debbie Riggs, as Pat Peters had argued, had lied repeatedly to the police and was not above suspicion. The inconsistencies and wild exaggerations among the witnesses against Skip, that Susan Hunt detailed, still stood. Will Bunch's claim the ATF had busted Darlene for selling drugs to her stepson as a way of breaking open this unsolvable case was a reasonable observation. His definition of "reasonable doubt"—"If you don't know, that is reasonable doubt; if you don't know who to believe, that is reasonable doubt"—gave the jury an easy out. John O'Connor's evisceration of jailhouse snitches Glen Shepard, Travis Small, Brian Atterbury, Frank Gile, Kevin Smith, and Bridgette Dornhoffer showed how the government had put on perjurer after perjurer to make its case.

The case went to the jury on February 26, 1997, but because it was a Friday and late in the afternoon the jury would not begin deliberations until the following Monday, March 1. Before they were sent home, Judge Stevens admonished them not to discuss the case with anyone and to avoid all media reporting about the case

During the trial there had been a noticeable presence of firefighters in the courtroom and even outside the courthouse on Grand Avenue. Not often, but on occasion, fire engine sirens could be heard wailing during the trial, circling the courthouse. Members of the fallen firefighters' families attended the trial every day. Their grief infused the courtroom. The unmistakable impression, from both the firefighters and the family members, was they wanted closure; they wanted this long nightmare over with and those on trial convicted and brought to a harsh justice.

A memorial to the six firefighters killed at the construction site had been built just off 87th Street, off to the side of what had become in the intervening years the completed Bruce R. Watkins Memorial Drive. That weekend after the closing arguments, a well-publicized candlelight vigil was held at the 30-41 Memorial. A major motif of this vigil was for the jurors to find the strength to convict the Marlborough Five. All Kansas City television stations featured coverage of the vigil.

Shortly after the jury began deliberations on Monday, there was an initial straw poll: four voted for guilty, one not guilty, and seven were undecided.

While the jury continued deliberations, the jury foreperson informed the court it wanted to review the audio statement Darlene Edwards gave wherein she said she drove two people to the construction site. At one point, the foreperson sent a note to the judge asking what the jurors should make of the fact an earlier grand jury had indicted these defendants. The only other piece of evidence the jury requested was to see the trial transcript of Becky Edwards's testimony. The defense team interpreted these requests as bad news.

The next day, after thirteen hours of deliberations, the jury took its first official vote, and found all defendants guilty.

One of the jurors told the *Kansas City Star* the jury could not tell which defendant did what, but they felt with so many government witnesses testifying the defendants made admissions of involvement, they must be guilty. The jury foreperson said the jurors agreed with the government's theory the defendants "wouldn't have said they did it if they didn't do it." He said the jurors could not believe dozens of witnesses would all be untruthful, saying, "It just didn't make sense for them to lie." The heart of the prosecution's case—the tonnage of the witnesses—had born fruit.

The verdict stunned the defendants. To a person, each thought the government's case was transparently fabricated and the jurors would see through the smokescreen of lies their attorneys exposed on cross-examination and highlighted in their summations. Bryan Sheppard broke down and cried. His attorney, John O'Connor, wept next to him. Darlene sobbed and almost passed out. Her attorney, Will Bunch, gently patted her back.

For the families of the firefighters, justice was served. The closure they long awaited was at hand. A great relief swept the courtroom as they hugged and consoled each other. For Becker and Agent True it was a shining vindication.

The courtroom cleared.

In a conference room in the courthouse, the defense attorneys held their first meeting with their convicted clients. The issue before them was whether to waive their rights to be sentenced by the jury or allow Judge Stevens to dispense their punishment. Something the judge recently said in chambers—that he knew none of the defendants had any intention of killing firefighters or anyone else—gave the attorneys hope the judge, more so than this jury, would not impose the maximum sentence allowed: life without the possibility of parole. So the unanimous decision was made to waive jury sentencing.

The next day all the defense attorneys, the five convicted, and both prosecutors met in court with Judge Stevens to formalize the defendants' option of waiving jury sentencing. The jury was not present. There was no objection from Becker. One by one each defendant waived the right to sentencing by jury.

The jurors were called in to the courtroom and promptly thanked for their service and dismissed.

The judge set the sentencing hearing for July 2, 1997. He said the presentencing reports on each defendant would be available May 5. These reports would detail the criminal history of each defendant. In the federal system, there are six criminal history categories. The lower the level of criminal activity, the better for the defendant when it comes to the judge applying the mandatory sentencing guidelines for the offense. A convicted person with no previous criminal history would be rated at Level I. A convicted person with thirteen or more criminal history points would be at Level VI.

There are a number of factors that go into determining the criminal history points, but the basics are the points are calculated by adding three points for each prior sentence of imprisonment exceeding one year and one month; adding two points for each prior sentence of imprisonment of at least 60 days but not more than 13 months; adding one point for each prior sentence of less than 60 days.

When the presentencing report came in all the Marlborough Five were rated at Level V.

A week later, Judge Stevens denied the defense motion for a new trial. In the order he issued, he showed his remarkable command of language and succinctness:

> The Court recognizes that the evidence in this case was not strong. There were two fires set on November 29, 1988, only one of which was charged in this case. No physical evidence linked any specific defendant to the offense. Rather, the government's case was built

primarily around Darlene Edwards's confession and numerous admissions against interest, referred to throughout the trial as "confessions," made by other defendants to various testifying witnesses. Many of these confessions required redaction, and many were inconsistent in their explanation of various details. Further while witnesses testified that each defendant confessed to being part of a group present at the setting of the fire, it was not clear from the confessions that all the defendants knowingly participated in the actual setting of the fire which resulted in the explosion, as opposed to the allegedly initial fire of a security guard's truck, and the extent of various defendants' participation, except Darlene Edwards, was left largely undefined.

After the conclusion of the firefighters trial, the government split $56,000 among more than fifty persons who provided information in the case. The government did not disclose how many of those fifty persons testified at the trial, since that information is considered confidential. Nor did the government disclose how much of the $56,000 was paid to the dozens of convicts and convicted felons who testified.

Aerial view of the explosion scene taken hours after the firefighters were killed. (Courtesy of KCPD)

Aerial view of the explosion scene looking west toward 71 Highway at top, 87th Street to the left. Across the highway is the west side where the earth-moving equipment was stored and where Debbie Riggs's pickup was torched. (Courtesy of KCPD)

Battalion Chief Marion Germann's badly damaged vehicle at the scene. Fire department driver Dean Gentry parked this vehicle behind guard Robert Riggs's station wagon just before the blast that killed the firefighters. (Courtesy of KCPD)

Construction company trailers in median of 71 Highway where Debbie Riggs claimed to see two prowlers; the trailers were located about a quarter of a mile from where she sat on the west side in among the earth-moving equipment. (Courtesy of KCPD)

One of the two dynamite lockers not broken into or badly damaged by the explosions. (Courtesy of KCPD)

Outside view of Debbie Riggs's torched, red Toyota pickup. (Courtesy of KCPD)

The charred remains of the cab of Debbie Riggs's pickup. (Courtesy of KCPD)

Interior of Debbie Riggs's pickup showing suspicious combustible items found within. The vinyl purse shown contained her driver's license, checkbook, and $6.51 in currency, all intact. (Courtesy of KCPD)

Front interior of Robert Riggs's Nissan station wagon with black smudges on the steering wheel and the windshield laced with spiderwebs. (Courtesy of KCPD)

Interview of Debbie Riggs by Detective Victor Zinn at police headquarters a few hours after the explosions. (Courtesy of KCPD)

At Fire Department Station House 30, photos of fallen firefighters. *Top row from left*: Gerald C. Halloran, and Thomas M. Fry. *Bottom row from left*: Luther E. Hurd, Michael R. Oldham, James H. Kilventon, and Robert D. McKarnin. (Courtesy of Joe O'Connor)

From left to right: Earl Sheppard, father of Frank and Skip Sheppard; Larry Baker, Frank and Skip's brother-in-law; Frank; and Skip on Father's Day, 1987. (Courtesy of the Sheppard family)

Author with Richard Brown at the federal prison in Coleman, Florida, 2013.
(Courtesy of Richard Brown)

Reporter Mike McGraw
(Courtesy of KCPT)

Cyndy Short, attorney
for Bryan Sheppard
at his resentencing.
(Courtesy of Cyndy
Short)

The 30-41 Memorial at 87th Street, close to the site of the explosion that killed the firefighters, was dedicated in 1991. (Courtesy of Joe O'Connor)

Sentencing

Before the sentencing hearing began on July 2, 1997, the judge met in chambers with the defendants and counsel for both sides. John Osgood, on behalf of the other defense attorneys, had filed a motion with Judge Stevens challenging the "proximate cause" of the firefighters' deaths. In the motion he argued it was not the arson that caused the firefighters' deaths but their own gross negligence.

The grand jury's indictment charged the five defendants with one count of aiding and abetting an act of arson to property used in interstate commerce, thereby causing death to public safety officers performing official duties, in violation of 18 US Code, Section 844, 1 and I (2).

The jury found the defendants guilty of this exact charge.

So the proximate cause of the firefighters' deaths was the arson these five engaged in perpetrating.

Because Osgood had written the motion he felt no need to expound on it. Pat Peters wanted to expand the judge's consideration of the proximate cause issue one step by bringing up the matter of "foreseeability." He argued the foreseeability element breaks the chain of proximate cause—that the arson caused the deaths—because no one could have foreseen or predicted "for the first time in recorded history a fire would cause ANFO to explode."

Shortly after Peters made his argument, the sentencing hearing began in a packed courtroom.

The convicted defendants entered the courtroom handcuffed and shackled, wearing orange prison jumpsuits.

To begin, Judge Stevens asked if there were any objections to the presentencing reports filed by the government.

Presentencing reports are filed by federal probation officers and are generally written to maximize a convicted person's past criminal history, to ratchet up the criminal level as high as possible. In this case, the same probation officer, Chi P. King, wrote the reports for all five defendants and somehow managed to give Richard Brown the same high level as all the other defendants.

Osgood was the only defense attorney to object, saying he thought Richard Brown being designated a Level V offender was unreasonable considering he had no felony convictions and with the exception of one misdemeanor offense, all of the other seven offenses attributed to him happened in the years after the deaths of the firefighters and those, too, were all misdemeanors. Giving him a Level V, Osgood said:

> violates the spirit of the sentencing guidelines where an eight-year period, such as this, has gone by before sentence is imposed, and then to use misdemeanor conduct during the interim to enhance, bring it all the way up to a V. And obviously I also mention I believe it is unusual punishment under the Eighth Amendment . . . I don't know of any other circumstance where somebody eight years ago has been charged and the sentencing guidelines have been used during the course of the time between the offense and the date of imposition of the sentence to bring that person up to a Level V with misdemeanor violations.

Osgood had spent nineteen years as a federal prosecutor and knew all about criminal levels in federal sentencing.

> A criminal history V, as the Court knows, is reserved for the most serious of offenders. The guidelines were designed and basically they are designed to rely on felony convictions to weigh the criminal history based on prior conduct. I do not believe the criminal V in this case truly and fairly and adequately represents this defendant's prior criminal history. His prior criminal history is really more in the nature of petty driving offenses primarily.

A fair criminal level for Richard would be Level II based on his actual criminal history even taking into consideration the misdemeanors he rang up during the eight years before he was charged with this crime, Osgood said.

The fact was if Judge Stevens ruled the convicted had committed first-degree murder, the criminal level assigned the defendants had no bearing. He would be compelled by the mandatory sentencing guidelines to impose a sentence of life without parole. On that basis, Osgood asked the judge to delay ruling on his objection on the unfairness of Richard's criminal level until that had been determined.

The judge then invited Osgood to argue his motion that the firefighters were responsible for their own deaths due to gross negligence. Osgood had filed a twenty-seven-page brief to that effect with the court. Judge Stevens said he had read it three times, the last time concluding at 11 p.m. the night before.

It was a bold and daring move for Osgood to take up this type of argument. But the stakes were high and he felt attacking the "proximate cause" of the firefighters' deaths was his best opportunity at mitigation for the defendants. His goal was to provide the judge with some justification for not imposing a life without parole sentence. To go this route, Osgood had to set aside that his argument would ensure the enmity of the firefighters' families not only for him personally, but for all the defendants. In the course of his argument the hatred the families felt for the convicted would congeal.

Osgood began by discussing a benchmark case in the Eighth Circuit Court of Appeals, the appeals court with jurisdiction over the federal court in Kansas City, known as *United States v. Ryan*.[1] Osgood said *Ryan*, an arson case, focused on the issue of the meaning of proximate cause in the statute. "I submit Congress put the word 'proximate cause' in the statute because when they wrote the statute they were familiar with felony murder rules and knew there has got to be some relationship between an act and a result."

The statute Osgood was referencing prescribed a penalty of up to twenty years if the arson resulted in injury and a sentence of up to life without parole or death if a firefighter were killed.

Osgood said Ryan owned a failing business and was having financial problems. (Dale L. Ryan was the manager of the Ryan Fitness Center in West Burlington, Iowa.) The building he owned was located in a built-up portion of the city in a commercial area. Around 8 p.m. one evening (January 1, 1990) he set his building on fire. When the firefighters responded the fire was raging. Two firefighters went inside and subsequently dropped their hoses to go to another area of the building. The building soon collapsed, killing both firefighters.

After a lengthy trial, in which Ryan's attorney argued the proximate cause of the firefighters' deaths was their dropping of their hoses, the jury found his arson was the proximate cause and convicted him. He was sentenced to 328 months, just over twenty-seven years.

Osgood cited this case not only because Ryan did not get sentenced to life without parole but also because the details of it contrasted so sharply with the details of the Kansas City firefighters case. In *Ryan*, there was no question the firefighters were there doing their job. "They responded to the fire properly, the way they were supposed to, went in and fought the fire and were doing what they could to put it out."

In the construction site fire, Osgood said, the firefighters from two pumper companies responded properly, put out the fire in Debbie Riggs's pickup, and then made a series of mistakes that would prove fatal to them.

"So what you have here is an argument that when these firemen arrived at the scene, Miss Riggs told them repeatedly there was ammonium nitrate and fertilizer in the trailer that was on fire," Osgood said.

> If they would have followed the procedure in the [Hazmat] book, what they should have done was evacuate the area, quarter it off and let the fire burn itself out or explode. The book itself says if the fire has reached the cargo area, do not fight fire, evacuate. They all had Hazmat training. They had been to school. They had the book. The book was carried in each of the fire trucks. Pumper 41 and Pumper 30 each had a copy of this book in the truck itself. . . . We believe that had they done what they were supposed to do, under their rules, regulations and procedures, that we wouldn't be here today.

The issue of negligence as opposed to gross negligence was up next.

> Now I think the Court has to deal with the issue of whether or not their acts were simply negligent; in other words, just careless or did it rise to a level above that. And I will concede at this point to the Court if it was simple negligence, I don't think I have an argument. I think the conduct might have risen to the level of reckless conduct such as to break the causal chain [of proximate cause].

Judge Stevens invited Osgood to hypothesize between a situation that was negligent and one that was grossly negligent. Osgood was ready for this one. He told the judge to picture his house on fire. In scenario A he dies in the fire because the fire truck has a flat tire on the way and doesn't get to him fast enough. One of the firefighters who was assigned to check the air pressure on the tires each week neglected to check them. That would be simple negligence. In scenario B he dies in his house as well, but this time it is because the firefighter driving the truck was drunk and has a wreck on the way. That would be reckless negligence.

To get to the nub of his argument about the gross negligence of the two pumper captains, Osgood said, "I submit when a trained official who has duties and responsibilities to the public, who has had training, who has a manual on board his unit telling him how to respond to that fire—"

> Judge: Let me get this straight, too. You mention that in your brief. Is it your suggestion that with that fire raging out there and equipment arriving by the minute and people there in great numbers, that proper conduct would have been for them to have stopped and turned on their reading lights and pull out the book and read the manual?
>
> Osgood: Actually, yes, Your Honor, because the manual was designed for precisely that. It has very large letters.
>
> Judge: Where does it say "Read during fire" in that thing?
>
> Osgood: You open the first page and it says ammonium nitrate and fertilizer is guide 46. You flip to guide 46 and it tells you right there. You can do it this quickly. Do not fight the fire, evacuate the scene. That is what it is designed for, made with large letters with guides for these kinds of emergency situations. You could read almost every guide in here on the way to the fire if you knew that's what you had. They were told they had explosives, no notwithstanding chuckles by some of the audience. That is exactly what this book is for. This book has probably saved firemen's lives. That is what it was designed for.

Encapsulating his argument, Osgood said the issue was whether the firefighters' improper response to dealing with the ANFO fire was of sufficient degree to make the proximate cause of their deaths their own fault.

The issue he was raising, he said, was not only a sentencing guideline issue, but a Fifth Amendment due-process issue under the US Constitution. "In other words, how far can we take criminal statute in terms of imposing criminal responsibility on somebody for acts that are beyond their control or are not contemplated or are not foreseeable?"

It was now Becker's turn to respond. He correctly stated only four of the deceased firefighters completed Hazmat training.

As a rebuttal witness, Becker called firefighter Mike Torrey. (He testified for the government at the firefighters trial.) As a firefighter at a nearby pumper station, Torrey had been called to the 71 Highway construction site about six times prior to the explosions, usually to put out brush fires or to douse an abandoned car that had been set on fire. Every time he went there, the dispatcher had warned his crew there were explosives at the site and to use caution. He knew Pumpers 30 and 41 had also made runs to the construction site and had been given the same advisory about caution.

Torrey, who had been a firefighter for twelve years, said he knew there were explosives contained in bunkers located toward the back of the site, so he knew to stay away from those. At no time was he ever told what was in the two trailers on the east side of the site.

Osgood asked him what the policy of the Kansas City Fire Department was if a trailer with explosives in it was burning. Torrey said, regardless of policy, he would stay away from such a trailer. He would evacuate.

So far so good for the point Osgood was trying to make, but then Pat Peters took over the cross-examination and asked Torrey if he thought Debbie Riggs warned the firefighters about explosives in the burning trailer.

Peters was doing his best to lead Torrey into saying these experienced firefighters would not have proceeded to the east side if they knew the burning trailer contained ANFO.

Peters's undermining Osgood's main case caused the judge to say, "the trouble I have with that is if we accept your proposition, then they couldn't have known that there was explosives there and, therefore, there was no intervening or, to use your word, supervening cause to block the conduct of your client and others as the cause of the deaths."

John O'Connor asked for a minute to confer with Peters. After this short conference, Peters had no more questions.

Becker then launched into a rebuttal of Osgood's argument about the proximate cause of the firefighters' deaths being their own gross negligence. "The *Ryan* case and other cases relating to criminal conduct by the defendants hold that the analysis of intervening cause does not apply," he said. "We will not excuse criminal conduct because of an intervening cause."

In the *Ryan* case, he said, the defendant used the foreseeability argument, claiming the firefighters panicked when they saw a wall of fire, dropped their hoses and then were killed by smoke inhalation. The jury did not buy it and neither did the Eighth Circuit Court of Appeals.

Becker said when Congress wrote the statue about arson resulting in death being punishable by up to life without parole or death, there was no intent to allow a defendant to use a proximate cause argument "to frustrate the purpose of the statute with artificial restrictions." Becker was making a legal argument based on the statute.

Bottom line: had these defendants not started an arson fire, there would have been no explosion to kill the firefighters.

Becker then asked the judge to make the following three findings: (a) the government has proven the defendants' conduct in setting the fire was a proximate cause of the firefighters' deaths; (b) the men killed were employed by the City of Kansas City as firefighters, and (c) they were performing their duties as firefighters at the time of their deaths.

Before making his ruling on those findings, the judge asked if any of the defense attorneys wanted to further address the proximate cause issue.

Osgood stepped forward. He said the court should make a finding whether or not it believes the firefighters were warned there was ANFO in the burning trailer and whether or not their actions in responding to that fire—instead of evacuating and cordoning off the area—were, in fact, reckless conduct. He said he wanted the judge to make a factual finding on those issues rather than a legal finding based on the arson statute.

> I submit to the Court to present this properly to the Eighth Circuit, the Eighth Circuit is entitled to know the Court's reasoning and rationale. And I believe that is embodied in Rule 32 of the Sentencing Guidelines, that the Court is required to make a factual finding, not a legal finding. What Mr. Becker is asking you to do is make a legal finding. I would ask you to articulate on the record what your factual finding is with respect to this negligence issue: a.) Were they told; and b.) What is the result of that knowledge in conjunction with what they knew and their training. And then the ultimate request, whether or not it makes a difference under the statute.

There would be no forcing Judge Stevens to explain his rationale. "I am not entirely sure that all of that is necessary from this Court in this proceeding, Mr. Osgood," the judge responded.

Pat Peters wanted to augment Osgood's proximate cause issue by going into the foreseeability aspect. He reminded the judge there was testimony at trial that fire had never caused ANFO to explode. And because it had never happened before it was an unforeseeable result.

"It has now," the judge said.

Following the lunch recess, the sentencing hearing resumed in open court. The next order of business should have been for the judge to hear opposing arguments on whether the deaths of the firefighters as a result of arson should be designated as first-degree or second-degree murder.

The arson statute allowed for either designation depending on various factors. One factor that could lead to the second-degree designation and avoid the life without parole sentence was if the perpetrator had no intent to kill anyone.

Instead of asking for argument on the first-degree/second-degree murder designation, Judge Stevens began the afternoon session by announcing his findings.

His findings were: the firefighters were not negligent; arson was the proximate cause of their deaths; the six killed were employed by the City of Kansas City as firefighters; they were performing their duties as firefighters at the time of their deaths.

"Now, having announced those conclusions, I will conclude, consistent with the findings, and recommendation of the probation office and the presentence investigation report, that the offense level with which we are dealing here is a Level 43," the judge said.

Judge Stevens, all on his own, without the benefit of argument by opposing counsel, had determined the offense level at 43, i.e., he deemed the deaths of the firefighters by arson as first-degree murder. For a Level 43 designation, the Sentencing Guidelines mandated a sentence of life without parole.

He then disingenuously invited the opposing sides to make any presentation regarding sentencing. One of the defense attorneys should have objected strenuously to this railroading of the defendants to a life without parole sentence before their arguments for a lesser sentence had been presented, but none did.

Becker jumped in at this point to say the Federal Rules of Criminal Procedure require the court to inquire if any immediate family members of the deceased firefighters wished to make a statement.

This was an awkward moment for Judge Stevens. His pell-mell rushing forward demeanor had caught up with him. The primary purpose of these statements was to give immediate family members an opportunity to speak about how the death of their loved one had so negatively affected their lives. Impact statements are also often used by family members to petition the judge to mete out the strongest punishment possible to the convicted, something Stevens had already announced.

In alphabetical order, the judge asked the immediate family members if they wished to address the court. The first four, the families of Thomas Fry, Gerald Halloran, Eugene Hurd, and James Kilventon, declined.

Debbie McKarnin, the widow of firefighter Robert McKarnin, stepped forward to the witness box and was sworn in. After thanking the court for the opportunity and saying she knew three of the deceased firefighters personally, she said:

When Bob and I were first married I used to be afraid for him going to fires and things like that. And I would ask him about that. And he would caution me and he would say, "Debbie, I am cautious when I go into fires. I think things through. We work together." And I wanted the Court to know they were not just out there to put out fires and make a big blaze. They were there because they thought they could do something good for the community.

She said with over a hundred of years of experience among the six firefighters, they would not have acted foolishly.

Her husband's mother died six months after he was killed and his father died two years to the day afterward.

Mrs. McKarnin thanked the judge for his understanding of the law and his wisdom and judgment and then said she wanted to talk about the penalties these defendants deserve. "I think that people should be held responsible for their actions and should be remorseful of those actions because they were desperate. Those were tragic, tragic things that happened. And to be laughed at and be thought of in a group of people as maybe a cool figure or something neat, you accomplished some great thing in your life, is terrible."

Send out a message to the community, she exhorted the judge, saying that means "a harsh, harsh penalty." The convicted should spend their days "working hard, breaking up rock, not watching color TV. And I guess that sounds harsh but I feel like the action was one that demands that."

The widow of firefighter Michael Oldham, Karen Oldham Cable, came forward and was sworn in. She had labored hard over the remarks she intended to address to the court. Over the intervening years, she had been the most active advocate of all the firefighters' relatives of bringing to justice the people, whoever they might be, who were responsible for killing the firefighters. She had kept in close contact with law enforcement as this seemingly unsolvable case finally led to the indictment of the Marlborough Five. She had also lobbied the Kansas City Council, the Missouri Legislature, and a subcommittee of the US Senate for recognition of this tragedy. She was a warrior in this cause, so much so that some of the members of the other firefighters' families found her too strident and shrill.

Without any preliminaries she began:

In the early hours of November 29, 1988 thieves came. Their purpose was to steal. But they took more than they had planned to—something more precious than earthly things. They took the lives of six firefighters. One of those brave men was my husband Mike Oldham. Mike was 32 years old and the father of our two children, Kyle who was 6 years old, and Jacqueline who was 3½. We were a young family just starting our lives and planning for the future. . . .

Until this trial I personally didn't know who was to blame or how to explain to my children why their dad was taken away. We have fought for quite a long time for a variety of things but now we come to fight for justice to be served, our most important fight yet. Even though there is no punishment great enough here on earth for those individuals, we ask the strictest punishment possible be imposed. The men that were killed were worth so much. They had rich lives. It was not due to money, it was because of the love they gave and shared with us. We ask the sentence for all five found guilty be life without parole for taking the lives of our loved ones Gerald, Eugene, Tom, Jim, Bob, and Mike.

Thank you.

When the judge asked if there were any other family members who wished to address the court, Leo Halloran, the younger brother of Captain Gerald Halloran, declared he would. He did not come in vengeance; he came to make one thing perfectly clear: his brother and the other five firefighters who lost their lives that night did nothing negligent.

His brother Gerald, he said, was cautious about everything—he drove cautiously, he worked cautiously, he had an analytical mind and knew danger when he saw it. Gerald was well versed in chemicals and had a very well-rounded knowledge of explosives.

It had been pure agony for Leo Halloran to sit in the courtroom and listen to the argument about proximate cause Osgood fashioned that was essentially based on the premise the firefighters killed themselves through their own gross recklessness:

I have heard Mr. Osgood's testimony today. Apparently he did some research for various expert witnesses. However, my opinion and common sense tell me the expert witnesses were the six firefighters who were killed. There is no way, absolutely none, that they would allow themselves, my brother and the other five veterans, to go near a trailer containing explosives.

Debbie McKarnin mentioned a hundred years. Actually doing some quick calculation, about 128 years. My brother had 38 years' experience. The two captains, Jim Kilventon and Gerald Halloran, had a combined experience of 66 years. And I think the least amount of time on the fire department of the other firefighters was I believe Eugene Hurd who had about nine or 10 years. If they had any knowledge, absolutely any inkling there was a blasting agent, you can call it fertilizer, ammonium nitrate, burning in that trailer, they wouldn't even have gone in there. They would have evacuated the area just like Chief German did after the first explosion.

These are the expert witnesses. Nobody else was there. These were the expert witnesses, the six firefighters, which I would conclude, and anyone with common sense would conclude, they were not negligent. They knew where the dynamite and the blasting caps were. They had made runs up there before. There was no danger. They were 250, 300 feet away. They were in heavy steel bunkers. They were not touched.

To bring in negligence at this point in time on these six dead men is like dancing on their graves. I think it is a desecration. I am offended and I believe our families are offended.

We are insulted by it. . . .

So your sentencing, that is up to the judge. I am not here to try to bring out revenge. I am just stating a fact. Again, the men were not negligent.

Thank you.

Leo Halloran's adamancy about the blameless conduct of the firefighters prompted Judge Stevens to reiterate what he announced previously, "I want to make sure that the record is clear. And it should be clearly implied from, if the Court did not expressly say, on the basis of the evidence here and the applicable law, any doctrine or rule of intervening cause does not apply to this situation and the deaths of these men were proximately caused by the convicted criminal conduct of these defendants."

Judge Stevens next wanted to determine if any of the convicted wanted to address the court, once again jumping the gun in his imitable rush forward.

"Excuse me," Osgood said. "You announced [a Level] 43 but did you mean to announce that as a starting point? We have had the argument [about proximate cause]. Now we move next to the guidelines and the drafter's comments [of the Sentencing Guidelines], whether or not it is appropriate to move from first to second degree. Are you prepared at this point to discuss that?"

Judge: If that is appropriate for discussion, I will give you that opportunity.
Osgood: I would like to.
Judge: Feel free.

Osgood said one of the things that prompted the defense to waive jury sentencing was the comment Judge Stevens made on the record in chambers that he did not believe these defendants intended to kill these firefighters when they set the arson fire. Osgood said if the judge "believed the government's case 100 percent, the convicted went to the construction site to engage in petty thievery; they did not set the fire with the idea of luring the firefighters there and blowing them up or killing them."

"They did not set a building on fire they thought was an occupied dwelling with someone in it to burn them to death," Osgood continued. "They merely set a fire. And had it been put out it would have been an act of vandalism, petty thievery, and arson."

The sentencing guidelines, Osgood said, state if the defendant did not cause the death intentionally or negligently, a downward departure from Level 43 "may be warranted." He said the extent of the departure should be based upon the defendant's state of mind, e.g., recklessness or negligence, the degree of risk inherent in the conduct, and the nature of the underlying offense conduct. He said the guidelines did not envision a departure below second-degree murder.

Osgood asked the judge to consider departing downward to a Level 33. Depending upon how the presentencing report rated the criminal level of the defendants, the term of punishment would amount to twenty-five to thirty years. "I would remind the Court that this is precisely what the judge did in the *Ryan* case. And *Ryan* was a more egregious set of facts than these, Your Honor."

Ryan's motive that led to the deaths of two firefighters, Osgood said, was profit and greed, plus he burned his building in the middle of town, knowing full well the firefighters would be responding and fighting the fire. Nonetheless, the judge departed downward to a Level 38 in sentencing Ryan. "In other words he split the difference between [Level] 43 and [Level] 33."

Stevens liked very much to show off his vocabulary, dropping in words like "phobic," "discommode," and "allocution" from time to time. Whether he did this out of vanity or as a subtle reminder he had a B.A. degree from Yale, only he knew. But this time he outdid himself: "You are distinguishing Ryan's greed and profit motive, is it your view this was some sort of eleemosynary [charitable] activity these people were engaged in?"

If Osgood made a botch of his closing argument at the trial, he was about to redeem himself with this impassioned, articulate pleading:

> Certainly not. I am speaking in terms of he [Richard Brown] has been convicted of this. I am not talking about guilt or innocence now. Based on the jury's finding, the best we have got is a bunch of thievery where they wanted to break into a trailer and see what was in it or steal something out of the sheds or the Caterpillars or something. That is not, in my mind, anywhere near as serious as a businessman with a balance sheet who is in debt, who sets his building on fire, knowing full well exactly what the consequences are going to be.
>
> Now, judge, in that case—and the Eighth Circuit accepted sentencing in that case at a level 38 as being appropriate. Under the drafter's notes to the [sentencing] guidelines that judge apparently felt that since he did not intend to kill those two firemen, it was appropriate to go below first-degree murder. First-degree murder here is the same sentence that the Court handed out in the murder-for-hire case in this court recently. It is the same sentence you should hand out in a kidnapping where the child is killed. These people did some terrible things and we have some tragic results but they are not cold, calculated, premeditated murderers, Your Honor. A Level 43 is for the cold, calculated, premeditated murderer. If you treat these in the same way you treat that, you in effect demean the total meaning of Level 43 and undercut, in my mind, its true message. We have five people here, again believing the jury verdict which we must do at this point, who did something far less serious than that. I think it is appropriate in light of all the facts and circumstances and in light of *Ryan* you go to level 33.

John Osgood had made as strong a case for second-degree murder as it was possible to fashion. The points Osgood presented made it imminently possible for Judge Stevens to back down and impose a downward departure. The fact the Eighth Circuit had upheld Ryan's downward departure gave Stevens the cover he needed.

The judge asked if any other defense counsel "had similar comments" to offer. None did, Osgood had made the case.

Becker said he would reserve his comments about whether these defendants deserve any mercy for a few moments, but first he wanted to address the Sentencing Guidelines. He said the guidelines' provision talks about the death being caused intentionally and knowingly. "When you speak of that in terms of felony murder, you have to put that in a context of our history of common law and holding persons responsible under the Doctrine of Felony Murder. You have to look at their conduct, the underlying felonious conduct, and, in this case, arson."

As to Ryan getting a downward departure, Becker thought it inappropriate.

Now back to the question of mercy. "It is a situation where they [the convicted] knowingly and intentionally set a fire and death resulted. Therefore, I believe a downward departure by the court would be inappropriate," Becker said.

That was all Stevens needed to hear. "I will abide by my previous announcement of the finding of a Level 43 and will not depart from that level. I do not believe that the authorities cited by Mr. Osgood as supplied by him are aptly applied nor do they apply in this situation."

It was now official: the Marlborough Five had been sentenced to life without parole. Each would soon be offered an opportunity to address the court, but before that would happen Becker wanted one more shot to put his animus for the convicted on the record.

"The defendants, personally, have no redeeming qualities. None of them has ever been gainfully employed but for a few weeks here and there," Becker said, asserting a blatant untruth for all of them except Frank. "None of these defendants has ever produced a positive thing for this society. When you compare that to the men who gave their lives on behalf of this community, as the court has heard from these family members, they have each left behind spouses, children, mothers and fathers."

The impact on the explosions was felt throughout the city, particularly on the south side where people were jolted out of bed, Becker said. The explosions caused millions of dollars of damage. But more importantly was the damage done to the firefighter community. "They will never again forget that six of their colleagues went to work that day and never went home to their families. On behalf of the fire department, on behalf of the families of these victims, on behalf of the United States, I ask you to sentence these defendants to life without parole."

It was time now at long last and for the first time in this drawn-out case to hear from the Marlborough Five. Frank Sheppard went first:

Yes, Your Honor, I do have some things I would like to say. Please excuse me. These are sensitive in nature but I know no way around this. This is hard for me to say, not because I am speaking in front of people, I am not used to this. It is because I am trying hard to hold inside me this downright hate and contempt I have for what is going on here today.

I guess I can understand your fears this crime would go unpunished and nobody would have to go away to prison, but, more importantly, this would go unsolved. Again, people, it is also very hard for me to feel sorry for you people, the families, you fellow firefighters, old friends. By this I mean this prosecution of the five of us by this court, the U.S. Attorney's Office, and all involved are wrong to say to you people, finally we got these killers. You all sat in this courtroom for six long weeks. You witnessed all of this. And if you were so full of hate and pain that you actually believed their pathetic evidence, then I guess this pathetic government is using you all just as badly as they are using us.

Leo Halloran, Cecilia Kilventon, Debbie McKarnin, Karen Oldham, Jewell Hurd, and Marietta Fugate, mothers and wives, I maintained my innocence from the very beginning of this tragedy but I have never had the opportunity to tell you personally, regardless of what the government maintains about how your husbands and sons died. Ladies, if I don't appear to be a God-fearing man, I guess that is between me and God. But God as my witness I had nothing to do with this—nothing.

This has been a long ordeal for all of us, you and us. It might be over for a while but sadly it is still unsolved. It is not solved.

That is all I have, Your Honor.

Skip Sheppard went next: "Just that my brother said it all and I would just like to maintain I am innocent of this crime. I will keep by that until I die."

Attorney Will Bunch spoke before Darlene. "I respect the judgment of this court, as you know, and so I can only say as an officer of this court, something I have never said before in sentencing, I do not believe my client is guilty. Thank you."

Darlene said she was very sorry loved ones had been lost, and "innocent people died but history is repeating itself because I am missing my family. I do hope someday this is truly solved, the guilty people do something, come forward. And I hope it is not too late. God bless you all."

In his statement, Bryan Sheppard said, "I would just like to say I am innocent of this crime. That is all I have to say."

The judge called next on John Osgood. He began by calling the judge's attention to the fact he made the Level 43 finding prior to hearing the arguments of defense counsel for a lesser sentence.

> Therefore, under the law it would be appropriate and I would be remiss in my duties if I didn't ask for reconsideration of those findings in light of what you have heard and what you have seen and particularly in light of what Frank Sheppard stood up here and said. I was, quite frankly, moved by what Frank Sheppard said. I think he has got a better handle on it than any of the lawyers in this courtroom.

Osgood said he did not understand how this court could ignore the *Ryan* sentencing.

Even though Stevens had made it abundantly clear he would not move off the Level 43 designation, Osgood, the bulldog, soldiered on, taking an altogether new tack in a desperate, last-ditch effort to change the judge's mind:

> The criminal justice system ought to provide some hope for everyone. There ought to be some light at the end of the tunnel for everyone. There are a variety of reasons for that. These defendants ought to be able to now move on to another segment of their lives . . . everybody ought to have some hope. The hope here would be you give a term of years at least of some fashion so at the end of that term of years there is some hope for release. Right now under these Sentencing Guidelines, if you impose a Level 43 sentence, there is no hope. We are treating these people the same way as if they set about in a cold, calculated, premeditated fashion to murder somebody.
> . . . And my client has told me from Day One he didn't do this . . . he took a polygraph examination and passed that polygraph examination. And I have come to know him pretty well and I don't believe he did this.

In his many years as a federal prosecutor, Osgood said he had never been involved in a criminal case with such flimsy evidence. He said he thought the verdict was essentially a backlash from O. J. Simpson walking free in October 1995.

If the judge truly meant what he said in chambers about knowing there was no intent by these defendants to kill anyone then he has to

follow that guideline or you should follow that guideline, the recommendation of the Sentencing Commission, and come down off of [Level] 43. Even if it is only a point, two points, come down and give a term of years so I can tell my client at least you are going to get out when you are 60 years old. Right now it is pretty blue, Your Honor. Please reconsider. Please reconsider.

Stevens made no response. He called on Richard Brown.

I want to thank my lawyer for representing me. He has done his best. I appreciate him trying to get these years knocked off, but I don't believe anybody that has done such a crime to hurt six whole families deserved to even go to prison. But at the same time other people commit a crime, I don't believe five innocent people, one is myself, should be taken from people they love and it hurts.

I sat in this courtroom all through the trial. I can't sleep at night. I am telling my mother, I am telling my wife, I am scared because the government drug me in here. Yes, I have done a lot over the years. I have drove on a suspended license and I have done a dozen things like that. I do not steal. I have not run around and robbed people. I do not do nothing of the sort. I do have a heart and I do have feeling. . . .

You know, you all sit over there and look at us which I can't blame you. I can't blame you firemen for getting up there. I respect you. But these individuals that convicted us, knowing that we are innocent, Dave True, you people know who they are. The Lord knows who they are. The Lord knows we are innocent. And I hope you do find the people who did do this because I will stand right behind you the whole way. Amen.

Before pronouncing sentence, Judge Stevens had an allocution of his own. He said it was undoubtedly the most difficult case he had ever had anything to do with as an attorney or as a judge. The case came to him on the eve of the opening of the trial due to the sickness of Judge Bartlett.

He said he found, having lived in Kansas City all of his life, it was quite difficult for him as a judge to not let the deep community feeling about this case affect "the level of fairness that these defendants and the government were afforded in the trial."

What Osgood said about him not believing these defendants had any intention of killing anyone he said was the truth. On the other hand, "I do believe that they conducted themselves in such a way and committed such act as to clearly and irretrievably make them fall under the statute which prohibited that conduct and set the sentence as penalty for it."

That was the reason, he said, why he announced the sentencing level and was now about to pronounce the sentence.

Each defendant, Stevens intoned, is sentenced, pursuant to the Sentencing Reform Act of 1984, to commitment to the custody of the Bureau of Prisons, "to be imprisoned for a term of his or her natural life."

In addition, as part of their sentence, the judge ordered each defendant to pay restitution of $536,000 to the Kansas City Fire Department, paid in installments to commence thirty days after the date of this judgment until paid in full.

All of the defendants were indigents. Any meager amount of money their families could place in their prison accounts would thus be subject to partial attachment. Osgood asked the judge to suspend execution of the restitution until their appeal of their convictions to the Eighth Circuit Court of Appeals had been ruled upon. (Each of the defendants was entitled to an automatic appeal and it was expected that would take about a year to resolve.)

Osgood said the defendants had the rest of their lives to make restitution, but right now they all have obligations and "what little bit of money they can have in their accounts would ease the burden on their families."

It was a reasonable, humane request, but Becker was having no part of it. "Most respectfully, in particular to Mr. Osgood's client, he has never met his obligation to his family and provided for them while he was on the street. So at this point to say he wants his funds available to him so he can provide to his family is somewhat disingenuous. I would ask the court to continue the sentence it just announced."

"I am not going to announce any alteration of that sentence at this time," the judge said.

PART II

THE SEARCH FOR JUSTICE

Appeals

Tom Jackman, the reporter who covered the firefighters trial for the *Kansas City Star*, separately interviewed each of the Marlborough Five at a federal holding facility in Leavenworth, Kansas, while they were awaiting sentencing. The day after they were sentenced, the newspaper ran his article under the headline, "Despite Conviction, Five Insist: 'We Didn't Set Blast.'"[1]

In the article each of them said they never made admissions about involvement in the firefighters case.

"They couldn't find no one else to pin the case on," Skip told him. "They just picked some bad lemons out of the neighborhood." He said the only time he ever said anything about the firefighter case was to say, "I'm glad I don't know anybody that had anything to do with this."

Was he sorry he did not testify at trial, Jackman asked Frank? "I regret it 110 percent. I feel that these people felt if the federal government indicted us, we must be guilty. Then, on my part, not to relieve these jurors of that shadow of a doubt against me as to why I'm not testifying. 'If he's not testifying, he must be guilty, he must be hiding something.'"

Richard Brown said it made no sense for Darlene to say he and Bryan walked back two miles from near the construction site to her house to ask her to take them to get gas when there was a QuikTrip visible from the construction site, "but they [the jurors] believed it." He also couldn't understand how burning the guard's pickup could possibly be viewed as a diversion "when they [the guards] had done left."

"I never in my life said anything of any sort that I had anything to do with this or anything," Richard said. "No part. The only thing I've ever said is that I was at home in bed."

Three months after the Marlborough Five were convicted, the *New Times*, an alternative weekly newspaper I owned and edited, published a two-part series on the firefighters case written by J. J. Maloney that ran to twenty thousand words. Part I was entitled "Frame-Up: The Firefighters Case" and Part II "Railroaded: Indictment and Trial."

Maloney, fifty-seven, was a former investigative reporter for the *Kansas City Star* and the *Orange County Register*. Five times articles he wrote for those newspapers were nominated for the Pulitzer Prize. In Kansas City his beat was organized crime; in California it was crime with a specialty in serial killers. During his twenty-five-year career as a journalist, he won numerous awards, including the American Society of Newspaper Publishers Award for the Best Investigative Story and the Silver Gavel, the highest award presented to a journalist by the American Bar Association.

Since 1990, in addition to fiction writing, he worked as an investigator and paralegal for Will Bunch, the attorney the US District Court appointed to represent Darlene Edwards in the firefighters trial. Maloney's work as Bunch's investigator on this case was approved and paid for by the court.

Because of J. J.'s association with the defense, I had misgivings about his reporting this story. Even though he had been editor of the *New Times* from 1991 to 1993, I had never met him and knew very little about him. He and Chuck Saults, *New Times* publisher, are friends. When Chuck approached me about J. J.'s interest in writing a feature about the case—a feature saying not one of the five people convicted had anything to do with the deaths of the firefighters—I doubted if someone who had been so involved could do a fair, unbiased job of reporting.

"You don't have to make up your mind now," Chuck told me. "He's going to send some copy in pretty soon and then you decide."

I paid scant attention to the firefighters trial. From the news media coverage, I didn't pick up any notion the ATF rigged the case against the five defendants, or the federal prosecutor knowingly used the perjured testimony of the government's key witness—Ronnie Edwards—to gain the grand jury indictment, or the judge was so pro-prosecution in his rulings and courtroom demeanor that the case was a farce in terms of its search for justice. When the guilty verdicts came down, I didn't pause to think about them.

How could the *Kansas City Star* and all the other media have missed out on what J. J. was now proposing to write?

A few days later, J. J. emailed the first three thousand words of the firefighters story. The copy, like the story it began to tell, was riveting. It reminded me of Norman Mailer's writing in *The Executioner's Song*. It was emotionless, understated, and flat (when I showed it to my wife she said it read as though J. J. had just sent in his notes); it used the weight of detail, fact, and organization, not theory or argument, to give the story forward momentum, a sort of staccato beat propelling it along.

Later in the afternoon on the day the copy came in, Chuck took me to a bar to meet J. J. Before long, I opened the question of bias. Could readers trust him, a member of the defense team, to be fair?

"I have no vested interest in Darlene Edwards or anyone else involved in this case. I wouldn't walk across the street to have a cup of coffee with her or any of the other defendants. I was paid by the federal court for my work on this case, not by any defendant or attorney involved," he said.

In Part I, "Frame-Up," Maloney sets forth the tortured, misguided eight-year search for the culprits responsible for igniting the explosion that killed the firefighters.

"All five of those convicted are almost certainly innocent of that crime," Maloney writes in the opening article. "The five became expendable because of the lives they'd led. . . . The firefighters case, in the end, became not so much a search for truth as a quest for closure. Over the years, the pressure for closure had grown intense."

Part I showed the way ATF Special Agent Dave True used tactics of entrapment, deception, intimidation, and inducements to bring this case to trial, all the while ignoring the mountain of evidence that pointed to guards Debbie and Robert Riggs.

Part II reported how Assistant US Attorney Paul Becker elicited the perjured testimony of Ronnie Edwards, Darlene's stepson, to secure the indictment of the Marlborough Five; how Becker defied court orders by withholding evidence from the defense until the last possible moment in order to prevent the defense to prepare adequately for trial; how Federal District Judge Joseph Stevens's bias in favor of the prosecution gutted the defense and made a mockery of justice.

Later in 1997, the Missouri Bar Association awarded Maloney its "Excellence in Legal Journalism Award" for his two-part series on the firefighters case that forcefully asserts the five defendants were wrongfully convicted.

Nine months after their sentencing, on April 15, 1998, the Marlborough Five's appeals were argued before a three-judge panel of the Eighth US Circuit Court of Appeals in the federal courthouse in St. Louis. Their trial lawyers represented them; the government was represented by US Assistant Attorney Paul Becker. It's the practice in the Eighth Circuit for the court to appoint the trial lawyers to represent the defendants on appeal. Doing so speeds up the appeal and saves the court the added expense of bringing in attorneys who will need a great deal of time to become familiar with the case.

The three-judge panel consisted of Circuit Judges James B. Loken and Donald P. Lay, and Robert W. Pratt, a federal district judge on loan from the Southern District of Iowa.

Appellate courts operate under a different standard than trial courts where the defendant is presumed innocent. Once a defendant has been found guilty, appellate judges are compelled to review the trial record in the light most favorable to the prosecution. In other words, the appealing defendant has been rightfully convicted and sentenced; unless the judges find a clear constitutional violation of the defendant's right to a fair trial, the verdict and sentence must be upheld.

The oral arguments were contentious. Judge Pratt sharply questioned Becker about the lack of any real evidence against the defendants and the government's extensive use of jailhouse witnesses. The defense attorneys argued during the hour-long hearing that Judge Stevens had denied the defendants a fair trial by denying their motions to try them separately and by not allowing the defense to recall ATF Agent True and guards Debbie and Robert Riggs. In addition, they argued it was improper to sentence the defendants to life without parole because the proximate cause of the firefighters' deaths was their own gross negligence, and also that Judge Stevens erred in not granting the defendants a downward departure in their sentences because the defendants did not "intentionally or knowingly" cause the deaths of the firefighters.

After the hearing there was a sense among the defense team that there was a chance the panel would overturn the convictions and order a new trial.

As the months passed by without any word from the Eighth Circuit Court, the hopes of the defense attorneys and the defendants continued to rise. But six and a half months later those hopes were dashed.

On October 30, 1998, in a twenty-six-page, unanimous decision written by Judge Loken, the convictions were upheld. "The evidence was sufficient for a reasonable jury to find the defendants set the fire that caused the fatal explosion."[2]

"To convict under the aiding and abetting statute, the government need only prove [each] defendant associated himself with the unlawful venture, participated in it as something he wished to bring about, and by his action sought to make the activity succeed. . . . We conclude the evidence was more than sufficient to convict each defendant of aiding and abetting arson in violation of 18 U.S.C.," the decision stated.

The day the Eighth Circuit Court decision was released, Paul Becker was in Washington, DC, receiving an award from US Attorney General Janet Reno for winning convictions in the firefighters case. The US Treasury Department had earlier given an award to retired ATF Special Agent Dave True for putting together the case against the five defendants.

In reading through the Eighth Circuit Court's decision, it was dismaying to see how frequently the written decision seriously misstates the facts of the case.

The ruling stated the defendants were the immediate suspects of police, which was far off the mark. Immediately after the explosion the police investigated a large number of individuals because of tips pouring in from often anonymous callers. In particular, the early focus of the investigation was on two of the woodcutters at the site; one of the primary detectives working the case, Victor Zinn, focused on Debbie and Robert Riggs.

The federal government, which conducted its own, separate investigation, focused on organized labor—and as late as 1994 Agent True said organized labor was the focus of the federal investigation. The words "organized labor" were not to be found in the Eighth Circuit opinion—although defense lawyers battled throughout the trial to be allowed to put Department of Labor Agent Gene Schram on the stand.

On the issue of actual innocence—and the effort by the defense to show a guard at the site (Debbie Riggs) set the fires to collect the insurance on her pickup—the Eighth Circuit panel obfuscated that issue by saying the defendants were allowed to rigorously cross-examine the government's witnesses, which is untrue—since the trial judge specifically forbade the defense from cross-examining Debbie Riggs about her admission to Prosecutor Becker (on the first day of trial) that, in the early 1970s, she paid her roommate to steal her car so she could collect the insurance.

In fact, a major issue on appeal was the trial judge refusing to allow the defense to call a witness (Greg Pugh, a mechanic for the City of Kansas City) who claimed he drove past the site two times before the fires and saw a pickup truck with its hood up—which would have impeached Debbie Riggs's testimony that her pickup was functioning properly that day, and no work was being done on it.

The trial judge ruled such testimony was too remote, and Pugh had not come forward soon enough (he contacted the defense during trial)—yet, many of the government witnesses came forward years later and testified to conversations that allegedly occurred while everyone present was either drinking or doing drugs.

The Eighth Circuit also misstated the evidence when it said, "A number of witnesses saw the defendants in various groups in the Marlborough neighborhood before and after the explosions."

Not one witness at the trial testified to seeing Darlene Edwards in the Marlborough neighborhood before or after the explosions.

In the Eighth's decision the following was presented as fact:

> The investigation into who caused the fires was frustrated by a lack of witnesses and surviving physical evidence. After years of dead ends, the explosions were reenacted on a national television program, "Unsolved Mysteries," accompanied by a well-publicized $50,000 reward, extensive local publicity, and a phone number for reporting tips. Defendants lived in Marlborough, a neighborhood adjacent to the construction site. Frank and Skip Sheppard are brothers, Bryan Sheppard is their nephew, Richard Brown is Bryan Sheppard's best friend, and Darlene Edwards was living with Frank Sheppard at the time of the explosion. Many callers reported that defendants had repeatedly boasted of starting the fires. These indictments followed.

The court is incorrect. The most damaging evidence against Darlene Edwards came after the ATF posted rewards in every prison and jail in Kansas and Missouri.

The evidence against Darlene was extremely dubious. Other than her own audiotaped statement wherein she exonerated herself and Frank, the primary witnesses against her were three jailhouse snitches, none of whose credibility the Eighth Circuit examined.

Obviously, the testimony of these three informants was far from convincing as to the guilt of Darlene—and therefore one has to conclude the "more than sufficient" evidence of guilt cited by the Eighth Circuit is the spillover effect of the dozens of statements allegedly made by her co-defendants. In other words, even the Eighth Circuit couldn't compartmentalize the evidence, so how could a jury be expected to?

The decision said the panel rejected the defendants' premise that the government's case lacked corroborating evidence:

> Becky Edwards, Darlene's daughter, testified that she heard all five defendants planning to steal from the construction site about one week before the explosion. Investigators found a gas can on the site that did not belong to the construction contractors, and a witness testified that Frank and Skip Sheppard had many gas cans as part

of their lawn mowing business. A number of witnesses saw the defendants in various groups in the Marlborough neighborhood before and after the explosions.

This was a misrepresentation of the evidence. Becky testified she heard Richard Brown and Frank Sheppard having such a discussion while five others, including Bryan, Skip, and Darlene, were present. Becky also testified, after the second explosion, she saw Darlene in her nightgown—at home.

Becky was the witness who testified about gas cans—which, she said, she and Darlene (not Frank and Skip) used to cut lawns. The can found at the construction site (a five-gallon military-type gas can) was never connected to this crime and was never tested for fingerprints or even gas residue.

Another glaring misstatement of the facts was when Judge Loken wrote, "Twelve witnesses testified to admissions by Frank Sheppard, and seven witnesses testified to admissions by Skip. As to each, the admissions were specific, detailed, and consistent."

There were eighteen witnesses against Frank and fourteen against Skip—figures it would not seem difficult for the judges to keep straight—but the assertion that the testimony against them was "consistent" showed a great disregard for the trial's transcript. There was nothing consistent about the testimony of the witnesses against these defendants. No two witnesses against any of the defendants testified to the same set of facts, and other than Becky Edwards, no witness put these five defendants together. The testimony of the government's informant witnesses of what happened and who did what was wildly conflicting. The actual statements of the witnesses name a large number of nondefendants involved in the crime.

Other issues appealed and denied included the restrictions Judge Stevens placed on defense counsel to cross-examine government witnesses; the prejudicial impact of allowing the government to show the jury photos of the dead firefighters; the government putting on false testimony that batteries were stolen from the site; the bias of Judge Stevens throughout the trial; the improper sentencing of the defendants to life without parole because the proximate cause of the firefighters' deaths was their own gross negligence; and the failure of Judge Stevens to not grant the defendants a downward departure in their sentences because the defendants did not "intentionally or knowingly" cause the deaths of the firefighters.

Concerning the last claim, the Eighth Circuit panel ruled Judge Stevens was aware of his "discretion to depart downward. Therefore, his refusal to depart is not reviewable on appeal."

After J. J. Maloney died at the end of 1999 from acute bronchial congestion, I started having conversations with three of the trial attorneys—Will Bunch, John O'Connor, and John Osgood—about what could be done now that the Eighth Circuit Court of Appeals denied the defendants any relief. Like me, they were convinced the federal government had used its enormous power to frame and convict five innocent people simply to close this case.

The only way to get this case back in court, they told me, was to hire an attorney to file a habeas corpus appeal in federal district court. It would be inappropriate for any of them to file the habeas appeal because a regular component of such appeals is making a claim of "ineffective counsel."

A habeas appeal allows a prisoner to claim the right to be released on various grounds. Among many other things, the prisoner may argue the sentence imposed violated the US Constitution or the laws of the United State; the trial court was without jurisdiction to impose such a sentence; the sentence was in excess of the maximum authorized by law; or the prisoner's trial attorney was so ineffective the prisoner was denied his constitutional right to a fair trial.

Unlike prisoners sentenced to die, those sentenced to life without parole are not entitled to an automatic habeas corpus appeal in federal district court. They are entitled to the appeal but are on their own; the government—as it must in death row cases—is not required to pay their attorney fees if they are indigent. So unless an indigent defendant can find an attorney willing to handle his or her appeal pro bono or to somehow raise the money to hire an appeal attorney, no appeal will be filed.

In a letter I wrote to each of the defendants in June 2000, I told them I was the editor of the weekly newspaper that published J. J. Maloney's two-part series on their case and I attended their sentencing hearing and their appeal before a three-judge panel at the Eighth Circuit Court of Appeals. "I am not a lawyer. I am just an interested journalist who believes all five defendants in the firefighters case were convicted wrongfully," and I was committed to helping see that injustice corrected.

I told them I had retained attorney Jonathan Laurans to review the trial transcript and all the filings related to their Eighth Circuit Court appeal to determine if he thought there were grounds for a habeas appeal.

(After his review, Laurans saw several constitutional issues for appealing the convictions.) If they were agreeable, Laurans would visit separately with each defendant and each could decide if he or she wanted him to represent them. Laurans was proposing to file the same appeal for each defendant. Because they were tried and convicted together there was a certain logic to this approach. (It turned out the issues Laurans raised on appeal applied across the board to each defendant.)

Time was of the essence. The appeal had to be filed by October 4, 2000, to be accepted by the district court. Each of the defendants signed on to have Laurans represent them.

Although Laurans was a young attorney, just thirty-five at the time, what moved me to hire him was a federal case he appealed and won in 1994 involving former Kansas Lieutenant Governor David Owen. Owen was charged and convicted of tax fraud and sentenced to a year and a day. In a habeas corpus petition, Laurans was able to show Owen had been inappropriately sentenced, winning his immediate release.

In the habeas petition Laurans filed with the US District Court for the Western District of Missouri on September 28, 2000, he made five claims for overturning the verdicts.

(1) Based on case law, i.e., precedents set by two other cases he cited, arson in many cases is not a federal offense because of the lack of impact on and nexus with interstate commerce.

(2) Any fact which increases the statutory maximum punishment for an offense must be pled in the indictment, submitted as an element in the jury instructions, and found by a jury beyond a reasonable doubt, rather than by the trial judge at sentencing by a preponderance of evidence.

(3) Ineffective assistance of counsel.

(4) Newly discovered evidence proves the innocence of the defendants and/or should have been presented at trial by counsel. (In an affidavit, a witness swore that guard Donna Costanza had confessed to coworkers that she started the fire to Debbie Riggs's pickup at the construction site.)

(5) Jury misconduct. (Darlene's mother, Doris Clark, swore in an affidavit dated September 22, 2000, that three days before the case went to the jury she overheard the widow of firefighter Luther Hurd telling a woman sitting next to her in the courtroom gallery that she had received a note from a male black juror that stated "everyone but the girl [Darlene] was going to be convicted.")

The appeal was assigned to Federal District Judge Fernando J. Gaitan Jr. Around the federal courthouse, he is not often seen outside his normally very quiet chambers. Tall, distinguished looking, and uncommonly soft-spoken, he was born in Kansas City, Kansas, in 1948. He went to Donnelly Junior College for two years and then finished up at Pittsburg State University in Pittsburg, Kansas, in 1970 with a B.S. degree. Four years later, he graduated from the School of Law at the University of Missouri–Kansas City. From there he took a job as an attorney at Southwestern Bell in Kansas City where he worked for the next six years.

From 1980 until 1986, he served as a circuit court judge in Jackson County and was then appointed to the Missouri Court of Appeals, Western District. President George H. W. Bush appointed him to the federal bench in 1991.

Judge Gaitan sat on the habeas appeal Laurans filed for almost three years, an inordinately long time to consider a petition with only five claims. What was most disconcerting was he held no evidentiary hearing to allow Laurans to argue his case.

His ruling denied all five claims and did not certify any of them. If he had certified one or more of the claims it would have meant that even though he did not see the merit, the claim or claims could be brought before the Eighth Circuit Court of Appeals for that court's review. Certifying a claim is a way for a federal judge to say one or more of the issues raised on appeal are complex enough that perhaps it deserves a fresh look by a three-judge panel. Without such certification, the habeas appeal was virtually dead.

CHAPTER 13

Affidavits of Recantation

After Judge Gaitan denied the habeas corpus appeals in mid-July 2003, I made an appointment to visit John Osgood at his law offices in Lee's Summit to see if there was any way forward to establish the innocence of the Marlborough Five. Nadine Brown, Richard's mother, had given Osgood a check for $9,500 back in June 2000 to conduct further investigation into the case. Osgood, a sole practitioner, agreed to provide his assistance pro bono. From time to time he hired investigator Mark Reeder to follow up on various tips that came along. So far nothing substantive had, and most of the money Mrs. Brown put up was depleted.

Other than one of the actual perpetrators coming forward and admitting to the crime, Osgood said, the only way to get the defendants back in court was to develop evidence so compelling of their innocence that no jury would have convicted them if they had known about it. In addition, the evidence presented could not have been discovered earlier by the use of due diligence, i.e., it had to be newly discovered evidence that Darlene's remained unknown until it was found.

We decided the best way forward would be to contact witnesses who testified at the grand jury or trial to see if any of them would recant. There was another group of witnesses the government did not called to testify that Osgood thought might also be good to approach. Between the two groups, there were over 150 names of people. Reeder made a list of the ones he would attempt to contact and I did the same. The two witnesses I wanted the most to interview were Darlene's daughter, Becky, and Darlene's stepson, Ronnie Edwards.

Neither Reeder nor I could track down Ronnie Edwards. Mark and I went to his father's house in Marlborough and were told by Steve Edwards he hadn't had contact with his son in over ten years. At his mother's house, her boyfriend, John Atterbury, told us he was so intimidated by Dave True—now long retired from the ATF—he wouldn't say anything about Ronnie and not to bother to come back when Ronnie's mother was home. I did go back several times when I saw her van in the driveway, but she never answered the door.

Simply locating the witnesses we wanted to interview took hours of traipsing through Marlborough. Dogs prowled many of the front yards, jumping up almost as high as the fences that kept them in as I walked by. In many yards, pit bulls were chained to pegs. The few times I was invited to enter one of those I feared the chain would snap.

About half of the people I was trying to contact had been witnesses at trial and had been paid about $1,000 each for their testimony. When I was able to make personal contact with any of them and ask if their trial testimony had been truthful, I was told of their fear of being prosecuted for perjury by the government if they made such an admission.

Some of the witnesses I spoke to were downright hostile. Osgood received a short letter, purportedly signed by Tracy Ownby—a witness against Skip—saying she had "important information that could change the outcome of the guilty verdict. Please contact me so we can talk in person." A postscript to the letter said the government had paid her $2,000 "to lie." When I did locate her she angrily denied writing the letter and told me to get off her property.

The first affidavit Mark acquired was from Alan Bethard.[1] He was the one whose charge for auto theft in state court was upgraded to a federal crime for his refusal to corroborate the testimony of his housemate Ronnie Edwards. Bethard stated both he and Ronnie were home in bed the night of the explosions. Also that Agent True offered him the entire $50,000 reward if he would corroborate what Ronnie had told them and testify to that at the grand jury and at trial. True also told him he would be released from jail shortly after testifying and he would be allowed to "reside in any city in the United States" as part of the government's witness protection program and the government would pay all relocation expenses.

Our reinvestigation got a major boost in mid-2004 when Carie Neighbors, who testified against Bryan and Richard, admitted to Mark she perjured herself at trial. We knew the type of pressure Agent True had exerted on Alan Bethard, Glen Shepard, and Travis Small—threatening to turn state charges pending against them into federal charges with much longer prison sentences—but we didn't know how he had gone about turning some of the nonfelon witnesses into perjurers.

In her affidavit, Neighbors said she was approached by Agent True in the weeks following the airing of *Unsolved Mysteries* after Mark and Mary Studna called the TIPS hotline to report Neighbors had heard admissions of guilt from Bryan and Richard. The Studnas hoped by calling in about

Neighbors they could share in the reward money.[2] Neighbors's affidavit stated in part:

> The first time Agent David True approached me at my residence he stated, "We know what you know and this is what you are going to say." After that Agent David True told me what I was going to testify to and told me that if I did not testify accordingly, he would have me prosecuted for contempt; I would receive a sentence for that offense of 18 months that would be served in a federal prison and my child [her 2-year-old son] would be removed from my care and custody.

She further stated True told her Bryan and Richard had made admissions to her at a party in Marlborough and later at Swope Park. She said every time she met with True, up to and including just moments prior to testifying at the firefighters trial, she attempted "to inform him that what he wanted me to say was a lie." Each time she did, True would threaten her with eighteen months of prison time and loss of her son.

At trial her testimony mirrored what True told her to say. "I declare those statements [her trial testimony] to be untrue and I would not have testified to them in federal court if it were not for the fact that Agent David True threatened me."

After the Marlborough Five were convicted and sentenced, Neighbors received a check from the government for $836.

Tracking down Joe Denyer, who testified against Darlene, was like trying to corner a shadow. From time to time I would get reports from Virgie Sheppard, Bryan's mother, that Denyer was sleeping in this or that abandoned house in Marlborough. I'd leave notes to him on the front porches to drop by Virgie's house. One afternoon in early January 2005, Virgie called me to say Joe was sitting in her living room with Valerie Rocha, one of Bryan's former girlfriends.

In a two-page affidavit witnessed by Rocha and Virgie, Denyer avowed, "The testimony I offered at trial was then and is now false and inaccurate . . . I wish to recant that testimony and come forward and make an offer that what I testified to was not true."[3] He said he gave false testimony "at the direction of federal agents" in return for assistance on a charge he was in jail for at the time.

During the session with Denyer, Rocha told me True approached her while she was in a drug-rehab program and offered her $400 in cash to say she overheard Richard and Bryan saying, "What are we going to do if we get caught?"

Rocha said she was called before the grand jury, but was abruptly dismissed when she would not testify to hearing any admissions from Richard and Bryan.

John Osgood's direction that Reeder and I focus on the not-called witnesses proved sound. I caught up with Larry Summers, one of Bryan's oldest friends, on a Sunday afternoon in his side yard in Marlborough during a cookout with a few other people. His wife very much resented my showing up and didn't want him to talk to me. We walked out to the front sidewalk. Summers told me—and a few days later swore in an affidavit—a Kansas City homicide detective interviewed him a few months before the firefighters trial. He said he told the detective he did not think Bryan had any involvement in the explosions. Summers recounted driving to the construction site with Bryan the afternoon after the explosions to check it out. "We drove around the site and looked around for a few minutes. . . . We were both amazed at the explosions. Bryan never said anything about his being involved in it. He was just curious like I was to see what had happened."

Two months after that interview, Agent True came to see Summers and asked him to sit in his car while they talked. "He struck me immediately as having a big attitude problem because he was very aggressive with me right off the bat," Summers stated. True told him he read the statement Summers gave to the Kansas City detective but he now wanted him to change his story. "He told me if I changed my statement to implicate Bryan that it would help the families of the dead firefighters." Summers said what he told the detective was the truth and he was not going to change it. "He [True] then reached into the glove box of his car and threw a subpoena right in my face and said he would see me in court. At this point I was scared. I got out of his car and went back inside and Agent True drove away."[4]

The subpoena ordered Summers to appear at the firefighters trial in two weeks. Summers ignored it and never heard from True again.

Buster Hower, Bryan's brother-in-law, had helped Bryan in the past with some of his legal fees. In 1995 when Bryan had a court appearance in Cass County on a charge of manufacturing meth, Hower helped hire an attorney to represent Bryan. Dave True was there with a film crew, urging the judge to set a higher bond but the judge threw the case out when Bryan's attorney established the "meth" the Belton police confiscated was only a bottle of Vida-Blend, an energy drink.

At the Cass County Courthouse, Agent True asked Hower what his relationship with Bryan was. Hower explained he was Bryan's brother-in-law.

After the Marlborough Five were indicted, True began calling Hower, asking him to pass along questions he had for members of the Sheppard family. True also called to try to verify information. Hower eventually told True he didn't want to continue to be a conduit between the ATF and the Sheppard family.

Shortly thereafter, two ATF agents showed up to question Hower at the interior-services business he owned in midtown Kansas City. When he told the agents he had nothing to say to them, "the agents appeared miffed," Hower stated in his three-page affidavit he swore to in February 2005. "Later that day two FBI agents showed up at my office. They said they had a tip that I matched a description of John Doe No. 2 in the Oklahoma City bombing that occurred the day before or two days before."[5]

The FBI agents asked him where he was the day of the bombing. He told them he was in his office in Kansas City meeting with his property manager. At one point during the thirty-minute interview, Hower told the FBI agents they weren't there about the Oklahoma City bombing but about his relationship with Bryan Sheppard.

Hower said a number of his business associates and clients soon became aware of the ATF and FBI agents' visits to his office and of his being questioned about the Oklahoma City bombing. "My business turned so bad I was forced to close it . . . I am now a general superintendent working as a carpenter."

No matter what else might be said about Agent True, he was tenacious in building his case against the Marlborough Five. His failure to turn Buster Hower into an inside source within the Sheppard family did not deter him; it was just a bump in the road.

True next turned to Debbie Howard, Bryan's girlfriend at the time of the explosions. Six months earlier Debbie had given birth to their daughter, Ashley. By this time, Bryan had been arrested for selling drugs to an undercover agent and was in detention. Debbie had moved on, glad to be rid of Bryan. She was now living with Ashley and a new boyfriend outside of Marlborough.

At the ATF office she told the agents during a lengthy videotaped interview she hated Bryan and if she could, in good conscience, tell them he was guilty, she would. But the truth was Bryan came home to his parents' house around midnight. She said she and Bryan argued before he left that night with Richard Brown and she was still angry when he came home.

In a letter she wrote to me in February 2006, she said after Bryan came in that night,

> We argued, made up, and fell asleep on the couch in Jack and Virgie's front room. I was living with them and was absolutely not allowed to sleep in the same room as Bryan. I say this because that is how I remember so clearly waking up a little after 3 a.m. I was extremely intimidated by Jack and I was scared he would catch me on the couch with Bryan.[6]

She wrote she got up then and went downstairs to her bedroom, leaving Bryan asleep on the couch. The next thing she remembered was being awakened by Virgie about 7 or 8 a.m. and being told to get dressed because the police were talking about evacuating the neighborhood. When she went upstairs, Bryan was still on the couch, half-asleep.

During her interview at the ATF office, the agents asked her repeatedly about the time of morning she claimed she woke up and left Bryan sleeping on the couch. "They [the agents] wondered if someone had put that in my head, and that I really didn't remember. I believe they had me doubting myself somewhat, but I remember looking at that clock and thinking, 'If Jack catches me, I'm dead.' That is why I went downstairs."

Debbie was subpoenaed to appear before the grand jury but her testimony did not vary from saying Bryan came home that night around midnight and she left him sleeping on the couch. The government did not call her as a witness at trial and, oddly, neither did the defense as an alibi witness for Bryan.

True had much better luck with Shannon Reimers, Richard Brown's younger half sister.[7] At trial she testified when she came back to Darlene's house after the second explosion she saw Frank and Darlene and one other adult, fully clothed, sitting in the dark in the living room. In an affidavit she executed on September 19, 2005, she swore she didn't know how they were dressed "because it was too dark in the room to tell." (The second explosion knocked out all the electricity in Marlborough.)

Agent True pursued her doggedly:

> I did not want to be a witness. Agent True kept coming to where I lived to try to get me to speak with him. He is a very intimidating person. Very stern. While I lived at three different places, he visited me at all of them in the months leading up to the firefighters trial.

. . . On one of Agent True's visits, after I had refused to let him in the house, he stuck his foot in the front door and dropped a subpoena on the floor.

Some days after receiving the subpoena, Shannon, twenty-two at the time, relented and told True she would meet with him at her mother's house in Independence, thinking her mother's presence would help her deal "with this imposing agent." But True, who arrived with another agent, nixed that idea.

The interview lasted for "two or three hours." True started off friendly "but before long he really begins to press for what he wants." She stated in her affidavit True "essentially gave me his version of what he wanted me to tell him."[8]

During the interview Shannon told the agents she believed Johnny Driver was in the living room with Darlene and Frank, but she was afraid to mention Driver's presence "because he scared me and it was not wise to mess with him." True told her there was no need to mention Driver when they took her taped statement "because he had already checked him out."

Agent True, she said, turned on the tape recorder "and took my statement in five to ten minutes. I told him what he wanted to hear just to get rid of him." She didn't see True again until the day she testified at trial.

On the morning she testified she was nine months pregnant and expecting to deliver at any time. Before she was called to the stand, she met with Paul Becker and True in an office outside the courtroom. "Mr. Becker said he wanted to go over my statement, but like Agent True before him, he essentially told me what he wanted me to say on the stand. I felt he was putting words in my mouth and I told him that."

Becker wanted her to testify Darlene had burned her car to collect insurance money, "but I had never said I saw Darlene do that. I had only said, out of spite for Darlene, that I had heard that she had burnt her car for insurance money."

Just as Becky Edwards had been the government's most important witness at trial, she was to me the most important person we needed to interview. I had been trying for months to make contact. Becky was now twenty-eight and the mother of two small boys. She was living with them and her common-law husband in central Missouri.

Becky had been traumatized growing up. Her feelings about her mother were extremely conflicted. She loved Darlene but her mother's toleration of Frank embittered her. When Darlene was arrested and sent to prison in 1995, Becky was left virtually homeless at age eighteen. Her experiences with Dave True had left her fearful and distrusting. She felt used. The ordeal of testifying at the grand jury and the firefighters trial had made her want to disappear. The last thing she wanted to do was to revisit those painful days.

So she resisted any contact with me. My only hope was to persuade her grandmother, Doris Clark, to ask Becky to call me. In the summer of 2005 I drove down to meet Mrs. Clark in her rural trailer home. Sitting in an easy chair with a Bible on the end table, the TV set tuned to a game show, Mrs. Clark, now a widower, was skeptical. She left the courtroom after the verdicts thinking all but Darlene were rightfully convicted.

We talked about the case for over an hour. I laid out how I thought all five were innocent, how each had iron-clad alibis, and how nonsensical it was for the government to say these drunks and dope users could have pulled off in five or ten minutes a Navy Seal–type raid on the construction site, starting fires on both sides of the construction site and not being seen by a single person. I made the case the guards at the site were the most probable perpetrators, and her daughter, unless we did something to prove otherwise, would spend the rest of her life in prison for a crime she and the others had nothing to do with. I told her I needed to understand how Becky had come to testify as she did.

A few weeks later Becky called me. We agreed to meet at noon a week later at the Applebee's restaurant on US 71 in Grandview, Missouri, a few miles south of the construction site. For this initial meeting I asked Susan Hunt, Skip Sheppard's trial attorney, to join us.

Becky is an attractive young woman, petite with long brown hair. I would have thought she was a teenager if I had not known her age. She is very shy—uneasy—and speaks in almost a whisper.

We had an awkward start. When the waitress came by, Becky said she wouldn't be staying long enough to eat and asked for a glass of water; Susan and I ordered soft drinks.

Feeling the need to press ahead, I gave Becky a copy of her trial testimony. Over the next forty-five minutes Becky told us how Agent True hounded her to testify. He threatened to prosecute her on drug charges unless she cooperated and said what he wanted her to say. She never heard the defendants speak specifically about the construction site where the firefighters were killed nor did she ever hear any of them speaking about the construction site explosions afterward—"and they were people given to bragging."

It was a good start, but I needed a lot more detail. She agreed she would read over her trial testimony and the next time we talked we could go through it. As I walked her to her car I saw why she was so pressed for time: her two young sons were waiting in her car.

On a Sunday afternoon a few weeks later, my wife and I drove to see Becky at her house in the woods about eighty miles southeast of Kansas City not far from Sedalia where she lived with her sons and their father, Marcus Torres. It was a major breakthrough to be invited to her house, and this time we would have a couple of hours. Her children were incredibly well behaved and Torres was welcoming. After a few minutes inside, Becky came outside with my wife and me and we sat at a picnic table.

The pain of the ordeal Becky experienced growing up, including seeing her mother being sentenced to life, was always just beneath the surface. Tears frequently trickled down her face. What was clear to my wife and me was there was a great deal to Becky. She had somehow survived her upbringing and was making a good life with her family.

Over the next month or so Becky and I worked on putting together her affidavit. I'd send her a draft, she would make changes. I'd send her the revised draft, she'd make changes or add new information. As we neared the final draft, I wrote her a letter on October 9, 2005, asking her if there were any other changes she wanted to make. "The important thing is that we get it right, totally right. If it takes us two or three more tries that's no problem. We are not in a hurry." On November 6, 2005, she signed her affidavit and Marcus Torres witnessed it.

Her affidavit contained sixteen assertions.[9] Beginning with No. 3 she explained how she had come to testify against her mother and the other defendants. After Darlene was sent to prison on her drug conviction in 1995, Becky moved in with her father in Marlborough. Agent True, KCPD Officer Jerry Ludwig, and another ATF agent began coming to see her at her father's house. The first two times she did not let them in, telling them through the door she was only eleven at the time of the explosions and could not remember anything worth mentioning to them.

A few weeks later when they returned, she decided to let them into the living room "in an attempt to get rid of them once and for all. As a minor, I wanted my father to be present during the questioning but the agents said he if stayed in the living room that he too would become involved in the firefighters case. My father did not want to get involved and went down to the basement."

Once they were in the house, True noticed she had a couple of marijuana roaches stuck inside the cellophane of a cigarette pack. He told her the ATF knew she smoked marijuana and took meth. He said the ATF could make her drug use "hard or easy" on her depending on whether she cooperated with them. (She told Susan Hunt and me at our first interview the day True caught her with the marijuana butts she had just quit using meth two weeks before. She also told us her mother allowed her to smoke crack at age eleven.)

Switching tactics, True questioned her about her mother and Frank's drug use and petty thievery:

> They said it was important that I told them something about them. Agent True told me to consider that my mother had not been a very good mother and had allowed me to suffer abuse from Frank Sheppard all those years. Agent True said he wanted me admit that my mom and Frank Sheppard were drug users. He said my admitting they were drug dependent might actually help them gain sympathy with a jury. Agent True told me he knew I did not want my mother in jail and that my admitting she was a drug user would make it easier on her.

Fearful of being charged with drug use, Becky agreed to admit her mother and Frank were drug users and petty thieves. "I did not feel as though I was admitting anything that was not common knowledge in our neighborhood and with the police and ATF. At the conclusion of this interview, I now assumed that I had given them what they wanted from me and that they would leave me alone."

But True was a long way from being finished with her. Some weeks later he ordered her downtown to the ATF office. This time he wanted her to say a lot more. He wanted her to tell him and the other agents she heard all of the Marlborough Five "having a meeting at my mother's house where they conspired to rob the 71 Highway construction site." Not only that, but he wanted her to say this meeting was held the night before or in the days immediately preceding the explosions at the construction site.

> I told Agent True that I had not heard any discussions about stealing any items on the night before or in the days leading up to the explosions at the 71 Highway site. What I did tell Agent True was that there was a steady stream of people in and out of my mother's house who were drug users and petty thieves. They did from time to time discuss potential thefts, but that I never heard any discussion of a theft at the 71 Highway site.

No matter what I told Agent True, it was never enough to satisfy him. He always wanted me to say more than I actually knew about this case.

True tried to get her to say more than she knew by speculating it would be actually good for the defendants to be convicted and spend some time in prison so they could get off drugs and straighten out their lives. He also told her if the defendants were acquitted by a jury there would be people out to get them, wanting to shoot them, and they would be safer in prison.

One thing True made clear to her was how much he wanted to solve this case so he could retire from the ATF. "He told me he very badly wanted to be able to say that he solved the case. Agent True always left me the impression that he wanted a notch on his gun no matter what the truth was."

True clearly wasn't making the headway he wanted with Becky so toward the end of the interview at the ATF office he brought her stepbrother, Ronnie Edwards, into the room. "Agent True said he was bringing Ronnie and me together so that we could get our stories straight. They wanted us to talk about a meeting at a gas station that I did not know anything about and about the theft of some walkie-talkies from the 71 Highway construction site. I told them I had never seen any walkie-talkies or knew anything about them," she stated in her affidavit.

"It became clear that Agent True was pressuring Ronnie, as he had been pressuring me, to make damaging statements about my mother and the other named defendants. Agent True using pressure on Ronnie made me furious. Agent True made it clear that Ronnie's past drug use could be used against him and that he risked never being able to see his son Derrick again," she stated in her affidavit.

And now to her grand jury testimony where she did swear she heard her mother and the other defendants plotting to steal from the 71 Highway construction site.

I was terrified to testify before the grand jury. I do not know how Prosecutor Becker got me to say what I testified to there. I was just too scared to disagree with anything he said I had told the ATF agents in all those interviews. I was completely intimidated by the entire situation, particularly by the fear that if I did not say what Agent True wanted me to say that I would be subject to drug charges.

The day the indictments against the Marlborough Five were returned by the grand jury, True and Ludwig, accompanied by camera crews from local TV stations, showed up at the infamous QuikTrip near the construction site where Becky was now employed. True told her they were going to be keeping "an eye on her." She was humiliated and embarrassed to the core by this negative attention. She quit her job that afternoon and soon made arrangements to move to Adrian, Missouri.

In Adrian, True tracked her down and served her with a subpoena to testify at the firefighters trial.

When she appeared at the courthouse to testify, True put her and about five or six other witnesses in a room and showed each of them a separate stack of documents that memorialized the various interviews conducted with them by police and ATF agents.

"Prior to that time, I had not seen any of these documents nor had I ever signed any statements. Agent True did not ask me to sign any of those statements that day. Instead he told me and the others to go over the documents before us and to line out any statements that we did not actually make or which any of us thought misrepresented what we had said," Becky stated in her affidavit.

When she asked True if her guardian, Michelle Carter, could be present while she reviewed the documents, True said no. "I remember it was a large stack of documents and that I underlined quite a large number of sentences that I designated as either I had not said or that I thought were untrue."

In the final declaration of her affidavit, Becky stated, "The day I took the stand at the trial I did not know what I was doing. I was so frightened and intimidated by this experience that I do not remember anything I said."

CHAPTER 14

Mike McGraw

Our primary purpose in getting affidavits from witnesses who testified at the firefighters trial was to see what caused so many of them to testify falsely. We were looking for a pattern that would make sense and that we could develop with other witnesses as we went forward. In terms of the people the government interviewed but did not call to testify, we wanted to determine what made that difference. In the latter case, we found, it was simply they refused to alter their stories, i.e., they refused to lie. In the former case, it became clear one overzealous government agent used intimidation to coerce false testimony.

If we could find enough evidence of this abuse of federal power, we hoped it would be grounds for returning to the Eighth Circuit Court of Appeals and asking to be allowed to file a successive, or second, habeas corpus petition that would seek to vacate the sentences and call for a new trial. It is extremely rare for federal appeals courts to grant a second habeas corpus petition. Less than 5 percent of such petitioners get what is referred to as "a second bite out of the apple."

As a fallback, we hoped we could interest the *Kansas City Star* in writing about the abuse that led to these convictions.

By mid-2005, Mark Reeder and I had developed six affidavits and I was working on putting one together with Becky Edwards. We had enough information about the coercive, intimidating tactics True used to pressure witnesses to testify falsely that it was time to try to get that publicly exposed. I also had a copy of a letter Frank Gile wrote to Bryan Sheppard in 1998 when Bryan was sent to the state penitentiary in Jefferson City where Gile was also incarcerated. At trial, Gile had testified against Richard Brown and had implicated Bryan. His letter read:

Brain [*sic*]: What's up? Not to much here I just talked to DJ he told me what house [the prison pod] you were in well bro I'm going to get straight to the point. I'm sorry for what happened but I can't change it or may be I can. Brain those weren't my words against you they were the governments words. You don't have to believe me but it's true. I wrote Nadine, Richard's mom about a week ago telling her just what I'm telling you. Brain I'm willing to help you beet this case with me I think you can because of some of the things the government did that I know about. It's your choice write and let me know if you want my help. If I don't get a letter I'll know not to fuck with you.

Frank

I thought our best bet would be for me to approach Mike McGraw, a Pulitzer Prize–winning investigative reporter at the *Star,* to see if he would agree the firefighters case deserved a second look. I had never met him, but I heard J. J. Maloney speak highly of him based on their days as young reporters on the *Star.* I think the main reason Mike agreed to meet was because he knew J. J. was convinced the government had convicted the wrong people.

While there is a great deal of ranting on Fox news and Rush Limbaugh–type radio shows about the liberal bias of the media in general, the *Kansas City Star* had been a paragon of conservative Republican values since its founding in 1880 by William Rockhill Nelson. It is as much a fabric of life in Kansas City as the Missouri River.

So if the *Star,* a newspaper that has won eight Pulitzer Prizes since 1931, agreed to dig into how the government had put together its case, the court of public opinion would be back open.

I met Mike at the *Star* on the afternoon of June 6, 2005. We sat at a table in the newspaper's deserted cafeteria. There are no airs about Mike, who was then in his mid-fifties. His friendliness is genuine. His closely trimmed white beard and wire-rim glasses give him the look of someone who would be more comfortable in a rocking chair sitting outside a Cracker Barrel or driving his old beat-up Ford pickup to his cabin in the woods.

For a person with his gift of congeniality, one would not suspect how driven and intent he can be, but under the surface is one of the most dogged reporters in the country. The Pulitzer Prize he won along with fellow reporter Jeff Taylor in 1992 for national reporting was for a seven-part series that documented waste, fraud, racism, and ineffective meat inspection within the US Department of Agriculture. One of the findings showed the USDA often refused to give black farmers loans and crop subsidies they qualified for, particularly in southern states.

When I called for the appointment, he told me he would give me an hour. Once we sat down, I never got the sense he was in a hurry. As I talked, he listened and took notes. I had written down a list of points I wanted to present, but my essential message was threefold: the people convicted were innocent and were framed by the government; the government had gotten the case backwards—the arson near the ANFO trailers was a diversion for the torching of Debbie Riggs's pickup; and the affidavits I was about to turn over were the tip of the iceberg into the corruption of the government's investigation.

At the time of this meeting, Mike was involved in a special project that would take him six months to wrap up. He was investigating a major financial scandal at the Housing and Economic Development Corporation in Kansas City. After that, he said, he would go to his editors and see if they would allow him to do some preliminary investigation into the firefighters case. Then he would get back to me. In the meantime, if there were more affidavits developed, I could send them to him.

My supplying Mike with affidavits carried no real weight with him or his editors. Any information or evidence of wrongdoing contained in the affidavits I provided would have to be independently verified. He personally would meet with every person involved and, if he felt the need, get his own affidavits. Mike would often videotape or audiotape his witness interviews. In the case of Becky Edwards, he spent a day driving down and back to Becky's grandmother's home in southern Missouri to interview her.

Between the time of our meeting in 2005 and Mike's first article about the case in 2007, the McClatchy Company purchased the *Star* from Knight-Ridder. By this time the editor of the *Star*, Mark Zieman, had approved Mike investigating the firefighters case, and there would be no disruption on his full-time assignment. Zieman had been Mike's special projects editor when the *Star* won the Pulitzer for the USDA series. (Zieman is now vice president of operations for McClatchy.) Even when the recession hit in 2008 and the *Star*, like newspapers across the country, was forced to slash newsroom personnel, Mike remained full-time on the firefighters investigation.

The first article Mike McGraw wrote about the firefighters case appeared in the *Kansas City Star* on February 18, 2007, ten years after the Marlborough Five were convicted. The front-page story was entitled, "New Questions Arise in Deadly 1988 Blast."[1] By this time McGraw had been reinvestigating the firefighters case for a year and had a number of revelations to make.

The news peg for the first story was that Assistant US Attorney Paul Becker had recently notified the trial attorneys for each defendant that Ed Massey, an ex-convict and former woodcutter at the construction site, had given new information about the case to the ATF during a three-hour interview on January 17. Massey told the agents he saw a woman he believed to be guard Donna Costanza running away from a burning pickup parked close to one of the ANFO trailers. Massey also told the agents guard Debbie Riggs offered him money on two occasions to set her Toyota pickup on fire to collect insurance.

In the letter Becker wrote to the defense attorneys, he stated, "Mr. Massey . . . saw a security guard, Donna Costanza, moving around the site. Mr. Massey stated that he saw 'flashes' on the pickup truck on the hill and the side of the road when he saw Ms. Costanza. Mr. Massey also stated that security guard Debbie Riggs had earlier asked him to set fire to her truck for an insurance fraud."

McGraw wrote that Massey approached the ATF after talking extensively with him about his allegations. The *Star* subjected Massey to two polygraph tests conducted by separate examiners; one of them, Charles Honts, was among the most prominent in the United States. Both tests found Massey had credible information that "indicated he saw the fire being set and that the five people now imprisoned were not on the site," McGraw wrote.

Becker told the defense attorneys he was making Massey's allegation known to them "out of an abundance of caution rather than any belief by the investigators or prosecutors of the veracity of Mr. Massey's current statements." He also pointed out that Massey, who was an early suspect himself in this case, passed a polygraph on December 1, 1988, denying he was at the construction site that night when the fire was set and saying he did not know who set the fire.

Massey told McGraw he was at the site that night because another woodcutter, Shawn Roma, asked him to meet him there to settle a dispute. (Roma, who lived close to the construction site, called police around 6 a.m. that morning—two hours after the firefighters were killed—and said Massey threatened to burn all of the wood at the site—a football field–size pile of wood—rather than allow Roma to harvest it.)

The reason he did not come forward at the time of the explosions, Massey told McGraw, was because he was a felon with a pending warrant and based on what he saw Costanza do he could be charged as an accessory to the crime. Massey said the reason he was coming forward now was because "I have carried around a lot of guilt for seventeen years because I still wonder if I could have stopped it."

In a telephone interview, Becker told McGraw the US Attorney's Office "has no intention of opening a new investigation, because we don't believe any of the information in the [ATF] report."

"Regardless of what Massey did or did not see the night of the explosion, he spent a lot of time on the highway construction site where the blasts occurred," McGraw wrote. "He cut firewood there nearly every day for two months and occasionally got into confrontations with security guards."

The claim that Massey saw guard Costanza starting a fire was not uncorroborated. McGraw reported Sandy DiGiovanni, a Kansas City real estate agent and former friend of Debbie Riggs and Costanza, told him Costanza admitted to her a few nights after the explosions she helped Debbie Riggs burn her pickup as part of an insurance scam.

McGraw also cited an affidavit attached to the habeas corpus appeals filed on behalf of the defendants in federal district court in 2000. The affidavit was sworn to by Jessica Vernon.[2] She averred Costanza told her she was responsible for setting the fire that caused the explosion that killed the firefighters. McGraw also reported that Johnny Ray Neil, Vernon's brother, had overheard Costanza making similar admissions. Neil informed the ATF in 1994 and later that year the Clay County Undersheriff Ron Nicoli that he overheard a conversation at Stack's Drive-In during which Costanza told his sister she and Debbie Riggs set Debbie's pickup on fire at the construction site the night the firefighters were killed for the insurance money.

McGraw's second article appeared in the *Star* three weeks later under the headline, "Jurors in Firefighter Deaths Didn't Follow Judge's Orders."[3]

The instructions Judge Stevens gave the jurors before they began their deliberations on the guilt or innocence of the five charged stated, "You must give separate consideration to the evidence about each individual defendant. Each defendant is entitled to be treated separately."

Despite those instructions, the jurors voted only once to convict all five defendants. One juror told McGraw, "We took one vote on all of them and didn't consider them separately."

Another juror told McGraw he and others might have voted to find Darlene Edwards not guilty if the jurors had known they could return different verdicts for each defendant.

The article also reprised the Ed Massey allegations about seeing guard Donna Costanza start a fire near the first ANFO trailer that exploded and referenced again the alleged admissions by Costanza to at least two people on separate occasions she helped Debbie Riggs set her pickup on fire as an insurance scam.

And then McGraw introduced new findings:

- False testimony by Becky Edwards, the daughter of Darlene Edwards. Becky Edwards said that an investigator pressured her and that she lied at trial about overhearing the defendants planning a theft at the construction site.
- Recanted testimony by prosecution witnesses Shannon Reimers, Carie Neighbors, and Joe Denyer. Like [Becky] Edwards, all three now say they lied at trial because federal agents threatened them or offered assistance in return for their testimony.

In the months following the *Star*'s revelations about false and recanted testimony, McGraw received numerous phone calls and emails from others involved in the firefighters trial who told them Agent True had used intimidation, threats, coercive tactics, and incentives to entice them to perjure themselves at the grand jury or at the trial—and many times both. Some resisted but many did not. In an article that dominated the front page of the newspaper on Sunday, June 29, 2008, McGraw told their stories.

"Did Pressure Lead to Lies? Numerous Witnesses Say Testimony Was Coerced," ran the headline in bold type.[4] "Today, *The Star* reveals that numerous witnesses now say they were pressured by a federal investigator to lie in the case against the [Marlborough] five," the article claimed. "Also today, *The Star* will introduce a new witness who points to another suspect in the fires."

For longtime readers of the newspaper, the boldness of these assertions was unprecedented. The *Star* did not take sides, but this day it did.

Finally, eleven years after the Marlborough Five were convicted and sentenced to life without parole, part of the massive frame-up the government engineered was coming to light, its assertions so detailed and authoritative the US Attorney's Office could not just fob them off.

In addition to the dominant front-page treatment, the article took up three full pages and ran to over forty-three hundred words. It began this way: "Carie Neighbors said they threatened to take away her son. Jerry Rooks said they warned him he'd get a stiffer jail sentence. Alan Bethard said they charged him with a more serious crime. Now those witnesses and up to 12 others—many speaking publicly for the first time—have told *The Kansas City Star* that a federal investigator in the firefighters explosion case pressured them to lie."

McGraw wrote that five who testified admit they lied to the federal grand jury or later at trial. The other seven witnesses said they refused to change their stories.

Asked for comment about the *Star*'s findings, Senior US Federal District Judge Scott O. Wright—the same judge who found the government's prosecution of Alan Bethard to be vindictive—said, "I think this is something the Justice Department really ought to look into." US Representative Emanuel Cleaver, a former mayor of Kansas City, said, "We need to go to the Attorney General and request that the investigation surrounding that explosion be reopened, and that if it is necessary, that we go back to trial."

Strong words.

Assistant US Attorney Paul Becker was not daunted by the *Star*'s revelations. To him it was all part of the job to threaten recalcitrant witnesses with their loss of freedom if they refused to cooperate in "solving a crime." He did concede, "It would be suborning perjury"—a felony—"if a federal agent pressured witnesses to lie at trial."

Becker acknowledged the case against the Marlborough Five was built in part on questionable witnesses who often gave conflicting testimony, but argued to McGraw that should be offset by the large number of witnesses who claimed the defendants made admissions of guilt.

Former ATF Special Agent Dave True had no comment.

The article moved on to a discussion of Ronnie Edwards, the government's key witness at the grand jury. McGraw wrote that over the years Edwards's accounts changed so many times "that even he couldn't keep them straight. Police records show that Ronnie Edwards told homicide detectives just two weeks after the explosion that he didn't know anything about it."

Somehow, nearly seven years later, Edwards was claiming as he stood outside the QuikTrip with Alan Bethard shortly after the first blast that he saw his stepmother, Darlene Edwards, along with Frank Sheppard, Skip Sheppard, Bryan Sheppard, and Richard Brown speeding away from the explosion site in Bryan's Ford Thunderbird being driven by Darlene.

"Despite his eyewitness account," McGraw wrote, "prosecutors never called Ronnie Edwards to testify at the trial. Becker said 'his prior statements were turned over to the defense, and he was certainly available for the defense to call [to testify at trial] if they chose to.'"

This was a misrepresentation. The defense desperately wanted to put Ronnie Edwards on the witness stand to show how the government's indictments had been cobbled together around his fantastically unreliable and perjured grand jury testimony. McGraw writes that the defense team was unable to locate Edwards, which was the case, but the article does not mention that when John Dawson, a retired Kansas City police sergeant hired by Will Bunch to subpoena Edwards, left his card at Edwards's door with a note asking him to make contact, Becker threatened to have Dawson arrested and charged with tampering with a government witness. Dawson did not try again to subpoena Edwards.

As part of his research for this article McGraw did track down Edwards at the house where he lived in Overland Park, Kansas, a close-in suburb to the southwest of Kansas City. Edwards told McGraw he did not see Darlene and the other defendants driving by the QuikTrip right after the first explosion because he was "at home in bed." Edwards said he was no longer sure the defendants are guilty, but declined to comment beyond that.

Moving on to the key witness at trial, McGraw reports Becky Edwards told him none of her trial testimony was factual. "She says [ATF Agent] True told her what he wanted her to say."

In his interview with her, she said "True pressured her for months. He followed her to work. He threatened to prosecute her for her drug use. . . . She said he got her to lie by convincing her that her physically abused, drug-addicted mother would be better off in jail."

Referencing the 2005 affidavit Becky swore out, "Becky Edwards recanted and said she never heard any discussion in 1988 of a theft specifically at the U.S. 71 site." McGraw quotes the affidavit where Becky averred, "He [True] always wanted me to say more than I actually knew about this case."

When McGraw asked her why she was recanting, she said she "had grown to realize that True had manipulated her," adding, "I grew up in a crack house, but I'm not stupid."

Ronnie Edwards, in another of his wild tales, told True that shortly after the explosions there was a party at his mother's house where Richard Brown and Bryan Sheppard were videotaped admitting committing the crime. Ronnie gave True the names of the people at the party. True began interviewing them but could not find one partygoer who said they heard any admissions.

One of the people at the party, Debra Cearley, told True there were no admissions and there was no one there with a video camera. "True didn't like anything I had to say," she told McGraw.

Another partygoer that night was Ronnie's roommate, Alan Bethard. He insisted to True he heard no admissions and volunteered to take a lie detector test. Bethard also refused to corroborate he was with Ronnie at the QuikTrip when Ronnie saw Darlene and the other four defendants speeding by.

"Bethard said True offered him the entire $50,000 reward if he would verify Ronnie Edwards's story. When he refused, Bethard said, True followed through on his threat to help move a stolen-car case against Bethard from state to federal court, where the penalties are harsher," McGraw wrote.

Becker would not tell McGraw whether he ever questioned Ronnie's story, "but he denied the government retaliated against Bethard. . . . We call it an inducement."

The article shifted to interviews McGraw conducted with numerous witnesses who were involved in the case one way or the other. While many he interviewed had no complaint about how Agent True handled himself, he found fifteen who did.

- Deborah Howard Foster, former girlfriend of Bryan's, says True tried to get her to change her story that Bryan was home in bed all night at the time of the explosions. Also True pressured her to give other incriminating information. She refused and was not called as a witness.
- Jerry Rooks, who testified at trial against Frank, Bryan, and Richard, said investigators pressured him to say Richard was involved in the crime. "They told me not to say Richard didn't have anything to do with it." Rooks added that he was told if he didn't cooperate he would do more time on a probation violation.
- Dave Dawson was on the government's witness list for the trial. He told McGraw he "fabricated some lies about one defendant" at the behest of federal investigators after they promised to assist him with a pending criminal charge. "When he refused to repeat those lies in court, Dawson said, he was charged in several armed robberies he said he did not commit."
- Carie Neighbors, a former girlfriend of Bryan's, told McGraw that True pressured her to testify she overheard Bryan and Richard Brown admitting to the crime. "He was awful," she said of True. "He told me basically that if I didn't testify, he would take my son away from me." She said True told her, "We know

what you know and this is what you know and this is what you are going to say."

- Shannon Reimers, Richard Brown's half sister, said she was also pressured by True to make false statements at trial. She now says her testimony was "inaccurate" and True intimidated her to such a point "I told him what he wanted to hear just to get rid of him."
- Larry Summers told McGraw that True encouraged him to say Bryan admitted involvement. "He told me if I changed my statement to implicate Bryan that it would help the families of the firefighters."
- Chuck Jennings says True told him not to cooperate with the defense attorneys or testify on Richard's behalf or he would face charges for past crimes.
- Joe Denyer, a homeless Marlborough man with a drug addiction, testified against Darlene. He said he lied at trial "at the direction of federal agents" who offered to help with legal problems while in jail.
- Valerie Rocha, a former girlfriend of Bryan's, said True approached her in a drug rehab program and offered her a $400 cash reward "to lie." She said True gave her "word for word what to say to the grand jury." When she was called before the grand jury, Rocha said she refused to lie and was abruptly dismissed.
- Dixie Cloughley, mother of Valerie Rocha, said True pressured her to incriminate the defendants.
- Mike DiMaggio, Shannon Reimers's former boyfriend, says ATF agents "threatened" him because he did not say what they wanted to hear.
- Johnny Driver, who was a jailhouse witness against Bryan in 1989, says True told him he would indict him for the firefighters crime if he did not implicate Bryan again.
- Jack Clark, brother of Darlene, told the *Star* he testified inaccurately to the grand jury that Frank Sheppard asked him to steal from the construction site. He said he gave that testimony because he was in trouble with the law at the time and federal agents pressured him.
- Buster Hower, Bryan's brother-in-law, said he was pressured by federal agents to stop helping Bryan with legal fees.
- Patti Smith, a former girlfriend of Skip Sheppard, testified against Skip but told True before the trial that based on what she heard Skip say his nephew Bryan was innocent. "But Smith said federal

officials told her they were not interested in information clearing Bryan 'because it was their job to prosecute.'"

The lone survivor to the explosion—other than guards Robert and Debbie Riggs—is Marion Germann, the fire department's battalion chief that night at the construction site. He told McGraw he has reservations about the case. "I've just always been uncomfortable with whether the right people went to trial." (In a phone interview in February 2007, Germann told me he was "very leery" of Debbie Riggs because she later claimed to have told his driver, Dean Gentry, what was in the burning trailer. "She never told him anything."[5])

In a sidebar article written by McGraw, "Security Guard Implicated Herself, a New Witness Says," Antonia Garcia, a friend of Debbie Riggs, swore in an affidavit that within days after the explosion that killed the firefighters, Debbie admitted her involvement in the crime.[6]

Garcia was now the fourth witness McGraw interviewed who implicated the guards.

There was actually a fifth witness who implicated Debbie Riggs who McGraw did not include in this article or any other he wrote. Another woman friend of Debbie's contacted attorney Cheryl Pilate, a defense and appeal attorney I hired in 2006 to try to find a way back into court to challenge the convictions.

Pilate introduced McGraw to this woman, but she showed such strong reluctance to having her name mentioned in the newspaper, McGraw did not refer to the contents of her affidavit, as I'm doing here. In a five-page affidavit with twenty-eight assertions she signed on July 28, 2007, she recounted being at Debbie's house with a few other women friends, including Donna Costanza, on the Sunday night before the explosions.[7] They were getting ready to watch a rented movie, *An Officer and a Gentleman*, when Debbie said she "was going to get rid of her pickup truck by burning it so that she could get the insurance money."

In a second sidebar article, this one headlined, "Trial Finds Guilt Despite Alibis, 'Snitch Testimony,'" the unreliability of jailhouse snitch testimony and testimony induced by the prospect of a $50,000 reward was taken up. From analyzing the trial transcripts and witness statements, McGraw found many of these witnesses contradicted each other. "Numerous witnesses put the defendants in different places at the same time. . . . They put Frank Sheppard in nine places at once; Bryan and Skip Sheppard, Darlene Edwards, and Richard Brown in three or four places at once."

Two days after McGraw's article ran, the lead editorial in the *Star*—"Questions, New Information Deserves More Legal Scrutiny"—called for further investigation into the case.[8]

"The 1997 trial of five Kansas Citians in what became known as the 'firefighters case' was one of the most unwieldy and contentious in the region's history. More than a decade later, with all five defendants serving life sentences, doubts about their guilt have grown substantial enough to warrant further investigation in the case," the editorial began.

"An exhaustive investigation by *Kansas City Star* reporter Mike Mc-Graw has raised more disturbing questions about the reliability of the government's witnesses, as detailed in Sunday's newspaper. At least 15 of these witnesses said an investigator for the U.S. Bureau of Alcohol, Tobacco, Firearms and Explosives pressured them to lie," it continued.

Then the editorial pointed the finger at the security guards. "In addition, at least four persons now say two security guards at the construction site have made statements suggesting their own involvement in the blast."

"A desire for 'closure' was a factor in a case that traumatized the city and went unsolved for nearly 10 years, but true closure can only be obtained through a fair and thorough process. Enough doubts exist that the Justice Department should reopen the case" were the parting words of the editorial.

Game on.

The next day the US Attorney for the Western District of Missouri, John F. Wood, caved.

"Sunday's *Kansas City Star* article indicates that some individuals have called into question their own prior statements regarding an arson case that my office tried in the 1990s," the statement his office released began.[9] (At the time of the indictment and conviction of the Marlborough Five, Stephen Hill was the US Attorney for the Western District of Missouri.)

While Wood had every confidence in the work of the investigators and the prosecutors in the case,

> our paramount goal is to ensure that justice is served in every case.
> We should ensure that all evidence is carefully considered. In order
> to ensure that these new assertions are reviewed and considered in
> a thorough and unbiased manner, on Monday morning I requested
> that the Department of Justice designate an attorney outside the U.S.
> Attorney's Office to review the assertions. We will fully cooperate
> with this review in order to assure that justice is done.

Wood's calling for a thorough and unbiased investigation was widely hailed. Senior Federal District Judge Scott O. Wright said Wood's request deserved to be granted. US Representative Emanuel Cleaver said, "If we don't reopen this case, I think this community will scream for justice. If we fail to investigate this now, it is one of the most blatant malfunctions of justice we have ever seen in this city."

Will Bunch: "It's a long awaited opportunity to correct an injustice." John Osgood: "I'm quite pleased and I think it's long overdue." Susan Hunt was incredulous: "You're kidding, I'm shocked." John O'Connor: "If the U.S. Attorney has doubts, we all should have some serious doubts."

CHAPTER 15

The Department of Justice Investigation

Two and a half months after US Attorney John Wood requested the Justice Department to conduct an investigation into the allegations of witness tampering, the *Star* ran an article on the front page of its Metro section that said anyone with new information about the firefighters case could report it by calling the DOJ's Inspector General's field office in Chicago.

It sounded as though the Justice Department had assigned the case to staff at the Office of Inspector General (OIG) in Chicago. It was a promising start to see OIG would be conducting the investigation.

Congress created the first OIG in 1976 to oversee the operations of the Department of Health and Human Services to fight waste, fraud, and abuse in Medicare, Medicaid, and more than one hundred other HHS programs. Two years later the Office of Inspector General Act was enacted, and twelve additional offices were set up, one for each of the cabinet departments. Over time, more than sixty other OIGs have been added to monitor a wide variety of government agencies and functions from the Small Business Administration to the Social Security Administration to the Tennessee Valley Authority. OIGs had become the federal government's watchdogs. Their staffs are fiercely independent and not beholden to the cabinet department or federal agency they are empowered to monitor for malfeasance.

The day the *Star* published the phone number for the OIG in Chicago, I called and asked for the staff person assigned to review the firefighters case. I was eventually put through to Pamela McCabe, who told me she was one of the people assigned to the case. She asked me what my interest was in calling her. I told her since the time the newspaper I edited published articles about the case in 1997, I was convinced of the innocence of all five defendants. I was more or less a self-appointed advocate for all five of them.

She said the investigation had not really begun, but the plan was to interview in person the witnesses McGraw had written about—no phone interviews. I told her about the seven affidavits I had that confirmed how Agent True used various forms of coercion. When I asked her if it would be all right to write to her about the case, she agreed. She said she would call me when she and another investigator came to Kansas City for the interviews.

Over the next week I put together a thirty-page synopsis of the case, laying out how the investigation had evolved over the eight years from focusing on organized labor to finally homing in on five ne'er-do-wells from Marlborough; how the government had principally used the perjured testimony of Ronnie Edwards to gain the indictments; how Agent True's theory of the case, as expressed in his pretrial report to Becker, was filled with inconsistencies, contradictions, and assumptions, with no account of what roles any of the five indicted played in the crime; how each of the convicted had iron-clad alibis; how Agent True repeatedly used coercive tactics or incentives such as a reduction in prison time to get witnesses to lie; how the guards at the construction site were the most obvious perpetrators of this crime.

Attached to my letter were affidavits from Becky Edwards, Alan Bethard, Joe Denyer, Larry Summers, Shannon Reimers, Buster Hower, and Carie Neighbors and the letter Deborah Howard Foster had written about Bryan being home asleep since around midnight on the night of the explosions.

Over the next few months, McCabe was finding how difficult it is to track down witnesses. She asked me to send her phone numbers and addresses. In late January 2009, I sent her information on twenty people, including Debbie Riggs in Texas and Robert Riggs at his Ameriguard offices in Kansas City. Alan Bethard and Johnny Driver were in prison in Missouri. Joe Denyer was living with his parents in Alabama; Jerry Rooks was homeless. I wasn't sure where Ronnie Edwards lived, but he was still in the area; Becky Edwards was no longer at her last cell phone number, but I would write to her. I gave her active cell phone numbers or addresses for the others on her list.

I suggested she might want to expand her interviews to include Kevin Lemanske, a guard at the construction site, and John Atterbury, whom True coerced in 1995 to sign a statement implicating all five defendants. I told her I thought the manner in which True threatened Atterbury would exemplify his tactics.

A few months after Atterbury told Mark Reeder and me he was too intimidated by True to talk to us, Mike McGraw explained Atterbury's re-luctance. Atterbury recently told McGraw the statement he signed for the ATF on January 24, 1995—in the presence of Agents True and Lobdell—was a complete lie. Atterbury said if he refused to sign the statement True would see to it that he would be charged in connection with the tragic 1989 deaths of Atterbury's wife and two young daughters.

On a Sunday morning, Atterbury was called away from the trailer he lived in with his family in rural Belton, Missouri, to give a jump-start to his brother's car. When he returned to the trailer, the fire department was there and the trailer had been consumed in fire. His wife and two daughters were being brought out in body bags. The state fire marshal ruled the fire an accident caused by a faulty space heater.

On February 10, 2009, I emailed McCabe about former ATF Agent True being at Mama Tio's, a bar in Marlborough, earlier that day. When Katie Sheppard, Bryan's sister, dropped by to get something to eat, Mike McCoy, the bar's longtime owner, told her True had just been in. McCoy told her True asked him specific questions about the four male defendants. True also told him he planned to sue reporter Mike McGraw and the *Star* for publishing articles about the firefighters case that misrepresented him.

On April 26, 2009, less than two weeks before the federal investigators would come to Kansas City to conduct witness interviews, the *Star* published another front-page story that directly implicated the guards in the arsons. Headlined, "Report Surfaces in 1988 Explosion That Killed Six Firefighters," it reported that a woman driving by the construction site not long before the first explosion had seen the small pickup on fire and two cars circling between the burning truck and Blue River Road.[1]

Eight months previously, the Midwest Innocence Project, which was based at the University of Missouri–Kansas City School of Law, agreed to take up the case on behalf of one of the defendants, Bryan Sheppard. Molly Frankel, an investigator for the project, was sifting through boxes of police reports at the Kansas City Police Department when she came across a report that piqued her interest. It was written by Detective John Fraise on August 2, 1990.

The *Star* article began, "Defense attorneys say they were never given key evidence that could have helped five defendants convicted in the 1988 explosion that killed six Kansas City firefighters. The attorneys say the evidence—a one-page police report—could have been used to implicate other suspects in the case and help prevent a guilty verdict in the 1997 trial that sent five defendants to prison for life."

Robert and Debbie Riggs testified at trial they did not learn of a fire at the construction site until the night manager at QuikTrip told them about it. Here was an eyewitness report from a credible person saying just the opposite.

The government's not turning over this police report constituted a major *Brady* violation even if the report was not withheld intentionally. Because it clearly implicated the guards in the arson of Debbie's truck it would have had blockbuster implications at the trial of the Marlborough Five.

In an email I wrote to McCabe the day before the *Star* article appeared, I said this police report shows both Robert and Debbie Riggs perjured themselves at trial. I pointed out that

> this police statement contained extremely important exculpatory information for all five defendants. It would have enabled their attorneys to mount an entirely different defense, a defense that would have cast major suspicion on the guards. It would have also allowed the defense to impeach the testimony of the guards. I would go as far as to say the government would have been obligated to pursue the guards as their prime suspects if this police report had been turned over to the defense.

Pamela McCabe was always friendly and pleasant to me, but also very guarded, keeping me at arm's length. Over the months leading up to her coming to Kansas City, we talked on the phone numerous times and exchanged dozens of emails, mostly about providing her with addresses and phone numbers of the people in the *Star* articles.

It was agreed we would meet at Pilate's office in Olathe on May 6, 2009, at 5 p.m. McCabe was accompanied by John Cox, an attorney in the criminal division of the US Justice Department in Washington, DC. A former FBI agent and assistant US attorney, Cox was clearly in charge. He said McCabe's association with the Office of Inspector General was "a coincidence." The investigation was being conducted by the Justice Department, not the OIG. Cox had worked with McCabe previously and had selected her as his assistant/investigator.

That was a bit of a surprise.

One of the first things Cox said about this assignment, after saying Becker had turned over thirty-eight boxes of case material to review, was that it was "no career enhancer." There would be no kudos for Cox to conclude the federal government used improper tactics in prosecuting the firefighters case. And that's exactly why the case should have been turned over to OIG.

Something else he stated was equally concerning: the two investigators had no subpoena power—they would not be able to force witnesses to testify under oath. If any witness told them to go away they would have to go away. If any witness refused to answer specific questions, that would be the end of those questions.

Cox, who is in his forties, is low-key, but all business. He wouldn't be one to loosen his tie or to take his suit coat off and throw it over the back of a chair. He and McCabe are both clean-cut, well-groomed, attractive people. They look like the FBI agents they both once were.

They showed no resistance as Pilate and I laid out our case that the government framed the Marlborough Five because they were paupers and expendable and that the guards should have been the ones prosecuted.

It appeared Cox had looked over the trial transcript. "What about all the bragging? Too many people reported hearing admissions."

Once again we were back where this case always turned, back to where Becker bought True's case just because he lined up so many witnesses who would testify about admissions, back to the jury convicting on the basis that with this many witnesses not all of them could be lying, and back to the Eighth Circuit of Appeals ruling the witness testimony was more than sufficient to convict each defendant.

As Cox and McCabe began conducting witness interviews at the federal courthouse in downtown Kansas City the next day, I began getting feedback from some of these people. The following is a summary taken from these phone calls I wrote up at the time:

- Nadine Brown, Richard's mother. I asked McCabe to include Nadine and she agreed. Nadine told them she was alone on the elevator in the courthouse early in the trial when True and Becker got on with her. They told her they both knew Richard was innocent but because he was refusing to cooperate in the investigation he was going down with the rest of the defendants. Cox, who did all the talking, told her he couldn't use that because there was no way to prove it. Nadine was in and out in less than ten minutes.
- Shannon Reimers, Richard's half sister. Cox, McCabe, and a third man who was introduced to Shannon as an investigator were at the

interview. Cox did most of the talking. He was "stern." McCabe was "nice and seemed sincere."

Early on, when Shannon said she knew her brother was innocent, Cox told her she didn't know that. She said she did know it and he again said she didn't. She said he was the one who didn't know it, but she did.

They wanted to know a good deal about Richard. Any trouble he'd ever been in. They were particularly interested in a beating he gave to a man at a picnic that resulted in the man being hospitalized. The man insinuated himself into their picnic. When the man, who was 6'2" and weighed 250 pounds, made a crude pass at Shannon, Richard took him on. Shannon's overall impression from this line of questioning was they wanted to make Richard look bad.

Cox wanted to know how the ATF got her to say what she said at trial. When she said she was young and inexperienced in dealing with government agents, Cox said, "Come on, Shannon, you weren't that young; you were 21 years old. A grown woman." She said the ATF pushed her around, badgered her, and she simply wanted to get rid of them. "I said what I said just to get them off my back," she told Cox.

When Cox began pointing out inconsistencies in her various statements, noting where she initialed changes she wanted made, he made me feel like "a big ass fat liar." (Before she testified True put all of her statements before her in a room outside the courtroom and told her to cross out any statements she didn't feel she'd made. She made liberal deletions.)

Shannon told them she was still afraid of True and was concerned he might try to come see her even though he has been retired all these years. Cox asked her why she would think that. She said because she heard True had been in Marlborough recently trying to intimidate people. How did she hear that, Cox asked? She said the old neighborhood is a close-knit one and word about True travels fast. She told them she heard True had been in Mama Tio's talking about suing people who said bad things about him.

Both Cox and McCabe vigorously denied True had been in Marlborough, saying, "He wouldn't do such a thing." They said they looked into that rumor, but it had never happened. Shannon said their voices changed, growing more animated as they said, "No, no, no that didn't happen."

• Debra Cearley, Alan Bethard's ex-wife. Ten to fifteen minute interview. The investigators essentially wanted to know if Dave True had done his job. Debra told them she had only spoken with True once and that the conversation was short and he was pleasant. She was only seventeen years old at the time of the explosion. When True interviewed her in 1994 or 1995, she was living in Tennessee.

Cearley did attempt to tell the investigators about detectives from KCPD using heavy-handed intimidation tactics on her earlier in the investigation. The KCPD detectives told her they suspected her of withholding evidence and that was against the law. Cox and McCabe were not interested in hearing about KCPD tactics.

• Mike DiMaggio, Shannon Reimers's boyfriend at the time of the explosion. His interview lasted fifteen to twenty minutes. Mike found the interview to be "not thorough." "They said they wanted to hear the facts, but then they didn't really go into any facts."

Mike was in jail and due to be released in four or five months when True approached him back in 1995. True told him he would get Mike's jail time extended if he didn't cooperate, which Mike knew to be an idle threat because he was serving the maximum amount of time.

Mike said he told the investigators the five defendants never had a chance because of all the witnesses the government badgered into testifying.

Although Mike's name had popped up on a number of police statements as a possible suspect, Cox and McCabe did not ask him for his alibi or to explain how his name got included.

• Dixie Coughly, Valerie Rocha's mother. Dixie's interview with the federal investigators "lasted fifteen minutes tops." McCabe and the man asked her about Bryan and Richard and Valerie. She told them her whole family, including Valerie and her mother, Joanna Jenson, hated Bryan because he had been abusive to Valerie when they were dating each other.

She told True and she told Cox and McCabe that Valerie had every reason to speak ill of Bryan and the fact she didn't only showed Bryan never said anything to her about being involved in the crime; Dixie told the investigators True went to Wisconsin to interview her mother, Joanna Jenson, and Joanna said rotten things about Bryan out of spite.

Before the trial True interviewed Dixie and her mom in the same room. During the tape-recorded interview True kept trying to play what her mother said about Bryan against what she said. "I told True what Valerie had told me: Bryan had told her he had not been involved in the explosion. During the interview True was browbeating me, asking me why I didn't support what my own mother was saying. After a while I cut the interview off and told True to go fuck himself and I left the room."

The investigators showed her three photos and asked her to pick out True. It had been so many years since she'd seen him she wasn't sure if she picked the right picture. Later on in the interview they showed her two more photos and asked her which one was True. "I picked the same photo I had the first time. They didn't tell me if I was right or not."

They asked her about Bryan and Valerie's relationship and how she knew Richard. "The man kept asking me the same set of questions—at least three times—he made me go back over my answers as though he was trying to catch me in some mistake. I think McCabe believed me but the man was a jerk."

• Debbie Howard Matthews, Bryan's former girlfriend and the mother of their daughter. Her interview lasted over an hour. They were friendly to her, once telling her she was not at all what they expected her to be. I said that almost sounds like an insult, and she said that's the way she felt. "I guess they expected some sort of trailer court specimen."

They asked her what she remembered about the night of the explosion. She recounted sleeping over at Bryan's parents' house in Marlborough and about 3 a.m. getting up from the sofa she was in with Bryan and going down to the basement to spend the rest of the night because Jack Sheppard, Bryan's father, didn't want them sleeping together. Jack was an early riser so she went down at 3 a.m. (At the time she was five months pregnant.)

They asked her if Bryan smelled of fire and gasoline. She said Bryan was always working on cars so sometimes he did smell of gasoline.

They asked her about Valerie Rocha and Larry Summers.

Then something rather strange happened. Cox produced a telephone message True wrote back in 1996 stating Debbie called him to tell him there was dynamite in the Sheppard's basement and she supplied a short diagram, indicating the dynamite was somewhere near the washer and dryer. Debbie told Cox she never called True about anything at any time and the Sheppard's washer/dryer was in the garage, not the basement. Debbie said they did not press the matter farther.

When I asked her about her overall impression of the interview she said, "It seemed to me that they were more interested in clearing True of any wrongdoing than finding out from me if Bryan was innocent."

I don't know how many other witnesses Cox and McCabe interviewed during their three-day visit to Kansas City, but I do know they never interviewed Alan Bethard, Valerie Rocha, Larry Summers, Buster Hower, Johnny Driver, Joe Denyer, Patti Smith, or Mike McGraw. I encouraged McCabe to sit down with Mike while she was in town and go over with him all the witnesses he reported on who claimed True pressured them to lie.

Cox and McCabe told Pilate and me they intended to interview Robert and Debbie Riggs last. I am fairly sure from the feedback I got from McCabe the Riggses were not interviewed.

Former guard Donna Costanza, then working for Prudential in real estate in Baltimore, was interviewed there but refused to answer any questions about her possible involvement in the arsons. Without subpoena power to compel her to answer questions under oath—and to face obstruction of justice and/or a perjury charges if she lied to federal agents—she had no reason to say anything.

As far as I know, neither Cox nor McCabe made another trip to Kansas City despite saying on their first visit they planned to return—several times if need be—to interview witnesses they missed on the first go-around.

After Shannon Reimers told me about Cox and McCabe both saying True had not gone to Mama Tio's, I went to the bar on a Saturday afternoon with Larry Baker, Frank and Skip's brother-in-law. We sat in a booth at the front with bar owner Mike McCoy. When I asked him if True had been there in February, he said, "He was sitting right where you are now."

Months began to pass and there was no word from the Department of Justice about the investigation Cox and McCabe were conducting. Any time McGraw would attempt to get an update from the Justice Department, he would be met with a terse "no comment."

During part of this long hiatus Pamela McCabe was out on maternity leave. Skip Sheppard, who had sent me a Christmas card at the end of 2008 that said, "God is going to be good to us this coming year. You just have to believe, and I do," was diagnosed with liver cancer and transferred to the Federal Medical Center at Butner, North Carolina, for treatment in early 2009.

Skip called me several times during the last three months of his life telling me how much he would prefer to die at home. As he lingered near death, his doctor at the medical center recommended a compassionate release. I spoke with the warden at Butner about releasing him or at least transferring him to the Bureau of Prisons medical facility in Springfield, Missouri, so his family could visit him before he died. The warden said there were five levels of red tape to go through for Skip to be eligible for compassionate release. I asked Pam McCabe to help cut through the red tape. I don't know if she tried. The last time I spoke with Skip he told me he felt bloated but okay. Several days later he died on July 25, 2009, at the Federal Medical Center in Butner. He was forty-nine.

His ashes were shipped back to Virgie Sheppard, his sister-in-law. On a hot, windy but clear Sunday afternoon in early August, with a minister leading the prayers, I joined a small group of mourners at the cemetery. Someone said at the end of the service that Skip was the first of the five innocent defendants to be freed.

Two years and a month after former US Attorney John Wood requested the independent review, the *Star* ran an editorial on August 24, 2010, questioning the long delay. "The scope of the review is unclear. The dearth of information and the length of time the review is taking are raising suspicions that getting to the truth may not be a high priority," it stated. "We hope that's not the case. US Rep. Emanuel Cleaver . . . summed up the situation: 'Justice delayed could be interpreted as justice denied.'"

On July 26, 2011, over three years after an investigation had been called for, the US Attorney for the Western District of Missouri, Beth Phillips, held a news conference and read a four-paragraph prepared statement:

> In July 2008, this office requested that the Department of Justice conduct an independent review of allegations raised by *The Kansas City Star* concerning the prosecution of *United States v. Sheppard*, et al. A team of experienced attorneys from the department of Criminal Division conducted an exhaustive review of the records and evidence in the case. The team traveled to Kansas City on multiple occasions to interview trial witnesses, law enforcement officers, and other individuals involved in the case. Their findings are compiled in a 20-page report that has been presented both to myself and to the Office of the Deputy Attorney General. Due to privacy requirements and the amount of confidential investigative material contained in the full report, a summary of the report has been released to the public.
>
> This summary of the department's findings, which was released today, states that the review team "did not find any credible support for *The Star*'s allegations."
>
> This thorough and impartial review vindicates our longstanding confidence in the professionalism of our attorneys and law enforcement agents. More importantly, it vindicates the credibility of the system of justice that resulted in five defendants being indicted,

convicted at trial by a jury of their peers, and sentenced to life in prison. The convictions and sentences were twice reviewed and affirmed. The public can be confident that justice was served.

The bottom line: there is nothing that calls into question the defendants' guilt of the crimes for which they were convicted.

Phillips took no questions.

It was a smart move after making several obvious misrepresentations in such a short statement. There was no team of experienced attorneys from the Justice Department Criminal Division—only John Cox. Pam McCabe is not a lawyer nor is she from the Criminal Division.

The claim Phillips made that the review team "did not find any credible support for *The Star*'s allegations" was unsupported in the 2½-page summary. There is no mention of the review team's failure to interview Becky Edwards, Alan Bethard, Joe Denyer, Johnny Driver, Valerie Rocha, Larry Summers, Chuck Jennings, Patti Smith, or Buster Hower—five of whom swore out affidavits turned over to the review team about Agent True's strong-arm tactics.

As she stood before the news media that day, Phillips had her own concerns. President Obama had announced just five weeks before he was nominating her for a federal judgeship in the Western District of Missouri. She was not about to place that in jeopardy by taking questions about how slipshod the review team's investigation had been. No, that was not an option. She would call the review "thorough and impartial" and walk out of the room.

The real bottom line of her prepared statement was the *Star* and Mike McGraw were prevaricators. Forget the fact McGraw backed up every one of his witness interviews with audiotape, videotape, or a signed affidavit.

The 2½-page summary stated, "Based on the information obtained during its review, the review team did not find any credible support for *The Star*'s allegations. Specifically, the review team found the following," and then listed five conclusions.

These conclusions were disingenuous on various levels. For one thing, nowhere in the summary does the review team name any of these witnesses or individuals it interviewed. Every conclusion is cloaked in obfuscation.

For another, the "from the throne" manner in which the summary was written was arrogant. Somehow during its three years of dawdling, the review team had come to see itself not only as investigators but as judge and jury. It wasn't just declaring its findings, it was issuing decrees with papal-like authority. The review team was not a post-conviction appeals court and it had no standing to make the type of judicial rulings that are reserved for federal appeals courts.

Pamela McCabe's name was missing from the summary. Instead of her, the summary listed Cox, Kevin Carwile, chief of the Capital Case Unit, and James Trusty, acting chief of the Organized Crime and Gang Section. Cox was listed as trial attorney for the Organized Crime and Gang Section. The summary was addressed to Lanny A. Breuer, the assistant attorney general for the Criminal Division of the Justice Department.

Breuer's career at Justice was tainted when it was revealed during Senate hearings in 2011 he had endorsed the ATF's disastrous "Fast & Furious" operation without informing higher-ups at the Justice Department. During 2006–2007 ATF agents allowed thousands of guns to enter Mexico illegally as part of a tragically flawed sting aimed at drug cartels there.[2] Senator Charles Grassley of Iowa called for Breuer's resignation. A number of heads rolled at Justice, but not his. (He resigned in 2013.)

In the first item the summary said the *Star* identified five trial witnesses who allegedly admitted giving false trial testimony due to coercion by the government. "Two of those witnesses agreed to speak to the review team. Both stated that their trial testimony was truthful." (The two who spoke to the review team were Shannon Reimers and Carie Neighbors.)

The other three who told the *Star* they gave false testimony at trial were Becky Edwards, Joe Denyer, and Jerry Rooks. Denyer and Rooks, both homeless, were hard to track down. Becky Edwards was another matter. At the time, she lived in central Missouri. There was no interview for McCabe I worked on harder to set up than the one with Becky. At one point, after Cox and McCabe's visit to Kansas City, I advised McCabe if she could commit to a date certain—with a three-day leeway—Becky would meet with her. McCabe never gave me a date.

In the second item, coercion of those not testifying at trial, the review team said it interviewed "each of the individuals it could locate and who would consent to an interview" and found "the government did not engage in conduct intended to improperly coerce those individuals to inculpate the defendants or to dissuade them from exculpating the defendants, and that the individuals either possessed no relevant information, or, in those instances in which they did, the Sheppard defense team had the information prior to trial."

The *Star* identified ten nontrial witnesses who said they were coerced to provide damning information about one or more of the defendants or who were told not to come forward with information favorable to a defendant. (Of those, the review team only interviewed three—Dixie Cloughley, Mike DiMaggio, and Dave Dawson.)

The other witness I most wanted the review team to interview was Alan Bethard. For a good part of the investigation Bethard was in prison in Missouri and easily available to the agents. The review team had no excuse for omitting him. Leaving Bethard out of the review showed bad faith. Both True and Becker used extreme coercive tactics in an attempt to get him to corroborate Ronnie Edwards's perjured grand jury testimony. And there were court records to prove it.

The review team also failed to interview Johnny Driver, Valerie Rocha, Jack Clark, Larry Summers, Chuck Jennings, or Buster Hower. All except Rocha were readily available.

The third item in the report concerned the prosecution's withholding of exculpatory information from the defense, i.e., *Brady* material, information that would tend to show the innocence of one or more of the defendants or would impeach a government witness. The review team had a dicey time spinning what it discovered in its investigation:

> The review team has concluded that the information from one of these individuals was disclosed in discovery [to the defendants' attorneys], while information from the other three appears not to have been included among the voluminous amounts of potentially exculpatory material produced by the government in this case. The review team has concluded that the information that appears not to have been previously provided would not have called into question the defendants' guilt of the crime charged.

The report disclosed that the government committed three *Brady* violations by withholding exculpatory information from the defense. In *Brady v. Maryland* (1963) the U.S. Supreme Court ruled one *Brady* violation was grounds for a new trial.

The fourth section of the summary dealt with the *Star*'s allegations against the guards. This also was a tricky area for the review team. When Cox and McCabe visited Kansas City, attorney Cheryl Pilate and I had laid out how duplicitous Debbie Riggs had been with Detective Zinn, lying repeatedly during her first interview with him. How Robert Riggs had been told the previous afternoon his hours were being cut back. About woodcutter Ed Massey saying he saw guard Donna Costanza start a fire near the ANFO trailer and of four people reporting she said she helped Debbie Riggs torch her pickup.

In this section of the summary, all names referring to other suspects were redacted and none of the witnesses the *Star* relied on to bring the guilt of the guards into question were named. "The review team has concluded that the information provided by these witnesses would not have called into question the defendants' guilt of the crimes charged."

This "conclusion" was not credible. In addition to the information provided by Gloria Nolen that so directly implicated the guards, there was the ATF report about Ed Massey seeing guard Costanza starting a fire near an ANFO trailer as well as the information four other people supplied about hearing Costanza claim responsibility for the arson of Debbie Riggs's pickup—had this information been known to the defense at the time of trial, the case against the defendants would have collapsed.

An even bigger reason for Beth Phillips to take no questions at the news conference was the revelation contained in the fifth and final paragraph of the summary:

> *Newly Discovered Information.* The review team identified several newly developed pieces of information, not previously known to the prosecution, that suggests that [redacted] may have been involved in the arson in addition to—and not to the exclusion of—the defendants. The review team has concluded that this newly developed information would not have called into question the defendants' guilt of the crimes charged.

The redacted space—29 characters long—seems about the right length for two names unless the reference was to a group of individuals. Regardless, the review team, most probably inadvertently, was throwing the case wide open. Claiming that other people may have been involved in the deaths of the firefighters meant the case had not been solved.

One would have thought the summary would have ended with a recommendation of convening a grand jury to consider indictment of these other perpetrators, but it did not.

The next day, the *Star* ran an article headlined, "More Perpetrators Possible in Firefighters' Deaths, Feds Say."[3] After reporting on the disclosure of possible other perpetrators, the article ate crow. "The same federal review, however, found 'no credible support' for allegations by numerous witnesses quoted in the *Star* that they lied or were coerced by investigators during a 1997 trial in the case."

The closest McGraw came to lashing out came later in the article when he pointed out that the summary report's conclusion that witnesses were not coerced and did not lie "is based on interviews with some witnesses who agreed to talk with investigators. The summary makes no reference to the signed affidavits by some witnesses recanting their testimony."

This mild protest demonstrated an amazing restraint by McGraw and his editors not to call the summary the whitewash it was. And there would be no editorials defending the intrepid reporter's four years of diligent investigation.

McGraw quoted a Justice Department spokesperson who refused to say whether the department is now investigating the new information about additional perpetrators. When McGraw asked her if the Justice Department planned to release the full report, the spokesperson said it could not be released without a Freedom of Information Act (FOIA)[4] request to protect "confidential, sensitive, law enforcement and investigative material." By this time the *Star* had already filed a FOIA request to obtain the twenty-page report.

It was quite a sleight of hand to release only a 2½-page summary of the review team's twenty-page report. Charles Davis, an associate professor of journalism at the University of Missouri who specializes in open-government issues, told the *Star* it is "highly unusual for federal officials to release a summary of such a document but not the entire report. That constitutes a game of hide-and-seek between reporters and government and creates a very unequal playing field. The full report could be highly redacted and released."

Sean O'Brien, a law professor at the University of Missouri–Kansas City who has been active in innocence cases for years, said the fact the review team found possible new suspects "is huge, but I see no reason to trust their conclusion that this new evidence is irrelevant to the convictions of the original defendants. If the truth is ever brought to light in this case, it will have to depend on people other than the government."

A few months later the Justice Department, responding to the FOIA request from the *Star*, sent the newspaper a highly redacted copy of the full report. It turned out to be seventeen pages rather than the twenty pages advertised by Beth Phillips. The first three pages were an introduction, providing background on the case: the arson, the investigation, pretrial disclosures, the trial, the *Star* articles, and the assignment of Cox and McCabe. The remaining fourteen pages were so redacted—several pages completely blacked out—the full report had no more information than the 2½-page summary. And once again, the names of the other possible perpetrators were concealed.

What was revealed in the introductory section was how much bias Cox brought to this assignment. By the time he wrote this report he had bought the government's case these defendants were guilty beyond a reasonable doubt and the government's investigation, while it may have been a bit aggressive, was just.

In the investigation section, Cox distorts the record to say Darlene made "a recorded confession" to law enforcement that she, Bryan Sheppard, and Richard Brown had driven together to the construction site on the night of the arson, implying she admitted being with them at the construction site. The distortion is that in her recorded statement she said, "I'm not staying here and playing if you are playing with gasoline. I'm not getting my funky ass blown up . . . and I left them there, period!" Cox also makes no reference to the much longer videotaped recording she gave to the ATF two days earlier where she told True she didn't know anything about the explosions and wanted to take a polygraph to prove it.

Cox claimed that in addition to Darlene's "confession," the government's evidence against her "was buttressed by her post-arson admission to three inmates, as well as testimony by her daughter." It showed a great disregard for the trial record to give any credence to the testimony of Bridgette Dornhoffer, Rosemary Quiroz, and Linda Mynhier. All were exposed on cross-examination as testifying against Darlene in an effort to cut their sentences; Dornhoffer was shown to have perjured herself on the stand. At the end of her cross-examination, Becky said she didn't really know what the truth was.

Before going into the great number of witnesses against the other defendants, Cox had one qualifier to get out of the way: "Testimony about the motive for the arson varied among witnesses, but the basic theme was that the defendants had set the fires to divert security guards at the site and/or to cover up evidence of their planned theft of items from the construction site."

He did not bother to try to explain how setting fires could possibly work to divert the guards or why they would want to divert guards who were no longer at the site.

Trial testimony from Robert and Debbie Riggs made it clear that other than Debbie claiming to see unidentified "prowlers" in the median on the west side—not on the side with the ANFO trailers—the guards saw no one at the construction site. Nonetheless, Cox quoted one trial witness who said Bryan told him they ran away from the east (ANFO) side as they saw two security guards approach. He quoted another witness who said Frank told him the fire was set as a diversion and they didn't know "explosives were in the dump truck." (Cox knew there was no dump truck and the explosives were in a trailer.)

Cox next references witnesses who also testified to various other inculpatory facts, including seeing the defendants congregated together in various groups shortly before and after the explosions and seeing Bryan Sheppard several hours after the explosions smelling of gasoline and smoke and appearing to have several abrasions.

No witnesses claimed to see Darlene anywhere but at home that night. Two witnesses claimed to see Bryan and Richard in Marlborough a couple of hours before the first blast. One witness testified Frank and Skip arrived at their mother's house in a pickup shortly after the first blast; another witness said he saw Skip outside Larry Baker's house shortly after the first blast. Karen Baird, the former massage therapist, was the one who claimed Bryan came by her house a few hours after the explosion smelling of gasoline. The credibility of her trial testimony was eviscerated on cross-examination.

One of Cox's favorite putdowns when discussing witnesses who made recantations to the *Star* was to dismiss a number of them as "not being credible." His report did not address the elephant in the room: the credibility of the record number of informant witnesses the government used at trial.

Once McGraw received the virtually useless full report, the only viable route left to the *Star* was to file a Freedom of Information Act request with the Justice Department for an unredacted copy of the report. Months passed before the Justice Department informed McGraw that based on privacy considerations there would be no release of additional information.

At this juncture, the *Star* had two options. To file a FOIA lawsuit against the Justice Department in federal district court in Kansas City—a suit that would cost many thousands of dollars with no guarantee of success—or agree to arbitration. The *Star* chose arbitration. In short order, McGraw was informed the FOIA arbitrators at the Justice Department had ruled against the newspaper. So that was that.

If nothing else, the DOJ's obstinacy demonstrated how keeping the report secret was vital to the overall damage-control campaign. To turn down the *Star*'s FOIA request was to flout the Obama administration's call for a new openness in government. On President Obama's first full day in office, January 21, 2009, he issued a memorandum to all the heads of executive departments and agencies of the federal government regarding the Freedom of Information Act:[5]

> A democracy requires accountability, and accountability requires transparency. As Justice Louis Brandeis wrote, "sunlight is said to be the best of disinfectants." In our democracy, the Freedom of Information Act (FOIA), which encourages accountability through transparency, is the most prominent expression of a profound national commitment to ensuring an open government. At the heart of that commitment is the idea that accountability is in the interest of the government and the citizenry alike.
>
> The Freedom of Information Act should be administered with a clear presumption: in the face of doubt, openness prevails. The government should not keep information confidential merely because public officials might be embarrassed by disclosure, because errors and failures might be revealed, or because of speculative or abstract fears. Nondisclosure should never be based on an effort to protect the personal interests of government officials at the expense of those they are supposed to serve. In responding to requests under the FOIA, executive branch agencies should act promptly and in a spirit of cooperation, recognizing that such agencies are servants of the public.
>
> All agencies should adopt a presumption in favor of disclosure, in order to renew their commitment to the principles embodied in FOIA, and to usher in a new era of open government. The presumption of disclosure should be applied to all decisions involving FOIA.

In this memorandum, the president directed the attorney general to issue FOIA Guidelines for the heads of executive departments and agencies "reaffirming the commitment to accountability and transparency." On March 19, 2009, during Sunshine Week, Attorney General Eric Holder issued those guidelines. Holder highlighted the FOIA "reflects our nation's fundamental commitment to open government."

The Obama administration's interest in open government turned out to be pure puffery. The *Nation* reported—based on an Associated Press study—that the Obama administration had set a new record for denying FOIA requests.[6]

CHAPTER 16

Life in Prison

Following their sentencings, Frank, Skip, and Richard were sent to the federal penitentiary at Leavenworth, Kansas; Darlene to the federal women's prison in Tallahassee, Florida. Bryan, who had been convicted on state drug charges and given three, seven-year sentences, was sent for four months to a state prison in Fulton, Missouri, and then in November 1997 to the state's maximum-security prison in Jefferson City, an old dilapidated prison known as "The Walls" that was built in 1836. Nine months later he was paroled on the state charges and sent to Florence, Colorado, to begin serving his federal life sentence.

The growth in federal prisoners has been exponential since 1980, soaring by over 720 percent from 25,000 to over 205,000 in 2015. During that time the amount of money the Justice Department spends on housing federal prisoners has grown by over 2,000 percent, from $330 million to $7.1 billion, taking up 26 percent of DOJ's budget.[1]

More than half of the rise in federal prisoners stems from drug convictions. Two other major causes behind this growth are mandatory minimum sentences and the elimination of parole after 1987.

To cope with this dramatic increase in prisoner population, the Bureau of Prisons went on an unprecedented building program, erecting massive prison complexes in remote rural areas throughout the United States. There are now 122 federal prisons and 11 operated by private prison corporations.[2] The District of Columbia and every state have a federal prison, most states more than one. Made of cement with limestone or sandstone facades, their high walls topped with razor wire, these new prisons present forbidding, desolate visages when you see them arise out of what once had been open farmland.

The one in Coleman, Florida, is a prototype of the new concept in federal prison construction. Set back over a half mile from a two-lane state highway is a complex of five prisons laid out in something of a horseshoe. Richard—along with fourteen hundred inmates—is now housed in one of the two maximum-security prisons. Down the road is the other max.

Around the bend are the medium-security and minimum-security prisons. Across the way, sitting by itself, is the women's prison, called Camp Coleman. In total, the prison population runs to just over seven thousand inmates.

Prisons are hellholes not only because they are so dangerous or because the food is lousy and health care is an afterthought, but because they are so regimented. There are regulations for everything—the time you get up, the time you eat, the time you go to work if you are lucky enough to have a job, the time you can watch TV or make a phone call, the time you can be in the yard outside, and the time you go to bed.[3] And then there is the constant noise: doors clanging open and shut, inmates shouting, TVs and radios blaring, creating something like the roar of a packed stadium, punctuated throughout the day by loud intercom messages.

In prisons for male inmates, affiliations within the prison population are usually race based. Generally speaking, blacks stick with blacks, whites with whites, Hispanics with Hispanics, Asians with Asians. It is quite common for there to be subsets within the various race groups. Within the white population, for example, there could be Aryan Brotherhood members as well as members of a group that calls itself the Dirty White Boys—the largest white gang in the federal prison system. Then again, you have your Skin Heads. All of these white groups are generally at odds with members of the Black Guerrilla Family, the Crips, and the Bloods to say nothing of the Latin American gangs or the Mexican Mafia.

Native Americans, although by far the smallest subset within federal prisons, nonetheless constitute their own group. They cell together, eat together, and worship together at the sweat lodge. As the smallest group, they generally steer clear of aligning themselves with any of the major groups, although in some prisons they align with Mexicans or whites. Nonetheless, they are not immune to infighting within their own Native group.

Each prison group has its own hierarchy and power structure. It would not be an overstatement to say that in matters of everyday life the interactions among the various groups rather than any control the guards assert determines if the prison functions on an even keel. If say, a black group member has a problem with one of the members of the Dirty White Boys, the leader—known as the "shot caller"—of the black group would approach the leader of the white group to work out a solution. If diplomacy fails, all hell can break loose. When all hell breaks loose, everyone loses because everyone in both groups—as well as those housed around them—is put on lockdown.

Lockdowns can last for a couple of days, a week, or a month depending on the severity of the disturbance involved. During this time period, prisoners are confined to their cells and put on dry rations—no recreation, no store privileges, no classes, no work, no visitors, and no phone calls—twenty-four hours a day in a cell until the prison administration lifts the lockdown. During the lockdown, all the cells in the prison are searched for contraband and many prisoners lose valuable personal items such as stingers (an improvised device to heat water), extra clothes, blankets, and double pillows.

It would be the exception for Frank, Richard, or Bryan to tell me he had gone a month without being in lockdown. Fights are the most common reason for lockdowns, but using this disciplinary tactic for far less serious disruptions is a not so subtle way of asserting the prison's control.

Another way of asserting control over prisoners is to move them from federal prison to prison every three or four years or so—sooner if the prisoner is a troublemaker. Bryan, because of his good behavior, was transferred from Florence to Leavenworth in early 2001, joining Frank, Skip, and Richard. One time when I went to visit Leavenworth with attorney John Osgood, I was allowed to see each of them one at a time. After that, when I went to visit on my own, I could only be on the visiting list of one of them.

Getting into a federal prison to visit an inmate is usually an ordeal. The guards seem to take a perverse delight in making the experience an unpleasant and time-consuming one. Several times my three-hour planned visit was shortened to forty-five minutes or less in filling out paperwork and waiting in an anteroom to be called. Gaining admittance at Leavenworth, which is thirty-five miles northwest of Kansas City, was easier than at the newer prisons. Its proximity to an urban center may account for why the guards are more accommodating there.

If you didn't know better and were just driving by, the penitentiary at Leavenworth could easily be mistaken for a statehouse with its domed top above the front doorway. The building would not be out of place on Constitution Avenue in Washington, DC. Along with the one in Atlanta, Leavenworth opened in 1903 as a maximum-security prison. Prior to that federal prisoners were housed in state prisons.

In 2005, when Leavenworth was converted to a medium-security prison, Frank, Richard, and Bryan were sent to Florence and Skip to Victorville, California. None of them liked being incarcerated at Florence and all asked for transfers. Racial tensions at Florence, where the Aryan Brotherhood smoldered, could erupt at a moment's notice. Stabbings and beatings went on almost weekly. It was not uncommon for brawling inmates to be shot by the guards in the yard towers.

In the roughly two and a half years the three of them were incarcerated in Florence, they saw a lot of violence and violent deaths on the yard. Although none of them were ever the direct victim of violence at Florence, they did not escape unscathed. In an interview with a criminologist in 2016, Bryan discussed the trauma of being surrounded by violence: "It's hard to see somebody stabbed to death in front of you, multiple times. Watching people being stabbed to death, beaten; it's not like on TV . . . I *lived it*. . . . Seeing it, watching the blood spill, hearing the moans and the screams and stuff is, is, I don't know how you would describe it other than traumatizing. Like the *Silence of the Lambs*, I can still hear the screaming."

In May 2007, Richard and Bryan were shipped to Big Sandy in Inez, Kentucky, not far from the West Virginia border. Frank's transfer request for Tucson, where Skip had just been sent, was approved. By the time Frank got there, Skip was suffering from liver cancer and would be transferred a little over a year later to the Bureau of Prisons Medical Center in Butner, North Carolina, where he would die in mid-2009. After just two years in Tucson, Frank was transferred to Pollock, Louisiana, in 2009.

In terms of personal safety, Big Sandy was almost as bad as Florence. Bryan regretted asking for the transfer, but Richard threw himself into his new surroundings, becoming in just a few months the shot-caller for the twenty-five or so Native Americans prisoners. Instead of working a prison job as he always had, Richard turned the cell he shared with Bryan into his center of operations. For the first time, these avowed best friends were hardly speaking to one another, and Bryan had moved to another cell.

How a prisoner does his time says a great deal about him personally. All Bryan ever wanted to do, regardless of what prison he was in, was work on his legal case: he wanted to prove the innocence of the Marlborough Five. He wrote dozens of letters to innocence projects; he spent most of the $250 his mother sent him each month making phone calls trying to track down new information. He was persistent. Over the years I've received over a hundred letters from him and more phone calls. He sends more greeting cards than a socialite.

Within days of arriving at Florence in 1998, he enrolled in the prison's General Education Development program. Four months later the State of Colorado awarded him his high school equivalency diploma. Later he completed courses in anger management and drug education.

Richard, on the other hand, was, if not fatalistic, more concerned with prison life itself, although he too did get a GED while at Florence. He was in prison and he knew he was going to be there for a long time, if not the rest of his life. He not only wanted to survive, but to make the best of it. He played sports and was in tip-top shape. He was determined if push came to shove, which it invariably does in prison, he would be the one still standing.

At 5'10" and 180 buffed pounds, Richard was a match for inmates much larger. He made some enemies in the Native American group by his rapid rise that put his life in danger. Some of the full-bloods deeply resented him. But just as he had a penchant for souped-up cars, he loved being in the fast lane, feeding on the tension swirling around him. He relished being the center of attention his new status conveyed.

Bryan wanted nothing to do with being an "inmate." He refused to participate in team sports. For his own protection, he lifted soda bags and bulked up, and at 6' and 200 pounds was quite capable of taking care of himself. His dream was to stay shot free—without any demerits—long enough to be eligible to be transferred to a medium-security prison, preferably Leavenworth, so his daughter, parents, and sisters could visit him. He was well on his way to qualifying for a transfer when word reached him and Richard that one of the Natives boasted he was going to stab Bryan for being standoffish, for not being part of the Native gang.

Unfortunately, one way to get at Richard was to menace Bryan. If this was an elaborate ruse to undermine Richard, it worked to perfection. When the inmate who threatened Bryan next showed his face, Richard beat him to a pulp right in the pod. Richard told Bryan he needed to save face by bashing the guy too. Bryan did. It was a big mistake that came with a severe penalty. For fighting, Bryan was transferred to Butner, North Carolina, where he spent seven months in an isolation cell twenty-three hours a day with one hour out for exercise. Richard was sent to Gilmore, West Virginia, for five months in isolation. With this serious shot on his record, Bryan's chances of a transfer to Leavenworth were out of the question. Richard's days as a shot-caller were over.

Of the Marlborough Five, Frank knew how to do time. His years in state prisons in Missouri taught him how to get along. He knew the drill. He was old enough and big enough that other prisoners basically left him alone. At Leavenworth he celled with Skip and nobody there wanted to mess with Skip.

Frank's innate charm never left him. He was apolitical. He could talk to anybody. He was friendly as long as he was sober. When he could he imbibed the rock-gut booze fellow prisoners made by fermenting various fruits. Drinking landed him repeatedly in "the hole." Going to the hole was simply the price he was willing to pay to keep doing what he wanted to do. Some things never change.

Not long after Frank arrived at Pollock, Richard was transferred there. By then, Richard's long-held animosity against Frank had run its course even though he was still convinced Frank and Skip stole his grandfather's riding mower and chain saw after his grandfather had a stroke. (Frank vehemently denies stealing from Richard's grandfather.) For a few months they celled together, but they were essentially incompatible.

In April 2010 Bryan was sent to McCreary, a maximum-security prison located in Pine Knot, Kentucky, a rural area in the southeast part of the state near the border with Tennessee. It was the first time in eight years Bryan was not in the same general population with Richard and that in itself was a relief. McCreary was far better run than Big Sandy. Bryan melded into the Native American group and began for the first time to appreciate and cherish his participation in the sweat lodge ceremonies. The only shot he got on his record there was for staying inside the sweat lodge too long after a guard showed up and announced an emergency count, requiring all prisoners to return to their cells at once.

Richard spent three years at Pollock and then was transferred in 2013 to the federal penitentiary complex at Coleman, Florida. Two years later, Frank was transferred to the maximum-security prison at Atwater, California. He likes being back in California. It reminds him of his days when he was in the army stationed at Fort Ord. "This place is okay," he wrote me in July 2016. "Great weather, even better than Pollock and much less rain."

Darlene began her incarceration at the federal prison for women in Tallahassee, Florida, but was transferred to Carswell, the women's prison in Fort Worth, Texas, in late 1998. Carswell, which is situated on the grounds of a former air force base, opened in 1994 as the only medical hospital for women in the Federal Bureau of Prisons system. The hospital is a five-story building. On the second floor are cancer and dialysis units. The third floor is for inmates with mental issues. The fourth floor is for the chronically sick and includes a hospice for those nearing death. The fifth floor is for inmates who require regular medical treatment.

In addition to the hospital, there is a medium-security prison where Darlene was assigned, a maximum-security facility that houses about 20 women, and a camp prison that houses about 320 minimum-security inmates in barracks on land outside the main prison compound. In all, there are about 1,300 inmates at Carswell, most, but not all, with various medical issues requiring regular treatment.

Darlene's transfer to Carswell coincided with the opening of the medium-security women's prison next door to the hospital. Bridgette Dornhoffer, one of the jailhouse snitches who testified against Darlene at the firefighters trial, was there when she arrived. This presented an awkward and dangerous situation for Dornhoffer. Other than pedophiles and child murderers, snitches are the most reviled of all prisoners.

Normally, a prisoner in Dornhoffer's predicament would put in for a transfer and wait out the transfer in segregated housing. But Dornhoffer, whose reward for testifying against Darlene had been to begin serving her federal time to run concurrent with her state time—an agreement that cut eighteen months off of her state time—filed separation papers with the Bureau of Prisons requesting Darlene be transferred. The BOP granted her request. Darlene was sent back to Tallahassee.

In 2001, after Dornhoffer finished serving her federal time, Darlene put in for a transfer back to Carswell. Her father was in the final stages of his battle with cancer and she wanted to be able to see him before he died. The plan for her parents to drive to Fort Worth for a visit was foiled when Darlene got a shot—a demerit—for telling an off-color joke to a prison guard. Part of her punishment was no visitors for the next six months. By the time she could have visitors her father was too sick to travel. The next year he died.

Four years later her mother, her children Tommy and Becky, and their five children visited Darlene at Carswell. That was the last time she saw anyone from her family.

Darlene has been a model prisoner throughout her period of incarceration. If she had not been given a life sentence, she would have long ago been eligible to live in a camp prison and have far more freedom.

In 1998 she signed on with UNICOR, or Federal Prison Industries, a wholly owned US government corporation established in 1934 to provide various types of jobs for inmates.[4] UNICOR operates over one hundred factories inside federal prisons throughout the United States. Factories manufacture clothing, textiles, electronics, office furniture, among others, for sale to the military or government agencies. Lately there has been a move among the private sector to outsource data entry jobs and call centers to UNICOR workers.

Over time, Darlene moved from the typing pool to the call center, handling information calls for various telephone companies. Her per-hour pay rose from 24 cents, to 60 cents, to 80 cents, to the top pay level of $1.06. For her longevity she received an additional 20 cents an hour. When she was promoted to supervisor she could make as much as $2.50

per hour with overtime. Some weeks she logged sixty or more hours. After UNICOR shut down operations at Carswell in 2010, she began working for the prison administration as a payroll clerk and a supply clerk, her pay cut to 17 cents an hour.

Part of the sentencing of the Marlborough Five involved restitution for the loss of two fire trucks and all the equipment involved. The court set restitution at $536,000. Over the years, Darlene has paid in over $14,500 in restitution, $10,000 more than any of her co-defendants.

In terms of education courses, Darlene enrolled in 120 and completed 119, including 160 credit hours in reading, 111 hours in yoga, over 60 in painting, 40 in ceramics, and other subjects as far-flung as ancient Egyptian history, the study of fairy tales, employment skills, and exercise for older adults. Darlene, like Bryan, has always been convinced one day she will walk free.

Darlene turned sixty-three in October 2017. For the last twenty-two years, she has been locked up. During her first two years, she was so depressed she gained 130 pounds. She went on a months-long diet and lost 50 pounds and then gained about half of that back. In a letter she wrote to me in August 2016, she said, "I had no medical issues until I got to Carswell. Then in the last eight years I have had a hysterectomy. I had my bladder lifted. I have neuropathy in both legs. I have spinal fractures [from her motorcycle accident in 1987] that never healed correctly. I now have a curved spine. I also have a severe case of sleep apnea and I have to sleep with a C-PAP machine that forces air into my lungs to keep me alive and breathing. I wear glasses now. I have a lot wrong with me but I'm alive," adding a smiley face at the end.

As a result of her declining health, she is now housed on the top floor of the hospital building, sharing a room, not a cell, with four other inmates, and is unable to work a job.

Interviewing the Original KCPD Detectives

During the summer of 2014 I spent six weeks in Kansas City interviewing a number of people connected to the firefighters case.

One of the people I always go see is Leo Halloran, the younger brother of Gerald Halloran, the captain of Pumper 30. We met at a Starbucks in midtown about 10 a.m. in early August.

Leo knows the firefighters case; it is in his bones. He sat through every day of the six-week trial. At the sentencing hearing, after attorney John Osgood argued the firefighters demonstrated reckless behavior in fighting a fire in an ANFO trailer and essentially killed themselves, Leo made an impassioned and lucid speech in defense of their actions.

He even took the time to attend a lengthy deposition Debbie Riggs gave in a civil suit. He was leery of her and her brother Robert then and remains so. The first time I met him in 2003, he told me that as he walked out of the courtroom after the convictions, he had serious doubts the right people had been found guilty.

When I mentioned at Starbucks I'd never been to the site where the firefighters were killed, he said let's go. He thought it was a place I should see firsthand.

On one of the hottest days of the year, Leo took me up to see where the enormous craters the explosions created had been. There was no sign of them now. To get there we climbed up a vertically steep hill covered in grass and weeds up to our waists. Although Leo was seventy-nine then, he is a tall, lean, determined man.

The plateau where the firefighters died is about the size of three or four football fields. The limestone the construction companies were blasting to turn into roadbed back in 1988 has been long ago mined out. A rock quarry not far away—just a quarter of a mile or so—is still in operation. We could hear the workers over there as we walked, and we could see the dust fly up as their trucks full of limestone came down the nearby hill.

The land on top is flat, desolate, and forlorn, an excellent habitat for rattlesnakes and copperheads. I had an eerie feeling as we walked around. Not far from the bottom of the hill we just climbed stands a memorial to the six firefighters. Leo told me he visits it several times a week. Near where the craters had been, he showed me the approximate place his brother's body was found.

Nothing marks that spot. He told me his brother's body was found draped over a piece of construction equipment just feet from where the first trailer exploded. About three hundred feet away, he showed me where the bunkers containing the dynamite and blasting caps were located and told me the body of a firefighter was found there, a walkie-talkie on the ground near him.

We were up there about thirty minutes before we decided to head back down. I made it a few feet down the steep hill when I noticed Leo wasn't with me; he had stopped and was sitting on a rock trying to catch his breath, sweat pouring down his face. He had an ashen look. I had a terrible feeling he was having a stroke or a heart attack. He sat still for a while, embarrassed. We made it back down the hill very slowly. We agreed to meet for lunch at a restaurant in Waldo, a thriving, older neighborhood a mile north of Marlborough. Leo was there when I arrived.

During my time in Kansas City I set up interviews with three of the four former Kansas City Police Department officers from the homicide division who were assigned to investigate the case the day of the explosions. Captain Gary Van Buskirk led the investigation; Sergeant Troy Cole supervised it; and Detectives Victor Zinn and John Fraise were the principal investigators. All but Fraise agreed to talk with me.

Victor Zinn agreed to meet me at 6 p.m. on August 4, 2014, at Kelly's Bar in Westport, a trendy midtown area known for its nightlife. After working seventeen years in homicide, including being a hostage negotiator for most of that time ("I never lost a hostage"), Zinn was now a Jackson County deputy sheriff nearing retirement. He had a cushy but low-paying and boring job at the county courthouse. He had stopped home on his way to our meeting to change into civilian clothes. I had told him I was planning to write a book about the firefighters case. He agreed to speak on the record.

Zinn is a tall, burly man, built like an ice block. His facial expressions alternate between a scowl and deadpan. On first impression, I thought the interview would be very short. I expected nothing but terse answers. This impression took a sharp turn when I ordered him a drink and he immediately replied, "I've got the next one."

He had been a KCPD detective for eighteen months when the explosions occurred. He lived within a half mile of the blast site and was awakened by the second blast. Figuring he would be soon called in, he dressed and went to the command post at Bannister Road. There he was assigned the task of interviewing Debbie Riggs. Detective William Wilson was assigned Robert Riggs. Debbie by then was already at her mother's house in Grandview so Zinn drove there and picked her up predawn.

While Wilson was interviewing Robert in an adjoining room, Zinn took Debbie to the video room to question her, not as a suspect but as an important on-site witness to the events that preceded the explosions. He did not Mirandize her and Wilson did not Mirandize Robert. (That would come later when their "stories started getting left-handed," he said.)

For this interview, he deployed his standard approach. He wanted her to tell a story—to get her to commit to a version—without any challenges from him. "Your job is to act like you believe everything you hear and that you are being empathetic."

As Debbie recounted the evening's events, he said he felt there was "something obviously wrong" about her story. She said from her vantage point on the west side of the construction site near the large equipment, she saw two large, heavy-set prowlers about 3:30 a.m. walking in the direction of Blue River Road. The trailers, according to Zinn, were about a third of a mile from where she sat. She said they were walking in behind the Brown Brothers' office trailers in the median that separates northbound and southbound 71 Highway. She said she had the car's dome light on, making up new assignment schedules for Ameriguard (the security company's hours had been cut back earlier the afternoon before) when she looked up and noticed the two prowlers.

The story about the prowlers did not make sense to Zinn:

> You see someone suspicious and you leave your pickup truck with the keys in the ignition, your purse on the seat and the handgun your brother loaned you for protection in the glove box? That just doesn't add up. And then instead of staying on the premises to guard the site against prowlers you drive with your brother to QuikTrip and buy rolls and coffee? There were a lot of things wrong about all of that.

Zinn described the visual test he and Fraise conducted that convinced him Debbie could not have seen prowlers from where she sat.

Despite his suspicions about both Robert and Debbie Riggs—and

Donna Costanza as well—Zinn never took the step to file a probable cause statement with the Jackson County prosecutor. With a team of nine detectives working the case under the supervision of Gary Van Buskirk, the investigation went in numerous other directions. The early posting of a $35,000 reward brought in hundreds of leads that had to be chased down. Although Zinn retained his interest in the Riggses, he said he was never allowed to approach them after they retained attorneys. "Once they lawyered up, the case was stopped cold."

After the first forty-five days, Zinn said the police investigation had no direction.

In the early stages of the investigation there was a general assumption labor unrest might be behind the explosion, a theory Zinn said he never supported. "It wasn't labor's M.O. They would idle a site, shut it down for a few days by putting metal shavings in the gas tanks of earth movers, but not go in for causing such an enormous explosion."

After nearly seven years of fruitless investigation, Zinn said KCPD was more than happy to turn the case over to ATF. "The ATF has a lot of resources, a lot of money. Their people are very educated. Their problem is they have no street smarts. I'm afraid to work with them. . . . The federal government [Labor Department and ATF] were all wrong about labor," he said.

Asked if he thought the people convicted were guilty, Zinn said, "The only thing they were guilty of was being who they were. Those five were railroaded to close a case that should not have been closed. Just look at the type of witnesses the government used against them. All the witnesses against the defendants were shaky. They had some blind masseuse who ran a prostitution operation on the side, a bunch of losers from bars, and many, many convicts."

So who caused the explosions? "There's no doubt in my mind that the Riggses did it. Anyone who reads the case file would know that, too."

The scenario he sees in his mind is Robert Riggs, concerned now about Ameriguard's hours being cut back, driving up to Bannister Road and coming up the access road to the east side of the site—where the ANFO explosive trailers are—and dousing the Mountain Plains pickup truck with gasoline, setting it on fire, and then driving back around to the west side where he douses Debbie's pickup with gasoline, sets it on fire, and then quickly heads for QuikTrip to build an alibi. The big miscalculation Robert makes is that the Mountain Plains pickup is almost touching the trailer full of ANFO and the fire he thought would be relatively harmless turns into a horrific explosion, killing six firefighters.

"Riggs set a fire on a piece-of-shit pickup to make it look like vandalism. Debbie is such a ding-a-ling she leaves her purse in the pickup. Robert tells her what to say: to invent a prowler story. Keep it simple, stupid, but even then I caught her in a number of lies about that."

Regarding the convicted defendants, he said they were such lowlifes all of them would be in prison today on other charges. He seemed to have no understanding of the inherent differences and antipathies within this group of five, of how Bryan and Richard, twenty years younger than Frank and ten years younger than Skip, operated in another orbit and did their best to avoid contact with them. Frank's reputation as an armed robber and as a habitual petty thief tarnished all the defendants.

A week later I called Zinn to ask him if he ever saw the police report John Fraise wrote up on August 2, 1990, recounting the observations of Gloria Nolen—mentioning Nolen told Fraise she saw a pickup fully engulfed in flames as she drove by the site and she also saw two white cars with spotlights scanning the area around the office trailers in the median of 71 Highway.

"I never saw that report. Things were drying up by the summer of 1990. It would have been up to Sergeant Troy Cole to do the follow-up on that report, but I never heard from Cole about it." He said Cole is "a good guy from Oklahoma."

Zinn mentioned a file cabinet with all the police reports about the firefighters case stored in it. A couple of years after the explosions the reports were all put on a floppy disc. He said it would be interesting to see if Fraise's report about Nolen is on that disc.

In another interview, this one on the evening of August 20, I showed Zinn the police report written by Fraise recounting what Gloria Nolen reported seeing the night of the explosions. About the report, Zinn said, "Somebody should have gone out and talked in person to this lady."

Later that night, around 11 p.m., Zinn had me follow him to the former construction site off of US 71. We got out of our cars below the Bruce R. Watkins Memorial Drive and stood on a shoulder of an off-ramp with cars whizzing by. He said this was approximately where Debbie Riggs was parked when she claimed to have seen the two prowlers. Our view was directly north toward Blue River Road, a distance we judged to be about a quarter or a third of a mile away.

As we looked at cars just beyond Blue River Road—where Debbie said she saw the prowlers near the construction office trailers—he asked me if I could identify the model of any of the cars passing. I could only tell a car from a truck. He said to suppose I could see a person walking north of Blue River Road, did I think I could determine the person's sex? I said I couldn't. Did I think I could see whether a person was wearing a hoodie? That was definitely not a possibility. Did I think there was any possibility, even if I saw a person with a hoodie, that I could see the person's hair sticking out of the hoodie? That was impossible. "But that's how Debbie described one of the prowlers—wearing a hoodie with his hair sticking out," Zinn said.

On a sheet of paper he drew a rendition of the site, showing where Debbie was parked, where the construction trailers were, and where she said the prowlers first appeared. On this map he drew in Debbie's view of the east side of the construction site. Between where she was parked on the west side, she would look over southbound 71, over the deep median separating the southbound lane from the northbound lane of 71, over the northbound lane, over a deep ditch just beyond that, and then her view would be of a steep hill with about a 35 percent grade up to the mesa of the east side where the rock quarry was situated as well as the ANFO trailers and bunkers of explosives. It would be impossible to view any movement on the east side from her perspective on the west. The east side was not illuminated. From the west side it would only be possible to see light introduced by some outside source, such as a vehicle or a fire.

A number of things continue to vex Zinn about the guards. He found it strange—or convenient for concocting an alibi—that instead of Debbie going to the command post for questioning that Robert drove her shortly after the second explosion to her mother's house in Grandview. And then when he goes and picks her up for questioning around 6 a.m. he finds "her story from the jump is absolutely fabricated." He said what she told him during their interview just didn't make sense—"it simply wasn't plausible."

"There's no explanation for why a criminal would set the initial fire on the east side and then go set her pickup truck on fire," he said. "This would be like someone who just robbed a bank walking across the street to shoot some innocent bystander for the hell of it." He added,

Even the craziest crime in the world has a motive, but what's the motive for a small diversion when the guards are already gone from the site? What's the motive for these five idiots [the five convicted]— these boobs—to blow up these trailers? If the guards are gone to QuikTrip why set the guard's pickup on fire as a diversion? Why leave Debbie's purse and Robert's gun in the pickup?

Motive: "In my way of thinking, the only people who had anything to gain from an incident on the construction site were the Riggses: their hours were being cut."

The notion that one of the five convicted carried a five-gallon can of gas, weighing about thirty-five pounds, up to the site doesn't ring true to Zinn. The terrain on the east side was extremely rugged and difficult to negotiate. "You don't set out on a robbery job with a can of gas. How many other buildings or places did these knuckleheads break into and never started a fire?"

In his opinion, Debbie Riggs, "a dingbat," is the weakest link among the guards and would be the most susceptible to immunity to tell what actually happened at the site that night. "It's important enough to finally know what happened that night to give her immunity."

Zinn thinks there are three reasons why the government has stonewalled the fact the wrong people were convicted. "The fact Skip Sheppard died in prison makes it so the government will never admit they convicted the wrong people. The lawsuit from his death would be enormous. Second, the public outcry would be incredible that all these years have passed without convicting the right people. Third, overturning these convictions would open the federal government up to many other cases where they coerced or coached people to testify."

Even after twenty-six years this case still eats at Zinn. "What bothers me is that the Fire Department and the families of the dead firefighters so readily accepted the case the feds put together to solve this case. After all those years everyone wanted to know who did this crime. Instead of charging the right people the feds got some scapegoats. . . . We just don't have the right people in prison."

Until his retirement from the KCPD in 1991, Gary Van Buskirk was in charge of the department's investigation into the firefighters case. He retired with the rank of major. I spoke with him by phone for about thirty minutes on the evening of August 6, 2014. He told me he was not feeling well enough to do an in-person interview.

I told him I was writing a book on the firefighters case because I thought the wrong people were in prison and the five convicted were innocent. I said the reason I was calling him was because in reading the early reports in the *Kansas City Times* and *Star* it appeared he had serious reservations about the credibility of both Robert and Debbie Riggs, although he was quoted several times in the early days of the investigation saying he did not consider either one of them suspects. He said you don't call people "suspects" in the press unless you want them to "run even faster to get a lawyer."

Although he said he "wasn't uncomfortable with the convictions" that resulted because of his extremely dim view of Frank Sheppard's criminal past, he, too, retained serious doubts about the guards' possible involvement.

He said the account the guards gave, particularly about only being away from the construction site 4½ to 5 minutes, "didn't pass the smell test." But on the other hand, he said, you have to have proof of guilt. "You just can't go with your own opinion." There was a total lack of evidence against the guards. "After all, they were the only two there. There is only so much you can do with no physical evidence."

Asked why the guards got off the police's radar so quickly, even after Detective Zinn's interview of Debbie Riggs the morning following the explosions caught her in numerous lies, he said there simply wasn't enough evidence to keep pursuing them "short of water-boarding them." Plus, he said, they both quickly hired lawyers and clammed up.

I asked him why he thought the Riggses lied so much about their actions that night. "To save their asses; to benefit themselves," he said.

When I mentioned I thought it was quite a coincidence Robert Riggs was notified during the afternoon before the blasts occurred that the construction company was cutting back Ameriguard's hours to patrol the site, he said he was well aware of that fact, adding immediately, "I don't believe in coincidences."

Asked if Robert Riggs's passing a police-administered polygraph exam cleared Riggs in his mind, he said, "I don't believe in polygraph tests. If you're a habitual liar and good at it, your heart rate doesn't change."

He asked me if I had spoken with Victor Zinn. I told him I had, and Zinn was adamant about the guards' guilt. "Vic felt that way from day one. But I told him you can't have tunnel vision until you get deeper into the investigation."

He suggested I contact former Sergeant Troy Cole, who he assigned to supervise the firefighters investigation. He took the time to look up Cole's phone number.

When I asked him if he ever saw the 1990 police report given by Gloria Nolen that placed the guards at the construction site while Debbie's pickup was ablaze, he said he had not. I asked him if such a report would have brought the investigation back to the Riggses, he said, "That would have re-opened the door for us on the Riggses. We would have some leverage to use against them."

He asked me to find out what police officer took that statement and to call him back. When I reached him by a phone two days later and told him the report was written by Detective John Fraise and signed by Cole, he said, "I'm seventy-five years old and I just can't remember if I ever saw that report."

I made numerous attempts to reach John Fraise, talking to his wife a couple of times, but he never returned my calls.

Troy Cole was out of town when I called, but I was able to leave a message on his answering machine. He called me the day he came back. We agreed to meet for lunch at Applebee's in Grandview off of US 71 on August 20.

Cole is an attractive, athletic-looking man with a crew cut. He has an open demeanor, smiles easily, and is low-key. I got the impression sitting across from him he had seen it all and had viewed a great deal of it with irony. When I told him I got his phone number from Van Buskirk, he asked about him and then said, "He was the best police commander in the history of the KCPD." He also said Zinn and Fraise were excellent detectives.

Cole, sixty-eight, retired from the KCPD in 1997 with the rank of sergeant, finishing his career working in intelligence for KCPD. He then worked thirteen years for a local insurance company in the fraud division. He retired for good in 2010 and now lives on four acres outside of Belton, Missouri.

He attended junior college in Oklahoma. He then went to work for the CIA at its headquarters in Langley, Virginia. Because of a CIA rule banning relationships among its employees, he left the CIA after two years to go to work for the Washington, DC, Police Department. He worked there two years. (He is married to the woman he met at the CIA.)

He moved to Kansas City and joined KCPD and was a patrol officer for a year and then was moved into intelligence work. After a few years there, mostly doing stakeouts for the FBI, he joined the homicide division and was there about seven years when the firefighters were killed. Just before that case broke he was finishing up the Bob Berdella investigation that began in April 1988. (Berdella raped, tortured, and killed at least six young men between 1984 and 1987. He was arrested in April 1988, convicted, and sentenced to life. He died of a heart attack in 1992.[1])

Asked if he thought the right people were convicted in the firefighters case, Cole said, "I was convinced the guards were involved, that the guards did it. As big of assholes as the Sheppards and Brown were, they didn't deserve to be in prison for life." He said one thing that impressed him a great deal about these defendants was none of them ever rolled over on the others to get a lesser sentence. "I thought it was weird none of these people took the get-out-of-jail card and testified against each other."

What made him so convinced the guards were involved? "Their demeanor. I felt they were lying from day one. Their stories didn't jive . . . I've been working homicide a long time and I know how to size people up and their stuff didn't add up. The fact their hours had been cut that day was a big red flag to me."

He also couldn't understand how the guards would leave the site and go to a convenience store when their job was to guard the site. He remembered the report from the woman (Vivian Rhodes) who told police the guards seemed unconcerned and in no hurry to return to the site after the QuikTrip manager told them about the fire at the site.

Something else that struck him as pointing to the guards was that Debbie's pickup was torched in such a way that the truck was totaled but somehow Debbie's purse and the gun in her pickup were untouched by the flames. "How could the gun and the purse not get burnt?"

As for Debbie Riggs claiming to have seen prowlers that night, he said, "I didn't buy the story of the intruders." He said to test her story he had Detectives Zinn and Fraise re-create the scene to see whether it would be possible to see prowlers where she said she saw them. "The re-creation demonstrated she had lied about seeing the prowlers," he said.

"The guards were the ones with the opportunity and they had the motivation to set these fires—Debbie to cash in on the insurance from her burnt truck and her brother to keep his hours from being cut," he said.

Cole was the one who early on ordered a polygraph test for Robert Riggs. When I asked him if that cleared Robert in his mind, he said, "Polygraphs don't mean shit."

I asked him why he didn't file a probable cause statement with the Jackson County prosecutor after catching the guards in so many blatant lies. "A probable cause filing is only for an arrest or to obtain a search warrant," he said. "You can't arrest somebody for lying. The Feds can but we can't. The problem with arresting the guards was lack of any physical evidence linking them to the arsons or any eyewitness accounts seeing them in the act."

He said he was only involved in the investigation for a few weeks and then a task force was formed with US Labor Department, ATF, and

KCPD. He assigned a couple of detectives to the task force but couldn't remember who they were. He said he still had some details to follow up on the Berdella case and he went back to doing that.

About the task force, he said, "I thought they were pursuing the wrong people. The case against the Marlborough defendants stunk. This was one of those occasions where the desire to solve the case overtook good judgment. I read some of the reports [about the five named defendants]. It was all 'he said, she said.'"

About the five being convicted, he said, "I was shocked when they were convicted. I did not expect convictions based on my own knowledge of the case."

We spent the rest of the interview discussing the August 2, 1990, report written by Detective Fraise recounting what eyewitness Gloria Nolen told him. He agreed the report would make it appear the guards were still at the site—and not at the QuikTrip—when the fire in the pickup was raging.

He said he did not remember seeing the report but because Fraise reported to him he would have signed it and passed it on. He said his signing reports for his detectives, particularly since he was not working the firefighters case then (because the task force was), was "pro forma." "By that time I wasn't working the case. John [Fraise] wasn't working the case either then." He said what probably happened was Fraise just happened to be in homicide when Ms. Nolen called in and he wrote up the report, gave it to Cole to sign, and Cole sent it to the task force. "I would have sent that report to the task force. I sign off on all such reports."

He said all such police reports are sent to two places. The original to the Record File (the master file for the case) and the other to the homicide file for the firefighters case.

I asked him how such an important report could have not brought investigative attention back to the guards. He said he had no idea, adding, "No one would file charges without having the whole police file, particularly knowing that the KCPD had initiated this investigation."

He said he "was surprised this report didn't get included in the court's file"—in the discovery file available to both the prosecution and defense.

He would only talk about Becker and True off the record. He did say he ran into True at some intelligence meeting a couple of months ago and True told him he just retired from Yellow Freight. True told him he went to work there "the day after I closed that case."

Resentencing of Bryan Sheppard

The US Supreme Court ruled in *Miller v. Alabama* on June 25, 2012, that sentencing minors to life without parole was a violation of the Eighth Amendment's prohibition against cruel and unusual punishment.[1] Because Bryan Sheppard was a minor at the time of the explosions he was entitled to a resentencing hearing in federal district court in Kansas City. Prior to *Miller*, a juvenile convicted of first-degree murder was automatically sentenced to life without parole.

"Mandatory life without parole for a juvenile precludes consideration of his chronological age and its hallmark features—among them, immaturity, impetuosity, and failure to appreciate risks and consequences," Justice Elena Kagan wrote for the majority in this 5–4 decision. "It prevents taking into account the family and home environment that surrounds him—and from which he cannot usually extricate himself—no matter how brutal or dysfunctional."

In *Miller*, it would still be possible for a juvenile to be sentenced to life without parole if the jury or sentencing judge deemed the juvenile "irreparably corrupt" or "permanently incorrigible." However, the high court stressed those sentences should be extremely rare. "Given all that we have said in *Roper*, *Graham*, and this decision about children's diminished culpability, and heightened capacity for change, we think the appropriate occasions for sentencing juveniles to this harshest possible penalty will be uncommon."

In the seven years leading up to the *Miller* decision, the US Supreme Court had been modifying its jurisprudence relative to juveniles, using the Eighth Amendment prohibition against cruel and unusual punishment as the catalyst. In 2005, the Supreme Court, in *Roper v. Simmons*, banned death-penalty sentences for capital crimes committed by minors—those under the age of eighteen.[2] The Supreme Court expanded its protection for juveniles in 2010, ruling in *Graham v. Florida* it was unconstitutional under the Eighth Amendment to sentence minors to life without parole for nonhomicidal offenses.[3]

Miller, in essence, was a logical expansion of the *Roper* and *Graham* rulings. In *Miller*, the Court concluded that imposing mandatory life without parole sentences on juveniles "contravenes *Graham*'s (and also *Roper*'s) foundational principle: that imposition of a State's most severe penalties on juvenile offenders cannot proceed as though they were not children."

Another way to view these favorable rulings for juveniles was to see them as the Supreme Court's long overdue repudiation of the myth of the juvenile superpredator, a myth popularized during the 1990s when crack cocaine was ravishing inner cities across the nation. *Roper*, *Graham*, and *Miller* marked the Supreme Court's catching up with the science that established children are drastically different from adults—that children are children.

John DiIulio, a Princeton professor, coined the term "superpredator" in 1995, predicting that a massive wave of juvenile offenders was about to be unleashed.[4] Writing for the conservative *Weekly Standard*, he estimated in the next fifteen years there would be 270,000 more young offenders on the nation's streets. Without disguising the inherent racism of his claim, he said these youngsters would be "radically impulsive, brutally remorseless," saying they would "pack guns instead of lunches" and "have absolutely no respect for human life."

Criminologist James Fox agreed with DiIulio, saying, "Unless we act today, we're going to have a bloodbath when these kids grow up."

State legislators across the country bought into the myth of the superpredator. By 1999 nearly every state had passed legislation that significantly increased the prosecution of juveniles as adults for purposes of sentencing and punishment, including sentences of life without parole.

The tough-on-crime politics and the legislation they inspired resulted in great disparities along racial lines in the implementation of mandatory life without parole sentences for juveniles. As the Phillips Black Project reported in 2015, the legislation to allow states to charge minors as adults:

> created a straight line from poorly funded schools to juvenile hall and on to the institutions of adult mass incarceration. Our nation's least-advantaged children, the children of poverty, mental illness, and historically discriminated against groups, have fared the worst under these policies. Children of color have been disproportionately adjudicated as delinquents and institutionalized while their peers were far more frequently allowed to work things out without

involving courts and jails. We stripped courts and prosecutors of the discretion required to provide treatment tailored to juveniles' individual needs, blinding our institutions to the reality that children are fundamentally different than adults. And we have sentenced thousands of our nation's youth to die in prison for crimes they committed before they were old enough to vote.[5]

By the time the *Miller* decision came down in 2012, it was clear the superpredator predictions were unsound. Before most states enacted new laws to punish juveniles, violent juvenile crime rates had already begun to fall in the mid-1990s. By 2000, the juvenile homicide rate stabilized below the 1985 level. Both DiIulio and Fox were proved wrong and admitted their mistake.

Nonetheless, the damage to juvenile offenders of capital crimes had been done. There were at the time of the *Miller* ruling over 2,700 juvenile defendants serving life without parole in state prisons and 40 in the federal system. Five states imprison some 60 percent of these prisoners: Pennsylvania, 450; Michigan, 360; California, 310; Louisiana, 300; and Florida, 218.

The *Miller* decision ruled the sentencing body should take into account a number of mitigating factors in determining the new sentence to be given those formerly sentenced to life without parole: the juvenile's "family and home environment"; the "circumstances of the homicide offense, including the extent of [the juvenile's] participation"; and the impact of "familial and peer pressure," the juvenile's "inability to deal with police or prosecutors (including on a plea agreement), or his capacity to assist his own attorneys," and the compelling "possibility of rehabilitation" for someone sentenced so young.

All of the factors involved various elements of the core assertion of *Miller:* juveniles are different from adults and should be viewed that way at sentencing, i.e., there are mitigating factors at the essence of being a juvenile that have to be considered in order for the sentence to be a fair one.

The Midwest Innocence Project (MIP) was representing Bryan when the *Miller* ruling took effect.[6] It voted to adopt his case in August 2008, a month after the *Kansas City Star*'s massive report documented how federal agents pressured over a dozen witnesses or potential witnesses to lie at the grand jury or at the trial.

Other than a police report uncovered by an investigator for MIP in April 2009 that placed the guards at the construction site while Debbie Riggs's pickup was ablaze, the organization represented Bryan in name only. No one from the group had ever come to see him or filed any motions on his behalf.

The report uncovered by MIP investigator Molly Frankel represented a major *Brady* violation because it contained information that tended to establish the innocence of the Marlborough Five and the report had not been turned over to the attorneys representing them at their trial. If there had been any real intent for MIP to insert itself into this case, this was the golden opportunity to file a *Brady* claim with the Eighth Circuit Court of Appeals and request a new trial.

Instead of doing that, the then-director of MIP, Tiffany Murphy, fired Molly Frankel on the spot for leaking a copy of the police report to Mike McGraw of the *Kansas City Star*.

Once a Supreme Court ruling is issued, defendants it affects, like Bryan Sheppard, have one year to file for a successive habeas corpus petition with the proper court of appeals. I was about to offer the job of representing Bryan to an appeal attorney in St. Louis when Cheryl Pilate, who had been representing Darlene since 2006, recommended Cyndy Short to me. This made a great deal of sense because Short, a defense attorney based in Kansas City, specializes in mitigation, and Bryan's resentencing would essentially be a mitigation hearing.[7]

Cynthia L. Short graduated from the St. Louis University Law School in 1987. After a short stint at a labor law firm in St. Louis, she joined the Missouri Public Defender System's Trial Division at its Kansas City office. Over the next three years she tried over fifty cases. In 1994 she moved to the Capital Trial Division and was promoted to lead counsel two years later. Now working exclusively on death-penalty cases, she created a model plan for mitigation investigation and presentation: how best to go about gathering a defendant's background information and putting it together into a compelling narrative to be presented at the sentencing.

In 2003, she opened CLS Mitigation and Consulting Services within the McCallister Law Firm, a plaintiff's firm established by her husband Brian McCallister in 1996. She began working as a mitigation attorney with lawyers appointed to death penalty cases in Missouri, Texas, Kansas, Utah, Illinois, and Washington and in federal cases in Missouri, Arkansas, Florida, Michigan, and Nevada.

Over the next eighteen years Short represented over one hundred people facing the death penalty. Not one of them was sentenced to death. As the mitigation specialist and co-counsel at the death-penalty trial for Levi King in 2006, King became the first capital defendant in twenty-four years not to be sentenced to death by a Texas jury. In the esoteric field of mitigation, Cyndy Short is a star.

In February 2013, Short agreed to represent Bryan at his resentencing. The next month she filed an application with the Eighth Circuit Court of Appeals to file a successive habeas corpus petition for Bryan and a request for the Eighth Circuit to appoint her as Bryan's counsel.[8] Because Bryan is indigent, the Federal Court for the Western District of Missouri was responsible for paying his legal fees.

The Eighth Circuit appointed Short on April 9, 2013, but did not grant permission to file a successive habeas petition pending the government's response to her application. Paul Becker, filing on behalf of the US Attorney's Office, informed the Eighth Circuit the government had no objection to the appeals court granting the successive petition. This was by no means a sign of generosity on Becker's part. The US Justice Department had advised all US attorneys it viewed the *Miller* decision as retroactive and not to oppose the request for successive petitions.

On September 9, 2012, the Eighth Circuit granted Bryan's request to file a second petition in federal district court.

Until this time it was not known what federal district judge would be handling Bryan's resentencing. Judge Fernando Gaitan was now on senior status and was away from the courthouse for months at a time. But because he was the judge who handled Bryan's original habeas corpus petition in the early 2000s, it would be his case if he wanted it. In something of a surprise, he took it.

On September 24, Short filed the successive habeas petition to Judge Gaitan and requested she be appointed Bryan's counsel for the resentencing. Three weeks later Gaitan granted her request. Becker, in stall mode, waited until February 5, 2014, to file his response, once again conceding that *Miller* is retroactive.

More months passed by until on August 25, 2014, Gaitan granted the successive habeas petition and transferred the resentencing to the criminal docket. Bryan's resentencing was now official: he was no longer under sentence of life without parole.

When Bryan first learned that he was eligible for a resentencing under *Miller*, he had conflicting emotions. He was thrilled by this fortuitous development and yet at the same time felt a strong sense of remorse that he was the only one of his co-defendants with such an opportunity. Richard Brown missed qualifying for the resentencing by just over four months. Bryan was afraid there would be deep resentment against him by Frank, Darlene, and Richard as well as their families.

Instead of resentment, all three of his co-defendants—and their families—were elated for Bryan personally. They also viewed the resentencing as a way to advance their own claims of innocence. Short would be filing a detailed discovery request with the court that included production of an unredacted copy of the Department of Justice report that named the possibility of other perpetrators. Because part of Bryan's resentencing hearing would delve into what actual role—if any—he played in the deaths of the firefighters, obtaining the Justice Department report was a crucial piece of evidence that could establish who was responsible for setting the arson fire near the ANFO trailer.

So that Short and her mitigation team could have easier access to Bryan, Judge Gaitan arranged through the Bureau of Prisons to transfer Bryan from the federal prison in Pine Knot, Kentucky, to the Leavenworth Detention Center operated by the Corrections Corporation of America (CCA). Bryan arrived at Leavenworth on September 12, 2014. By that time the resentencing had been set for August 4, 2015. Short filed a motion with Gaitan to delay the resentencing so she could have adequate time to prepare.

In November, Short filed a discovery request with Judge Gaitan that asked for an unredacted copy of the Justice Department report. Becker opposed. Six months later, Gaitan denied the request.

The State of Louisiana, which faced the prospect and expense of holding resentencing hearings for three hundred juvenile defendants sentenced to life without parole, filed a petition with the US Supreme Court on September 5, 2014, challenging the retroactivity of *Miller*. The Supreme Court granted the petition four months later and heard oral arguments on *Montgomery v. Louisiana* on October 13, 2015.

Even though the Justice Department deemed *Miller* to be retroactive and no US Attorney's Office had opposed the granting of a new sentencing hearing for any of the defendants in the federal system, Becker, on June 8, 2015, filed a request for a stay of Bryan's resentencing pending the outcome of the *Montgomery* case.

Judge Gaitan granted the stay on July 28, placing Bryan's fate in limbo but allowing him to remain at CCA in Leavenworth.

During the interim, Cyndy Short filed a much more extensive discovery request, virtually asking for the government to provide its entire case file, including an unredacted copy of the Justice Department report. Becker filed a response, arguing that the discovery requested did not relate to the *Miller* resentencing factors and there was no statutory or any other legal basis for the production of the items sought.

The *Montgomery* case was fast-tracked at the Supreme Court. In a 6–3 decision written by Justice Anthony Kennedy, *Miller* was ruled retroactive on January 25, 2016.[9] One remedy Justice Kennedy advanced for states concerned about the cost of the resentencing hearings was simply to parole the defendants.

There was no fast track operating in Judge Gaitan's chambers. He waited until June 2, 2016 to return Bryan's case to his docket. In the order he wrote, he denied Short's entire discovery request, stating,

> The Court agrees that the government is not required to disclose this information. Defense counsel states that the information is necessary so that she "can investigate the circumstances of the offense and the nature and characteristics of the defendant." But what counsel fails to realize is that the granting of the [habeas] motion and the sentencing of Sheppard does not mean that the entire criminal case has been reopened and the issues relating to Sheppard's guilt or innocence revisited.

In his next sentence he finds himself on a slippery slope when he writes, "*Miller* does not direct counsel to investigate the circumstances of the crime, rather it simply states that this is one of a number of factors which the Court should consider in sentencing a juvenile." In other words, despite *Miller* stating the circumstances of the crime are one factor that should be considered, he does not intend to provide Short with the discovery needed to do that.

The final issue Gaitan addressed in his order was the rescheduling of the resentencing. Now that the *Montgomery* ruling was in place, the stay Becker asked for was "moot." Short's request for more time to prepare her mitigation case was likewise moot because of all the time that passed since she made that request.

The court arranged for Short and Becker to meet on June 30 to agree on a new date for the rescheduling. Becker, of course, is in no hurry to proceed and Short still wanted more time to prepare, so they settled on a date to be determined in mid-February 2017.

The next step for Short was to file a budget request with the court. She asked the court to approve 321 hours of her attorney time, 112 hours for a mitigation expert, 25 hours for a victim outreach expert, 60 hours for a forensic psychologist, as well as travel expenses for her to interview Frank Sheppard at a federal prison in California, Richard Brown in Florida, and Darlene Edwards in Texas.

In an order issued by Judge Gaitan on July 14, 2016, he approved all of her budget requests. The total expenditures came to around $80,000, with $48,000 of that in compensation for Short. In approving her budget, Gaitan wrote, "However, the Court would caution counsel as it has done before, that this is not a capital case, this is a resentencing hearing conducted pursuant to the Supreme Court's decision in *Miller v. Alabama.*"

He stated further that the

> resentencing hearing will focus on the six factors which the *Miller* court identified: 1.) "the background and mental and emotional development of a youthful defendant"; 2.) susceptibility "to influence and to psychological damage"; 3.) "the character and record of the individual offender [and] the circumstances of the offense"; 4.) "the family and home environment that surrounds him"; 5.) "the extent of his participation in the conduct and the way familial and peer pressure may have affected him"; 6.) the "juvenile's potential for rehabilitation and capacity for change."

In addition to the *Miller* factors, Gaitan stipulated he would also look at the factors identified in 18 U.S.C. 3553, the instructions for imposing a sentence in federal court.[10] The first two were the same as two of the *Miller* factors: the nature and circumstances of the offense and the history and the characteristics of the defendant. But the next four set a different, harsher tone: the need for the sentence to reflect the seriousness of the offense and promote respect for the law and provide just punishment; to afford adequate deterrence; to protect the public from further crimes of the defendant; to avoid unwarranted sentencing disparities.

"Counsel is strongly advised to focus her investigation and preparation on these [two sets of] factors, as they are the ones which the Court will rely on in resentencing Mr. Sheppard," Gaitan informed Short.

Since the time of the *Miller* decision in June 2012, at least seventeen defendants who were juveniles when they were sentenced to life without parole in federal court have been resentenced.[11] If they entered those resentencing hearings thinking or hoping that *Miller* would provide a panacea, only a few of them left the courthouse feeling that. Two, both from the Federal District of Arizona, had their life sentences reimposed; another from that district was resentenced to fifty-nine years. A defendant from Nevada was resentenced to eighty years. Four were given new sentences of between forty and forty-two years; seven were given between thirty and thirty-seven years, and two received twenty-five years. One of those resentenced to twenty-five years was Ralph Brazel out of the Middle District of Florida. He had served twenty-five years and was soon released from prison.

Ten of the forty federal defendants were barred from relief because even though their sentences had the effect of being for life, they had been sentenced by a judge or a jury to a set number of years rather than to mandatory life without parole. Three others were barred for not filing in a timely manner. The remaining ten cases, including Bryan Sheppard's, were pending.

Nine days prior to the resentencing hearing, Short and Becker each sent the court a "sentencing memorandum," laying out their arguments for the sentence Bryan should receive.

Short's memorandum covered seventy-one pages, listing in great detail Bryan's troubled upbringing, the traumas he had endured at ages fourteen and fifteen, and his record of rehabilitation. She ended the memorandum by writing, "Therefore, we respectfully request that Bryan Sheppard's sentence for the offense of conviction be found to have been completed and that he be released immediately." She supported her argument by citing, in addition to *Miller*, two dozen other cases that bore on the sentencing of minors. In addition, she provided the judge with sixty letters of support for Bryan's release and videos of eighteen people who spoke about Bryan's past and his rehabilitation.

For the first time in his twenty-two-year engagement with the firefighters case, Becker was fighting an uphill battle. The *Miller* decision required that before sentencing a juvenile to life without parole—which was what Becker argued the judge should do—the sentencing judge take into account how children were different and how those differences weighed against irrevocably sentencing them to life in prison. Also that *Miller* recognized a juvenile's greater possibility of rehabilitation.

In the more than two decades Bryan had spent in prison—even though he was under a life sentence—he had tried to better himself by learning to read, getting his GED, and taking dozens of courses to improve his character; he had been alcohol and drug free since 2003; he had embarked on a spiritual journey that connected him to his Native American roots. Chi P. King, the same probation officer who had written his presentencing report for Judge Stevens in 1997, amended her presentencing report in December 2016 to inform Judge Gaitan that Bryan had completed every program offered at the prison, had been assigned as an in-house trustee at CCA since May 2015, and that his case worker considered him a "model prisoner."

"The government recommends that Bryan Sheppard be sentenced to a term of life imprisonment based on the severity of his offense," Becker's sentencing memorandum began. "The devastation caused by the defendant in setting a fire which caused the deaths of six Kansas City, Missouri, firefighters far surpasses any mitigating factors of his juvenile status at the time of the crime when he was at age 17 years, 8 months and 24 days. That is he was 114 days from legal adulthood." The only two cases Becker cited in his memorandum were *Miller* and the case that made *Miller* retroactive, *Montgomery v. Louisiana*. In other words, he did not advance any other cases that supported his recommendation of sentencing Bryan to life without parole.

Becker also argued that the judge should set aside Bryan's juvenile status and his rehabilitation because "the defendant continues to insist he did not participate in setting the fire which killed the six firemen." Further, he has failed to accept responsibility for the crime and has never apologized to the families of the fallen firefighters. This refusal to accept responsibility, Becker argued, was proof of Bryan's "irreparable corruption" and was the basis for sentencing Bryan to life without parole.

His age at the time of the crime is irrelevant. "This is necessarily so because a defendant's immaturity and lack of judgment explain why he committed the crime which resulted in his conviction. If, as the defendant maintains, he did not commit the crime, then as a matter of logic any explanation mitigating the conduct is moot," Becker wrote.

Bryan's rehabilitation could be discarded as well. "If the defendant denies the existence of his crime, then his supposed rehabilitation is just a catalog of his activities, not a demonstration of his reformation following the offense."

Despite what Becker contends to the contrary, *Miller* applied to Bryan for the simple fact that he was sentenced under mandatory guidelines to life without parole for a crime that occurred when he was a juvenile.

Becker misstated *Miller* on two separate levels when he wrote that "*Miller* envisioned a brutal home environment from which an impressionable youth could not extricate himself. Nothing could be further from the facts of this case."

In *Miller* it didn't matter how brutal or dysfunctional the home environment was, however, the more brutal or dysfunctional the more of a mitigating factor it would be. To claim that Bryan, who ran away from home at age thirteen to avoid his father's corporal punishment and spent the majority of the next few years living in the basement of a drug dealer's house, did not suffer greatly from a dysfunctional household is to misstate the known facts of Bryan's upbringing. Yes, his parents and siblings loved him, but both his parents were chronic alcoholics and abdicated their responsibility as parents, forfeiting their control over him, essentially allowing him to run wild. As a result, Bryan from age fourteen on suffered one traumatic experience after another—being shot in the chest, being the one to find his grandfather dying of a self-inflicted gunshot wound, and getting his front teeth knocked out in a car accident—all before he turned sixteen.

For some reason, Becker kept pointing out how close Bryan was to being eighteen, as though his nearness to that age makes his *Miller* claim less potent. "While a less than ideal home life might theoretically impact or slow the development of a young child's judgment, that ability to reason is surely well formed by the time one is a hair's breadth from 18," Becker wrote. (The actual science now is that the brain doesn't mature until around age 25.[12])

Considering the last thing Becker wanted was for the resentencing to reopen the validity of Bryan's guilty verdict and that Judge Gaitan had made it clear that the resentencing hearing would not take up the matter of Bryan's claim of innocence, it was difficult to understand why the prosecutor would peg his argument for a life sentence around Bryan's claim of innocence.

Toward the end of the twenty-four-page sentencing memorandum, Becker referenced a far more fertile basis for imposing a harsh sentence on Bryan when he detailed thirteen other federal cases where juveniles who had been sentenced to life without parole came up for resentencing under *Miller*. Excluding two who were resentenced to life, Becker showed that the average new sentence for these defendants was forty-two years. In the information provided, Becker omitted the case of Ralph Brazel out of the Middle District of Florida, who was resentenced in 2013 to twenty-five years and was shortly released thereafter because he had served twenty-five years.

Becker's sentencing memorandum prompted Short to file a motion in opposition. If Becker intended to make Bryan's denial of his involvement in the crime as the basis for sentencing him to life without parole, then she should be allowed to put on an innocence defense. "Mr. Becker's assertion that a failure to accept responsibility for the crime of conviction demonstrates irreparable corruption certainly opens the door to important mitigating which may explain why Mr. Sheppard has not accepted responsibility."

As part of this innocence claim, Short wrote that she would like to put on a tape recording of Darlene Edwards recanting her claim that Bryan and Richard came to her house the night of the explosion asking her to take them to get gas and dropping them off at the construction site; Bryan's alibi for that night, supported by the testimony of his mother and his girlfriend at the time, Debbie Howard Matthews; Bryan's passing a polygraph exam in 1989 about his noninvolvement in the explosion; Bryan's refusal in 1997 to take a plea deal offered by Becker of a five-year sentence in return for his testimony implicating his co-defendants; the affidavit of Becky Edwards wherein she swore that Agent True threatened her with drug charges if she did not implicate the Marlborough Five at trial and that everything she testified to was a lie; the affidavit of Carie Neighbors swearing that Agent True coerced her to lie about Bryan at trial under threat of charging her with obstruction of justice and having her two-year-old son placed in social services; KCPD Detective Victor Zinn's belief that the guards at the construction site were involved in the explosion and that none of the Marlborough Five were implicated; and a rundown of the wildly conflicting testimony provided at trial by witnesses who implicated Bryan.

In a conference call on the Friday before the resentencing hearing, Judge Gaitan spoke with Becker and Short.[13] During the phone conversation, Becker did not declare how he would handle Bryan's failure to accept responsibility, which occasioned Judge Gaitan to make it clear if Becker persisted in that argument, Short would be allowed to put on evidence of Bryan's innocence. The judge did elicit from the prosecutor that Bryan had been maintaining his innocence for the last twenty-five years.

In chambers before the hearing began on February 15, Becker abandoned the argument that Bryan's refusal to admit his involvement was an aggravating factor. The judge then declared that there was no reason for Short to put on any evidence about why Bryan had not accepted responsibility.

The last time Bryan Sheppard had been in a federal courthouse was July 2, 1997, the day Judge Stevens sentenced him and his co-defendants to life without parole in the old courthouse—built during the Great Depression—at 8th and Grand in downtown Kansas City. The new courthouse, named for former Supreme Court Justice Charles Evans Whittaker—who had been a federal judge for the Western District of Missouri—opened a year later at 400 E. 9th Street, overlooking the Missouri River. Built of granite, limestone, glass, and terrazzo, the eleven-story crescent-shaped structure makes an impressive architectural statement.

The resentencing hearing was held in a packed courtroom at 9 a.m. on February 15, 2017, with Judge Fernando Gaitan presiding. A low railing, spanning the middle of the large, airy courtroom, separated the judge's high bench from the rows of pews occupied by about a hundred spectators. Seating for the family and friends of the fallen firefighters was on the left side, directly behind the table occupied by the government's attorneys, led by Assistant US Attorney Paul Becker. Family, friends, and supporters of Bryan Sheppard sat on the right behind the table reserved for his attorney and three of her staff. To accommodate the overflow audience of about twenty-five other spectators, a separate courtroom was connected by an audio and video feed.

Before Judge Gaitan made his entrance, Bryan made his through a side door on the right side of the courtroom. Dressed in an orange jumpsuit, with "INMATE" stenciled in large letters on his back, he was escorted—manacled hand and feet—into the courtroom by two US marshals. As he shuffled to his seat at the defense table, he gave a furtive glance to his mother and sisters in the second row, sitting directly behind Mike Mc-Graw and other reporters.

Instead of an air of anticipation, the mood in the courtroom on both sides of the gallery struck me as one of trepidation, the firefighters' side dreading the possibility of one of the Marlborough Five escaping a life sentence and Bryan's supporters fearful that Judge Gaitan would impose a sentence of life without parole or one up to forty-two years, as the other federal *Miller* defendants had on average received.

When Judge Gaitan opened the hearing he did so in a tone so hushed that his microphone could barely project his voice to the gallery. It seemed as though everyone in the courtroom picked up immediately on this subdued aura, including prosecutor Becker, who would be the first to address the court.

The format for the proceedings was akin to a mini-trial, minus the opening statements by the prosecution and the defense. The government would go first, putting on its witnesses, and then Cyndy Short would call hers. Cross-examination was permitted. The government would make a closing statement, Short would make hers, and Becker would be entitled to a rebuttal.

The only witnesses Becker called were three family members who would deliver "impact statements" regarding the loss they suffered and continue to suffer as a result of the deaths of their loved ones. Only two of the six families were represented. That in itself made its own kind of subtle, ambiguous statement.

Debbie McKarnin, the widow of Robert McKarnin, said her family was decimated by her husband's death and finished by saying, "This man should stay in jail for the rest of his life." Her daughter Cassandra McKarnin said the death of her father gave her a life sentence and that the "punishment should last a lifetime, too." She said the play about the fire-fighters case that ran in Kansas City during February 2016, *Justice in the Embers*, was "a personal torture" to her.[14] (The entire cast of the play attended the hearing in support of Bryan.) Janice Offil, the sister of Michael Oldham, said, "Bryan Sheppard deserves to stay where he is."

Bryan Sheppard was the first witness for the defense. By the time he took the stand, he had been waiting nearly three years at the Corrections Corporation of America holding facility in Leavenworth, Kansas, for this day to arrive. During those years his father had died and his mother's health had deteriorated steadily. Virgie Sheppard—who suffers from chronic obstructive pulmonary disease, cirrhosis of the liver, and kidney issues—was now wheelchair-bound with so many physical ailments that everyone who knew her considered her survival something of a miracle that could not last much longer.

Other than the opportunity for one or two family members to visit him for an hour on Friday nights—something his family members could only afford to do once a year while he was in various federal prisons—Bryan found living at CCA disorienting and nerve-racking. Instead of having a cellmate for a year or more at a time, at Leavenworth he had forty or so come and go during his time there. A number were in and out in a day or two. Like him, these cellmates were inmates awaiting proceedings in federal court, many of them for probation violations.

Jobs and programs were scarce at CCA. After five months of applying for work, Bryan got a job as an orderly in his unit, responsible for cleaning the common areas, including the showers and day room. He was soon promoted to head orderly. He took all the programs offered, completing a twelve-week course on addiction with thirty other inmates. He followed that with a three-week course entitled "Accepting Responsibility in a Finger-Pointing World." After he finished all the courses offered, his counselor gave him some computer-generated ones he did on his own. Among the letters of support Cyndy Short sent Judge Gaitan on Bryan's behalf were three written by CCA employees—his unit manager, case manager, and counselor. Anyone who knows anything about the inner workings of penal institutions would grasp how unusual and rare such endorsements are.

As the date for the resentencing approached, Bryan's anxiety level—always just below the surface since he had entered prison twenty-two years ago—spiked. He could not sleep more than an hour or two at a time. On the morning of the hearing, he woke at 4 a.m., waited to go to breakfast an hour later, and at 5:30 a.m. was escorted to the receiving and discharge area. There he sat until 8 a.m. when two CCA guards manacled his wrists and shackled his feet before putting him in a van and driving him the thirty-five miles to the federal courthouse. Once at the courthouse, two US marshals took him to a holding cell just outside the courtroom.

Short began her questioning by saying to Bryan, "Mrs. McKarnin and Ms. Offil have just told the judge about the terrible loss suffered by their families. The loss was felt across the Kansas City community. What do you want to say to the families of the firefighters and to the Kansas City Fire Department community?"

Even though Bryan knew this question was coming—and all the other ones Short was intending to ask him—and had rehearsed his answer with her in private, he could not find his voice. After an agonizing amount of seconds had passed, he asked for some time to compose himself, saying, "This is kind of tough."

When he did respond, he choked out, "I want them to know that I pray for them every day as I pray for my own family." He paused, swallowed several times trying to gather himself. "I know it is of little comfort to the families. I am very sorry for the loss everyone in this room has suffered."

"Take a deep breath," Short said.

"I have a lot more to say, I just can't get it out," Bryan said.

Short moved on to ask him about his relationship with his mother. This induced outright sobbing. After another long pause, he said, "I feel like I'm about to have a heart attack."

As Short questions explored less emotional areas—such as his work history in prison, all the programming he had done over the years, his commitment to sobriety—Bryan settled in. He had always had a job in prison; he began programming immediately; he had been sober since 2003.

If paroled, how would he cope with the challenges ahead? He would surround himself with positive people, ask for help when he needed it, attend AA meetings regularly, stay connected to his Creator, work a steady job, and do volunteer work, trying to help the less fortunate.

During cross-examination, Becker did not challenge any claims Bryan made about his prison record, but he did ask him what he thought the sentence should be for someone who killed six firefighters. This caught Bryan by surprise. Before he could formulate an answer, Short objected and Judge Gaitan agreed that asking for speculation was inappropriate.

The next witness, Janice McMillan, a lifelong friend of his mother's, had known Bryan all his life. She described the Sheppard family Bryan grew up in as dysfunctional, riddled by alcoholism and domestic violence. Despite his home life, Bryan was a fun-loving kid, "always laughing," and "never mean." Other witnesses who had known Bryan since he was a child and had stayed in touch with him through the years spoke of his difficult upbringing and the incredible turnaround he had made in his life while incarcerated.

This was a theme reinforced by his brother-in-law, Buster Hower, and his son-in-law, Steven Keeney. "Bryan will always have a bed in my home and a seat at my table," Keeney said.

The only light moment in the proceedings occurred while Becker was cross-examining Father Gerald Waris, a retired Catholic priest who had volunteered to serve as Bryan's chaplain because CCA offered no Native American religious services. Father Waris described how he had been visiting Bryan twice or more a month for the last three years and had gotten to know Bryan as a very caring, humble, and spiritual person. During cross-examination, Becker asked him a series of questions that indicated he did not grasp how the priest had come to be Bryan's chaplain, something he had explained when Short was taking his testimony—which caused Father Waris at one point to say he thought the last question was "irrelevant." The judge, smiling, intervened to say, "Father, that's my job to determine," bringing on a ripple of laughter.

Two expert witnesses testified for the defense.

Lori Sexton, an assistant professor in the Department of Criminal Justice at the University of Missouri–Kansas City, has a Ph.D. in criminology, law, and society from the University of California, Irvine. She interviewed Bryan for three hours two times at CCA. Asked if Bryan, in her opinion, was amenable to rehabilitation and was prepared to reenter society, she said, "Based on the documents I have reviewed and the interviews I have conducted with Mr. Sheppard, it is my expert opinion that Mr. Sheppard has proven extremely amenable to rehabilitation, will continue to rehabilitate himself if released from prison, and poses minimal risk to the community. Mr. Sheppard has endured his punishment and adjusted to prison in a way that prepares him well for successful reintegration to society."

She said his adjustment to prison "has been quite remarkable. His favorable institutional record, with only 10 minor disciplinary infractions over two decades, demonstrates his decision to be a good citizen."

From her interviews with Bryan she found that as a youth he had exhibited the classic hallmarks of adolescence: underdeveloped sense of responsibility, recklessness, impulsivity, needless risk taking, and vulnerability to negative influences, outside pressure, and peer pressure.

"What did your evaluation reveal about the transient nature of these hallmarks of adolescence," Short asked.

"His character was not well-formed, therefore he has greater prospects for reform," Dr. Sexton answered.

Short asked her what were the factors that predict successful reintegration to society that apply to Bryan. She said his age now, forty-five, was a positive predictor. With regard to recidivism in particular, she cited an analysis of Bureau of Justice Statistics data on prisoners released between 2005 and 2010 that reveals a downward trend in recidivism that begins around age twenty and becomes more pronounced by age forty.[15] "If released at the age [of] 45, Bryan's risk of recidivism is low not just because of his hard-earned rehabilitation and his strong support system, but also by virtue of his age," she said.

Dr. Marilyn Hutchinson, a forensic psychologist, met with Bryan two times for three hours in December 2016 and met with his mother for an hour. Short began by asking her if she believed, based on her interviews with Bryan, that at age seventeen was he "irreparably corrupt, that is incapable of rehabilitation?" No, she did not.

Short: In forming her opinion, did she take into account developments in adolescent neuroscience?

Hutchinson: Yes, I did.

Short: Could she give the court an overview of the relevant brain research?

Hutchinson: The brain does not complete growing until mid 20's. In particular the pre-frontal cortex—the executive functioning, the part that is about being an adult—does not finish. It is responsible for planning, motivation, judgment, decision making, evaluating consequences, weighing risk and reward, perception, control of emotions, inhibition of impulses, recognizing deception, working memory and moral judgments—all the things that kids can't do—and we expect competent adults to do.

Short: Would Bryan's brain have been fully mature 114 days later when he turned 18?

Hutchinson: No. His frontal cortex development was far from complete. His impulses ruled him. He was focused on pleasure in the moment. He was reckless in the extreme. He smoked marijuana and drank every day. At age 17 he impregnated two girls during the same time span; he moved from house to house; he could not read, and had no regard for returning to school.

Short: Is there an additional factor that also impacted his impulsiveness, difficulty with school and substance use?

Hutchinson: Yes, he had ADD, attention deficit disorder.

Short: Were there events in Bryan's life that further complicated his life beyond his neighborhood, ADD, and immature brain?

Hutchinson: He underwent three tragedies within four months that would have felled almost anyone—let alone a 15-year-old who had little or no family support. He was shot in the chest by an emotional and impulsive 14-year-old girl; he was in a serious car wreck, driving underage, that knocked out his front teeth and caused severe damage to his girlfriend who broke many bones in her face and ribs; he heard and then found his grandfather who suicided. He was living there and came to find him in the living room, gun in hand. This prompted the decline of the somewhat minimal support he had been receiving from his mother—as she increased her alcohol consumption after the death of her father.

Short: What did you understand about Bryan's response to these tragedies?

Hutchinson: He reported being very guilty about the car accident, grieved about his grandfather—one stable fixture in his life—and confused about the young woman who shot him. He distracted himself with substance use.

Following several questions about Bryan's vulnerability to peer pressure, Short asked Hutchinson who Bryan was after he was first charged by the state for the firefighters crime in 1989 and subsequently released.

Hutchinson: He was a lost young man who had been working steadily for a couple of years since he was first charged; who had managed to get some control of his life but was still partying; he was with only one woman, who was living at his parents while she was pregnant; he was still at risk. He was not a criminal and he was pulling out of the chaos of his adolescence.

Short: And who was he when he was arrested in 1995?

Hutchinson: He was more lost than ever. He had plummeted into major drug use. He had just been arrested for meth distribution and hoped for treatment to try and get his life back. No treatment was available when his status as a suspect in the fire was reported.

Short: What has he done since incarcerated?

Hutchinson: Grown up—and made use of any and all possibilities the federal correctional system could provide him.

Short: Could you elaborate?

Hutchinson: At the time of his incarceration, due to his ADD and probably some LD (learning disorder), he had never learned to read. He learned to read and passed his GED. Despite being housed in some of the most violent prisons in the U.S. he has stayed largely violation free, has never associated with any gangs and worked on his recovery. He has a total of nine write ups in the BOP (Bureau of Prisons) for very minor offenses in the past 20 years. He has refused psychotropic medication for his anxiety and depression knowing the dangers his own genetics holds for addiction and knowing what drugs did to his family members. He controls his moods with spiritual practices and exercise. He completed almost every possible training and rehabilitation program that has been available to him at any institution in which he has been placed.

Short: What has motivated this young man to fight this hard during a life sentence?

Hutchinson: Family; daughter; grandchildren; supporters; hope. He has always believed in his innocence and that he would eventually be released. He wanted to be ready for whatever could be possible.

Short: What plans does he have if he is released?

Hutchinson: He wants to work, buy land and give back to repay in his own way the many people who have assisted him in this legal fight. He plans to search out deserving people and provide them working transportation given his ability to repair cars.

Short: Do you have any fears about his future ability to be a responsible citizen?

Hutchinson: Not one.

The final witness for the defense was Bryan's daughter Ashley Kenney. Now twenty-eight, she was six years old when Bryan was incarcerated on a drug charge. Over the years, she has visited him in numerous prisons, sometimes bringing her young daughter with her. At CCA, Bryan met his two-year-old grandson for the first time.

When Short asked her about her relationship with her father, Ashley said they had formed a very close father-daughter bond and that Bryan had become an important part and positive force in her life and the lives of her children and husband. "I am very proud of him and know the kind of man he is," she said. "He's a great example of how you can turn your life around."

After a short recess, closing arguments began just after 1 p.m. Becker went first. Each counsel was allotted thirty minutes. Becker would only take ten.

He began by asking the judge to follow what the Sentencing Guidelines demanded for abetting an arson that led to the deaths of public servants performing their jobs. Those guidelines call for the imposition of a life without parole sentence.

"Some crimes are so severe and lasting that the punishment should be severe and lasting," he said, arguing that while Bryan "has enjoyed having a family, the families of his victims have had that chance taken away from them forever."

He said *Miller* had no application "to this defendant" who had never accepted responsibility for the crime, reneging on the agreement that he would not take this tack and at the same time opening the door for Short, in her closing argument, to broach the subject of Bryan's innocence.

One of the stipulations in the Sentencing Guidelines is that the sentence should provide respect for the law. Becker said it was far from fair for Bryan to be the only one of the five convicted to get a reduced sentence, particularly when co-defendant Richard Brown was only a few months past the age of eighteen when the firefighters were killed.

Becker spent most of his time going over the other *Miller* cases that had already been concluded in various federal courts. As he referenced the thirteen sentences meted out that added up to an average of forty-two years, Judge Gaitan took notes.

Cyndy Short is in no way what anyone would consider an aggressive advocate. She would be one to raise an eyebrow, but not her voice. Organization and clarity rather than flare govern her demeanor. She is prepared. She had worked hours on her closing comments and had them before her on her laptop screen as she began in a low, conversational voice to make her argument:

> On one side of the courtroom are members of our community who see the horrific loss of six brave men and cannot imagine that any sentence less life could reflect the seriousness of the offense.
>
> Retribution is the penological justification for a life sentence if you are a member of the community that lost these men.
>
> On the other side of the room are members of the community who see injustice when they look into the well at us. They are committed to the sincerely held belief that Bryan Sheppard is innocent. They cannot see any penological justification for Bryan Sheppard's continued prison sentence.
>
> I stand in the well and I am sworn to work within the bounds of the law as I address you this afternoon.
>
> We have learned over these last two decades that a legal conviction and actual innocence are not mutually exclusive. When they reside together and the Court is asked only to resentence, innocence is not a bar to that legal obligation. I want the Court to know I understand this.
>
> But as Bryan's counsel it would be immoral for me not to bring innocence into the well of this courtroom.
>
> As a society we expect those who commit crimes to accept responsibility for their actions, to express remorse and when that does not occur, it is natural to argue as Mr. Becker has, that the failure can only be a reflection of an irreparably corrupt man.
>
> However, here the failure to accept responsibility is not the reflection of Bryan Sheppard's irreparable corruption. It is a reflection of his belief in our system of justice. It is a reflection of his youthful misunderstanding that there is no armor to protect the innocent in trial. It is a reflection of his character because he rejected opportunities to save himself to trade his freedom for a lie. [Bryan's refusal to take a plea deal of a five-year sentence for testifying at trial against his co-defendants.] His refusal to take the inducement cost him everything.

All of what she said so far was prelude and to a certain extent a direct rebuttal to Becker's closing argument. Now she was about to make the legal argument for why Bryan should be sentenced to time served and released forthwith.

Bryan Sheppard is here today standing before you convicted of aiding and abetting an arson that damaged or destroyed property. He was not convicted of murder. Although neither the judge nor the jury found that there was a plan to kill or an intention to kill or that the lives lost were taken with malice aforethought, Bryan Sheppard was sentenced as if he had planned a murder, intended a murder, and/or acted with malice aforethought.

Your role today is to turn an unconstitutional sentence into a constitutional sentence under the Eighth Amendment.

The sentence is unconstitutional not as the result of innocence, but as the result of his youth on the day that a fire was set which led to an explosion which killed six innocent men.

Short said that the questions before the court are taken from *Miller* and *Montgomery*. She said those cases instruct that the court must ask "whether the evidence used to convict Bryan of aiding and abetting an act of arson reflected transient immaturity or irreparable corruption"; whether "Bryan is among the very rarest juvenile offenders, those whose crime of conviction reflects permanent incorrigibility or is he among those youth whose transient immaturity gives way to his capacity for rehabilitation?"

To answer those questions, Short said the government had offered "no evidence of irreparable corruption and Bryan's prison history stands as compelling and overwhelming evidence of his capacity for rehabilitation." Second, "the government has never alleged and certainly never proved during the trial that Bryan Sheppard took any action to kill any person," or "hurt or kill any firefighter" or that he "acted with malice aforethought." Nor did the government ever allege that Bryan was aware of the contents of the trailer that exploded or that he knew that a fire set near a trailer would set off an explosion that would lead to injury or death.

Citing another US Supreme Court case, she said, Justice Breyer was clear in *Graham* that a juvenile may not ever receive a sentence of life if he neither killed nor intended to kill.

Further, she said, "Judge Stevens reaffirmed in his comments at the 1997 sentencing that he saw no evidence that any of the convicted acted intentionally or with malice aforethought."

Because there was no intent to kill anyone, including firefighters, she said the only analogous homicide classification is "reckless homicide," which falls under second-degree murder. Because the Sentencing Guidelines in 1997 mandated a sentence of fifteen to twenty years for reckless homicide, "the constitutional sentence for Bryan Sheppard falls within this range and should not exceed 20 years."

Turning to his rehabilitation, Short said, "On the other side of his conviction he began to grow up; he demonstrated good citizenship; he went to school; he found a worship community; he chose sobriety; he worked; he followed the rules; he nurtured relationships with people who mattered; he worked on all of these with no hope; he worked on all of these things while he was a lifer," Short stated. "He represents the very essence of why the United States Supreme Court decided *Roper* and *Graham* and *Miller* and *Montgomery*."

Short concluded by stating:

Bryan has been behind bars for nearly 22 years. He will be 46 years old next month. The constitutional sentence under the totality of the circumstances is 20 years. This sentence will meet the mandate of (18 USC) 3553 as it is sufficient but not greater than necessary. A 20-year sentence also meets the constitutional mandate of *Miller* which requires that the youthful offender has a meaningful opportunity to reintegrate into society, into his family and to create a meaningful life.

Becker was entitled to a make a rebuttal but did not.

Judge Gaitan closed the hearing by stating he would take the matter of the resentencing under advisement and would render his decision on March 3.

Once again, the courtroom was packed with observers when Judge Gaitan entered at 2 p.m. on March 3, 2017, to render his sentencing decision. Bryan, as before, was dressed in an orange jumpsuit and shackled. The mood in the courtroom was hushed and suspenseful.

It is amazing the sheer power the US Constitution invests in federal judges. Appointed for life, they are free of the constraints of the ballot box. Except for the occasional reversal by an appellate court, federal judges' rulings are virtually bulletproof.

Judge Gaitan had it within his power to resentence Bryan Sheppard to life without parole or to a term as high as forty or more years, or to a term that would have the effect of setting him free.

During the sixteen days between March 3 and the resentencing hearing, Judge Gaitan had written a twenty-two-page order that in the next fifteen minutes he would read into the record in his emollient voice. He began by stating the background of the case that began in late 1988 with the deaths of the six firefighters and which led eight years later to the convictions of the five defendants and their sentences to life without parole.

The judge then stepped back to give a broader historical overview, noting that over the last seven decades, the law regarding juveniles has been evolving. He mentioned the Federal Youth Corrections Act that Congress passed in 1950. The act established an alternative-sentencing system for juveniles that focused on treatment and rehabilitation. That act was repealed in 1984 by the Comprehensive Crime Control Act, which initiated much sterner treatment of juvenile offenders.

During the 1980s and early 1990s, the myth of the child as a "superpredator" took hold, he explained, leading to the enactment of the Violent Crime Control and Law Enforcement Act in 1994, authorizing the federal prosecution of juveniles as adults for certain crimes of violence and increased penalties for juveniles in possession of a gun or ammunition.

Two Supreme Court cases in the late 1980s dealt with the execution of minors. In *Thompson v. Oklahoma*, the Court ruled it was unconstitutional to execute a person who was under the age of sixteen at the time of the offense.[16] The next year, 1989, the Court ruled in *Stanford v. Kentucky* that it did not violate the Eighth Amendment's prohibition against cruel and unusual punishment to execute any person who committed murder at sixteen or seventeen years of age.[17]

With that background in place, Judge Gaitan said, "In the almost twenty years since Sheppard's sentence was imposed, the Supreme Court has issued numerous opinions regarding the sentencing of juveniles." He cited *Roper*, the 2005 Supreme Court case that barred capital punishment for juvenile offenders who were older than fifteen but younger than eighteen when they committed the crime, finding that "juveniles are categorically less culpable that the average criminal."

Five years later in *Graham*, he said the Supreme Court held that mandatory life without parole sentences violated the Eighth Amendment when imposed on juvenile, nonhomicide offenders.

> The Court in *Graham* noted that no recent data provide reason to reconsider the Court's observation in *Roper* about the nature of juveniles . . . developments in psychology and brain science continue to show fundamental differences between juvenile and adult minds.

The Court in *Graham* concluded that "a categorical rule gives all juvenile, non-homicide offenders a chance to demonstrate maturity and reform. The juvenile should not be deprived of the opportunity of judgment and self-recognition of human worth and potential."

And then he brought up the *Miller* decision. "The Court in *Miller* explained that the previous decisions in *Roper* and *Graham* found that 'children are constitutionally different from adults for purposes of sentencing.' Because juveniles have diminished culpability and greater prospect for reform 'they are less deserving of the most severe punishment.'" In 2016, he said, the *Montgomery* decision made Miller retroactive.

Before getting into the *Miller* sentencing factors involved in Bryan Sheppard's case, the judge noted that the deaths of six Kansas City firefighters were a major tragedy and the gravest on record for the local fire department. He then said:

> There was compelling and moving testimony presented at the resentencing hearing from Debbie and Cassie McKarnin, the wife and daughter of Robert McKarnin. Cassie McKarnin testified that "the impact of this crime lingers though my entire lifetime and the entire lifetimes of everyone who loved those six men." Janice Offill also testified regarding the effect of losing her brother Michael Oldham has had on her and her family.
>
> There is no denying that the crime which the defendants were convicted of resulted in a tragic loss of six lives. However, the Court also cannot ignore the statements made by the trial judge, that he did not believe that the defendants intentionally with malice and forethought set out to kill the firefighters. The Court also cannot ignore that the evidence showed that the defendants went to the construction site that night to steal and that the fire was set merely to cover up or destroy evidence of their theft. There was no evidence that the defendants set the fire with the purpose of luring the firefighters to the scene with the thought that they would be killed when the trailers exploded. Indeed, there was no evidence that it was foreseeable that the trailers would explode. The ATF (Alcohol, Tobacco, and Firearms) expert testified at the trial that he was not aware of any other instances in the United States where a trailer containing ANFO caught fire and exploded, so it was unlikely that the defendants knew when they set the fire that it would cause an explosion.

With that said, Judge Gaitan made his first finding: "The Court concludes that the circumstances of the offense dictate that a sentence of less than life in prison without the possibility of parole should be imposed on Bryan Sheppard."

The next section of his order dealt with Bryan's character. After going through all of his arrests leading up to his being sentenced in state court in 1996 to seven years for selling methamphetamine, he shifted his focus to Bryan's rehabilitation while in prison the last two decades. He quoted Dr. Lori Sexton testifying that Bryan's "adjustment to prison has been quite remarkable." He also named a number of the programs Bryan had completed in prison. He followed this up with his second finding:

> The Court finds that the relatively few criminal convictions Bryan had before being convicted of the instant offense and Bryan's record of good conduct while in prison demonstrate that he falls with the category of "the juvenile offender whose crime reflects unfortunate yet transient immaturity" and does not indicate that he is the "rare juvenile offender whose crime reflects irreparable corruption." This factor thus also weighs in favor of a sentence less than life in prison.

In regard to Bryan's mental and emotional development, the judge quoted from the assessment written by Dr. Marilyn Hutchinson, the forensic psychologist who testified at the resentencing hearing. She had delved into Bryan's chaotic upbringing, his illiteracy, his attention-deficit disorder, his almost total lack of impulse control, his dangerous risk-taking, and his susceptibility to peer pressure.

"The Court finds that Bryan's background and mental and emotional development—his recklessness, immaturity and impetuosity—are all factors which weigh in favor of imposing a reduced sentence," the judge stated.

Next, the judge took up the three traumas Bryan suffered when he was fourteen and fifteen—being shot in the chest, being in a terrible car accident, and being present when his grandfather committed suicide in the next room. "The Court finds that Bryan was susceptible to undue influence of friends and family members and that combined with the incidents of psychological damage that he suffered weigh in favor of a sentence of less than life without the possibility of parole."

Concerning Bryan's upbringing, the judge found that "Bryan's abusive and dysfunctional family and home environment and the use of alcohol and drugs at a young age are factors which also weigh in favor of a sentence of less than life in prison without the possibility of parole."

Addressing the issue of Bryan's claim of innocence, the judge stated:

Although he was convicted, Bryan Sheppard has consistently maintained that he is innocent of the charges. Also of note is that several of the witnesses who testified against Bryan Sheppard at the trial have since recanted their testimony. Additionally, during the trial, the extent of the various defendants' participation, except for Darlene Edwards, was left largely undefined . . . the lack of evidence regarding Bryan's participation in the crime, and the negative way that familial and peer pressure affected Bryan are factors which also weigh in favor of a reduction in sentence.

Turning now to Bryan's extensive record of rehabilitation while in prison, the judge stated, "Mr. Sheppard's extraordinary rehabilitation efforts over the years that he has been incarcerated are another factor which weighs in favor of a reduction in sentence."

During the reading of the order, as the judge kept reiterating that the *Miller* factors under consideration weighed in favor of a reduction in sentence, Bryan got the feeling, he told me the next day by phone, that "something good was about to happen."

In regard to all of the other *Miller* cases the government detailed at the resentencing hearing where the average new sentence was forty-two years, "the Court finds these cases to be of limited assistance because even the government admitted 'none parallel the facts of this case,'" the judge said.

And now the ruling: "After consideration of all of the *Miller* factors discussed above, the evidence, testimony and arguments presented at the resentencing hearing and review of the voluminous materials presented by Sheppard's counsel, the Court finds that Bryan Sheppard should be sentenced to 20 years in prison," the judge ordered.

There was a gasp from the audience. Tears flowed from Bryan's mother, his daughter, and his sisters. Against great odds, Bryan would be free for the first time in nearly twenty-two years.

As part of his release, the judge stipulated that Bryan would be placed on supervised probation for five years and would remain responsible for paying restitution of $536,000 to the Kansas City Fire Department.

As soon as the judge left the bench, Bryan and Cyndy Short hugged and two US marshals quickly escorted Bryan from the courtroom and placed him in a holding cell where Short joined him for an hour before guards from CCA escorted him back to Leavenworth.

Three days later, he was released from CCA at 4:30 p.m. In the mail he was handed on his way out was a card from Tracy Kilventon, the wife of James M. Kilventon, the son of one of the captains killed in the explosion in 1988. "I hope you adjust well when you get out and make the most of every day."

Instead of walking out the front door where Cyndy Short, his daughter Ashley Keeney, and reporters and TV crews were positioned, two guards took him out a back door and placed him in a van. They drove him about a mile to the nearly deserted parking lot of a Kmart and released him, driving away and leaving him standing there on his own.

"I didn't know what to do," Bryan told me. "I thought about running off and hiding." He was there for about ten minutes when Cyndy Short drove up in a van with Ashley to pick him up. TV cameras recorded the reunion.

A friend of Short's had arranged for a suite in a hotel on the Country Club Plaza for Bryan to spend his first night of freedom with his daughter, her husband, and their two young children. His mother was in a room across the hallway.

The terms of his five-year probation required Bryan to wear a sweat patch for drug testing for the first 120 days, changing patches once a week; pay $100 a month in restitution to the KCFD beginning April 1, 2017; obtain medical coverage within sixty days; secure full-time employment within sixty days; live within the immediate Kansas City area for the first six months; sleep at the same house for the first sixty days.

Bryan was afraid of returning to Marlborough so Short graciously offered him lodging at her home north of the river. He got a job in late April working as a handyman for a company that repairs patios. His brother-in-law, Buster Hower, a contractor, also began hiring Bryan for various projects.

The day after Bryan was sentenced to time served, the *Kansas City Star* ran a letter from his daughter, Ashley Keeney.[18] Below is an excerpt:

> I wish I could say that I feel nothing but joy and relief. But looking across the aisle in the courtroom, I realized my father's release would not only bring happiness to me, but also would bring further suffering to the families of the fallen firefighters. I don't want my joy to cause someone else's suffering. I think especially of Cassandra McKarnin, the daughter of one of the firefighters.

During the resentencing hearing, both Cassandra and I took our turns on the witness stand. We both spoke of the pain and loss we've experienced by not having our fathers present for the past several decades. But I know that Cassandra's loss is greater than mine. I have been able to continue a relationship with my father over the phone and through glass walls, and I've been sustained by the hope that he might one day be released. But there is nothing Cassandra can do to bring her father back.

I have mourned the loss of my father's time. She mourns the loss of her father's life. This is a breathtaking reality, and I can see her pain is only made worse every time my family speaks up to once again claim that my father is innocent. I understand that her family's wish to keep my father in prison is one way of having a sense of closure for the loss she has experienced. Nothing I say or do can ease their suffering, but I do believe there is another way forward.

My hope is that the families of the firefighters and the families of the defendants can come together and seek real justice in this case. I hope and pray that we can all look beyond our suffering long enough to notice one of the biggest problems that still exists in this case: the government has in its possession the names of two additional suspects that may have been involved in this horrible crime.

All of our families, both the firefighters and the defendants, have the right to demand that the government name the suspects, charge them and bring them to trial. For the firefighters community, that's the only road to real justice and closure in this case.

And for my family, we believe strongly that once the new suspects are tried, the case against my father will fall apart, and we can finally prove his innocence. . . .

Today my prayer is that Friday's ruling can bring us together so that we can seek justice for all, for the families of the victims and for the families of the wrongfully convicted.

On April 25, 2017, James and Tracy Kilventon sat for a television interviewed with Mike McGraw at the local public TV station. "I like to think that the court system works, but in this it didn't, at least it hasn't yet," Kilventon said. He said his doubts about the case began during the 1997 trial. "There was really no evidence to put him [Bryan Sheppard] there at the crime scene."

Kilventon said he has questions about the witnesses the government put on because some of them received consideration on pending legal problems in return and that some of those witnesses have since recanted their testimony.

"I'm not 100 percent sure they [the five defendants] are not guilty, but I lean toward that," Kilventon said. "I guess this would be a good time to see if the other [firefighter] families would like to talk to me."

Something that continues to bother him is the refusal of the Department of Justice to release an unredacted report of the investigation the DOJ conducted over a three-year period that found no credibility in *Kansas City Star* articles that asserted numerous witnesses were pressured to lie. The report, which was released in 2011, also referenced two other possible perpetrators who were unknown to investigators at the time of the trial.

"Whole pages [of the DOJ report] are just completely blacked out of it," Kilventon said. "It names new suspects and they won't let us see it."

"All six families [of the firefighters killed in the explosion] need to see what's in there," Tracy Kilventon said, adding that she and her husband would be willing to sign on to a lawsuit seeking release of the full report if one is ever filed.

Not long after Bryan's resentencing, Cyndy Short met with attorneys at one of Kansas City's most prestigious law firms, Shook, Hardy and Bacon, to begin preparing a Freedom of Information Act lawsuit to be filed in federal district court seeking release of the full DOJ report and all documents related to the investigation. In December 2017 the FOIA suit was filed. Jane Brown, an assistant US attorney, filed the government's response opposing the suit. Senior US Federal District Court Judge Ortrie D. Smith will preside. Oral arguments are expected by late summer 2018.

CHAPTER 19

New Evidence

My son, Joe O'Connor, has been running the website kcfirefight erscase.com since 2005. For the last few years, he's also been working on a documentary about the case and doing a great deal of independent research and sharing it with me.

The case files at Cyndy Short's offices did not have any of the photos from the crime scene or any of the more than 450 exhibits the prosecution entered at the firefighters trial. In 2013, Joe sent a Freedom of Information Act request to the ATF, seeking copies of the crime scene photos and the government's case file. He also sent a Missouri Sunshine Law request to the Kansas City Police Department requesting the photos.[1]

The ATF, after a year's delay, turned down Joe's FOIA request, but around that same time Sergeant Jamie Brown, the public information officer with KCPD, informed Joe he had located the crime scene photos and invited him to come take a look. Joe, who was then thirty-eight and lives in Washington, DC, flew to Kansas City and met with Sergeant Brown on July 17, 2015.

There were about seventy-five photo negatives in the evidence room. Some of the negatives were of the mangled fire trucks, others the gaping craters created by the two blasts. A series of photos showed the yellow lockers where the dynamite and blasting caps were stored. Photos of the open lockers established that the dynamite and blasting caps were undisturbed.

There were a number of photos of vehicles. Several were of Robert Riggs's damaged Nissan station wagon. The first blast, the one that totaled Battalion Chief Germann's car, cracked the Nissan's windshield, lacing it with spider webs, and blew out the Nissan's back window.

Another series of photos showed Debbie Riggs's Toyota pickup from both the outside and the inside. One interior photo showed her vinyl purse, some sort of yellow garment, and what looked like a plastic shopping bag in the debris of the passenger seat of the badly charred pickup. All except the purse, the garment, and the plastic bag were in ashes. The fire had been so intense that all that was left of the passenger seat was the metal coils; the steering column had melted and collapsed with the key to the ignition still in it.

Joe marked fifty of the seventy-five negatives for development and paid the fee involved. He now had developed copies of the negatives as well as digitized copies. He did not know if any of these photos had any significance beyond helping him illustrate the crime scene in his documentary, but he sent copies of all the photos to Mike McGraw and me. (Mike McGraw retired from the *Star* in 2014. For the next three years, he worked as a special projects reporter for the local public television station, KCPT, up until he died of cancer on January 6, 2018.)

In February 2016 Joe returned to Kansas City and met with former detective Victor Zinn. When Joe mentioned to him the photo showing that Debbie's purse had somehow survived the fire in her pickup, Zinn told him that the issue of her purse in the pickup always troubled him—he'd never known a woman to go off and leave her purse behind, even during a carjacking. The photo of the purse began to gnaw at Joe.

Mark Kind, a third-year law student who did research for Darlene's attorney, Cheryl Pilate, had recently completed an exhaustive spreadsheet of the entire case file, annotating all the witness interviews and police reports by date. The report, which ran to 781 entries, was a roadmap of the entire investigation from the time Robert Riggs called in the fire until December 1, 1996, when Special Agent True interviewed an inmate who claimed Frank Sheppard made admissions to him about the blast and stealing walkie-talkies from the site.

In reviewing the spreadsheet of investigative activities, Joe saw that Debbie Riggs had gone to the KCPD property room on December 11, 1988—less than two weeks after the explosions—and retrieved her billfold that contained her driver's license, a checkbook, and a small amount of currency in bills and coins totaling $6.51. The police retained her small vinyl purse and the cloth items that survived the fire.

"When I saw that her plastic driver's license and dollar bills had survived the fire in her pickup," Joe told me, "I wondered how those items could not have been consumed in a fire that raged for a minimum of seventeen minutes before the firefighters put it out."

Another police report, this one written by Detective Doug Clark on the day of the explosions, concerned Debbie's pickup.[2] Clark inspected the pickup at a police service station near downtown later that day. In his report, Clark refers to a small vinyl purse that contained Debbie Riggs's driver's license. "Contents of the purse were undamaged," Clark wrote.

"Purse received minor fire damage to the exterior. . . . Purse returned to the police property room as evidence."

Also recovered near the purse were two other partially burned items: a yellow garment and "a white cotton like substance." Clark noted that these items smelled "heavily of gasoline."

Clark concluded his report by stating his belief that the fire in the pickup was "incendiary," caused by the igniting of a flammable liquid tossed into the driver's side of the pickup. He sent the yellow garment and the white cotton item to the Regional Criminalistics Laboratory for analysis. The lab reported back the next day that the items were contaminated with evaporated gasoline.

When Joe enhanced the interior photo of Debbie's pickup by removing shadows and highlights he saw what looked like a charred fifty-page or so road atlas. He pictured Robert holding the burning atlas vertically under the purse and the yellow sweatshirt until those items began to burn and then placing the purse and sweatshirt in the cab with the smoldering atlas beside them to keep the items on fire.

The photos of Robert's station wagon lend credence to this theory. In addition to showing a heavily cracked windshield, they revealed heavy, black smudge marks on the steering wheel, indicating that the palms of Robert's hands were covered with some dark substance, quite possibly ashes from Debbie's pickup.

Shortly after the first explosion, Robert and Debbie returned to the west side of the construction site, leaving Battalion Chief Germann and his driver Gentry up on the access road. In a statement Robert gave to Detective Clark four days after the explosions, he said he and Debbie then stayed for a while behind the heavy equipment near Debbie's pickup before he dropped her off on 71 Highway near the 95th Street command center.[3] He said he then drove back to Debbie's pickup to retrieve "a revolver he had left there. He said he was at her pickup at the time of the second explosion."

Where Robert's gun was the night of the explosions is a matter of doubt. In her original interview with Detective Zinn, hours after the explosions, Debbie said only Robert was armed that night. Four days later both Debbie and Robert switched that story to saying Debbie had left the gun in her pickup when they went looking for the prowlers. The problem with this claim is that if the gun had been in the burning pickup, its barrel would have melted and its wooden handle would have been consumed in the fire, i.e., there would not have been a gun to retrieve.

Joe postulates that Robert always had his gun with him and the real purpose of his return to the pickup was to toss the incriminating garment and purse into the cab, light the items on fire, and hope that the fire would consume them, creating the appearance that the items had been destroyed in the original fire that engulfed Debbie's pickup.

Joe's theory is that in liberally dousing her pickup with gasoline, Debbie got some drops on her purse and sweatshirt. With Debbie's sweatshirt and purse tinged with gasoline, Robert did not want to risk approaching the command post at 95th Street so on the fly he concocted the story of returning to Debbie's pickup to retrieve his gun.

Robert was smart enough to know that there was no safe place at the construction site to hide the purse and the sweatshirt. Police would be combing the entire area for clues in a matter of hours. His problem ended up being that he didn't have enough time to wait around to see if the purse and sweatshirt were consumed in the makeshift fire.

At this point, things were happening too fast for the Riggses not to begin making critical mistakes.

As it turned out, Robert and Debbie were no-shows at the command post. If they had shown up there, they would have not been allowed to drive any farther in his badly damaged Nissan. The police would have been able to begin questioning Robert and Debbie either at the command post or after driving them downtown. Debbie would have been wearing the clothes that most probably smelled of gasoline.

Instead they took 87th Street east to most probably Blue Ridge Road to drive the three miles to their parents' home in Grandview. Robert had to have been driving with his head out the window because the front windshield was so shattered it was impossible to see through.

That Riggs exited the construction site via 87th Street was supported by what witness Terry Keen told police.[4] Keen said that about three minutes after the second explosion, he was about three blocks west of 71 Highway when he observed a vehicle with its driver's side window blown out "going at a high rate of speed on 87th Street. The vehicle was driven by a white male, 28 to 35 years of age . . . as the vehicle went through the intersection of 87th and 71 Highway the driver shielded his face." (Robert Riggs was thirty-four then.) Keen said he thought the driver was trying to hide his face from being identified by a police officer who was taking flares out of the trunk of a patrol car parked by the intersection. Keen said the vehicle drove beyond I-435 toward Blue Ridge on 87th Street.

After dropping Debbie off at their parents' house and probably cleaning himself up some, Robert eventually drove back to the command post at 95th Street; he had been away from the construction site for about an hour. As soon as he arrived, he was driven downtown for his police interview.

Once at her parents' house, Debbie ended up having only an hour or less to shower and change clothes before Detective Zinn arrived unannounced predawn, about 6 a.m., to escort her downtown for her interview.

To test his theory that the purse and the sweatshirt were burned in a separate and later fire—sometime after Debbie's pickup had been engulfed in flames and doused by the firefighters—Joe sent an email to the International Association of Arson Investigators—the leading certifying body for arson experts in the United States—asking for an arson expert to analyze the interior photos of Debbie's pickup. When no one responded to subsequent emails, Joe drove to the group's headquarters in Crofton, Maryland, about ten miles west of Annapolis. He spoke with the office manager who told him the association did not do arson investigations, but that it would provide him with referrals. A few days later, a representative called and gave Joe the names of three firms that conduct arson investigations.

Joe opted to contact EFI Global (Engineering Fire and Environmental Services).[5] Headquartered in Humble, Texas, EFI has offices in over forty states, Canada, and Brazil. Joe was impressed that prior to joining EFI in 2015, one of their arson experts, Bradley Henson, had been the fire marshal of Olathe, Kansas, a suburb to the southwest of Kansas City. For six years, Henson had been the chair of the Eastern Kansas Arson Task Force. During his thirty-year career, he had investigated over 440 fires and had worked with the ATF and the FBI. Another plus was that Henson was certified as an arson expert in Kansas, Missouri, and Illinois.

In an email Joe wrote Henson on March 4, 2016, he did not reveal that the photos he was attaching were from the construction site where six Kansas City firefighters were killed in 1988. He told him that it was known that gasoline was used to ignite the fire in the pickup's cab and that the fire blazed for at least seventeen minutes before firefighters put it out.

Referring to the interior photo of Debbie's pickup, he said, considering that everything in the pickup had been reduced to ashes and metal, how could the white purse and other items shown not been consumed in the fire?

Three days later, Henson emailed his report.[6]

Comments
After reviewing the photographs you submitted, I concur that the fire originated in the passenger compartment of the vehicle. As you

stated, you already confirmed gasoline was used to ignite the contents of the compartment. The damage in the photographs reaffirms there was an accelerated fire in the compartment. The total consumption of combustibles in the compartment is consistent with the time frame stated before the fire department extinguished the fire.

The contents that were in question did not have the degree of fire damage as the rest of the contents. There should not have been any remains of any combustibles as a result of the fire. It would be assumed that the items would have been consumed by the fire and any remaining pieces would have been exposed to copious amounts of water from firefighting operations. As shown in the photographs, it would have been impossible for those items to have been present at the time of the fire nor should they have been in the condition found if they had been in the original fire.

It appears the items you referenced were damaged by a separate fire event. This is based on the amount of damage the items sustained as compared to the total consumption of combustibles from the vehicle fire.

I have two opinions on the difference in damage to the items:

1. The items were found in another area of the vehicle or area and placed in the passenger compartment of the vehicle by fire personnel who extinguished the fire. This is a normal procedure to clean up loose items found at the scene of a vehicle fire and place them in the vehicle to be disposed of when the vehicle is removed from the scene.
2. The items were burned at a different fire event. The items were then returned to the scene and placed in the vehicle after the fire department cleared the scene. The motive to why this might have occurred is unknown at this time.

These opinions are based solely on the photographic evidence submitted. The conclusions drawn in this report are based on an analysis of the information collected during the site visit and investigation. Information or data that becomes available at a later date may justify the modification of the results and/or conclusions at that time.

EFI Global, Inc.
Bradley Henson, IAAI-CFI, ECT, CI,CFEI
Fire Investigator

Reviewed by:
Ronald Krupp, IAAI-CFI, CFEI
District Manager

The first opinion Henson advanced—that firefighters placed the purse and other items back in the cab of the pickup after extinguishing the fire—does not make sense because the guards were present when the firefighters put out the fire in Debbie's pickup. If they had come across her purse, they would have simply handed it to her.

The second option—that the purse and other items were burned in a different fire after the firefighters cleared the scene—is left as the only viable explanation.

Whether or not Joe's theory about how the purse and sweatshirt were set on fire is correct in all its detail, I think he has come up with what could be called the smoking gun in terms of proving the involvement of at least Debbie and Robert Riggs in the burning of Debbie's truck. And if that is established, it isn't much of a leap to speculate that they are linked to the east side arson as well.

Back into play comes Ed Massey, a woodcutter at the construction site, who told the ATF in 2007 that he saw Donna Costanza—Debbie's significant other and fellow guard—moving around the east side of the site around 2:30 a.m. Massey said he then saw "flashes" and saw Costanza running away from a burning construction company pickup parked near the rear door of the first ANFO trailer that exploded. Massey also said Debbie Riggs had previously twice offered him money to set fire to her pickup to collect insurance.

Also back into play comes Gloria Nolen, the passerby who reported seeing the guards at the construction site while Debbie's pickup was ablaze. Likewise the reports from Sandy DiGiovanni, Jessica Vernon, and Johnny Ray Neil, who told police that Costanza made admissions about setting Debbie's pickup on fire.

Affidavits sworn to by two of Debbie's women friends—only one of which was reported on in the *Star*—reveal that Debbie made admissions about burning her pickup as part of an insurance scam two nights before the explosions and several days after the explosions.

In an attempt to move the secondary-fire evidence forward, Joe sent an email to Sergeant Brown, the public information officer for KCPD on July 19, 2016, asking if he would be permitted, in the company of an attorney and a forensic expert, to examine the purse and the other items from Debbie's pickup.

I found photographic evidence in a picture you provided of a "secondary-fire event" unknown to investigators and I would like to see if the physical evidence supports this observation or not.

In photograph "AA002" [the interior photo of Debbie's pickup] items appear with suspicious burn patterns and a curious lack of fire damage if they were in a blazing truck fire. Arson expert Bradley Henson of EFI Global analyzed the photo and he too thought the items may have been burned in a second-fire event not known to the original investigators.

. . . There is a pressing public interest to find closure in this case. If this photographic evidence of a "secondary-fire event" matches the physical evidence, KCPD detectives will have a fresh opportunity at solving Kansas City's biggest mystery. The physical evidence may tell a drastically different series of events not known until now. Let's let modern forensic science sort this out.

Sergeant Brown responded on August 5, saying he found out the day before that he needed to speak with the US Attorney's Office "to discern who from their office needs to be present along with, potentially, prior defense counsel." Brown said his understanding was that the US Attorney's Office should handle the evidence review portion of the request. He said he would be dealing with the records portion.

Brown's response prompted me to send a certified letter on August 8, 2016, to Tammy Dickinson, the US Attorney for the Western District of Missouri that began, "There is evidence in the possession of the Kansas City Police Department that could establish the innocence of the five people convicted in 1997 in the tragic deaths of six Kansas City firefighters."

The evidence, I told her, was a white vinyl purse, a yellow sweatshirt, a plastic bag, and what looks like a paper road atlas all with varying degrees of burn damage found inside guard Debbie Riggs's pickup. These items were shown in the photo "AA002" and somehow survived a fire that raged for at least seventeen minutes before firefighters put it out, a fire that left the interior of the pickup in ashes and charred debris.

I informed her that Bradley Henson, an arson expert, concluded from looking at the photo that "the items were burned at a different fire event. The items were then returned to the scene and placed in the vehicle after the fire department cleared the scene. The motive to why this might have occurred is unknown at this time."

"If you will allow the full development of the evidence, I believe you will have a rare opportunity to correct these wrongful convictions and bring the actual perpetrators of this terrible tragedy to justice," my letter ended.

Dickinson never responded, but in September 2016, Sergeant Brown informed Joe the US Attorney's Office does not wish to be involved in the handling of the evidence concerning the purse and sweatshirt, among others, that point to a "secondary fire."

The stonewalling continues.

Going forward, there are various pathways open for the remaining defendants—Richard Brown, Darlene Edwards, and Frank Sheppard—to win their freedom.

For Richard, who missed being eligible for resentencing under *Miller v. Alabama* by just over four months, there is growing research in neurobiology and development psychology that the brain does not complete developing until a person's mid-twenties.[7] The Illinois Appellate Court has already acted on this realization. In an order issued December 24, 2015, it vacated the life without parole sentence of Antonio House, who was nineteen at the time of the two murders for which he was convicted. "We find the designation that after 18 an individual is a mature adult appears to be somewhat arbitrary," the court wrote in ordering a new sentencing hearing for House.

More significantly, the challenge of extending the benefits of *Miller* to young adults older than seventeen received its first recognition at the federal level on March 29, 2018, when a US district court judge for the District of Connecticut vacated the life without parole sentence of Luis Noel Cruz and ordered a new sentencing for him. In 1994, when Cruz was eighteen, he killed two men as part of a gang retaliation. In her order, District Judge Janet C. Hall wrote:

> The court concludes that the hallmark characteristics of juveniles that make them less culpable also apply to 18-year-olds. As such, the penological rationales for imposing life imprisonment without the possibility of parole cannot be used as justification when applied to an 18-year-old.
>
> The court therefore holds that *Miller* applies to 18-year-olds.

Decisions by federal judges from one district are not binding for judges in other districts—such as the Western District of Missouri—but they do provide attorneys such as Cyndy Short, who is now representing Richard Brown, with an authority to cite when seeking a resentencing for their clients.

In terms of the three defendants as a group, a 2012 case out of the Northern District of Ohio Eastern Division, which is incredibly similar to the firefighters case in many of its particulars, offers an opportunity for a new filing in federal district court. In *United States v. Antun Lewis*, the court ordered a new trial for Lewis "in the interest of justice because the verdict is against the manifest weight of the evidence."[8]

An ATF special agent led the investigation. Lewis was indicted by a grand jury on October 1, 2008, on one count of arson in violation of 18 U.S.C. 844, the same statute under which the Marlborough Five were indicted. Eight children and one adult were killed in a house fire in 2005. During the three-week trial, the government's key witness was a career felon who claimed he acted as the lookout when Lewis set the house on the fire. For his testimony, the lookout was given immunity from prosecution in the arson; current felony charges pending against him for kidnapping, aggravated burglary, and attempted felonious assault were reduced to misdemeanors and he was given probation; the ATF paid him over $20,000 in relocation expenses.

One of the other key witnesses was a prostitute who received over $1,000 in payments from the ATF.

There was no evidence linking Lewis to the arson. To make its case, the government called six jailhouse informants who claimed Lewis made admissions to them while incarcerated.

During the trial, the government advanced two separate motives for the arson.

In granting Lewis a new trial, the court stated its reluctance to overturn a jury verdict:

> However, the court finds that this is one of those few cases where the integrity of the system is at stake and the court is required to overturn the jury's verdict as being against the manifest weight of the evidence. Here, a conviction for a crime of this magnitude rests almost exclusively on the word of suspect witnesses, career criminals, and jailhouse informants who can easily insert themselves into the facts of a case given its high-profile nature. This is a case where the defendant at one point was facing the death penalty and now a life sentence; the stakes demand some measure of confidence, and the record simply does not provide it.

Another possible avenue for appeal for the remaining defendants was opened by Federal District Judge Gaitan during Bryan Sheppard's resentencing when he predicated the twenty-year sentence he handed down on the basis that there was no intent by Bryan (or the other defendants) to kill anyone in setting the fire at the construction site. This took the crime from first- to second-degree murder, which carried a sentence of fifteen to twenty years in 1997.

The new evidence uncovered by my son that points to Robert and Debbie Riggs's involvement in setting her pickup on fire could be grounds for the Eighth Circuit Court of Appeals to grant the defendants a second habeas corpus petition and a new trial.

If the Freedom of Information Act lawsuit that Cyndy Short is working on with Shook, Hardy and Bacon—that seeks an unredacted copy of the DOJ report that names two other perpetrators—is successful, the release of those names has the potential of cracking open the case against the Marlborough Five.

No matter what else happens, this case will not be closed until the Marlborough Five are exonerated and the actual perpetrators are brought to justice.

Cast of Main Characters

Baker, Diddi, wife of Larry Baker and sister of Frank and Skip Sheppard

Baker, Larry, brother-in-law of Frank and Skip Sheppard

Bartlett, D. Brook, US federal district judge originally assigned to try the case but was forced to step aside for health reasons

Becker, Paul, assistant US attorney who prosecuted the Marlborough Five

Bethard, Alan, refused to corroborate the testimony of star grand jury witness Ronnie Edwards and was prosecuted for it

Brown, Ed, father of Richard Brown

Brown, Ken, president of Brown Brothers Construction, the general contractor at the construction site

Brown, Nadine, mother of Richard Brown

Brown, Richard, one of the Marlborough Five, close friend of Bryan Sheppard

Bunch, Will, trial attorney for Darlene Edwards

Clark, Doris, mother of Darlene Edwards

Cleaver, Emmanuel, II, mayor pro-tem of Kansas City at time of explosion and now a US representative

Cole, Troy, KCPD sergeant who supervised the early investigation

Collins, Norm, president of Mountain Plains Construction

Corriston, Kelly, former girlfriend of Richard Brown who testified against him at trial

Costanza, Donna, guard at construction site

Cox, John, Department of Justice attorney who investigated charges the *Kansas City Star* made of witness tampering

Denyer, Joe, friend of Bryan and Richard who testified at trial against Darlene and later recanted his testimony in a sworn affidavit in 2005

Dickinson, Tammy, former US attorney for the Western District of Missouri

Edwards, Becky, Darlene Edwards's daughter and key prosecution witness at trial

Maloney, J. J., wrote two ten-thousand-word articles about firefighters case for the Kansas City *New Times* in May 1997

Martindale, Frederick, confessed to KCPD detectives in 1991 to killing the firefighters

Massey, Edward, woodcutter at construction site who years later claimed he saw guard Donna Costanza start the fire at the ANFO trailer

McCabe, Pamela, investigator who assisted John Cox in the Department of Justice reinvestigation

McGraw, Mike, investigative reporter for the *Kansas City Star*

McKarnin, Robert, apparatus operator for Pumper 41

Miller, Dan, an assistant Jackson County prosecutor who assisted US Assistant Attorney Paul Becker in the prosecution of the Marlborough Five

Neighbors, Carie, witness against Bryan Sheppard and Richard Brown who recanted her testimony

Neil, Johnny Ray, told ATF that in 1994 he overheard Donna Costanza saying she torched Debbie Riggs's pickup the night the firefighters were killed

Nolen, Gloria, passerby who reported seeing Debbie's pickup ablaze while vehicles with spotlights shining were still at construction site

O'Connor, John P., trial attorney for Bryan Sheppard

O'Connor, Joseph B., webmaster of kcfirefighterscase.com who uncovered new evidence that possibly linked Robert and Debbie Riggs to the arson of Debbie's pickup

Oldham, Michael, firefighter for Pumper 41

Osgood, John, trial attorney for Richard Brown

Pederson, Amy, her call to the ATF in 1994, implicating Richard Brown, caused Special Agent Dave True to pivot away from labor toward people in Marlborough

Peters, Pat, trial attorney for Frank Sheppard

Phillips, Beth, US attorney for the Western District of Missouri when a Justice Department review team exonerated ATF Special Agent Dave True of tampering with grand jury and trial witnesses

Pilate, Cheryl, post-conviction attorney for Darlene Edwards, 2006–2012

Pugh, Greg, passerby who drove by construction site twice several hours before the first explosion and saw the hood of Debbie's pickup and four people nearby

Reeder, Mark, private investigator for the defense

Reimers, Shannon, half sister of Richard Brown and prosecution witness at trial who later recanted her testimony

Riggs, Debbie, sister of Robert Riggs and guard at construction site

Riggs, Robert, president of Ameriguard, the security company at the construction site

Romi, Nancy, sister of Darlene Edwards who testified at trial against Richard Brown

Schram, Eugene, investigator from Department of Labor, Racketeering Division

Sheppard, Bryan, one of the Marlborough Five, nephew of Frank and Skip Sheppard, who was set free on March 6, 2017, after serving over twenty-two years

Sheppard, Frank, one of the Marlborough Five, brother of Skip Sheppard and uncle of Bryan Sheppard

Sheppard, Naomi, mother of Frank and Skip Sheppard and grandmother of Bryan Sheppard

Sheppard, Skip, one of the Marlborough Five, brother of Frank Sheppard and uncle of Bryan Sheppard

Sheppard, Virgie, mother of Bryan Sheppard

Short, Cynthia L., attorney for Bryan Sheppard at his resentencing

Stanton, Melvin, guard at construction site

Stevens, Joseph E., senior US federal district judge at trial of Marlborough Five

True, Dave, ATF special agent in charge of the investigation that led to the indictment of the Marlborough Five

Van Buskirk, Gary, KCPD homicide captain who led early investigation

Wall, Phil, chief dispatcher for KCFD

Waris, Gerald, a Catholic priest who was Bryan Sheppard's chaplain at CCA Leavenworth

Wood, John F., US attorney for the Western District of Missouri who called for the Justice Department to conduct an independent reinvestigation of the case

Wright, Scott O., senior US federal district judge at Alan Bethard's trial

Zinn, Victor, KCPD homicide detective during early investigation

Timeline

9-6-88:   Construction of the Bruce R. Watkins Memorial Drive begins, a $200 million project to link US 71 at 87th Street to downtown Kansas City, ten miles away.

10-20-88:   Brown Brothers Construction, the general contractor for the project, hires Ameriguard, a six-person security company run by Robert Riggs, to guard the west side of the construction site where it stores its large earth-moving equipment.

10-26-88:   Mountain Plains, the subcontractor responsible for the blasting operations on the construction site's east side, hires Ameriguard to guard the east side of the site.

11-28-88:   Around 3 p.m. Brown Brothers informs Robert Riggs that Ameriguard's hours are being reduced from 6 p.m. to 6 a.m. to 7:30 p.m. to 5 a.m.

11-28-88:   Around 9:30 p.m. Debbie Riggs calls guard Melvin Stanton and tells him to report to work; around 10 p.m. he takes up his post on the east side of site where the ANFO trailers are located.

11-28-88:   Around 11 p.m. Robert Riggs sends guard Melvin Stanton home.

11-29-88:   At 3:41 a.m. Robert Riggs calls the Kansas City Fire Department to report a fire in a pickup truck on the west side of construction site, adding there were "some explosives up on a hill that I also see now is burning."

11-29-88:   At 3:48 a.m. a pumper crew of three out of Fire Station 41 arrives at the west side of the construction site and proceeds to put out the fire in the pickup. Captain James Kilventon informs dispatch that there is another fire in progress on the east side and requests that another pumper company be sent.

11-29-88:   At 3:53 a.m. a pumper crew of three out of Fire Station 30 arrives and proceeds directly to the east side of the construction site where a semitrailer containing ANFO is on fire.

11-29-88:   At 4 a.m. Captain Gerald Halloran of Pumper 30 asks the dispatcher if he could "confirm that there is explosives in this trailer or not." Dispatch tells him that Pumper 41 had advised "we have additional information on the original call that there were explosives in that area, use caution." In response, Halloran tells dispatch to send Pumper 41 up. Kilventon hears the transmission and informs dispatch, "We're en route now."

11-29-88: At 4:06 a.m. Battalion Chief Marion Germann and his driver arrive, parking on an access road about 350 feet away from the burning semitrailer.

11-29-88: At 4:08 a.m., as Germann reaches for his radio to order the firefighters to abandon the site, the ANFO trailer explodes, instantly killing all six firefighters.

11-29-88: At 4:48 a.m., a second ANFO trailer explodes with much greater force than the first one, causing millions of dollars in property damage, mostly within a ten-mile radius of the blast site.

12-2-88: A memorial service for the six fallen firefighters is held at Arrowhead Stadium, home of the Kansas City Chiefs of the National Football League, with about twenty thousand mourners in attendance.

9-27-89: Bryan Sheppard, an eighteen-year-old, is indicted by the Jackson County Prosecutor's Office and charged with six counts of second-degree murder for causing the explosion that killed the firefighters.

12-28-89: All charges against Sheppard are dropped when his attorney establishes that the jailhouse informants who implicated him in the deaths of the firefighters were lying.

8-20-90: A passerby reports to KCPD homicide that on the night of the explosion she was driving by the construction site and saw on the west side a pickup engulfed in flames and two white cars with spotlights shining around the area of the pickup. No one from homicide follows up on this lead.

2-10-95: The TV program *Unsolved Mysteries* features the deaths of the firefighters and encourages viewers to contact the TIPS hotline with information, announcing a $50,000 reward. Simultaneously, reward posters are posted in all the jails and prisons in Kansas and Missouri. In the weeks that follow, over 150 people, more than 60 of them convicts or ex-convicts, call the hotline.

3-14-95: The *Kansas City Star* runs a front-page story saying the government's investigation is focusing on the Sheppards—Bryan and his uncles—and Darlene Edwards, mentioning items that "may have been stolen" from the construction site.

6-12-96: A federal grand jury returns indictments against Frank, Skip, and Bryan Sheppard, Darlene Edwards, and Richard Brown.

3-2-97: After a six-week trial, the jury convicts all five defendants.

5-15-97: The Kansas City *New Times* publishes Part I ("Frame-Up") of J. J. Maloney's articles about the firefighters case; Part II ("Rail-roaded") is published a week later.

7-2-97: Senior Federal District Judge Joseph Stevens, the trial judge, sentences all five defendants to life without the possibility of parole and restitution of $536,000 each to the Kansas City Fire Department.

8-30-98: The Eighth US Circuit Court of Appeals denies the direct appeal for each defendant.

10-4-99: The US Supreme Court denies certiorari, i.e., refuses to hear an appeal of the Eighth Circuit's decision.

7-11-03: US District Judge Fernando Gaitan denies the habeas corpus appeal for each of the Marlborough Five.

2-18-07: The *Kansas City Star* begins publishing a series of front-page articles by investigative reporter Mike McGraw that cast doubt on the guilt of the Marlborough Five and point to the possible involvement of the guards in the crime.

6-29-08: "Did Pressure Lead to Lies? Witnesses Say Testimony Was Co-erced," McGraw's article reports on how ATF Special Agent Dave True had used coercive tactics to pressure fifteen people to lie at the grand jury and/or trial.

7-3-08: Local US Attorney John F. Wood calls for the Department of Justice to conduct an independent investigation into the *Star*'s allegations of witness tampering.

7-25-09: Skip Sheppard dies of liver cancer at the Federal Medical Center in Butner, North Carolina. He was forty-nine.

7-26-11: In a 2½-page report issued by then US Attorney Beth Phillips, the Department of Justice review team finds no "credible sup-port for *The Star*'s allegations." The review states that it discov-ered that others may have been involved in the arson that killed the firefighters, but those names are blacked out. Freedom of Information Act requests by the *Kansas City Star* to obtain the names of the other possible perpetrators are denied by the Jus-tice Department.

7-25-12: The US Supreme Court rules in *Miller v. Alabama* that sentenc-ing minors to life without parole is a violation of the Eighth Amendment's prohibition against cruel and unusual punishment. Because Bryan Sheppard was a minor at the time of the explosions, he is entitled to a resentencing hearing in federal district court in Kansas City.

3-7-16:   Arson expert Bradley Henson of EFI Global reports that several items in Debbie Riggs's charred pickup could not have survived the intense fire that engulfed her pickup and were most likely placed inside the vehicle after the firefighters put out the fire in her pickup.

3-3-17:   US District Court Judge Fernando Gaitan sentences Bryan Sheppard to twenty years, but because he had already served twenty-two years, he is released from custody three days later.

Acknowledgments

My thanks for the publication of this book go to Kim Hogeland, acquisitions editor at the University Press of Kansas in Lawrence. It was extremely important to me that a book of this nature—a book that essentially argues that the federal government wrongfully convicted five innocent people for a crime it could not solve but wanted to close—would go through the rigorous editorial procedures of a respected university press.

Back in early February 2016, I approached Kim with a rough draft of the book. She thought the manuscript had potential but needed a good deal of work. She was particularly concerned about the critical, judgmental tone of the book. She pressed me over and over to let the facts speak for themselves, to allow readers to draw their own conclusions. What she stressed through her comments was that there is a crucial line that must be drawn between my being an advocate for the Marlborough Five and my being the author of a book about a terrible miscarriage of justice.

As part of the vetting process at a university press, there is a peer review that involves soliciting the opinion of two "readers," who are asked to determine if they believe the manuscript is worthy of publication. Daniel S. Medwed, professor of law and criminal justice at Northeastern University, and Brant Houston, a journalism professor at the University of Illinois, both provided strong endorsements and said they thought this was a story that deserved to be told. Each, in different ways, made suggestions about how to improve the manuscript. I found those suggestions invaluable going forward and I thank them for their insights.

The final step toward publication at the University Press of Kansas is the vote of the faculty editorial board. When Kim told me on October 20, 2017, that the board was unanimous in giving the go-ahead on publication, I could not have been more gratified and grateful.

I owe a great debt of thanks to my friend John Brady, author of *Bad Boy: The Life and Politics of Lee Atwater* and most recently of *Frank & Ava: In Love and War*, for patiently, kindly, and constructively going through draft after draft of this book.

No one, though, has been more crucial to me writing about the fire-fighters case than Mike McGraw. His articles in the *Kansas City Star* broke new ground time and again in uncovering how flawed the investigation into this crime was ever since the ATF took over the investigation in 1994 and focused exclusively on indicting the Marlborough Five. Sadly, Mike died from a particularly aggressive form of cancer on January 6, 2018. I will miss him for the rest of my life.

One of the most pleasant surprises I had in doing the research for this book was the candor expressed by the former Kansas City, Missouri, homicide officers involved in the early investigation into the deaths of the firefighters. Their comments about how the investigation went awry and why are, to my mind, the most convincing in the book.

My son Joe O'Connor has pushed me for years to tell the story of these false convictions and has done a great deal of research and investigation on his own that I have incorporated into this book. Over the last couple of years, Joe, more than anyone else, has been working to develop evidence that will exonerate the Marlborough Five. And he's not done yet.

I'd like to thank UMKC law professor Sean O'Brien for meeting with me numerous times to discuss the legal aspects of this complex case. And the same is true for Jonathan Laurans, John Osgood, and Cyndy Short.

Thanks to my sister Paula O'Connor for her diligent proofreading and tremendous encouragement and support throughout this endeavor.

I was greatly assisted in the final stages of putting this book together by Larisa Martin, production editor at the University Press of Kansas, and by Martha Whitt, whose copyediting greatly improved this book.

I also owe a huge debt of thanks to Father Gerald Waris, a friend of mine since high school, who volunteered to become Bryan Sheppard's chaplain at CCA. He's walked with me every step of the way in seeking justice for the Marlborough Five.

One ancillary benefit of researching and writing this book is how my life has been enriched by getting to know so intimately Richard Brown, Darlene Edwards, Bryan, Frank, and Skip Sheppard, as well as Richard's mother and father, Nadine and Ed Brown, and Bryan's mother, Virgie. Another friend for life I've made along the way is Leo Halloran, the brother of Captain Gerald Halloran of Pumper 30.

Finally, my fervent hope is that in showing how the government went about so blindly railroading five innocent people, the US Attorney's Office will finally get around to indicting the actual perpetrators of this tragic crime and bring real closure to the families of the fallen firefighters.

Notes

PROLOGUE

1. Jim Dwyer, Peter Neufeld, and Barry Scheck, *Actual Innocence: When Justice Goes Wrong and How to Make It Right* (New York: New American Library, 2000) 166–167.
2. The National Registry of Exonerations, A Project of the University of California Irvine Newkirk Center for Science and Society, University of Michigan Law School, and Michigan State University College of Law (https://www.law.umich.edu/spe cial/exoneration/Pages/Exonerations-in-the-United-States-Map.aspx).
3. "DNA Exonerations in the United States," *The Innocence Project*, https://innocen ceproject.org/dna-exonerations-in-the-united-states/.
4. The two-part articles written by J. J. Maloney, "Frame-Up" and "Railroaded," are viewable at http://www.kcfirefighterscase.com.
5. Sworn affidavit of Carie Neighbors, June 2004.
6. Mike McGraw, "Did Pressure Lead to Lies?" *Kansas City Star*, June 29, 2008.
7. The Missouri Sunshine Law was passed by the state legislature in 1973 and made a part of the Missouri Constitution (https://ballotpedia.org/Missouri_Sunshine _Law).
8. Report by arson expert Bradley Henson of EFI Global (Engineering Fire and Environmental Services), March 7, 2016.

CHAPTER ONE: THE LAST ALARM

1. Details about the night of the explosion and its immediate aftermath are taken from the KCFD dispatch tape and from articles published subsequently in the *Kansas City Star*.

CHAPTER TWO: WHAT WENT WRONG?

1. Quotes for this section about firefighters and information about the internal operations of a firehouse are taken from the *Kansas City Star* article, "Living on the Firing Line," published December 3, 1988.
2. Quotes and details about the six firefighters are taken from an article in the *Kansas City Star*, "Families, Friends, Pay Tribute to City's Fallen Firefighters," December 3, 1988.

3. Author interviews with various firefighters at Fire Station 41, August 6, 2014.

4. *Emergency Response Guidebook: A Guidebook for First Responders during the Initial Phase of a Dangerous Goods/Hazardous Materials Transportation Incident* (Washington, DC: Department of Transportation, 1973).

5. Brian Ellison, Matthew Long-Middleton, and Glenn Frizell, "Freedom, Inc.," *Central Standard*, February 9, 2016, http://kcur.org/term/freedom-inc#stream/0.

6. "Bruce R. Watkins, Kansas City, Missouri Leader and Successful Black Entrepreneur," blackmissouri, July 14, 2008, http://blackmissouri.com/digest/bruce-r-watkins-kansas-city-missouri-leader-and-successful-black-entrepreneur.html.

7. Partha Das Sharma, "Priming of Explosives for Effective Blasting," *Mining and Blasting*, May 14, 2013, https://miningandblasting.wordpress.com/2013/05/14/priming-of-explosives/.

8. "Oklahoma City Bombing," History.com, http://www.history.com/topics/oklahoma-city-bombing.

CHAPTER THREE: INVESTIGATING THE CRIME

1. "The Union Station Massacre," *Kansas City Star*, July 10, 2014, http://www.kansascity.com/news/special-reports/kc-true-crime/article706028.html.

2. From Robert Riggs's deposition taken on April 18, 1979, in conjunction with the lawsuit filed against him by William Hinton.

3. Kevin Lemanske (former Ameriguard guard), interview by ATF Special Agent Dave True, April 4, 1994.

4. Robert Riggs, interview by KCPD Detectives William Wilson and Joe Chapman, November 29, 1988.

5. Debbie Riggs, videotaped interview by Detective Victor Zinn, November 29, 1988.

6. Victor Zinn (former detective, KCPD), interview with author, August 4, 2014.

7. Robert Riggs, videotaped interview by Detectives William Wilson and Joe Chapman, written up by Detective Larry Sprouse, November 29, 1988.

8. Report by Police Officer Lee Edwards, November 29, 1988.

9. Police report by Detective Ed Glynn of interview with Vivian Rhodes, December 1, 1988.

10. Of the $35,000 reward, $25,000 was provided by an anonymous Kansas City donor and $5,000 each was donated by the Heavy Constructors Association and the Missouri Arson Hotline, a group underwritten by state insurance firms, according to the *Kansas City Times* as reported on December 1, 1988.

11. Gary Van Buskirk (former captain, KCPD), phone interview with author, August 6, 2014.

12. Report by KCPD Detective Victor Zinn, December 1, 1988.

13. Under cross-examination at the firefighters trial, Robert Riggs admitted the gun was not a collector's item.

14. Victor Zinn (former detective, KCPD), interview with author, August 4, 2014.

15. A claim stated on Ameriguard's web site, http://ameriguard.org/#services, accessed December 5, 2017.

16. Melvin Stanton, interview by Detective John Fraise, February 22, 1989.

17. Information revealed by Debbie Riggs in a civil suit deposition taken on October 4, 1989.
18. In sworn affidavits taken in the summer of 2007, these two friends averred Debbie's admissions.
19. Police report of the call to KCPD homicide department made by Gloria Nolen to Detective John Fraise on August 2, 1990.
20. Report by ATF Special Agent Dave True of his interview with Johnnie Ray Neil, June 1, 1993.
21. Report by ATF Special Agent Dave True of his interview with Jessica Vernon, which was attended by Special Agent Eugene Schram of the Department of Labor, February 4, 1994.
22. Report by Detective Don Emerson of his interview of Debbie Riggs, February 10, 1995.
23. Report by Detective Don Emerson of his phone interview with John Collum, February 13, 1995.
24. Report of ATF Special Agent Dave True's interview with Robert Riggs, April 17, 1990.

CHAPTER FOUR: INVESTIGATING THE MARLBOROUGH NEIGHBORHOOD

1. Author letter and email interviews with Frank Sheppard and Darlene Edwards.
2. Author in-person, letter, and email interviews with Richard Brown.
3. Polygraph of Richard Brown by Officer Harold D. Oldham, December 9, 1988.
4. Sworn affidavit of Becky Edwards, November 6, 2005.
5. Tom Jackman, "Inquiry Returns to Early Focus: After Several Years, Those Investigating the '88 Blast Look at Previous Suspects," *Kansas City Star*, March 14, 1995.

CHAPTER FIVE: THE MARLBOROUGH FIVE

1. Accounts of how the various members of the Marlborough Five spent the day before the blast that killed the firefighters are taken from in-person interviews the author conducted with Richard Brown, Bryan Sheppard, Frank Sheppard, and Larry Baker, Frank and Skip's brother-in-law, as well as letter and email responses from Richard, Bryan, Frank, and Darlene over the years.
2. Biographical details about Skip Sheppard are taken from the author's in-person, phone, and letter interviews with Skip up until his death in 2009. His brother, Frank Sheppard, and his sister-in-law, Virgie Sheppard, also provided the author with information about Skip's background.
3. Biographical detail about Darlene Edwards was provided to the author by her through letters, emails, and phone calls.
4. Biographical details about Bryan are taken from author in-person, phone, and letter interviews with him and in-person interviews with his mother.
5. Biographical details about Richard are taken from author in-person, phone, email, and letter interviews with him and in-person interviews with his mother.

1. Author in-person interviews and by letter, phone, and email with Bryan Sheppard.
2. Author in-person interviews and by letter, phone, and email with Richard Brown.
3. Author interviews with Darlene Edwards by phone, letter, and email.
4. Darlene Edwards, videotaped interview by ATF Special Agent Dave True, February 17, 1995.
5. Darlene Edwards, audiotaped interview by ATF Special Agent Dave True, February 19, 1995.
6. Becker turned down the author's request to interview him for this book. I had proposed interviewing him in person or by submitting questions in writing.
7. Amanda Honigfort, "Harry Truman: The 'Senator from Pendergast' Got His Start with Missouri Political Machine," *St. Louis on the Air*, July 15, 2014, http://news .stlpublicradio.org/post/harry-truman-senator-pendergast-got-his-start-missouri -political-machine. Honigfort described how after Truman gave his maiden speech in the US Senate, Senator Huey Long (D-LA), stood and loudly said he wanted to welcome "the senator from Pendergast."
8. "Kansas City Group Fights Jailing of 20," *New York Times*, October 29, 1991, http:// www.nytimes.com/1991/10/29/us/kansas-city-group-fights-jailing-of-20.html.
9. "How Federal Grand Juries Work," NPR, October 26, 2005, https://www.npr.org /templates/story/story.php?storyId=4975837.
10. William J. Campbell, "Eliminate the Grand Jury," *Journal of Criminal Law & Criminology* 64, no. 2 (1973): 174.
11. Sol Wachtler, quoted in Josh Levin, "The Judge Who Coined 'Indict a Ham Sandwich' Was Himself Indicted," *Slate*, November 25, 2014, http://www.slate.com /blogs/lexicon_valley/2014/11/25/sol_wachtler_the_judge_who_coined_indict_a _ham_sandwich_was_himself_indicted.html.
12. Retired ATF Special Agent Dave True turned down the author's request to interview him for this book. I had proposed interviewing him in person or by submitting questions in writing.
13. Ronnie Edwards, interview by Detective Ron Randol, December 12, 1988.
14. Ronnie Edwards, videotaped interview by Detectives John Fraise and Victor Zinn, February 17, 1989.
15. Ronnie Edwards, interview by Detectives Doug Clark and Joe Herrera at the KCPD Bomb and Arson Unit, January 25, 1995.
16. Ronnie Edwards, grand jury testimony, September 27, 1995.
17. Affidavit of Alan Bethard, August 3, 2004.
18. Court transcript of Alan Bethard's trial in federal court, February 14, 1997.
19. ATF Special Agent Dave True's summary of the case against the Marlborough Five, "Recommendation for Prosecution," October 14, 1996.

CHAPTER SEVEN: THE TRIAL OPENS

1. Hans Sherrer, "99.8% Conviction Rate in U.S. Federal Courts Can Make Japanese Prosecutors Jealous," *Justice Denied*, May 17, 2016, http://justicedenied.org/word press/archives/3190.

2. Alexandra Natapoff, *Snitching: Criminal Informants and the Erosion of American Justice* (New York: New York University Press, 2011), 89.

3. Justin Rohrlich, "Why Are There Up to 120,000 Innocent People in U.S. Prisons?" *Vice News*, November 10, 2014, https://news.vice.com/article/why-are-there-up-to -120000-innocent-people-in-us-prisons.

4. Sherrer, "99.8% Conviction Rate."

5. Information from the US District Court Criminal Docket—Western District of Missouri, *United States v. Sheppard et al.*, April 25, 1997.

6. Ibid., August 27, 1997.

7. "Severance of Charges," *Criminal Law and Procedure B*, https://crimb.weebly.com /severance-of-chargesseparate-trials-for-co-accused.html.

8. Information about the pretrial activity is taken from J. J. Maloney, "Railroaded: The Firefighters Case, Part II," *Kansas City New Times*, May 22, 1997, http://kcfire fighterscase.com/content/railroaded-part-ii-firefighters-case.

9. "Brady Rule," Legal Information Institute, Cornell Law School, last updated October 2017, https://www.law.cornell.edu/wex/brady_rule.

10. All of the information about the trial is taken from the trial transcripts and from Maloney, "Railroaded." The full transcript is available at http://kcfirefighterscase .com/trialtranscript.pdf.

11. "Federal Judges on Senior Status," Ballotpedia: The Encyclopedia of American Politics, https://ballotpedia.org/Federal_judges_on_senior_status.

12. Christin J. Jones, "A Guide to the Offer of Proof," American Bar Association, August 31, 2016, http://apps.americanbar.org/litigation/committees/trialpractice/arti cles/summer2016-0816-a-guide-to-the-offer-of-proof.html.

13. Geoffrey Nathan, "What Are the Federal Sentencing Guidelines + Chart 2017," FederalCharges.com, https://www.federalcharges.com/what-are-federal-sentencing -guidelines/.

14. "S.668 (98th): Sentencing Reform Act of 1984," GovTrack, https://www.govtrack .us/congress/bills/98/s668.

15. "S.1762, Comprehensive Crime Control Act of 1984," Congress.Gov, https://www .congress.gov/bill/98th-congress/senate-bill/1762.

16. US Sentencing Commission, "An Overview of the United States Sentencing Commission," n.d., https://isb.ussc.gov/files/USSC_Overview.pdf.

17. Ethan Brown, *Snitch: Informants, Cooperators, and the Corruption of Justice* (New York: Public Affairs, 2007), 25–26.

18. "The Anti-Drug Abuse Act of 1986," GovTrack, https://www.govtrack.us/congress /bills/99/hr5484.

19. Brown, *Snitch*, 29.

20. Ibid., 30.

21. Ibid., 31.

22. For information about Northwestern University's Center for Wrongful Convictions, see http://www.law.northwestern.edu/legalclinic/wrongfulconvictions.

23. Rob Warden, "The Snitch System: How Snitch Testimony Sent Randy Steidl and Other Innocent Americans to Death Row," Center on Wrongful Convictions, Northwestern University School of Law, Winter 2004–2005, http://www.law.north western.edu/legalclinic/wrongfulconvictions/documents/SnitchSystemBooklet .pdf.

24. For information about the National Registry of Exonerations, see https://www.law .umich.edu/special/exoneration/Pages/about.aspx.
25. For information about the Death Penalty Information Center, see https://death penaltyinfo.org/.
26. "Frequently Asked Questions," Innocence Project, https://www.innocenceproject .org/contact/.
27. Jim Dwyer, Peter Neufeld, and Barry Scheck, *Actual Innocence: When Justice Goes Wrong and How to Make It Right* (New York: Doubleday, 2000).
28. Ibid., 165–167.
29. "DNA Exonerations in the United States," Innocence Project, https://www.innoc enceproject.org.dna-exonerations-in-the-united states/.
30. Statistics tracking the government's use of cooperating witnesses—felons who testify for reductions in sentences or to have pending charges dismissed or informants who are incented by reward money—at trial are not compiled by any government entity or any professional organization. The author queried numerous scholars who have written extensively about the use of informants at trial. Professor Alexandra Natapoff informed the author that a federal prosecutor in Cleveland called six jailhouse informants to testify at the trial of Antun Lewis, who was convicted on February 14, 2011, of setting a house fire that resulted in the deaths of eight children and one adult. In her book *Snitching*, Natapoff referenced a 2006 case where Ann Columb and her three sons were convicted in federal court in Louisiana of running one of the largest crack operations in the state based on the testimony of thirty-one jailhouse snitches. Prior to sentencing, all charges were dropped when it came out that the informants had conspired en masse to lie to obtain cuts in their sentences. Ethan Brown, author of *Snitch: Informants, Cooperators & the Corruption of Justice*, directed the author to the case of Euka Waldington, who was convicted in 1999 in federal court of three counts of drug conspiracy and sentenced to two concurrent life sentences based primarily on the testimony of eleven felons who received significant reductions in their sentences for cooperating with the government. Leonard C. Goodman, Waldington's trial and appeal attorney, told the author in an email dated October 15, 2017, that the government used twelve cooperating witnesses at Waldington's sentencing hearing.
31. Jessica Smith, "The Bruton Rule: Joint Trials and Codefendants' Confessions," *North Carolina Super Court Judges' Benchbook*, UNC School of Government, May 2012, http://benchbook.sog.unc.edu/sites/benchbook.sog.unc.edu/files/pdf/The%20 Bruton%20Rule%20Joint%20Trials%20%26%20Codefendants%27%20Confes sions.pdf.

CHAPTER EIGHT: THE CASE AGAINST THE MARLBOROUGH FIVE

1. Biographical details about Frank Sheppard were accumulated over the years by the author's email and letter interviews with him.
2. All the information about trial testimony is taken from the trial transcript, which runs to 4,071 pages. The full transcript is available at http://kcfirefighterscase.com /node/4.

3. Becker's motion was obtained by the author on January 27, 2017, through the filing of a Freedom of Information Act request to the US Justice Department.
4. Ron Chapman, "Proffer Agreements in Federal Criminal Cases," blog post, September 16, 2008, http://www.justiceflorida.com/proffer-agreements-in-federal-criminal-cases/.
5. Author interviews with Becky Edwards.

CHAPTER NINE: THE DEFENSE

1. John P. O'Connor, phone interview with the author, April 5, 2017.

CHAPTER TEN: CLOSING ARGUMENTS AND VERDICT

1. On July 23, 1997, Becker filed a Rule 35 motion with US District Court for the Western District of Missouri for reduction of sentence for John White; for Whitelaw Becker promised him that he would try to get his habeas corpus petition—which had been rejected by US District Court Judge Fernando Gaitan in 1996—reviewed again. After the firefighter trial, Judge Gaitan denied it again.

CHAPTER ELEVEN: SENTENCING

1. *United States v. Ryan*, Eighth Circuit Court of Appeals, 1998, http://caselaw.findlaw.com/us-8th-circuit/1253264.html.

CHAPTER TWELVE: APPEALS

1. Tom Jackman, "Despite Conviction, Five Insist: 'We Didn't Set Blast,'" *Kansas City Star*, July 3, 1997.
2. The full opinion of the Eighth Circuit Court is available at http://kcfirefighterscase.com/edwards_et_al_opinion.pdf.

CHAPTER THIRTEEN: AFFIDAVITS OF RECANTATION

1. Sworn affidavit of Alan Bethard, August 3, 2004.
2. Sworn affidavit of Carie Neighbors, June 2004.
3. Sworn affidavit of Joseph Denyer, January 2005.
4. Sworn affidavit of Larry Summers, July 2004.
5. Sworn affidavit of Buster Hower, February 2005.
6. Debbie Howard Foster, letter to author, February 2, 2006.
7. Author's numerous in-person interviews with Shannon Reimers.
8. Sworn affidavit of Shannon Reimers, 2006.
9. Sworn affidavit of Becky Edwards, November 6, 2005.

CHAPTER FOURTEEN: MIKE MCGRAW

1. Mike McGraw, "New Questions Arise in Deadly 1988 Blast," *Kansas City Star*, February 18, 2007.
2. Sworn affidavit of Jessica Vernon, September 26, 2000.
3. Mike McGraw and Michael Mansur, "Jurors in Firefighter Deaths Didn't Follow Judge's Orders," *Kansas City Star*, March 8, 2007.
4. Mike McGraw, "Did Pressure Lead to Lies? Numerous Witnesses Say Testimony Was Coerced," *Kansas City Star*, June 29, 2008.
5. Marion Germann (former KCFD battalion chief), phone interview with author, February 2, 2007.
6. Mike McGraw, "Security Guard Implicated Herself, a New Witness Says," *Kansas City Star*, June 29, 2008.
7. Sworn affidavit of another friend of Debbie Riggs, July 28, 2007.
8. "Questions, New Information Deserves More Scrutiny in 'Firefighters Case,'" *Kansas City Star*, July 1, 2008.
9. Statement released by US Attorney John F. Wood, July 2, 2008.

CHAPTER FIFTEEN: THE DEPARTMENT OF JUSTICE INVESTIGATION

1. Mike McGraw, "Report Surfaces in 1988 Explosion That Killed Six Firefighters," *Kansas City Star*, April 25, 2009.
2. For more on the "Fast & Furious" debacle, see "ATF's Fast and Furious Scandal," *Los Angeles Times*, December 15, 2010. http://www.latimes.com/nation/atf-fast-fu rious-sg-storygallery.html.
3. Mike McGraw, "More Perpetrators Possible in Firefighters' Deaths, Feds Say," *Kansas City Star*, July 27, 2011.
4. For more information about FOIA, see the National Archives website at https:// www.archives.gov/foia.
5. "President Obama's FOIA Memorandum and Attorney General Holder's FOIA Guidelines: Creating a 'New Era of Open Government,'" U.S. Department of Justice, last updated August 21, 2014, https://www.justice.gov/oip/blog/foia-post-2009 -creating-new-era-open-government.
6. Ted Bridis, "Obama Sets New Record for Withholding FOIA Requests," *PBS News Hour*, March 18, 2015, https://www.pbs.org/newshour/nation/obama-administra tion-sets-new-record-withholding-foia-requests.

CHAPTER SIXTEEN: LIFE IN PRISON

1. Nathan James, "The Federal Prison Population Buildup: Options for Congress," Congressional Research Service, May 20, 2016, https://fas.org/sgp/crs/misc/R42937 .pdf.
2. "Our Locations," Federal Bureau of Prisons, https://www.bop.gov/locations/.
3. The Admission and Orientation Handbook for the federal prison at Coleman,

Florida, runs to sixty-nine pages; https://www.bop.gov/locations/institutions/cop
/COP_aohandbook.pdf.

4. Nathan James, "Federal Prison Industries," Congressional Research Service, July 13, 2007, https://fas.org/sgp/crs/misc/RL32380.pdf.

CHAPTER SEVENTEEN: INTERVIEWING THE ORIGINAL KCPD DETECTIVES

1. "Robert A. Berdella," *Murderpedia*, http://www.murderpedia.org/male.B/b/berdel
la-robert.htm.

CHAPTER EIGHTEEN: RESENTENCING OF BRYAN SHEPPARD

1. "*Miller v. Alabama*—Mandatory Life without Parole Sentences Are Unconstitutional for Juveniles," National Conference of State Legislatures, February 24, 2015, http://www.ncsl.org/research/civil-and-criminal-justice/miller-v-alabama-mandatory-life-without-parole.aspx.

2. *Roper v. Simmons*, 543 U.S. 551 (2005), http://caselaw.findlaw.com/us-supreme
-court/543/551.html.

3. *Graham v. Florida*, 560 U.S. 48 (2010). For a summary, see "*Graham v. Florida*,"
CaseBriefs, https://www.casebriefs.com/blog/law/criminal-law/criminal-law-keyed
-to-kadish/defining-criminal-conduct-the-elements-of-just-punishment/graham-v
-florida/.

4. Steve Drizin, "The 'Superpredator' Scare Revisited," *HuffPost*, April 9, 2014, https://
www.huffingtonpost.com/steve-drizin/the-superpredator-scare_b_5113793.html.

5. Phillips Black Project, "Juvenile Life without Parole after *Miller v. Alabama*," Juvenile Sentencing Project, July 8, 2015, https://juvenilesentencingproject.org/phillips
-black-project-juvenile-lwop-after-miller/.

6. For information about the Midwest Innocence Project, see http://themip.org/.

7. "Defending the Damned—CLS Mitigation & Consulting Services," Insider Exclusive, http://insiderexclusive.com/defending-the-damned-cls-mitigation-consulting
-services/.

8. Randal S. Jeffrey, "Successive Habeas Corpus Petitions and Section 2255 Motions after the Antiterrorism and Effective Death Penalty Act of 1996: Emerging Procedures and Substantive Issues," *Marquette Law Review* 84, no. 1 (Fall 2000), http://
scholarship.law.marquette.edu/cgi/viewcontent.cgi?article=1342&context=mulr.

9. "*Montgomery v. Louisiana*," ScotusBlog, January 25, 2016, http://www.scotusblog
.com/case-files/cases/montgomery-v-louisiana/.

10. "18 U.S. Code § 3553—Imposition of a Sentence," Legal Information Institute, Cornell Law School, https://www.law.cornell.edu/uscode/text/18/3553.

11. For information about the status of resentencing hearings in federal court the author consulted with legal staff at the Office of the Federal Public Defender, who compiled the information from searching Pacer and the federal court's online docketing system.

12. A. Rae Simpson at MIT writes: "According to recent findings, the human brain

does not reach full maturity until at least the mid-20s. The specific changes that follow young adulthood are not yet well studied, but it is known that they involve increased myelination and continued adding and pruning of neurons. As a number of researchers have put it, 'the rental car companies have it right.' The brain isn't fully mature at 16, when we are allowed to drive, or at 18, when we are allowed to vote, or at 21, when we are allowed to drink, but closer to 25, when we are allowed to rent a car." Simpson, "Brain Changes," Young Adult Development Project, http://hrweb.mit.edu/worklife/youngadult/brain.html.

13. Cyndy Short, interview with author.

14. *Justice in the Embers* ran on weekends from February 4 through February 20. The play was a production of StoryWorks KC, a community engagement project of the local public TV station, KCPT, the Living Room Theatre, and the Center for Investigative Reporting. Adapted by playwright Michelle T. Johnson, the play dealt with new evidence uncovered by Mike McGraw that put the convictions of the Marlborough Five in doubt. Each performance was followed by an open discussion that permitted members of the audience to address questions to Johnson, McGraw, Cyndy Short, and the cast about the case. For each performance, the one-hundred-seat Living Room Theatre was sold out or nearly so. The role of Bryan Sheppard was played by actor Moses Brings Plenty, an Ogala Lakota born on the Pine Ridge Reservation in South Dakota. The setting for the play was the detention center in Leavenworth where Bryan was awaiting his resentencing hearing. (For more information about Moses Brings Plenty, see http://www.imbd.com/name/nm2511354/bio.)

15. For information about the Bureau of Justice Statistics, see https://bjs.gov/.

16. *Thompson v. Oklahoma*, 487 U.S. 815 (1988), Legal Information Institute, Cornell Law School, https://www.law.cornell.edu/supremecourt/text/487/815.

17. *Stanford v. Kentucky*, 492 U.S. 361 (1989), Legal Information Institute, Cornell Law School, https://www.law.cornell.edu/supremecourt/text/492/361.

18. Ashley Keeney, "Firefighters, Families Should Seek Justice Together in 1988 Explosion," *Kansas City Star*, March 4, 2017, http://www.kansascity.com/opinion/readers-opinion/guest-commentary/article136357608.html.

CHAPTER NINETEEN: NEW EVIDENCE

1. For information about Missouri's Sunshine Law, see https://ago.mo.gov/missouri-law/sunshine-law.

2. Report by KCPD Detective Douglas Clark, November 30, 1988.

3. Report by KCPD Detective Douglas Clark, December 3, 1988.

4. Police report written by Detective Joseph Chapman, December 7, 1988.

5. For more information about EFI Global, see https://www.efiglobal.com/.

6. Report by fire investigator Bradley Henson of EFI Global, March 7, 2016.

7. Vincent Schiraldi and Bruce Western, "Why 21 Year-Old Offenders Should Be Tried in Family Court," *Washington Post*, October 2, 2015, https://www.washingtonpost.com/opinions/time-to-raise-the-juvenile-age-limit/2015/10/02/948e317c-6862-11e5-9ef3-fde182507eac_story.html.

8. *United States v. Antun Lewis*, 850 F.Supp.2d 709 (N.D. Ohio 2012), https://www
   .gpo.gov/fdsys/pkg/USCOURTS-ohnd-1_08-cr-00404/pdf/USCOURTS-ohnd
   -1_08-cr-00404-1.pdf.

Bibliography

SOURCES

"The Anti-Drug Abuse Act of 1986." GovTrack, https://www.govtrack.us/congress/bills/99/hr5484.

"ATF's Fast and Furious Scandal." *Los Angeles Times*, December 15, 2010, http://www.latimes.com/nation/atf-fast-furious-sg-storygallery.html.

"Brady Rule." Legal Information Institute, Cornell Law School, last updated October 2017, https://www.law.cornell.edu/wex/brady_rule.

Bridis, Ted. "Obama Sets New Record for Withholding FOIA Requests." *PBS News Hour*, March 18, 2015, https://www.pbs.org/newshour/nation/obama-administration-sets-new-record-withholding-foia-requests.

Brown, Ethan. *Snitch: Informants, Cooperators, and the Corruption of Justice.* New York: Public Affairs, 2007.

"Bruce R. Watkins, Kansas City, Missouri Leader and Successful Black Entrepreneur." http://www.BlackMissouri.com, July 14, 2008.

Caldwell, Laura, and Leslie S. Klinger. *Anatomy of Innocence: Testimonies of the Wrongfully Convicted.* New York: Liveright Publishing, 2017.

Campbell, William J. "Eliminate the Grand Jury." *Journal of Criminal Law and Criminology* 64, no. 2 (1973): 174.

Chapman, Ron. "Proffer Agreements in Federal Criminal Cases." Blog post, September 16, 2008, http://www.justiceflorida.com/proffer-agreements-in-federal-criminal-cases/.

Death Penalty Information Center. https://deathpenaltyinfo.org/.

"Defending the Damned—CLS Mitigation & Consulting Services." Insider Exclusive, http://insiderexclusive.com/defending-the-damned-cls-mitigation-consulting-services/.

"DNA Exonerations in the United States." Innocence Project, https://www.innocenceproject.org.dna-exonerations-in-the-united states/.

Drizin, Steve. "The 'Superpredator' Scare Revisited." *HuffPost*, April 9, 2014.

Dwyer, Jim, Peter Neufeld, and Barry Scheck, *Actual Innocence: When Justice Goes Wrong and How to Make It Right.* New York: Doubleday, 2000.

"18 U.S. Code § 3553—Imposition of a Sentence." Legal Information Institute, Cornell Law School, https://www.law.cornell.edu/uscode/text/18/3553.

Ellison, Brian, Matthew Long-Middleton, and Glenn Frizell. "Freedom, Inc." *Central Standard*, February 9, 2016, http://kcur.org/post/freedom-inc#stream/0.

Emergency Response Guidebook: A Guidebook for First Responders during the Initial

Phase of a Dangerous Goods/Hazardous Materials Transportation Incident (Washington, DC: Department of Transportation, 1973).

"Families, Friends, Pay Tribute to City's Fallen Firefighters." *Kansas City Star*, December 3, 1988.

"Federal Judges on Senior Status." Ballotpedia: The Encyclopedia of American Politics, https://ballotpedia.org/Federal_judges_on_senior_status.

"Frequently Asked Questions." Innocence Project, https://www.innocenceproject.org/contact/.

Honigfort, Amanda. "Harry Truman: The 'Senator from Pendergast' Got His Start with Missouri Political Machine." *St. Louis on the Air*, July 15, 2014.

"How Federal Grand Juries Work." NPR, October 26, 2005, https://www.npr.org/templates/story/story.php?storyId=4975837.

Kansas City Firefighters Case. http://www.kcfirefighterscase.com.

"Kansas City Group Fights Jailing of 20." *New York Times*, October 29, 1991.

Jackman, Tom. "Inquiry Returns to Early Focus: After Several Years, Those Investigating the '88 Blast Look at Previous Suspects." *Kansas City Star*, March 14, 1995.

———— "Despite Conviction, Five Insist: 'We Didn't Set Blast.'" *Kansas City Star*, July 3, 1997.

James, Nathan. "Federal Prison Industries," Congressional Research Service, July 13, 2007, https://fas.org/sgp/crs/misc/RL32380.pdf.

———— "The Federal Prison Population Buildup: Options for Congress." Congressional Research Service, May 20, 2016, https://fas.org/sgp/crs/misc/R42937.pdf.

Jeffrey, Randal S. "Successive Habeas Corpus Petitions and Section 2255 Motions after the Antiterrorism and Effective Death Penalty Act of 1996: Emerging Procedures and Substantive Issues." *Marquette Law Review* 84, no. 1 (Fall 2000).

Jones, Christin J. "A Guide to the Offer of Proof." American Bar Association, August 31, 2016, http://apps.americanbar.org/litigation/committees/trialpractice/articles/summer2016-0816-a-guide-to-the-offer-of-proof.html.

"Juvenile Life without Parole after *Miller v. Alabama*." Juvenile Sentencing Project, Phillips Black Project, July 8, 2015.

Keeney, Ashley. "Firefighters, Families Should Seek Justice Together in 1988 Explosion." *Kansas City Star*, March 4, 2017, http://www.kansascity.com/opinion/readers-opinion/guest-commentary/article136357608.html.

Levin, Josh. "The Judge Who Coined 'Indict a Ham Sandwich' Was Himself Indicted." *Slate*, November 25, 2014, http://www.slate.com/blogs/lexicon_valley/2014/11/25/sol_wachtler_the_judge_who_coined_indict_a_ham_sandwich_was_himself_indicted.html.

"Living on the Firing Line." *Kansas City Star*, December 3, 1988.

Maloney, J. J. "Frame-Up" and "Railroaded," http://www.kcfirefighterscase.com.

McGraw, Mike. "New Questions Arise in Deadly 1988 Blast." *Kansas City Star*, February 18, 2007.

———— "Did Pressure Lead to Lies?" *Kansas City Star*, June 29, 2008.

———— "Security Guard Implicated Herself, a New Witness Says." *Kansas City Star*, June 29, 2008.

———— "Report Surfaces in 1988 Explosion That Killed Six Firefighters." *Kansas City Star*, April 25, 2009.

——— "More Perpetrators Possible in Firefighters' Deaths, Feds Say." *Kansas City Star*, July 27, 2011.

McGraw, Mike, and Michael Mansur. "Jurors in Firefighter Deaths Didn't Follow Judge's Orders." *Kansas City Star*, March 8, 2007.

"*Miller v. Alabama*—Mandatory Life without Parole Sentences Are Unconstitutional for Juveniles." National Conference of State Legislatures, February 24, 2015,

"*Montgomery v. Louisiana*." ScotusBlog, January 25, 2016, http://www.scotusblog.com /case-files/cases/montgomery-v-louisiana/.

Natapoff, Alexandra. *Snitching: Criminal Informants and the Erosion of American Justice*. New York: New York University Press, 2011.

Nathan, Geoffrey, "What Are the Federal Sentencing Guidelines + Chart 2017." Federal Charges.com, https://www.federalcharges.com/what-are-federal-sentencing-guidelines/.

The National Registry of Exonerations. A Project of the University of California Irvine Newkirk Center for Science and Society, University of Michigan Law School, and Michigan State University College of Law, https://www.law.umich.edu/special/ex oneration/Pages/Exonerations-in-the-United-States-Map.aspx.

"Oklahoma City Bombing." History.com, http://www.history.com/topics/oklahoma -city-bombing.

"Our Locations." Federal Bureau of Prisons, https://www.bop.gov/locations/.

Phillips Black Project. "Juvenile Life without Parole after *Miller v. Alabama*." Juvenile Sentencing Project, July 8, 2015, https://juvenilesentencingproject.org/phillips -black-project-juvenile-lwop-after-miller/.

"President Obama's FOIA Memorandum and Attorney General Holder's FOIA Guidelines: Creating a 'New Era of Open Government.'" US Department of Justice, last updated August 21, 2014, https://www.justice.gov/oip/blog/foia-post-2009-cre ating-new-era-open-government.

"Questions, New Information Deserves More Scrutiny in 'Firefighters Case.'" *Kansas City Star*, July 1, 2008.

"Robert A. Berdella." *Murderpedia*, http://www.murderpedia.org/male.B/b/berdel la-robert.htm.

Rohrlich, Justin. "Why Are There Up to 120,000 Innocent People in U.S. Prisons?" *Vice News*, November 10, 2014, https://news.vice.com/article/why-are-there-up-to -120000-innocent-people-in-us-prisons.

"S.668 (98th): Sentencing Reform Act of 1984." GovTrack, https://www.govtrack.us /congress/bills/98/s668.

"S.1762, Comprehensive Crime Control Act of 1984." Congress.Gov, https://www.con gress.gov/bill/98th-congress/senate-bill/1762.

Schiraldi, Vincent, and Bruce Western. "Why 21-Year-Old Offenders Should Be Tried in Family Court." *Washington Post*, October 2, 2015.

"Severance of Charges." *Criminal Law and Procedure B*, https://crimb.weebly.com/sev erance-of-chargesseparate-trials-for-co-accused.html.

Sharma, Partha Das. "Priming of Explosives for Effective Blasting." *Mining and Blasting*, May 14, 2013.

Sherrer, Hans. "99.8% Conviction Rate in U.S. Federal Courts Can Make Japanese Prosecutors Jealous." *Justice Denied*, May 17, 2016, http://justicedenied.org/word press/archives/3190.

Simpson, A. Rae. "Brain Changes." Young Adult Development Project, http://hrweb
.mit.edu/worklife/youngadult/brain.html.

Skarbek, David. *The Social Order of the Underworld: How Prison Gangs Govern the
American Penal System.* London: Oxford University Press, 2014.

Smith, Jessica. "The Bruton Rule: Joint Trials and Codefendants' Confessions." *North
Carolina Super Court Judges' Benchbook.* UNC School of Government, May 2012,
http://benchbook.sog.unc.edu/sites/benchbook.sog.unc.edu/files/pdf/The%20
Bruton%20Rule%20Joint%20Trials%20%26%20Codefendants%27%20Confes
sions.pdf.

"The Union Station Massacre." *Kansas City Star,* July 10, 2014.

US Sentencing Commission. "An Overview of the United States Sentencing Commission," n.d., https://isb.ussc.gov/files/USSC_Overview.pdf.

Vollen, Lola, and Dave Eggers. *Surviving Justice: America's Wrongfully Convicted and
Exonerated.* San Francisco: Voice of Witness, 2005.

Warden, Rob. "The Snitch System: How Snitch Testimony Sent Randy Steidl and
Other Innocent Americans to Death Row." Center on Wrongful Convictions,
Northwestern University School of Law, Winter 2004–2005, http://www.law.north
western.edu/legalclinic/wrongfulconvictions/documents/SnitchSystemBooklet.

COURT CASES

Brady v. Maryland, 1963

Cruz v. United States, 2018

Graham v. Florida, 2010

Miller v. Alabama, 2012

Montgomery v. Louisiana, 2016

Roper v. Simmons, 2005

Stanford v. Kentucky, 1989

Thompson v. Oklahoma, 1988

United States v. Antun Lewis, 2013

United States v. Ryan, 1991

United States v. Sheppard et al., 1997

Index

2009 story implicating the security
guards in firefighters case, 226–227
2011 article on possible other perpetrators
in the firefighters case, 237
Keeney, Ashley, 203, 280, 288–289
Keeney, Steven, 276
Kelly, Paul Henry and Hazel, 47
Kennedy, Anthony, 267
Kilgore, Stephen, 91, 122, 128, 132, 145, 149,
150
Kilventon, James H., 3, 4–5, 9, 10–11, 12, 175
Kilventon, James M., 289–290
Kilventon, Tracy, 288, 289, 290
Kind, Mark, 292
King, Chi P., 168–169, 269–270
King, Levi, 264–265

Lackland, Richard, 25
Laddish, Tim, 103
Landon, Lisa, 89, 128–129, 149
Laurans, Jonathan, 196–197, 198
Lay, Donald P., 192
Leavenworth Detention Center, 97, 266.
    See also Corrections Corporation of
    America (CCA)
Leavenworth federal penitentiary, 242, 244,
246–247
Leeds Farm detention center, 56
Lemanske, Kevin, 18, 19, 121–122, 225
Lett, Harold, 59, 101–102
Level 43 designation. See offense level 43
Lewis, Antun, 299, 318n30
life without parole sentencing, juvenile
justice and, 261–263
Living Room Theatre, 322n14
Lobdell, Pete, 34, 111, 226
Loken, James B., 192, 195
Ludwig, Jerry, 207, 210

Mafia, 61, 62
Maggard, Monica, 113, 114, 153
Mall, Christine, 104, 143, 150
Maloney, J. J., 189–191, 196, 212
Mama Tio's bar, 226, 229, 232
mandatory-minimum sentencing
    cooperating witnesses and, 82, 83–84
    overview and history of, 82–83
Marburger, Kathy, 107, 108, 120, 142, 153
Markey, Bill, 11
Marlborough Five
    appeals (see Marlborough Five appeals)
    biographical sketches of, 40–54
    Dave True's continued investigation of
    following indictment, 62–63

Dave True's overall strategy in building a
    case against, 55
Dave True's pretrial report on, 68–73
dynamics among, 37
events in the making of, 31–32, 34, 35–36
events of November 28, 1988, and, 37–40
federal grand jury and the indictment of,
    62, 63–67, 68
imprisonment in 1995 on unrelated
    charges, 55–60
investigators' creation of distrust and
    discord among, 56–57, 58–60
J. J. Maloney's New Times article on,
    189–191
lives and experiences in federal prisons,
    242, 244–249
physical impairments of, 37
postsentencing interviews with Tom
    Jackman, 189
remaining pathways to exoneration,
    299–301
sentencing hearing (see sentencing
    hearing)
trial of (see Marlborough Five trial)
use of jailhouse snitches to build a
    case against, 55 (see also jailhouse
    informants)
See also Brown, Richard; Edwards,
    Darlene; Sheppard, Bryan; Sheppard,
    Frank; Sheppard, Skip
Marlborough Five appeals
    to the Eighth Circuit Court, 191–196
    habeas corpus appeals, 196–198, 215
Marlborough Five defense attorneys
    habeas corpus appeal and, 196
    John Osgood's arguments for a lesser
        offense level at the sentencing
        hearing, 178–181, 183–184
    Marlborough Five appeals to the Eighth
        Circuit Court and, 191, 192
Marlborough Five trial
    assignment to defendants, 74–75;
        closing arguments, 135–145;
        Darlene Edwards's taped
        interview with the ATF and,
        100–101, 102; debate on admitting
        Debbie Riggs as a defense witness,
        122–125; debate on admitting
        Greg Pugh as a defense witness,
        125–126; decision not to have
        the defendants testify, 133; Judge
        Stevens's bias against the defense,
        80–82, 101, 106–107, 113, 119, 120,
        121, 123–125, 126–127, 129, 130,